1942

Australia's greatest peril

BOB WURTH

MACMILLAN
Pan Macmillan Australia

First published 2008 in Macmillan by Pan Macmillan Australia Pty Limited
1 Market Street, Sydney

Reprinted 2008, 2016

Copyright © Bob Wurth 2008

The moral right of the author has been asserted.

All rights reserved. No part of this book may be reproduced or transmitted by any person or entity (including Google, Amazon or similar organisations), in any form or by any means, electronic or mechanical, including photocopying, recording, scanning or by any information storage and retrieval system, without prior permission in writing from the publisher.

National Library of Australia
Cataloguing-in-Publication data:

Wurth, Bob, 1947-

1942: Australia's greatest peril/author, Bob Wurth.

ISBN: 9781405038607 (pbk.)

Curtin, John, 1885-1945.
World War, 1939-1945 – Australia.
World War, 1939-1945 – Japan.
Australia – Politics and government – 1939-1945.
Nineteen forty-two

940.5426

Every endeavour has been made to contact copyright holders to obtain the necessary permission for use of copyright material in this book. Any person who may have been inadvertently overlooked should contact the publisher.

Typeset in 13/15 pt Granjon by Post Pre-press Group
Printed in Australia by McPherson's Printing Group

Cartographic art by Laurie Whiddon

1942

*For Angus and Elea
and their friends.
Thankfully, all born of a different era.*

Invasion is a menace capable hourly of becoming an actuality. I tell you bluntly that the whole world may very well shake within the next few weeks under the blows that full-scale warfare will strike – and Australia cannot escape a blow. We face vital, perilous weeks fraught with exceedingly important happenings for Australia.

– John Curtin

No matter what happens, in order to win we simply cannot allow the enemy to use Australia. If the enemy is not able to prepare themselves yet, then we can take Australia.

– Baron Captain Sadatoshi Tomioka

Fundamentally, however, the army opposed the invasion of Australia and Hawaii on the grounds that they would extend national strengths beyond their limits . . . Reflecting on the bitter experience of the China Incident, the chances were high that an invasion would extend over the whole of the Australian continent.

– *Senshi Sosho*, Japan's official war history series, Pacific area army operations (1).

CONTENTS

Foreword		*xi*
Maps		*xiii*

1	A sea of tranquillity	1
2	A gesture of great struggle	9
3	The coming conquests	23
4	Blossoms raised to fall	35
5	Glorious victory	47
6	A nation exposed	57
7	Invasion planning	69
8	Dawn of a fearful year	79
9	Plotting against Australia	93
10	The indefensible continent	104
11	An illusion of superiority	116
12	Australia attacked	133
13	A day of decision	146
14	A clash of philosophies	160
15	Scorching Australia	176
16	Australia's reprieve	188
17	Bold, new targets	203
18	The boy who saw the Japanese	212
19	Rowboat reconnaissance	221

20	From chaos to confidence	237
21	A scene of dreadful carnage	251
22	The submariners' revenge	261
23	Return of the hero gods	273
24	Savagery and dishonour	285
25	Turning the tide	298
26	Death of an empire	315
27	Surrender	328
28	Not the war but the game	345

Epilogue – Boys, resting peacefully	364
Notes	373
Select Bibliography	421
Acknowledgments	435
Index	445

Foreword

For 40 years after federation, Australians were obsessed with the nightmare of a Japanese invasion. As one of the furthest flung members of the British empire, and occupying such a lightly peopled continent, it was not surprising that Australians were convinced that an Asian nation would one day contest their occupation.

The Japanese attack on Pearl Harbor and Singapore in December 1941 seemed to confirm those historic fears. Although the British government dismissed Australian concerns, predicting that the Japanese were more likely to strike westward towards India, Australian political and military chiefs prepared for the worst, conscious that they had insufficient defence forces to repel a serious invasion.

For much of 1942, the Australian government of John Curtin scrambled desperately to assemble sufficient forces to defend the continent and prepare its people for the possibility of invasion. In London and Washington, Churchill and Roosevelt were determined to ensure that Australian appeals for assistance would not divert attention from the war against Germany.

This fundamental divergence of interest between Australia and its two great power protectors saw bitter disputes erupt between Curtin and Churchill during the first half of 1942, as Curtin demanded the recall of Australian forces to protect their homeland. Despite the arrival of some American forces under the command of General Douglas MacArthur, and the distant cover provided by the carriers of the US Navy, the defence of Australia during those dangerous months depended overwhelmingly on its own forces.

In the event, the invasion of Australia never eventuated. This has led some historians to conclude that Churchill had been correct in dismissing it as a serious possibility. Some have argued that an invasion of Australia was never on the Japanese agenda. Some have even gone so far as to argue that Curtin deliberately played on Australian fears during 1942 in order to boost the Australian war effort.

In contrast, Bob Wurth draws on a multitude of Japanese sources to show how an invasion of Australia became a very real possibility in the wake of the unexpectedly easy Japanese success in destroying much of the American Pacific fleet, along with the British warships, *Prince of Wales* and *Repulse*, before the subsequent run of Japanese victories from Burma to Bougainville. With the fall of these vast territories, and the defeat of their defenders, the path to Australia had been cleared.

There were powerful voices in Tokyo calling for their commanders to capitalise on their victories by also taking Australia out of the Allied equation. Prolonged debates ensued between Japanese naval and military officials before the issue was finally settled. In the event, it was decided that Australia was a territory too big and too far. Japan would try to isolate rather than invade Australia. Instead of being a tyranny, distance proved to be Australia's best defence.

In his immensely readable and historically rigorous book, Bob Wurth brings those far-off days to life in dramatic fashion, providing a new and important perspective to the ongoing debate. It is a story that all Australians should read.

Professor David Day
University of Aberdeen

MONGOLIA
MANCHURIA
RUSSIA
Hokkaido
Sea of Japan
JAPAN
Peking
KOREA
Honshu
Tokyo
Hiroshima
PACIFIC OCEAN
Shikoku
Kyushu
Shanghai
CHINA
INDIA
Okinawa
Iwojima
Formosa
Hong Kong
BURMA
Philippine Sea
Hainan
South China Sea
Rangoon
Luzon
Manila
THAILAND
Saipan
Bangkok
Philippine Islands
INDO-CHINA
Guam
Camrahn Bay
Leyte Gulf
Gulf of Thailand
Truk
Davao
Palau
Kota Bharu
Kuantan
Tarakan
MALAYA
Singapore
Borneo
Sumatra
Celebes
Kavieng
New Guinea
Rabaul
DUTCH EAST INDIES
Ambon
Batavia
Bandung
Java
Java Sea
Papua
Lae
Tjilatjap
Dili
Port Moresby
Torres Strait
INDIAN OCEAN
Koepang
Timor
Bali
Milne Bay
Darwin
Bachelor
Adelaide River
Great Barrier Reef
Coral Sea
N
W
E
S
Wyndham
Cairns
Broome
Townsville
SCALE
0
1000 miles
Mackay
AUSTRALIA
0
1000 kilometres
Rockhampton

The Bay of Hiroshima

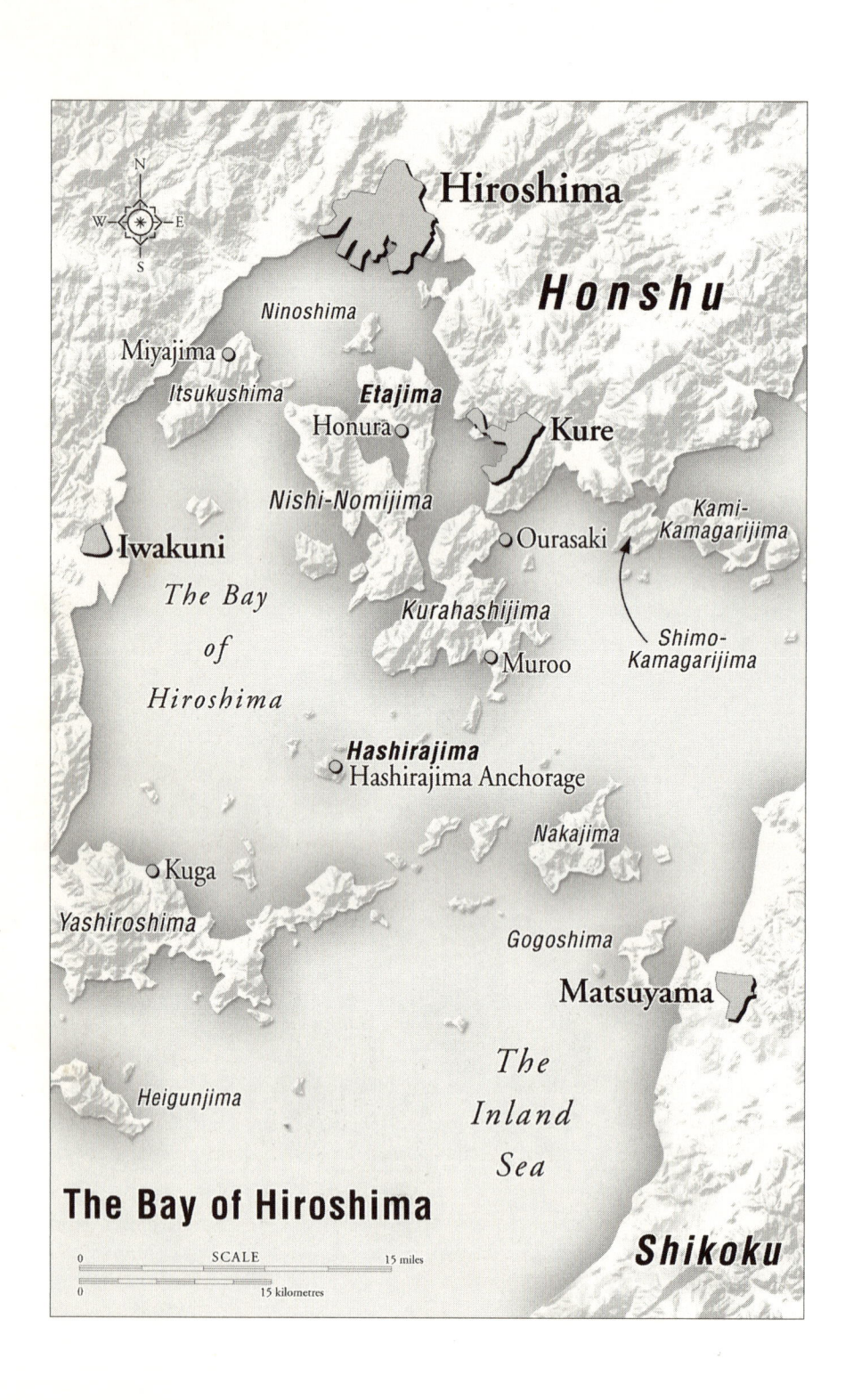

PACIFIC OCEAN
Admiralty Islands
Kavieng
0
200 miles
0
200 kilometres
Bismarck
Sea
Wewak
New Ireland
N
W
E
S
Rabaul
NEW GUINEA
Tol Plantation
Madang
New Britain
Bougainville
Kieta
Finschhafen
Lae
Buin
PAPUA
Salamaua
Balale
Solomon
Sea
Gulf of
Papua
Owen
Stanley
Range
Gona
Buna
Kokoda
Kokoda Track
Port Moresby
Torres
Strait
See Kokoda Track inset
Milne Bay
AUSTRALIA
Coral
Sea
SCALE
30 miles
30 kilometres
Gona
Buna
Popondetta
Kokoda
Deniki
Isurava
Oivi
Awala
Kagi
Myola
Menari
Efogi
Ioribaiwa
Nauro
Ilolo
Owers' Corner
Port
Moresby
The Kokoda Track

1

A SEA OF TRANQUILLITY

'Where is the place of the battleships?'

The old boatman is perspiring, stooped over a cargo of boxes which he is unloading from the ferry to the breakwater jetty. He stops and shakes his head; his craggy face breaks into an uncomprehending smile.

He must be in his eighties. Surely he lived through the war. His granddaughter, who has just arrived on the same fast ferry as my companion and I, translates while the old man listens and wipes his brow. It's mid-summer and Japan is suffering a relentless heatwave.

I start again: 'I'm here to find the place of the great ships. The Hashirajima anchorage. You know, the place of the *Yamato*, the *Nagato* and the grand fleet . . .'

'Ah yes, yes. *Yamato*!' he smiles in instant recognition. 'Over the other side. Go straight!' he says, pointing to a gap in the distant hillside, covered from top to seashore in dense fir forest and undergrowth. It's a wild-looking place. But the old man assures us that it's only a 20-minute walk – 'more or less' – to our destination.

1942

Tiny Hashira island, Hashirajima to the Japanese, floats in the languid heat haze on the Seto Naikai, the Inland Sea between Japan's main islands. The journey here has been memorable: endless islands on a stormless sea, a sea like a great lake. The furthest islands are wrapped in haze, the closest are of dark, deep green, almost black, some with craggy valleys, many with brilliant white beaches. Each island is a different shape, smooth and rounded, or jagged and jutting; scattered by the hand of nature in a semblance of *karesansui,* the zen gardens of sand, rock, and gravel.

It was from their sequestered anchorage at Hashirajima in the Bay of Hiroshima – so far from the Pacific on one side and the Sea of Japan on the other that it was unlikely to be menaced by enemy submarines or aircraft – that the warships of Japan headed out to their terrible missions in World War II.

The history of the Imperial Navy is embedded in this great bay. From high points in modern Hiroshima, you gaze across to the port of Kure, once a massive naval base, with the naval academy opposite on the island of Etajima, surviving with its grand buildings, much as it was during the war.

Following the bay to the south west is today's airbase at Iwakuni, from where the Kamikazes flew. Hashirajima is but a remote dot lost in the distance over the sparkling sea.

Several hundred civilians now live on Hashirajima island. A cluster of little houses and shops squats around a small, attractive harbour, where fishing boats bob in crystal clear water behind the breakwater. Big dark fish swim about the deep bottom and you wonder why the locals need go out in boats at all. Modest timber houses, one stacked upon the other in a single strip, rise behind the little town up a steep, green slope. Above, dense foliage is broken and softened by a precariously steep rice paddy.

Today, the fishermen and village folk of Hashirajima are at home, remembering the dead, conversing with them, raising a glass of sake, and putting one out for them too, along with a few treats. Obon is the annual Buddhist festival of ancestors. Young sailors and soldiers going off to war would say, *at least I'll be seeing you again in the Obon season.* It's a fortuitous time – perhaps – to attempt to unravel the motives of some of the departed, especially the war dead, to remember their deeds and actions, the bravery and the heinous idiocy behind some of their plans.

A few small places on Hashirajima offer accommodation, but not to foreigners. It is the language problem, they explain, embarrassed. And we don't know your customs. You might not like the food. Perhaps they also suspect the motives of foreigners – particularly Australians – who visit this remote place because the Australians have been here before in force.

I am here to fathom the character and logic of those officers of the Imperial Japanese Navy who planned their Pacific campaigns here before and during the war. It has become abundantly apparent in the course of my research that influential elements of this great navy wanted to invade Australia in 1942, although they never got as far as issuing the orders to invade. The evidence is overwhelming from the Japanese side, though, that such an invasion was a serious possibility.

It's a mystery how they would have rationalised this idea, even though their naval force was one of the largest in the world. Japanese warships were already heavily committed in the Pacific. Australia was 7000 kilometres away; it was not only remote, but its long coastline would have made it impossible to control completely; it lacked significant oil reserves and oil was the fuel the Japanese needed most.

Consequently, some Australian historians find the idea that Australia was even threatened with invasion preposterous; they think that such a plan, if it existed, was a fantasy cooked up by middle ranking or junior officers. 'In fact, of course, there was no invasion,' one prominent Australian historian has written, 'there was never going to be an invasion. But the people of Australia did not know that then, and most of them don't know it still.'

Yet evidence of the Japanese navy's bellicose intentions towards Australia was not hard to find once I began looking. References to an invasion appear often in Japanese diaries, memoirs, archives, and official histories, and many of them turn on the planning that was undertaken at this remote naval anchorage off Hashirajima.

My companion is a Chinese Singaporean who knows Japan and the Japanese and is not judgmental – even though, as a youth, he witnessed the bloodied heads of his countrymen on stakes in the streets of Singapore.

We set off, past the enticing crescent-shaped beach near the harbour, to trek across the island. The shady part of the beach under the cliff is a lure in the heat, but we ignore it. Passing the ramshackle houses of fishermen, the narrow road leads us up through a riot of green foliage, where forest fir, bamboo, and vines fight for the sun. Multi-coloured birds swoop through the undergrowth, and brown butterflies the size of small bats flit past.

The hot air throbs with the dry chorus of cicadas. Climbing upwards, we pass a few poor fields of melon and yam. Perhaps the season has finished. The narrow road twists and turns and, at the top, comes to a Tori gate: it frames the way through long grass to a tiny Shinto shrine, smaller than a house, and looking the worse for its years; the nearest shrine on land for the men of the great ships.

Now we are walking downhill, encouraged by occasional glimpses of the Inland Sea. The landscape flattens out: more dry fields and paddies. The heat is intense, and we have to stop frequently for water.

The coast is hidden by a long parallel sand hill covered by grass. We trudge on. 'Let's head in that direction,' my friend, 20 years my senior, says, and he strikes off at right angles through a dry paddy, heading towards the hidden sea. Scaling the sand hill, he calls out: 'You have found it. This is what you are looking for!'

Below the dune lies a long, white, sandy beach of a brightness that makes me squint. Offshore lies our goal – the Hashirajima anchorage, erstwhile haven of the Combined Fleet.

Overwhelmingly it is a soft, calm turquoise seascape of peace and serenity. A coastal trader glides away in the shimmering distance, seemingly floating above the surface of the sea. In a blink of an eye she is gone, consumed in the heat haze.

Tranquillity masks the past and you force yourself to recall that this is the place where they deliberated like successful gentlemen in a debating society the violent subjugation of nations for an ever expanding Japanese empire.

This is the secret place, hidden remotely in the twisting aquatic alleyways of a great inland sea, out of public gaze, once forbidden to the local fishermen on pain of severe punishment. Even the islanders tilling their fields on this uninhabited side of their home were meant to avert their eyes.

The panorama is of islands of differing hues of blue, one stacked upon another, and overhung by cotton wool clouds. In the foreground, not far away, is a small, steep island covered in foliage to the very water's edge and linked to Hashirajima by a narrow sand spit. To our right, the remains of an old concrete jetty and a grand semi-circular staircase rising from the empty beach to nothing.

Naval officers in their whites came ashore here, amusing themselves on fishing and shooting parties while ratings set out canvas chairs and picnic baskets and sake above the beach. The conversation in early 1942, when Japan's war was going so well, invariably turned on where to go next. *Should we capture India after Burma, Hawaii, or perhaps Australia?*

Japan began her war with 11 carriers and ten battleships, and within the first four months Japanese carrier fleets ranged triumphant and barely molested from Pearl Harbor in the Pacific to Ceylon (now Sri Lanka) in the Indian Ocean.

In my mind's eye, I struggle to imagine the battleships, carriers, cruisers, destroyers, and the rest, as many as 80 Japanese warships of all sizes anchored in this serene bay. Perhaps eight big battleships, including the squat old flagship *Nagato*, with her massive bridge and communications pagoda towering above the main deck like a haphazard vertical steel city. She was the first battleship in the world equipped with 16-inch guns, even before the US Navy.

Standing here decades ago, you would have heard from across the water the strains of the ship's band practising on the *Nagato*'s afterdeck. Each day, at 12.05 p.m., it played for 30 minutes the favourite repertoire of the venerated commander-in-chief of the Combined Fleet, Admiral Isoroku Yamamoto.

While the band played, officers took lunch in Yamamoto's wardroom, a formal Western meal that began with soup and ended with dessert, was served off crisp white linen, eaten with silverware, and washed down with a fine rice wine. The Imperial Navy was British in many ways.

Japan's army was trained by German instructors, its navy by the British. This heritage left lasting differences of mentality. As Winston Churchill observed, before the war the Imperial Navy tended to be more cautious and moderate in outlook than the Imperial Army. Army officers rarely went abroad, except to make war, cultivating a more narrowly arrogant, nationalistic spirit. But naval officers frequently visited foreign ports and knew something of the world outside Japan. They were much aware of the power of the British and American fleets. Such was the impact of their British training that they even gave some of their orders in English, rather than Japanese.

In this tranquillity, I remind myself that it was out there, aboard the *Nagato*, that Admiral Yamamoto worked on his plan to knock the United States out of the war from the start, through the attack at Pearl Harbor.

In 1942, a few months after that successful assault, the sleek new battleship *Yamato* replaced the *Nagato* as Yamamoto's flagship. The *Yamato*, all 65,000 tonnes of her, dominated the anchorage, her silver-white hull sparkling on the water. If you stood on her bridge, crewmen exercising on the forecastle below appeared ant-like. The massive triple turrets with 18-inch plus guns were the biggest guns on any ship in the world. As the world's largest battleship, she was a potent symbol of the might of the Imperial

Japanese Navy although, even new, she was obsolete as a major weapon of war. Like most of these great ships, she would go to the bottom.

Drenched in perspiration, for the temperature is about 37 degrees Celsius, we make our way back across the island to the oasis of the shady beach on the other side. As we trudge the air is rent by the wailing of an old wartime air raid siren. My companion says, simply, 'noon'.

High above and beyond sight an American fighter jet from the Iwakuni base sends its intrusive, reverberating roar across the Inland Sea. A farmer passes in a tiny truck, and politely offers us a ride. My companion, independent as ever, pleasantly declines for us.

At last, descending quickly through the forest, we reach the crescent-shaped beach near the ferry.

I sit on a tiny granite rock out in the water, my feet in the icy Inland Sea, my head in the shade of the cliff-face, and I begin drafting the opening of this book.

A party of four or five well-dressed Japanese tourists wind their way around the cliff base on a rough path and pause, greeting us in good English. I stop my scribbling, and bow from my tiny rock.

'May I ask, what are you doing?'

'I'm writing about Japan threatening to invade Australia and the great ships of the war at Hashirajima.'

An older woman in the group smiles. 'Australia? That's nice,' she says in a non-committal tone. She changes the subject: 'I haven't been home here since my childhood. Isn't it really beautiful?'

When Japan was utterly shattered after the surrender, stunned and wearied Japanese servicemen began returning to what was left of their homes. The Allied victors these vanquished people saw were mostly from Australia. Some 13,500 Australians temporarily occupied this region of the Inland Sea, known as Hiroshima Bay.

Hiroshima city, about 40 kilometres north, was a wasteland.

The nearby port of Kure was a smashed, desolate place. Battered, rotting, half-sunk warships littered the bay. The Australian troops occupied bomb-damaged barracks and began to feel the bitter cold of their first miserable winter; two Australian cruisers and two destroyers suddenly appeared at the anchorage.

The shy local women and their demoralised menfolk at first had little to do with the dominating and initially arrogant occupiers. But the children were readily taken in by the Australians' gifts of food and good humour, and many adults followed their lead as life improved after wartime and enemies often became friends.

Back in Kure, a few days after my visit to Hashirajima, I ask an expert on the occupation era, Professor Takeshi Chida, if the Australians were accepted by the Japanese. 'They were not liked by the men,' he replies in Japanese, 'because the Australians took away the most attractive women.'

To the men of the former Imperial Navy, the workers of the Kure naval base, the survivors from the bombing, especially devastated Hiroshima – who had all at one time dreamt of Japan's glory – nothing could have been more perverse than the presence of the enemy in their slouch hats.

2

A GESTURE OF GREAT STRUGGLE

The *Nagato*'s bow swung gently into the breeze in the calm waters off Hashirajima. With its single engine straining, a Nakajima float plane catapulted into the air from the battleship's deck.

It was 19 October 1941, a pleasant autumn day in the south of Japan, and staff officer Captain Kameto Kuroshima was on the most important mission of his life.

The fabric-covered biplane that carried him dipped and turned, then ascended slowly over Hiroshima Bay, passing south of Kure, identifiable by its distant pall of dirty smoke and by a great industrial stain on the sea. The prospect of war had brought a large influx of labour to the port city; it was a giant naval base, armoury, and shipyard now toiling at maximum capacity.

In the open cockpit, the pilot set a course for Tokyo at the Nakajima's maximum speed of 160 kilometres per hour. Kuroshima had long hours before touchdown in Tokyo Bay to think about his awesome responsibility.

The wind buffeted his gaunt, pale face, which was protected by goggles and leather helmet. He clung firmly to his precious satchel. Inside was a document marked 'AMO Operation', prepared by

Admiral Yamamoto, commander-in-chief of the Combined Fleet, and intended for the navy's most senior commanders.

Its secret contents: an extraordinarily bold, highly risky plan to destroy the United States' Pacific Fleet in a raid on its Hawaiian base at Pearl Harbor.

Japan had been in conflict in China since 1931. By the end of July, 1941, she had also subjugated Indochina by placing unbearable pressure on the weak Vichy government. Next, she had demanded massive concessions and a significant Japanese presence in the oil-rich Dutch East Indies (as Indonesia was then known). Thailand also was threatened under the guise of a protective Japanese hand.

The United States, alarmed at Japan's sudden expansionism and her treatment of the Chinese, had cut all trade with Japan; Britain, Australia, and the Netherlands had followed suit. The United States demanded that Japan withdraw its forces from China and Indochina. The Japanese demanded recognition of their expanded territorial rights. In Washington, diplomatic 'conversations' between the two soon broke down.

Japan's war was at tipping point. A new, extremist cabinet was being formed with aggressive General Hideki Tojo as prime minister, sealing the nation's entry into the larger global conflict. Tojo, from a low-caste Samurai family, had been one of the military leaders of Japan's occupation of Manchuria, and then, from 1940, war minister. He had long believed in the mastery of Japan over all Asia.

Two weeks earlier, a liaison conference between the army, navy and the government had decided to prepare for war against the West: 'Our Empire, for the purpose of self-defence and self-preservation, will complete preparations for war, with the last ten days of October as the tentative deadline, resolved to go to war with the United States, Great Britain and the Netherlands if necessary.'

The armed forces dominated the Japanese government, which had no power to interfere in military planning operations. Liaison conferences had no chairmen and the key participants all reported separately on important deliberations to the emperor if they wished to. Discussions were random, rather than structured, and could continue from morning until the early hours of the next day, often becoming heated. When decisions were eventually made, they went to cabinet for endorsement. But the civilians would never challenge the militarists: approval was never refused.

The Imperial Japanese Navy beat obedience and duty into its men from the moment they entered its service. At the Imperial Navy Academy on Etajima island, near Kure on Hiroshima Bay, the treatment of cadets was exceptionally harsh. The most minor infraction, whether real or perceived, resulted in a direct punch to the face. A cadet in a hurry who failed to salute a superior could expect four heavy blows to the head.

Officers remember their academy education as 'Spartan and thrashing'. For every 10,000 young men who sat the academy's entrance exam, only 200 were likely to be accepted. The cadets rose at dawn or even earlier, and washed in cold water, even in the freezing winter when snow lay on the surrounding mountains. The day was filled with military drill and academic training. Forced runs to the highest peak of Mount Furutaka, behind the academy, were routine. Cadets also spent many hours rowing longboats on the Inland Sea, shifting their oars until their hands and backsides were bloodied where the skin had worn away.

Admiral Yamamoto is especially honoured here at Etajima with a larger than life-size bronze bust. A lock of Yamamoto's hair sits alongside locks of hair from Japan's Fleet Admiral Heihachiro Togo and Admiral Horatio Nelson of the Royal Navy. Since 1888, Etajima had bred proud, professional officers like Yamamoto, officers who demanded much of the men who served under them, and received their loyalty and devotion in return.

As Captain Kuroshima's plane landed in Tokyo Bay, he steeled himself for the task ahead. He knew that he was expected to return to the *Nagato* within a few days with the full agreement of the war planners at Naval General Staff for the controversial AMO operation.

If it was adopted, Yamamoto's plan would automatically herald war with America. The United States would receive a crushing blow at the very outset. Yamamoto thought such a surprise attack was the only way in which Japan might quickly gain the superiority needed over the greater firepower and industrial capacity of the US. A shock blow would place Japan in a position to reach a peace settlement with the US after a limited, short war. In the meantime, Japan would have gained all the land and natural resources that she needed to survive.

Yamamoto and his chief of staff, Admiral Matome Ugaki, knew Pearl Harbor well. Both had been midshipmen on the cruiser IJNS *Azuma* which made training and goodwill visits to Pearl Harbor, Sydney and other Pacific ports before World War I. Yamamoto had also worked in the US and had toured the country at length. As a 27-year-old naval commander, he had been an aide to the Japanese ambassador in Washington in 1921 during talks that produced the Washington Treaty. The treaty limited Japan to three capital ships for every five maintained by Britain and America; terms regarded as humiliating by the Imperial Japanese Navy.

Although Yamamoto's plan to attack Pearl Harbor was complex, Captain Kuroshima was convinced that it was also brilliant. In the operations room of the *Nagato* a week earlier, the staff officer had witnessed three days of war games that demonstrated it had a good chance of success.

Kuroshima, later rear admiral, had a great grasp of operational detail. His colleagues, who thought him slightly weird, called him Ganji because his gaunt appearance reminded them of Gandhi, the ascetic Indian leader. His devotion to his work was intense and slavish, and he often locked himself away in his darkened cabin with his head buried in his hands for long hours. When ideas came to him, he turned on the light and scribbled notes on pieces of paper which were strewn on the floor about him. Dishes and dirty ashtrays piled up, disgusting his fellow staff officers. He emerged with detailed operational plans in his head, which he then dictated without the use of notes.

In Tokyo, Captain Kuroshima was driven to the navy ministry where naval ratings snapped a salute as his car entered the tall gates. The building, which stood in a spacious compound, with a garden featuring statues of past naval heroes, had been constructed in the Victorian era, and its decorative design of red and white bricks gave its façade a fanciful look. The ministry covered two extensive, rambling floors, and was situated near Hibiya Park, just two blocks to the south of the Imperial Palace.

The navy minister, Admiral Shigetaro Shimada, had his office in this building, but the real power here resided in the chief of the Naval General Staff, Admiral Osami Nagano, a heavy-set, balding man with thick eyebrows, who had studied at Harvard during World War I. Like Yamamoto, he kept civilians in the government in the dark, and enjoyed direct access to Emperor Hirohito, Japan's supreme military commander.

Army and navy ministers also reported directly to the emperor, merely informing the prime minister of the fact that they were doing so. Over the years, many of these army and navy ministers had taken their orders from the armed forces chiefs. Under the constitution, these ministers had to be officers on active duty. If a government failed to please the army and the navy, the military's high command simply told one of their ministers to resign. It then refused to replace him, precipitating a terminal political crisis.

Clutching his satchel, Kuroshima bounded up the granite steps of the navy ministry, and clattered over the stone floor to the great ornate central staircase. The building was busy with people. Footsteps echoed in the cavernous entrance as Kuroshima climbed, passing a venerable trophy of war, the wheel of a Russian warship captured at Tsushima in 1905. He strode down a long corridor, where portraits of former naval ministers in full dress uniform gazed down, and entered the operations room of the Naval General Staff. This was a large, plain room surrounded with maps and charts; other charts lay out on a central table.

Sadatoshi Tomioka bowed as Kuroshima entered. Three generations of Tomioka's family had served in the navy, beginning with his paternal grandfather during the Tokugawa Shogunate. His father had entered the naval academy at Etajima as a cadet, and had risen to become its director, serving with sufficient distinction to be made a baron. His son had inherited his title. An urbane man, comfortably padded with flesh, Baron Captain Sadatoshi Tomioka exuded the confidence and security of one who knew exactly what to do and say under any circumstance; yet, he knew that today he would find his impeccable manners sorely tested.

Tomioka headed the operations section in the first section or bureau of Naval General Staff. It was responsible for the assessment and development of naval war plans. By rights, the planning for major naval operations should have emanated from this office, and the officers aboard the Combined Fleet at Hashirajima should have carried those plans forward, acting with independence and on their own discretion only once they were in action. But in the heated and exhilarating madness of war talk that was consuming the armed forces in Japan, everything had been turned on its head. The men on the flagship now had greater clout.

Tomioka knew exactly why Kuroshima had come and what he wanted, and he dreaded the proposal in the officer's satchel. He was vehemently opposed to Yamamoto's plan to attack Pearl Harbor, privately referring to his guest Kuroshima as 'Yamamoto's foggy staff officer'. Yamamoto's plan outlined the Pearl Harbor operation in great detail, discussing the breadth of the deployment, the number and type of ships, the number of aircraft, the possible route, weather and the expected outcome. Tomioka politely read the report through. He was aware of its thrust from previous discussions and from war games held the previous month.

'This is highly speculative,' he told Kuroshima. 'To be successful the maximum damage must be inflicted on the fleet at Pearl Harbor and to achieve this, the American fleet must be caught in

Pearl Harbor. This is the major point of speculation.' Tomioka rightly worried that the fleet might have left by time the Japanese planes arrived at their target.

He and his staff had been busy putting together their own plans for the navy's involvement in the proposed southern operation, a string of invasions of the Philippines, Malaya, Hong Kong and elsewhere, with which Japan would launch its offensive in the Pacific.

'It's imperative to get oil resources from the southern areas,' Tomioka now insisted, pacing and gesturing as he spoke. Any operation that detracted from this goal at the outset of war would be vigorously opposed by Naval General Staff, he warned. Of key importance was the number of ships needed for the assault operations throughout the south seas. Yamamoto's plan would rob the southern operation of desperately needed aircraft carriers.

Kuroshima acknowledged the work being done on the southern operation. 'But the United States Navy has the potential power at Pearl Harbor to attack the Japanese flank as soon as the southern operation is launched. This could endanger the success of the entire operation to the south.'

Tomioka stood his ground; no elements of the navy could be spared for Pearl Harbor. The idea was simply impossible. The fundamental concept of any war with the US was that there would be one decisive battle in which the US Fleet would attempt to enter Japanese waters and would be decimated. 'That's just old, traditionalist thinking!' Kuroshima flared.

His opponent was quietly and calmly furious. Not so much about the rash way in which things were being done by Kuroshima and the Combined Fleet people, but about the craziness of the breathtaking proposal they had concocted.

Tomioka and his planners estimated that for every 100 combat-ready warships the United States owned, Japan had only 75. They calculated that in the event of war between the two, Japan's fleet strength would drop to about 50 per cent of America's by 1943, and to 30 per cent or less by 1944. In aircraft production, the US potential was more than ten times greater than Japan's. Kuroshima argued that this was why the Imperial Navy needed to deliver a crushing blow to the American fleet at the outset. Further destruction of the enemy's strength must follow in subsequent operations. Seeking a decisive sea battle before the disparity between the strengths of the Japanese and US navies widened was paramount. Yet Tomioka had grave doubts.

The operations chief was not without considerable influence. That fact that he was a baron with links to the imperial family gave him far greater standing and authority than his rank of captain suggested. Within a couple of years, he would become a rear admiral.

Yet even the Japanese establishment was now caught up in the patriotic call for war with the United States and Britain. The issue had become a matter of survival and national face. So Tomioka was not at all opposed to war as such. He felt that Japan had three options – war, delay, or surrender to the demands of the Americans. The second option would be fatal, as Japan was already acutely low on oil. The third would mean the end of Japan's aspirations to become a great colonial power, standing proudly alongside the world's most powerful empires.

The baron, often touted as a conservative or a traditionalist, was indeed one of the hawks at Naval General Staff, along with other hardline section chiefs Shingo Ishikawa and Toshitane Takada. They had argued heatedly with senior General Staff officers who were reluctant to support the Japanese advance into Indochina during 1941. Now they strongly insisted on war with America, prompting more moderate colleagues, such as the vice navy minister, Vice Admiral Shigeyoshi Inoue, to complain, 'It's like a captain is guiding the navy.'

Nevertheless, Tomioka feared that once the war in the Pacific started, there was no plan to end it. 'The reality that drove itself home continuously was that though Japan could control Oriental waters and take care of herself near home where she might even win brilliant victories, she had in the final analysis no way to defeat America and her potential power.'

Now, the tension mounted as Tomioka and Kuroshima exchanged arguments, each trying to knock down the other's main points. 'Pearl Harbor must be attacked!' Kuroshima thundered. Tomioka, the cultivated officer, fought to retain his impeccable self-control. But the two raised their voices and almost came to blows. Both knew the critical implications in the outcome of their argument and neither was prepared to give ground.

Admiral Yamamoto was a gambler, brilliant at poker, and Kuroshima had a gambler's ace up his sleeve. He suddenly revealed that his commander-in-chief, a highly popular officer, would resign forthwith along with his entire Combined Fleet staff if the Pearl Harbor plan was not adopted.

Tomioka was thunderstruck. He could never be responsible for such a scandal at a time like this. He judged that the time had come to refer the issue to his superiors. Kuroshima and Tomioka filed into the office of Tomioka's bureau head, Vice Admiral Shigeru Fukudome, an officer with an inscrutable face; after a brief discussion, he referred them to the vice chief of the Naval General Staff, Vice Admiral Seiichi Ito.

Until now, Fukudome and Ito had not voiced strenuous objection to Yamamoto's Pearl Harbor proposal, although they had spoken of the risks involved. Tomioka saw his two superiors as indecisive fence-sitters. He thought that they were, in fact, against the proposal, but did not possess the willpower to take a strong position against Yamamoto.

Captain Kuroshima flaunted the warning of Yamamoto's resignation. The issue was immediately referred higher to the chief of the Navy General Staff, Admiral Nagano. Tomioka had little time for Admiral Nagano, who, he thought, had never expressed clear-cut ideas about Pearl Harbor from the moment the plan was first raised months earlier. He just wasn't a forceful enough character of the type needed to lead a nation into war.

Nagano had been holding out hope that negotiations in Washington would result in a settlement. He had the power to stop Yamamoto's scheme, but as Tomioka put it, he was 'rather the type to leave things to his subordinates'. Since taking over the role of chief of the Navy General Staff, Nagano had allowed his pro-German staff officers to have their say in the navy's decision-making process. Now he was faced with a dilemma. He had no wish to see Yamamoto and his staff officers resign. Such an event would demand a complete reorganisation of the Combined Fleet at a critical stage as the navy went on full war footing. More importantly, if Yamamoto resigned it would raise serious questions about Nagano's own leadership.

Nagano meekly sent word to his vice admirals, who passed the news on down to Tomioka that he was advised to accept and adopt Yamamoto's plan to attack Pearl Harbor. To Tomioka's disgust, Kuroshima's day of argument and threat had succeeded. Now the wheels were well and truly set in motion towards war.

Naval General Staff agreed to draw up formal orders for Yamamoto's audacious assault, to be approved by the emperor. The opening of Japan's proposed War of Greater East Asia had just been significantly widened and made far more hazardous. With deep regret, Tomioka himself immediately drew up the brief outline in his office with Captain Kuroshima looking on. Filled with foreboding, he brushed his own name to the order before taking it to his chief.

As Kuroshima quickly made his way from the navy ministry out in to the busy streets of Tokyo, Tomioka opened the drawer in his desk and took out his service revolver. He was convinced that the Pearl Harbor carrier attack force would be discovered before launching one aircraft, probably on the last day of its voyage across the Pacific as the fleet closed on the island of Oahu.

He checked that the revolver was fully loaded and held the pistol in his hand for a time before replacing it in his desk drawer. If the worst came to the worst, he told himself, he would blow his brains out. The baron, the son of a vice admiral, could not live with his name on the Pearl Harbor attack order if it became the greatest naval disaster in the history of the Imperial Japanese Navy, ending Japan's war before it began.

*

In Australia, there was rising concern about Japan's intentions, as strident Japanese leaders and newspapers accused Western nations of 'encircling' Japan. But human nature being what it was, many Australians were preoccupied with the war in Europe and especially with the progress of fighting in the Middle East and North Africa.

Throughout 1941, soldiers of the Australian Imperial Force had distinguished themselves in Libya, Greece, Crete, Syria and at Tobruk, in military operations principally directed by the British. Some of these operations had been successful, but there were notable disasters. In Greece, Australian troops fought a thankless and costly fighting retreat; on Crete, some 3000 members of the 6th Division left to defend the island were taken prisoner by the invading Germans.

In September, the 6th Division was fighting to hold back General Erwin Rommel's Afrika Corps in the siege of Tobruk, near Bardia in North Africa. Australian troops were being killed and wounded in numbers. They had been in action for many months under harsh conditions, and the British were resisting Australian efforts to pull the men out.

The commander of the 6th Division was a distinguished soldier. Lieutenant-General Sir Iven Mackay had been wounded at Gallipoli, and knighted for his outstanding leadership of the Australians at Tobruk in World War II. He was a well-educated man with a prim, even sombre, presence, and a particular dislike for the Australian Labor Party.

In August 1941, Mackay had been recalled to Australia from Palestine by the conservative government of Robert Menzies, and promoted to commander-in-chief, Home Forces. His attention now was focused squarely on the looming threat from Japan in the Pacific. The more he examined the situation, the more he was appalled at the ramifications. In late October, he found Australia to be 'virtually naked, militarily ... because all I can see is more than 12,000 miles of Australian coastline, and so little wherewithal for defending the points that really matter'.

By the time Mackay reached this conclusion, Menzies had resigned and the conservative parties had been replaced in government by the Australian Labor Party. John Curtin, who became prime minister, was untested. He was 56, almost the same age as the Japanese prime minister, but as men they could not have been more different. Curtin was the eldest of four children of Irish-born parents. He was largely self-educated, spending large amounts of time as a youth reading 'serious' books in the public library. He was a socialist who gained an interest in journalism by writing for socialist publications. At 26, he became secretary of the Timber Workers' Union of Victoria, and soon became the union's federal president.

During World War I, Curtin ran the trade union movement's anti-conscription campaign, and at one point was jailed for three days for failing to enlist. He became editor of the *Westralian Worker* in Perth in 1917, married and settled down. In 1928, Curtin was elected to federal parliament. As leader of the Opposition from 1935, his major role was to attempt to unite his faction-riddled Labor party as war with Germany loomed.

Curtin reached office already exhausted by his labours. Shortly before his elevation to prime minister in October 1941, Curtin wrote in tones of resignation to his wife, Elsie, at home in Cottesloe, a beachside suburb of Perth almost 4000 kilometres away:

> I find I am growing old, as the song says. We cannot avoid what life brings. To me the finest occurrences have been you and the two children. I dreamed about [son] Jack last night. I'm afraid my nerves need a rest. And here crisis follows crisis and there is no spell at all. More than ever before my nature is crying out for a holiday from strife ...
>
> But enough of complaint. Let me look at the credit side. And you alone have supplied that. I have had a kindly life ... I have supreme happiness in your love and loveliness. And no man has ever had more than that.

Curtin could fall into the blackest moods worrying himself sick about war, threats to Australia and the lives of combatants. The early pacifist was anointed chief warrior overnight and the pressures of this weighed mightily. In his blackest moods he sought solace from trusted friends and advisers, no longer turning to alcohol, as he did, to his detriment, in his union days. Suddenly, though, Curtin would emerge with renewed vigour and determination. He had long been wary of Japan. Even earlier in the year, in another letter to Elsie, John Curtin showed that he understood the thinking of the Japanese leadership:

> Japan is ready and waiting the day of maximum opportunity. This is dependent on how Britain stands up and on the Japanese reading of the USA policy. My own view of America is that Great Britain and the Atlantic Ocean mean much more to that country than does Australia and what is called Oceania. And that means Australia would be mad not to exert the maximum precautions in and on all the stepping places and approaches to ourselves.

As prime minister, he at first endeavoured to maintain the peace, while fearing the worst. 'Australia wants peace in the Pacific,' he told parliament. 'She is not a party to any policy of encirclement and never has been . . .'

Curtin knew his country's vulnerability to Japanese attack. The threat was highlighted towards the end of October, when Japan's Axis partner, Nazi Germany, publicly urged Japan to invade Australia. In a broadcast picked up in London, the spokesman for the German Admiralty, Rear Admiral Friedrich Lutzow, said:

> Should Britain be defeated, as certainly she will, then Australia will be incorporated in to the New Order for the Pacific . . . the vast coasts of Australia are flat so that surprise landings can be undertaken at any point. The help which Great Britain can offer Australia is indeed questionable.

The provocation came as Curtin and his minister for external affairs, Herbert 'Doc' Evatt, were holding secret peace discussions with the Japanese ambassador in Australia, Tatsuo Kawai, a former spokesman for Japan's Foreign Office and an ardent believer in Japan's right to colonise much of Asia.

Evatt, asked to respond, commented: 'The invitation to Japan to invade us is nothing short of an invitation to Japan to commit national suicide.' These were bold words without substance. Before the attack on Pearl Harbor, the possibility of American military involvement with Japan was by no means certain. And both Evatt and his leader were well aware that Australia had sent the cream of her armed forces overseas to help Britain, leaving her own flank dangerously exposed.

3

THE COMING CONQUESTS

Towards evening, as the sun was about to set, Captain Kuroshima's Nakajima biplane circled the fleet at Hashirajima, and touched down on a stretch of calm water by the stern of the battleship *Nagato*. Overhead, the arm of a crane appeared, and winched the aircraft aboard.

Kuroshima, pulling off his leather helmet and goggles, stepped out onto the deck, and was greeted by a smiling bear of a man with a crumpled face and a head tending towards baldness. This was Vice Admiral Ugaki, Admiral Yamamoto's chief of staff. Kuroshima saluted and grinned. His promotion to rear-admiral now seemed assured.

Ugaki couldn't hide his pleasure at the success of the mission. The vice admiral, another trained at Etajima, was hard-drinking, intelligent, belligerent and determined. He was more than a patriot; he was an unapologetic militant and a man of fierce pride, utterly convinced of the righteousness of Japan's cause and the need to go to war with the United States. When other senior officers had prevaricated over Yamamoto's plan to attack Pearl Harbor, he had been disgusted. And when Yamamoto's air chief,

Vice Admiral Chuichi Nagumo, who would play an essential role in the attack, had opposed the raid, Ugaki had urged Yamamoto to replace him.

After the success of Kuroshima's mission, there was still much planning to undertake – and perhaps some major obstacles to overcome – before the raid on Pearl Harbor became reality. Within a week, Baron Tomioka travelled down to the *Nagato* for further discussions. He was bound to contribute positively to planning the attack that he had tried so hard to prevent; he resolved to work for the success of the plan, just as every loyal Japanese naval officer would.

Tomioka was escorted to the commander-in-chief's cabin, where he found Isoroku Yamamoto full of enthusiasm. They talked for two hours, then adjourned for the usual gentlemen's luncheon, while the ship's band played on the afterdeck. Afterwards, Tomioka joined the Combined Fleet's staff officers in a planning session, chaired by Ugaki, which lasted more than four hours.

The baron presented a letter from his immediate superior, Vice Admiral Fukudome, which said the new prime minister, General Tojo, had not yet expressed his opinion of the Pearl Harbor plan. On the other hand, Fukudome quoted Emperor Hirohito as saying that there should be 'a clean slate' and national policy should be re-examined. Fukudome noted that negotiations with the Americans had not progressed, adding direly: 'I desire you who are in the active service to prepare wholeheartedly, expecting the worst.'

The Combined Fleet staffers were encouraged, but Ugaki wanted still more. After a generous dinner with Tomioka and other officers aboard the flagship, Yamamoto's chief of staff retired to his cabin. He mulled over the continuing negotiations in Washington, venting his frustrations in his diary: 'Who would dare draw back, reducing our demands, under the present situation? There is no alternative just before a war is going to break out. Procrastination means falling into the enemy's trap.'

Tomioka left the *Nagato* the following day, feeling uneasy. He could only place his faith in Ugaki's experience. He thought that Yamamoto's right-hand man was one of Japan's best officers and a recognised authority on naval strategy. And yet, Tomioka was troubled. His colleagues at Naval General Staff 'thought that Japan might be able to come through', as they put it:

> They figured that England might drop out of the war, that Japan would be successful in the South, that Japan might destroy many units of the US Fleet and that Japan would be able to secure the southern regions. All this would lead to a prolonged war which the US would weary of, and eventually make peace with Japan.

This was hardly a resounding endorsement for starting a war. As Tomioka's train rumbled north on the long journey back to Tokyo, he engaged his assistant, Yugi Yamamoto, in animated discussion about Japan's options. In his heart, he knew that winning a protracted war against the might of the United States was impossible.

Back in the capital, Tomioka reported to Fukudome, chief of the operations division. His boss had a reputation as a moderate, because of his opposition to the Tripartite Pact with Germany and Italy and his much earlier preference to avoid war with America. But now, Tomioka found to his surprise and alarm, Fukudome was coming around to the Combined Fleet's way of thinking.

The desperate hope was for a short war. Naval General Staff officers anticipated that after the strike on Pearl Harbor the US would be forced by mounting pressure of public opinion at home to seek out the Japanese navy in a great all-out naval battle. For decades Imperial Navy hawks had dreamt of this decisive engagement.

Timing of such a battle was the crucial issue: it would need to occur within 18 months of the outbreak of war, while Japan was still well equipped with ships and planes and firepower.

Faced with Fukudome's support for Yamamoto's plan, Tomioka

set aside his doubts about its logic. Above all else, it had become a matter of face for Japan. He convinced himself of one truth to which his racing mind had kept returning as his train rumbled back to Tokyo: 'It is better to strike and be defeated than to wait and fall from self-collapse.'

Big things were happening in the capital. On 1 November, Admiral Yamamoto was called to an urgent conference, where he learned that the new prime minister was not opposed to the Pearl Harbor attack.

The Combined Fleet had been out at sea undergoing rigorous training, especially at night attacks in which the navy felt it excelled. There was little sleep for crewmen during these exercises. The men were pushed until they almost dropped.

Soon the fleet was again off Hashirajima and masses of planes began attacking the multitude of ships at anchor, simulating bombing, torpedoing, and strafing. Vice Admiral Ugaki was in a buoyant mood, noting with pleasure that the pilots' skill had much improved. He knew now that the final decision on war would be made on 1 December, and that the navy had established X-Day, the attack on Pearl Harbor, as 8 December, 1941.*

'Everything is O.K.,' Ugaki wrote passionately in his diary:

You die,
You all die for the sake of the land.
I, too, will die.

The next time he flew to Tokyo to visit the navy ministry for talks, he found that all the doubters about Pearl Harbor were apparently feeling better. Ugaki recorded that the atmosphere of every department 'seemed to be very cheerful and aggressive, with active, lively business underway'.

---

* 7 December in the United States, including in Hawaii.

On 3 November, Emperor Hirohito had lengthy discussions with the military's high command about the opening of the war. He worried deeply about the success of the operation, at this meeting recognising the strategic role that Australia would ultimately play in the outcome. The following day the emperor called in his key aide, the lord keeper of the privy seal, Marquis Koichi Kido, a staunch ally of the new prime minister, and told him that two things bothered him about Japan's war plans:

'Suppose we invade Thailand, won't we need to provide a clear justification for that? How is the research on this matter going? And in the event that airplane and submarine interdiction occurs from bases in Australia, do we have countermeasures so we can be sure of uninterrupted acquisition of oil and supplies?' The questions indicated Hirohito's keen sensitivity to the strategic weakness in Japan's position in the South Pacific.

On 5 November, the emperor, symbolically dressed in his army uniform, sat stiffly on a dais at one end of the palace chamber while at the other end of the room, the participants in the imperial conference – the army, navy and government leaders – sat facing each other at two long, brocade-covered tables, their knuckles on knees. In the following discussion, which had been called to endorse war against the United States and Great Britain, and which lasted nearly four hours, Hirohito did not speak one word, whatever reservations he might have harboured.

The prime minister, General Tojo, said Japan had made a special effort to reach agreement in diplomatic negotiations with the United States in Washington, but had not been able to get the Americans to reconsider their demands. As a result, Tojo said: 'We must now decide to go to war, set the time for military action at the beginning of December, concentrate all our efforts on completing preparations for war, and at the same time try to break the impasse by means of diplomacy.'

The chief of Army General Staff, General Hajime Sugiyama, a grizzled and aggressive extremist despite his bland countenance, pushed for immediate war. He said that if the start of war was delayed, the ratio of arms between Japan and the US would become more and more unfavourable to Japan as time went on.

Sugiyama was a most experienced army officer and politician, a man whose influence and authority arose not simply from his rank. Born of a Samurai family in Fukuoka prefecture, he had been minister for war and the armed forces during the 1930s, and had impressed the British embassy in Tokyo with his friendliness, wide experience and commonsense. In fact, he had a long history of belligerency, having been a key supporter of Japanese aggression in China.

He told the conference, 'We are fully confident of success, given close cooperation between the Army and the Navy.' Whether he knew it or not, the general had put his finger on one of the main weaknesses that would emerge in the Japanese campaign.

General Sugiyama explained the proposed targets and military strengths across the Pacific, adding finally: 'There are other forces in India, Australia and New Zealand, which I assume would participate sooner or later ... The operation is planned to start in Malaya and the Philippines simultaneously, and then to move towards the Netherlands East Indies; and that entire operation will be completed within five months of the opening of the war.'

Yoshimichi Hara, 74, was Emperor Hirohito's mouthpiece at these imperial conferences. He was president of the Privy Council, a group of distinguished advisers to the emperor, and he was not in favour of war. After several hours of discussion, Hara asked for some simple explanation of the proposed southern operations and how successful they were likely to be.

He pointed to a chart in his hand: 'India and Australia are excluded from this map. Although it is said that there is a force of well over 200,000 men and some aircraft in these areas, there are also warships. Can we destroy their fleet in a short period of time?' Sugiyama replied: 'We can destroy their fleet if they want a decisive battle. Even if we destroy it, however, the war will continue long after the Southern Operation.'

Tojo ruled that Japan was resolved to go to war in early

December. Hirohito did not demur. The participants bowed deeply as the emperor left the chamber. The following day Admiral Nagano secretly issued Imperial Japanese Navy Order No. 1, commanding Admiral Yamamoto to make preparations for war 'for the sake of its [Japan's] self-existence and self-defence.'

Civilian Foreign Minister Shigenori Togo watched the inexorable slide to war but couldn't get information from the services, as the military would not abide civilian 'interference', even at liaison conferences. Future military operations were the exclusive province of the High Command, neither the government nor the Diet:

> This predominance of military opinion had, with the passing of time, come to have a seriously crippling effect on the operations of the government. The trend to military intrusion into political concerns had been intensified with the growth of the concept of total war – figures relating to military strength were clothed in secrecy...

War fever gripped Tokyo. A liaison conference between the army, navy, and government was called on 15 November. The foreign minister, Shigenori Togo, reported on the continuing, fruitless negotiations in Washington and his own discussions in Tokyo with the US ambassador, Joseph C. Grew.

One of the policy documents approved by the liaison conference was a proposal for hastening the end of the war that had not yet begun. It envisaged 'a quick war', destroying American and British bases in eastern Asia to secure a powerful strategic position and control of vital materials. The policy called for Japan, Germany and Italy to work for the surrender of Great Britain: 'The connection between Australia and India and the British mother country will be broken by means of political pressure and the destruction of commerce, and their separation will be achieved.'

That afternoon the liaison conference reconvened at the Imperial Palace for war games. In the emperor's presence, the opening blows of Japan's Pacific campaign were rehearsed on large tables laid out with maps.

Four days later in Melbourne, a teleprinter clanked out a message in the office of Military Intelligence at Victoria Barracks. It was a secret diplomatic message in code from Togo to all Japanese diplomatic missions overseas. The foreign minister advised diplomatic missions to be prepared to burn their code books: 'Owing to the pressure of the international situation, we must be faced with a generally bad situation.' They were to expect a weather broadcast from Tokyo that would include secret directions.

At his expensive residence at Auburn, in Melbourne's leafy eastern suburbs, Japan's senior diplomat in Australia read his superior's message with growing despair. Tatsuo Kawai had become Japan's first minister to Australia in March 1941, a time of great tension between the two countries. Although he had been a strident apologist for the military subjugation of China during his previous post as the foreign ministry's spokesman in Tokyo, since taking up his external posting he had repeatedly denied that Japan had any territorial ambitions on Australia. A month after his arrival, he told the *Sydney Morning Herald*: 'The Japanese Government has no intention of moving down on Australia by military force... No responsible leaders in Japan have ever expressed a desire for Japan to attack Australia militarily.'

Friends and family would later recall Kawai as a man of two faces. Like many other Japanese diplomats, he was a complex, sophisticated personality who felt at ease in Western surroundings. But, atypically, he was his own man. At times, he could be quite rebellious and he encouraged his staff to probe and question, rather than accept everything at face value, including Japan's official policies.

He was a host of considerable charm, good humour and grace. At sumptuous dinners at *Carn Brea*, his Californian-style mansion in Auburn, his guests frequently included politicians, captains of industry, press barons and journalists, judges, and other opinion makers. The Japanese ambassador worked hard to persuade these influential Australians towards sympathy for Japan's international plight, while also attempting to turn the dominion away from its traditional ties with Britain. At the same time, he retained a number of military spies on his staff, and through them a network of contacts and agents around Australia.

Even though he remained a fervent nationalist, Kawai gradually came to admire the Australian character deeply. Australians, he considered, were generally honest and forthright, if not a little immature. One particularly direct, laconic, and humble man left a lasting impression on the Japanese diplomat. As leader of the federal Opposition, John Curtin had begun a series of long, secretive meetings with Kawai.

The ambassador was pleasantly surprised at how frankly they could discuss each country's major concerns and ambitions without diplomatic inhibition. Curtin proposed further meetings, and became involved in an intense round of debate with Kawai, on which he briefed Prime Minister Menzies. In pushing Japan's viewpoint, Kawai could be intimidating, yet as time went on he softened under Curtin's calm and unpretentious manner. According to the Japanese consul in Melbourne, Kawai's friend Tsuneo Hattori, they felt able to 'bare their hearts to each other'.

The Curtin family cottage at Jarrad Street, Cottesloe, still stands, although it awaits proper preservation. Any student of history can follow the sunny route that John Curtin loved to take, passing over the gentle slopes of the golf course, across the dunes to the beach. In 1937, he walked here with his daughter, gazing out to the Indian Ocean. China was in crisis, with renewed incursions by Japanese troops now turning into full-scale warfare.

After the Great War, Curtin had dedicated his life to preventing Australia from taking part in another conflict. Elsie, 19, could see that her father was preoccupied, and asked him what the matter was. Curtin, she soon learned, feared a Japanese invasion of

Australia: 'I was just thinking what we would do if we saw the Jap fleet coming in past the island right now. I can see it as clearly as the waves... the only question now is when.'

In July 1941, Curtin and his wife invited Tatsuo Kawai to dine with them at Jarrad Street. They extended this hospitality at a time when Japanese troops had just occupied southern Indochina. The politician was criticised for having the 'Jap' at home, but the evening cemented a friendship between the two families that would last generations.

From the time Curtin had become Opposition leader, one of his chief concerns was Japanese aggression and expansionism, and the build-up of Japan's armed forces.

Ten days after Kawai and the Curtins dined at Cottesloe, a foreign ministry cable from Tokyo made reference to a growing rift between Australia and Great Britain, evident particularly within Curtin's Australian Labor Party, a rift which Japan thought it could exploit: 'We shall place emphasis on propaganda work towards the Netherlands East Indies and Australia, since we wish to have access to the former's oil supply in the future, and to encourage the movement for independence in the latter.' The Japanese had misread completely Australian nationalism as a trend towards independence from Britain. Curtin's party, well stocked with men of Irish Catholic descent, certainly had issues with Britain, but Japanese observers greatly overstated the situation.

Curtin appeased Japan up until mid-1941, as did most Australian politicians, especially Prime Minister Menzies, who criticised his counterpart for issuing dire warnings about Japan's intentions. 'I do not believe in the inevitability of a conflict in the Pacific', Menzies stated from London in March 1941 when both sides of politics in Australia were issuing dire warnings. 'There is no difficulty which is not capable of being resolved with frankness.'

Even so, few Australians realised the extent and depth of the Japanese threat.

One senior military officer who had been to Singapore, and had witnessed the British there behaving as if the prospect of war 'was as remote as the moon', went out of his way to issue a wake-up call. At Victoria Barracks in Melbourne, the new deputy chief of General Staff in the Australian Army, General Sydney Rowell, pulled out an unmarked writing pad and began composing a series of unofficial letters.

In spite of the obvious worsening of the strategic position, Rowell had seen the most unwarranted optimism in some political and departmental circles. 'Indeed, the public at large seemed oblivious to the dangers that lay ahead, and they were given no warning by the political authorities. We were forbidden to issue any instructions to commands that war with Japan was inevitable.'

He knew that Australia had no operational force immediately available to meet the Japanese threat. Deeply concerned about this, disobeying instructions, he took it on himself to write personal letters to all general officers under his command. He warned that the implications for Australia 'were clear for all to see'. General commands 'would be well advised to look over their plans for the defence of vital areas'.

Late in the spring of 1941, the new prime minister of Australia was given an alarming insight into the looming threat from Japan. Such was Tatsuo Kawai's respect and trust for Curtin's 'distinctive character', as Kawai called it, that the Japanese ambassador did something that no Japanese diplomat at that time would have dreamt of doing.

He travelled to Canberra and went to see Curtin privately at Parliament House. It was 29 November 1941, and Japan's fleets were secretly heading towards military targets all over the Pacific. When Curtin asked the ambassador, simply, 'Is it to be war?', according to Curtin himself, Kawai replied: 'I'm afraid it has gone too far; the momentum is too great.' It was a direct answer that gave Curtin's war effort a flying start.

A vast battle fleet had slipped lines at Hashirajima and headed out of the Seto Inland Sea towards the Pacific. The 'main body', as it was called, comprised the battleships *Haruna* and *Kongo*, the heavy cruisers *Atago*, *Maya*, *Takao*, and ten destroyers. The fleet would sail for the southern Chinese island of Hainan, where it would collect troopships bound for the invasion of Malaya and the Philippines.

Its commander, Vice Admiral Nobutake Kondo, had his flag aboard the *Atago*, a fast and powerful heavy cruiser, notable for its ten eight-inch guns. Kondo's last act at Hashirajima had been to say farewell to Admiral Yamamoto aboard the *Nagato*. For days, there had been farewells at Hashirajima and onshore at Kure, where all the top brass had gathered at command headquarters overlooking the bay. Much sake had been drunk and many rousing speeches given.

Kondo had one of the most difficult tasks at the opening of Japan's war. He was ordered to destroy enemy fleet and air strength in the Philippines, Malaya and the Dutch East Indies, and to act as surface escort to the army's forces, supporting their landings in these places as well as in Thailand. He was also to prepare for the invasion of Timor and Burma, while destroying enemy ships in South-East Asia generally.

Japan's ultimate aim was the complete domination of Asia and supremacy in the western Pacific. But first she needed to take the Philippine islands, because of their strategic position, and the Dutch East Indies and Malaya for their natural resources, particularly oil and rubber.

Kondo had raised vigorous objections to the Hawaiian adventure because it extended the navy beyond its capabilities and depended too much 'on innumerable factors beyond Japan's control'. His objections had been overruled, as was his suggestion that the United States be left alone, at least in the initial stages of the war, so that Japan could engage the British and the Dutch without distraction.

Notwithstanding these rebuffs, every ounce of his energy was now consumed by his responsibility for the initial invasions. He would acquit himself triumphantly. Indeed, as his successes grew in number, Admiral Kondo would set his sights on Australia.

4

BLOSSOMS RAISED TO FALL

The switchback road curves this way and that, climbing the steep mountain beyond Kure. There are glimpses of the Inland Sea between the trees. 'Ah, there it is,' my Japanese guide says, and through the foliage, beside a path leading to a shrine, a glorious scene unfolds.

'That is Base P, Kurahashijima, the island of the midget submarine special attack base. You see that beach on the island? They practised in their midget submarines around there and on the other side. And you see those old buildings, like warehouses, along the waterfront. The midget submarine men used them during the war.'

The boys of the midget submarines were an intense, even melancholy lot. So I had expected something dark and foreboding, but their little island looks more like a pleasant resort. At one end there is an idyllic park, and a deserted sandy beach leading into dense jungle-like foliage. At the end of the long beach, there's a swimming enclosure and, beyond the park, a sizeable village of tightly packed houses.

The base, which is largely demolished now, has been replaced by Ourasaki Park. There's a large stone monument there. Its inscription, in Kanji, says that 2600 men were trained in 'special submarine' warfare, and that 439 died during the war.

Another large stone tablet reminds visitors that the 'special submarines' were 'a highlight of the early part of the war'; that after travelling a long distance, they infiltrated Pearl Harbor and attacked the US main fleet. 'Next they invaded Madagascar in the west and Sydney in the south. They shocked the English and Australian fleets and greatly shook the morale of all their men.'

Japan's infamous midget submarines were conceived by a naval engineer in the late 1920s. Their creator envisaged a special attack craft capable of surreptitiously entering well-protected anchorages and harbours where large submarines were prone to detection. The first prototype, built and tested at the Kure naval torpedo laboratory made its debut before the navy's high command in 1935. It wasn't until 1940 that the two-man midget was sufficiently developed to undergo sea trials.

The A-class two-man midgets destined for Pearl Harbor were larger than their name suggests, almost 24 metres in length and nearly two metres in diameter. They displaced 42 tonnes, and their electric motors, fed by batteries running almost the entire length of the ship, gave the craft a particularly fast submerged-speed of 24 knots. In theory, the midgets packed a considerable punch with two 18-inch torpedoes in the nose. But they were inherently crude, unsafe, and unreliable.

At first, the craft were lowered by crane over the back of a ship, but it quickly became clear that the mother ship easily could be detected. This resulted in a revolutionary idea – the midgets would be carried on the backs of much larger submarines that could dive with the smaller craft attached. The defect of this solution was that it removed highly effective weapons of war from combat in favour of highly ineffective ones.

It did not take long to demonstrate that the scheme was hare-brained and wasteful of valuable military resources, both human and material. But the midget sub programme continued nevertheless. In essence, it continued more because of senior-officer admiration of the warrior spirit of the young crews, who knew they were going to die, than of the midget submarines as an effective weapon of war.

At Base P, the trainees were shown maps of Hong Kong, Singapore, Sydney, San Francisco, and Pearl Harbor. One wrote that during training in 1941 he had been told by a tutor: 'Learn the peculiarities of these harbours and commit them to your memory.'

These young men, barely out of school, were taught to operate crude two-man midget subs and *Kaiten* human-guided torpedoes, particularly grotesque weapons that meant certain death for their operators. They would learn how to drive themselves to destruction on a live torpedo. There were many accidents in training, some fatal. Is it any wonder that some of the trainees, so repeatedly branded as fanatics wanting to die in battle for the emperor, in fact desperately wanted to live?

It is late 1941; in Japan, war with the Allies now seems certain. The newspaper headlines are screaming about the aggression of the West, and Western economic sanctions against Japan are beginning to bite. A small boy named Kazutomo Ban is walking at his mother's side through streets near Nagoya, a port and industrial city on the Pacific coast of Honshu island. They are accompanying his brother Katsuhisa to the railway station, to see him off to war.

Katsuhisa, 22, has achieved the honour of becoming the first naval officer from his home town of Takahama, a small port town on the Sea of Japan. His cap bears the distinctive brass crest of the Imperial Japanese Navy, an anchor topped by the cherry blossom insignia of the midget submariners, and he wears his crisp uniform with undisguised pride. Intelligent, strong, and handsome, he has already demonstrated outstanding ability in his midget submarine training, serving as a member of the recovery team when a sub was lost during training off their base near Kure.

As they near the station, his mother struggles with her emotions,

1942

and Katsuhisa talks animatedly to her. For his mother, this farewell is all too familiar. The boys' father, a poor lumberman, was a highly decorated army sergeant in the Russo–Japanese War, and their other brothers, all six of them, are fighting in China. This time, saying goodbye has a particular finality. All of them, even the child clutching his mother's hand, know it. 'I thought it was almost certainly the last time I would see him,' Kazutomo recalls.

'My mother talked a lot, and I was never allowed to listen in. But I remember at the station how distressed she was, and I remember feeling awkward at the burden she seemed to be bearing.'

Katsuhisa tells his mother that it is his duty never to return.

He is embarrassed by her grief. The poor woman is supposed to be grateful to lose a son in the service of the emperor. With four years of war in China, Japan is becoming a nation of grieving mothers.

In Wakayama City, Itsuo Ashibe is also saying goodbye to his older brother. Mamoru Ashibe is destined to share the same midget submarine in Sydney Harbour as Katsuhisa Ban. Two of Itsuo's brothers have already been killed in the war. But Itsuo is closest to Mamoru. The pair share a special bond: 'He didn't tell our parents or our other brothers, but he told me, "It's a secret – I'm going to be the first one to attack the enemy's warships and I'll die a glorious death",' Itsuo recalls.

For those assigned to the midget submarines, this talk of certain death for emperor and country was a way of life. It wasn't morbid bravado or patriotic exaggeration; it was a code drilled into them by their superiors and their peers.

Yet the novice submariners could be as wild and fun-loving as the young Australian servicemen who outraged decent Sydneysiders with their public drunkenness and pranks.

Ashibe, who knew he'd die in war, lived life on the edge. During 1941, he had such serious problems with alcohol that he was hospitalised. He wrote to his sister Mikiyo: 'From the look of things, I think I will be out of hospital in a week. I have much navy business to attend to, too, so I am taking plenty of rest and praying day and night so that I can go back to my naval ensign [duties] without further delay.'

He was filled with a sense of duty: 'Sister, I will forbid myself to consume any more alcohol from now on. How happy will Mother be, knowing that starting from my next leave she need not send me any sake?' He often worried about his mother. With all her sons in the services, she was alone. As his inevitable departure grew closer, Mamoru wrote to Mikiyo from his base near Ourasaki, pleading, 'Whenever you are free, please do go and see her.'

Keiu Matsuo was a particularly promising member of the midget submarine squads. In October, 1941, this intelligent and quietly spoken young submariner was chosen for special reconnaissance work.

Pacing the deck of the Japanese luxury liner *Taiyo Maru* in a merchant navy uniform, Matsuo had the rare honour to be privy early to Japan's deepest military secret – that the Imperial Navy and its air wing were about to smash the United States Pacific Fleet.

The *Taiyo Maru*'s voyage took her from Japan to Hawaii, but instead of travelling via the most direct route, the liner sailed north-east into the cooler waters of the Pacific before turning on a southerly course for her destination. This course took the ship well away from traditional sea lanes and patrolling aircraft from US bases in the Pacific.

While the paying passengers lounged on deck, Matsuo and two other officers of the Imperial Navy spent most of their time on the bridge. Commander Toshihade Maejima was an expert on submarines, and Lieutenant Commander Suguru Suzuki was an aircraft specialist. Working in relays, the three took meticulous notes of everything they saw and experienced, day and night, including the weather, wind and sea conditions and any sightings of aircraft and shipping.

Matsuo was his friend Maejima's assistant, and the two of them had helped to develop midget submarine strategy. Their ideas and enthusiasm had brought them to the notice of the navy's top brass, and they had been ordered before Admiral Yamamato to explain how they envisaged the subs could be deployed in combat. The midget submarine was by then in full production at Kure; already almost 20 had rolled off the production line. The submariners had quickly convinced Yamamoto that the midgets could strike at the enemy on their very doorstep, and then be recovered successfully. This would prove to be enthusiastic nonsense.

On a sunny Saturday, the *Taiyo Maru* slipped through the narrow Honolulu harbour entrance and made towards Pier 8. It was 1 November 1941. For the last ten days and nights the three spies had been on alert, and had had little sleep. They had intensified their watch as the *Taiyo Maru* approached the island of Oahu, noting every American aircraft and ship.

Matsuo and Maejima were there to judge the capacity of the US base for resisting submarine attack. The Imperial Navy obtained the observations of the land-based spies, masquerading as consular officials and diplomats, but also needed timely reports from its own naval people on the spot. Matsuo and his two colleagues had sighted no patrol craft north of the island of Midway, and reconnaissance aircraft north of Oahu appeared to extend not much further than 200 miles. They had sighted no other vessels during their voyage to Honolulu using the north-easterly course.

In a matter of weeks, Japan's great attack fleet would take the same circuitous route to its target.

From the *Nagato*, off Hashirajima, Yamamoto and Ugaki took the admiral's barge over to the *Akagi*. The carrier, with her 92 aircraft, was about to sail for Hitokappu Bay in the northern Kurile islands, the assembly point for the Hawaiian expedition. She would be Vice Admiral Chuichi Nagumo's flagship for the striking force attacking Pearl Harbor.

Yamamoto had been the *Akagi's* first captain. As he and his chief of staff were piped aboard, every officer was assembled on the flight deck to welcome the commander-in-chief. Americans must not be underestimated, he warned. They represented the most powerful enemy Japan would ever meet and the men must be prepared for any eventuality. Admiral Ugaki thought that he saw on the listeners' faces 'unshakable loyalty, determined resolution, even a degree of ferocity'.

Two days later, as Ugaki stood on the deck of the *Nagato,* he focused his glasses on an unusual-looking submarine in the distance. It was the big sub *I-22,* flagship of the first submarine division, also headed out on the Pearl Harbor adventure. She was carrying a midget submarine on her deck. The idea of incorporating midgets in the massive assault on Pearl Harbor had originated among young officers of the special attack squads who did not want to be left out of the action.

Keiu Matsuo was one of them, but he was still aboard the *Taiyo Maru* as it steamed back to Japan. Fate would intercede for some of the other young submariners, as well. Katsuhisa Ban and Mamoru Ashibe would not strike the first blow at the enemy at Pearl Harbor. Instead they would be assigned to the attack on Sydney Harbour the following year. But Ashibe did not yet know that, and wrote what he thought would be his final letter to his mother at Wakayama.

He enclosed his life insurance policy and made arrangements for his suitcase to be collected from the base: 'It will start to get cold, Mother, so take care of yourself, and hope for the day that the three of us [including his brothers who will also die] will serve with distinction. I have nothing to regret. This letter will be the last. Say hello to our relatives. Mamoru.'

This farewell letter was sent from the navy headquarters at Kure, where the midget submarine teams had assembled after their final training. All these young men were bachelors from large families with plenty of brothers; few had ever had girlfriends. It was intended that their deaths would not leave their parents childless, or bereave families of their own.

Although they had not volunteered for the suicidal 'special

attack' units, they seemed to accept their fate enthusiastically, at least according to their proud superiors. As Japanese of the era described it, the young men were like cherry blossoms dropping to the ground just as they reached their prime. Admiral Ugaki, patron of the midget-submariners, committed this idea to verse in his diary. 'Gone with the spring/are young boys like cherry blossoms...'

Right from the start of his navy training at Etajima academy in April 1937, Kazuo Sakamaki, now 23, had been taught that the most important thing was 'to die manfully on the battlefield': 'None of us was a volunteer. We had all been ordered to our assignment. That none of us objected goes without saying: we knew that punishment would be very severe if we objected; we were supposed to feel highly honored.'

Sakamaki was the son of a schoolteacher. The name, Kazuo, his parents gave him meant 'peace boy'. He grew up in a remote, quiet village surrounded by beautiful hills and gentle rivers on Shikoku island, the smallest of Japan's four main islands. Then, in April 1941, Sakamaki was made an ensign and told to report with 23 others to a submarine support vessel, the *Chiyoda*, anchored off Kure. In mid-November 1941, the young men were granted a week's leave. Sakamaki wrote how 'an indescribable fear of real war' crept into his mind. Saying goodbye to his family was not easy:

'I was unable to look them straight in the face and smile with them. That they were proud of me I did not doubt. But the thought of never seeing them again was overpowering. When I had to part from them, the moment which had been reserved for glory was an hour of agony.'

On 16 November, the young men of the special attack squads gathered in the assembly room at Kure. Vice Admiral Mitsumi Shimizu, commander-in-chief of the Sixth Fleet Submarines, entered the hall. 'You are herewith directed to take positions of readiness for war with the United States of America,' he said.

Sakamaki was stunned: 'The effect was like a sudden magic

blow. A sheet of paper was handed to each one of us. It was a written order which had been just given orally. With this paper in our hands, there was no longer any doubt. 'War with America!' The thought was gripping ... I walked downstairs in a daze, as if a heavy hammer had struck me in the head. "It has finally come," I thought. My whole body was filled with a strange pain.' Sakamaki and an Etajima classmate, Ensign Hirowo, walked solemnly through the busy city of Kure. When Sakamaki said it was their last night in Japan, Hirowo morosely replied: 'You are right. When we go, we cannot expect to return.'

Earlier, in a discussion with their commanding officer, Yamamoto had expressed concern about rescuing the men from the midget submarines after the attack on Pearl Harbor. He told Shimizu to cancel the midget sub involvement if the admiral thought it would be a suicide mission. Shimizu spoke with some of the boys, who were enthusiastic, before deciding to proceed.

Before departing, the submariners had their pictures taken and wrote short mottoes and verse expressing their willingness to die in combat. At noon on the 17th, the flagship of the first submarine division, the *I-22*, slipped out of Kure leading four other *I*-class submarines attached to the midget or 'special attack' force. One of them was the *I-24*, carrying the midget sub commanded by Sakamaki, who wrote of his depression: 'I, Kazuo Sakamaki, was being buried as of that moment. A skipper of a secret submarine going out in the service of his country was dictating that letter. I swallowed tears in my mouth.'

When Admiral Ugaki, from the deck of the *Nagato*, observed the *I-22* departing, he returned to his cabin and wrote enthusiastically in his diary of the men who manned the midgets:

> The surprise attack on X-Day will be an entirely unexpected storm. No one can predict what results they will bring about. Young lieutenants were seen on their deck smiling.
>
> They expect never to return alive; they are ready to die at the scene of battle. Their preparedness is admirable. Our old

'death-defying spirit' never changes. We can rely fully upon them.

Lieutenant Kazuo Sakamaki was not smiling: 'I stood on the deck and watched the coastal hills disappear in the deepening darkness. When I realised that this was my last glimpse of Japan, I could not help tears flowing out of my eyes.'

The submarines headed out east across the Pacific while the great aircraft carrier fleet, maintaining radio silence, took the separate, longer north-easterly route towards Hawaii. Most of Japan's carriers were committed to the opening devastating blow, including the *Akagi*, *Kaga*, *Hiryu*, *Soryu*, *Zuikaku*, and *Shokaku*. The fleet consisted of 31 ships while the carriers were armed with a total of 353 aircraft.

The Pearl Harbor fleet was not detected by the Allies, but another Japanese naval force was. On Monday, 1 December, six days before the outbreak of war with Japan, the world heard a report from Manila that a Japanese fleet, estimated at up to 70 ships, and headed by cruisers and aircraft carriers, had been observed in the region of Japanese islands, not far from British North Borneo.

In Canberra, Prime Minister Curtin told newsmen at a private briefing that the British expected an immediate attack on Thailand and Curtin had recommended that British forces, including Australian troops, 'go in first'.

The following day, the Melbourne *Herald*'s senior correspondent in Canberra, Joe Alexander, wrote in his diary that he was disturbed by off-the-record information from Curtin. Prime Minister Winston Churchill had sent Curtin a personal message stating he had sent US President Franklin D Roosevelt a strong plea to continue the conversations with the Japanese:

> He said the British War Cabinet was divided . . . I pressed Curtin for an interpretation of Churchill's attitude and he said it

amounted to this: 'Unless America collaborated Britain should let Thailand rip.' This is disturbing and forecasts another terrific condonation by the Allies of Japanese aggression.

On 2 December, the *Japan Times* carried a news item from the Domei agency in Bangkok headed AUSSIES PREPARING TO INVADE THAILAND: 'The international situation surrounding Thailand is becoming worse every moment. Reuters reports that 50,000 Australian troops have already completed preparations for the invasion of Thailand.'

Soon, there were reports from Singapore of two large, heavily escorted Japanese fleets rounding Cambodia Point and steaming up the Gulf of Siam, apparently towards Bangkok, although their destination could be Malaya. American intelligence also indicated that 125,000 Japanese troops had concentrated in Indochina.

In Tokyo, Australia now entered the equation for three operational planners engaged in estimating the Allied strategy. They were two colonels, Takushiro Hattori and Ichiji Sugita from the operations section of Army General Staff, and the naval captain, Baron Sadatoshi Tomioka. The men agreed that the US, Britain, and Russia would try to isolate Japan politically and economically, and that the enemy would also endeavour to check and counter-attack Japan's advances to the south by reinforcing Singapore and the Philippines.

They also agreed that the Allies would 'endeavour to secure communication with Australia, India and other remaining strategic areas in the Far East'. They correctly guessed that Britain could not spare too many of her forces for the war against Japan because of her war with Germany. They were not entirely sure about the approach the USA would adopt, but correctly told their superiors that war with Germany and Italy probably would be the Americans' first priority.

Neither the British nor the Americans were prepared to strike the first blow by instigating attacks on those Japanese fleets that they knew were on the move. The Western world seemed to hold its collective breath.

President Roosevelt sent a personal message to Emperor Hirohito in a final attempt to prevent war, but it was too late. In Washington, the government's top officials, monitoring intercepted Japanese diplomatic messages, soon knew that the talking had finished, and that the future lay in the hands of the generals and admirals.

5

GLORIOUS VICTORY

The small figure of Isoroku Yamamoto, clad in a dark, unadorned uniform, slumped in a canvas chair, dozing peacefully.

All around him, in the operations room of the *Nagato*, there was barely restrained tension.

On 2 December, Admiral Yamamoto had issued a message to all ships of the Combined Fleet, especially those closing on the Hawaiian Islands. The message read simply, '*Niitaka-yama no bore* 1208' (climb Mount Niitaka 1208). Now, in the early hours of Sunday, 8 December, Japan's war operations were about to begin.

The emperor had told Yamamoto: 'The task facing the Combined Fleet is of the utmost importance, and the whole fate of our nation will depend on the outcome...' But the admiral was at peace. Everything that he could have done had been done. For the first time in months, he had even put in an appearance at his family home in Tokyo, to dine with his wife Reiko and their four children. Reiko, plump and solid, had been ill, but got up immediately and prepared a meal.

The admiral in recent weeks had spent the night with former geisha Chiyoko Kawai, his true love for many years, at an elegant inn on Itsukushima, a beautiful island offshore from Iwakuni on the Inland Sea. Yamamoto had never attempted to keep his friendship with Miss Kawai a secret, even inviting her aboard the *Nagato*.

Now, while Yamamoto slept in a corner of the operations room, the young staff officers around him nervously but quietly shuffled through reports and examined charts and maps, talking in whispers, worrying that there was some vital detail they had overlooked. Yamamoto and Ugaki had allowed their staff officers enormous freedom of thought and expression. When the young men wanted a raging debate about naval options and policies, they asked their seniors to vacate the room so that they could express themselves freely. Their superiors would obligingly trot out of the operations room and wait to be called back.

At last, a wireless officer burst in with the first news of the army's landing in rough seas at Kota Bharu, northern Malaya; news of a successful landing on the north coast of Luzon, north of Manila soon followed. But it was Pearl Harbor that they all wished to hear about.

At 3.00 a.m., Admiral Ugaki rose from his bunk. He observed his usual morning ritual, bowing to the photographic portraits of the emperor and empress displayed in his cabin; then he lit a cigarette.

About 300 kilometres north of Pearl Harbor, the carriers of Admiral Nagumo's strike force swung into the wind, and the first of 353 planes began taking off. The cheers of crewmen rung out in the pre-dawn darkness. Commander Mitsuo Fuchida was in the lead plane: 'One by one I counted them. Yes, the battleships were there all right, eight of them! But our last lingering hope of finding any carriers present was now gone. Not one was to be seen. It was 0749 when I ordered my radioman to send the command, "Attack!" He immediately began tapping out the pre-arranged code signal: "TO, TO, TO . . ."'

Admiral Ugaki was smoking impatiently when the *Nagato*'s aviation staff officer, Commander Akira Sasaki, burst into his cabin. 'At 0319 wireless TO is being sent repeatedly,' the breathless officer blurted. Ugaki hurried into the *Nagato*'s operations room.

At Pearl Harbor, the Japanese airmen began blasting the battleships and airfields of Pearl Harbor, meeting little resistance in the air. The absence of the American carriers would be a significant blow to the Imperial Navy's plans, yet Fuchida was elated: 'The effectiveness of our attack was now certain, and a message – "Surprise attack successful!" – was accordingly sent to [the flagship] *Akagi* at 0753. The message was received by the carrier and duly relayed to the homeland. But, as I was astounded to learn later, the message from my plane was also heard directly by *Nagato* in Hiroshima Bay and by the General Staff in Tokyo.'

Back in the operations room of the *Nagato*, Yamamoto woke from his siesta. Radio messages in the form of telegrams from aircraft and ships were now coming over the speaker on the wall and the officers listened enthralled as Japan's initial victory unfolded. Ugaki later wrote in his diary:

'I torpedoed enemy battleship with great war result' or 'I bombed Hickam Airfield and got a great war result', which were wirelessed by our friendly planes, as well as enemy wireless messages which were most interesting. We can see the fighting so clearly. Enemy consternation is beyond description... While they were at their breakfast table, great masses of Japanese airplanes came like bolts from the blue; I can imagine their utter surprise.

The young staff officers shook hands with each other, bursting with elation and relief. Yamamoto tried to hide his emotions but couldn't, according to one of his favourites, Commander Yasuji Watanabe. Chief steward Omi poured sake and served dried squid. Thousands of kilometres from Pearl Harbor, the brains of the Combined Fleet toasted their own success.

En route to the Hawaiian islands, submariner Kazuo Sakamaki permitted himself to think only of success in the task ahead. But he was almost finished off before he reached Oahu. He was washed overboard from the deck of the *I-24*, and was saved only because he was able to grasp a rope tethered to the ship.

From the mother sub, Sakamaki and his comrades could see the lights of Honolulu, and pick up jazz music playing from a wireless station on shore. The seas were calm, with a waning but bright moon. But when it was time for action, the young submariner received a second shock. The gyrocompass on his midget submarine was not functioning; Sakamaki and his crewmate, Petty Officer Kiyoshi Inagaki, insisted on going anyway. They entered the midget, which was released underwater about 16 kilometres south-west of Honolulu.

Trouble struck immediately. Sakamaki had difficulties with the trim, and the midget sub almost toppled over. He was desperately afraid of surfacing and being spotted by an American warship. The sub eventually righted itself, and Sakamaki looked through the periscope. To his horror, they were headed in the wrong direction, and US patrol craft were moving across the harbour entrance.

They were spotted by an old four-stacker destroyer, USS *Ward*, patrolling off the harbour entrance. She began firing four-inch shells, the first shots of the war with Japan. The submariners heard an enormous crash, and then white smoke filled the sub chamber, as a depth charge from the destroyer exploded nearby. Its force knocked Sakamaki out, but he recovered consciousness, regained his feet, and squinted through the periscope to see warships charging again.

By daybreak, Sakamaki was disoriented. He saw the harbour entrance and headed straight for it. Torpedo planes and dive bombers were now descending on the battleship row around Ford Island, and on Hickam Field: 'I saw several columns of black smoke! I was hot throughout my body . . . I shouted to my aide: "They've done it!" . . . The scene greatly aroused my companion, who shouted: "The air raid! Look at it!" He shouted with joy: "The air raid! A great success! Look at the smoke! Enemy ships are burning. We must do our best too, and we will!"'

But the midget was depth-charged again, nearly turning the sub over. Sakamaki surfaced her, and a mighty bang shuddered along her length. The sub was stuck on a coral reef, exposed to the destroyers. Using maximum power, Sakamaki eventually motored the craft back into deep water.

Compressed air and gas from the batteries now leaked into the chamber, and the air inside the sub was dangerously foul. Exhausted, the two men made another futile attempt to penetrate the harbour entrance. They were depth-charged again, and ran aground on the reef several times. Sakamaki felt tortured; 'bitter tears' rolled down his face incessantly.

At last he gave up, reluctantly setting the midget towards the agreed rendezvous point with a mother sub, something the submariners had quietly agreed they would never do. Choking, Sakamaki collapsed in the toxic air, falling into unconsciousness. Inagaki had already collapsed. By now, their ship was on the surface, drifting in the dark, its top hatch open.

They had agreed to set off demolition charges and kill themselves rather than let the sub fall into enemy hands. But there was a last-minute change of plan, one that Sakamaki doesn't explain in his published account. The crew took the option of escaping, rather than staying to die in the explosion. According to Sakamaki, they lit the fuse and clambered up the hatch and onto the deck. Large waves crashed around them. In the early light, they could make out the shore.

The two young men jumped into the surf. Minutes passed and Sakamaki, swallowing sea water, realised that the demolition charges had failed to explode. 'I wanted to go back, but there was no strength left in me,' he wrote. 'Then I saw my aide no more. He was swallowed up by the giant waves. I lost consciousness.'

Sakamaki awoke on the beach to find an American standing over him with a pistol. The 'peace boy' had just become the United States' first Japanese prisoner of war.

*

1942

The US battleships *Arizona*, *California* and *West Virginia* were sunk or sinking. The *Oklahoma* had capsized. The *Nevada* was heavily damaged and burning, and the *Maryland*, *Tennessee* and *Pennsylvania* were also damaged. Many other American warships had been struck and were on fire. More than 2400 Americans, mostly navy men, were dead or dying, including 1000 sailors trapped in the *Arizona*.

The *Akagi* and its vast fleet turned towards Japan for the voyage to a peaceful anchorage off Hashirajima. The battleship *Nagato* was now underway, sailing with other ships to offer protection to the returning carrier strike force. But the protection wouldn't be needed, and she would soon return to the peace of Hashirajima.

Eighty minutes before the Pearl Harbor attack, the Japanese had landed troops in northern Malaya and southern Thailand. It was the start of a string of almost unbelievable successes. In less than eight hours, the Japanese attacked and bombed the Philippines, Singapore, Hong Kong, Guam, Midway and Wake and other islands.

Emperor Hirohito's Imperial Rescript, issued after the attacks began, declared war on the United States and the British Empire:

> To cultivate friendship among nations and to enjoy prosperity in common with all nations has always been the guiding principle of Our Empire's foreign policy. It has been truly unavoidable and far from Our wishes that Our Empire has now been brought to cross swords with America and Britain.

WAR IS ON! screamed the banner headline of the *Japan Times*. Stunned crowds gathered on the streets. After four bitter years of conflict in China, a new, far greater war was thrust upon the Japanese people, but there was celebration. If Japan were to submit to US demands to withdraw its forces from China and elsewhere, 'the prestige of our empire would be compromised', Prime Minister Tojo explained to the Japanese people.

In Washington, President Roosevelt, seeking formal political support for the declaration of war with Japan, read a message to a hastily assembled joint sitting of Congress: 'Yesterday, December 7, 1941 – a date which will live in infamy – the United States of America was suddenly and deliberately attacked by naval and air forces of the Empire of Japan.'

John Curtin, in a hotel room in Melbourne, was told of the Japanese attacks at 5.30 a.m. on Monday, 8 December. After attending an emergency meeting of the war cabinet that morning, he told a lunchtime rally at the town hall that for the first time in history, it looked like an enemy could enter Australia and break down the nation's defences. That night, Curtin addressed the nation in a broadcast: 'Men and women of Australia, we are at war with Japan.' The leaders in Tokyo had ignored the convention of a formal declaration of war and had struck 'like an assassin in the night', Curtin said. The Pacific Ocean was now reddened with the blood of Japan's victims:

> These wanton killings will be followed by attacks on the Netherlands East Indies; on the Commonwealth of Australia; on the Dominion of New Zealand; if Japan can get its brutal way.
>
> ... Each must take his or her place in the service of the nation, for the nation itself is in peril. This is our darkest hour. Let that be fully realised.

In Tokyo, members of Naval General Staff had displayed gentlemanly calm before the storm. On the eve of the Pearl Harbor attack, the most influential staff officers gathered at the *Suikosha*, the naval officers' club in the capital. This was an elegant old three-storey mansion with imposing columns at the portico, built on the former estate of the feudal lord Daimyo Hisamatsu. A Shinto shrine was located in one corner of the rambling compound, which contained a traditional Japanese garden as well.

As the hours ticked down to war, the navy's elite enjoyed a fine dinner, serenely discussing what it would mean for Japan. The party comprised the old war horse Admiral Osami Nagano, chief of Naval General Staff; his deputy, Vice Admiral Ito; Vice Admiral Fukudome, who had formerly been Yamamoto's chief of staff; and the war operations planner, Baron Tomioka. These officers could hardly be called friends: indeed the atmosphere of disrespect among them was almost palpable. Fukudome, for instance, thought Ito lacked 'aggressiveness and a fighting spirit'. And like Tomioko, Fukudome had reservations about his chief. Nagano was 'an impulsive type', prone to saying 'I'll take care of it', when he didn't really understand the fine detail of a proposal.

After the war, Tomioka told the Americans that most of this leadership knew that while the power of the United States could be controlled in oriental waters, Japan, in the final analysis, had no way to defeat America: 'The Japanese naval officers who knew America realised the tremendous power she could eventually generate – power that Japan could not hope to match let alone defeat. The best that they figured to do was to keep America in check, not defeat her.'

The sake at the navy officers club flowed freely at dinner. Next morning, Nagano and his group woke early and went downstairs to the club's dining room for breakfast. First news of the offensive was received by Admiral Nagano's party between 4.00 and 5.00 a.m., long after the first dramatic reports of success had been heard on the *Nagato*.

Arriving at the navy ministry building more than two hours after the Pearl Harbor attack began, the admirals and Tomioka found their staff officers ecstatic at its success, yet concerned about a possible counter-attack on the Japanese carrier fleet. When word came through that the fleet had escaped unscathed, the mood at naval staff headquarters grew even brighter. 'The officers were wild with joy over the news,' Fukudome recalled. 'They were not particularly surprised but they were greatly impressed by the achievement of the task force.'

It was the dawning of a new era. A junior officer wrote enthusiastically: 'Nothing could hold back our Imperial Navy, which kept silent for a long time. But once it arose, it never hesitated to dare to do the most difficult thing on this earth. Oh, how powerful is the Imperial Navy!'

Nagano listened approvingly and with growing pleasure to the incoming reports and eventually sent a telegram of congratulations on the 'glorious victory' to the flagship at Hashirajima. Ugaki was handed the message and deferred answering, commenting that 'this result should be counted, in my opinion, as only a trivial one'. Quite suddenly, there had been a shift in influence and power within the Imperial Navy. Officers of the Combined Fleet would strut their ascendancy and those in Naval General Staff soon would be scrambling to keep up.

The Japanese southward advance was like a series of rolling shock waves. Japan's troops were pushing down the Malay peninsula. At its southern end, Singapore had been bombed but remained a solid barrier. Two great British battleships, the *Prince of Wales* and the *Repulse*, had arrived at the island not a moment too soon.

In London, the British prime minister, Winston Churchill, met Admiralty officials in the war cabinet room, trying to measure the consequences of the entry of Japan into the war. As he noted later, the situation was grave, but not hopeless: 'We had lost the command of every ocean except the Atlantic. Australia and New Zealand and all the vital islands in their sphere were open to attack. We had one key weapon in our hands. The *Prince of Wales* and the *Repulse* had arrived at Singapore.'

Aboard the *Nagato*, Yamamoto and Ugaki scrambled to send ships and aircraft to intercept the two battleships when they left Singapore, heading north along the east coast of the Malayan peninsula towards the Japanese troop landings. But the British ships were without air cover, as none could be spared. On 10 December, the Japanese admirals heard the stunning news that land-based Japanese torpedo bombers had sunk the British battleships near Kuantan, in eastern Malaya. Singapore, long the 'bastion' protecting Australia's north, was now exposed. The Japanese forces off Malaya had suffered little damage: three Japanese planes shot down and several forced to land in Indochina. Writing in his diary, Ugaki exclaimed: 'No greater victory than this will be won!'

Throughout all this action, Admiral Ugaki bizarrely took a particular interest in the fate of one small group – the ten midget-submarine crewmen who took part in the Pearl Harbor raid. The midget subs had proved totally ineffective weapons. It was doubtful that even one of their torpedoes hit a ship. Yet, in his diary, Ugaki had far more to say about the subs and their crewmen, than about the successful air attack or the 50 Japanese pilots who had been lost: 'I shall be very happy if these midget subs will return, but if they don't, who will make public their pains and merits? I regret that their efforts can only be estimated by enemy situations at a later time.'

When he learned that none of the crewmen reached the mother submarines waiting off Oahu, he was distraught. 'My heart aches to think of that. I heartily regret that their immortal spirit will remain in the dark.' The mission proved fatal for nine of the ten crewmen of the midget submarines who participated in Pearl Harbor. Kazuo Sakamaki was the sole survivor. Although he lived, his shame at not dying was so great that he tried to take his own life.

Today, in the Educational Museum of naval history at the Etajima academy, there is a photograph commemorating the 'Nine Heroes', the midget submariners of Pearl Harbor. Photographs of the young men who were killed in their submarines are arranged around a painting of Battleship Row. Even Sakamaki's assistant, Kiyoshi Inagaki, is there.

The tenth man, Sakamaki, is missing. We are told simply that another submariner was 'captured after losing consciousness'. Even today among such extravagant memorialisation of Japan's deceased sailors and naval officers, there is no room for his name or his image. Despite his harrowing wartime experiences and his psychological suffering as a veteran, the Japanese navy has still not forgiven Sakamaki for surrendering at Pearl Harbor.

6

A NATION EXPOSED

Japan's initial triumphs were at once spectacular and terrifying. It was as if nothing could halt the Japanese advance. Only in hindsight would it be realised that the loss of relatively antiquated battleships at Pearl Harbor would in time have little effect on the US Navy's combat capabilities, while the addition of a few new carriers would enormously increase US power.

For now, British, Indian, and Australian forces were in retreat through the plantations and jungles of Malaya, while further landings in the Philippines pointed to a sure conquest of the archipelago. With the occupation of Thailand and the capture of vital oilfields in Borneo, the war was going remarkably well for Japan, and further victories were assured.

In Tokyo, the improvement in public morale was marked. In the early days of the war, the Japanese people were generally intoxicated with victory, the foreign minister, Shigenori Togo wrote. 'The feeling was widespread that the years of suffering [in the China war] could be permanently consigned to oblivion.'

Despite two hard years of war, Australia's armed forces were shockingly unprepared to meet Japan's sudden threat. Most of their men were overseas defending British interests, leaving the forces in Australia significantly depleted. The AIF's battle-seasoned divisions – the 6th, 7th and 8th – were still in the Middle East. Two other brigades from the 8th Division were in Singapore and Malaya.

Put simply, the Commonwealth had not made Australia's own defence its first priority. At the US embassy in Canberra, American diplomats had long observed Australia's lopsided defence logic with increasing incredulity and alarm. In September 1940, the US minister, effectively ambassador, in Canberra, Clarence E. Gauss, had reported to Washington:

> It can truthfully be said that Australia has weakened her own defences and security for the Empire cause in a measure, which unless rapidly repaired, holds the possibility of serious consequences.

Since nationhood, the dominion had fought Britain's wars on the expectation that if Australia was threatened, she would be defended by the motherland. That traditional thinking would be overturned suddenly, but until it was, many Australians continued to live with a false illusion of security.

Prime Minister Curtin was desperate to awaken Australians to the imminent Japanese threat. He took the opportunity at a war savings bonds lunch in Melbourne: 'Today the war rages in Australian waters; the enemy is seeking the earliest possible hour in which he can set foot on our soil.'

This bleak warning was based on Curtin's view of a most secret report on the defence of Australia and adjacent areas, compiled by defence chiefs at the PM's request. It advised that a Japanese attempt to seize the naval and air base of Darwin could become a strong possibility, and also reported that Sydney, the coastal industrial regions of New South Wales and the munitions-producing city of Lithgow, were threatened:

The most probable form of attack on mainland Australia [is] naval and air bombardment of important objectives (such as industrial works at Sydney, Newcastle and [Port] Kembla by a fast capital ship and cruisers with or without aircraft carriers. Sea-borne raids against selected land objectives was possible.

The report presented to war cabinet on 11 December, considered any attack on Darwin would probably come from the air. However, there were qualifications: 'Sea-borne raids were considered unlikely in view of the size of the army garrison, but an attempt to seize Darwin would become a strong possibility in the event of the defeat of the Allied naval forces or the capture of Singapore and the Netherlands East Indies.' In the wider region, the defence chiefs thought that in an initial southward thrust, the Japanese would probably attempt to occupy New Guinea and New Caledonia. The capture of any of the south-east outlying islands would provide the enemy with bases for the development of attacks against the mainland of Australia. The greatest threat then would be to Darwin, with its naval and air force base and to the exposed northern coastline of Australia:

> The target was an attractive one and, in spite of the fact that it would be necessary for naval enemy forces to penetrate the Malay barrier, an attack by bombardment squadron or carrier borne aircraft was a strong possibility . . .

The Malay barrier, so called, was the line of defence stretching from Malaya, down through the East Indies and Timor to Cape York peninsula.

On 11 December, three days after the start of Japanese hostilities, Australia's war cabinet announced the immediate call-up of a further 100,000 army personnel. Cabinet approved the evacuation of Australian women and children from Darwin, and from the Australian territories of Papua and New Guinea, especially Port Moresby and Rabaul. The significant bulk of forces within

Australia were already in the south of the country, and a considerable force had to be maintained there for the protection of the Newcastle–Sydney–Port Kembla–Lithgow centres, essential for war production. Only a limited number would be moved north as reinforcements.

The British prime minister, Winston Churchill, soon would imply that Curtin and his senior military advisers were ill advised and panicky about Japan's intentions. Yet the critical assessment of the threats to Australia came mainly from British service chiefs seconded to Australia. Before the outbreak of war with Germany, Prime Minister Menzies, believing that Australian officers lacked necessary wartime experience, had recruited British officers for high-ranking duties.

The chief of the Air Staff in Australia was Sir Charles Burnett, who had served with the Royal Flying Corp in World War I. The acting chief of the Naval Staff was Commodore John Durnford, a younger officer on secondment from the Royal Navy. He replaced another Briton, Admiral Sir Ragner Colvin, who had retired through illness. Only the chief of the Army Staff was Australian-born. General Vernon Sturdee, the son of a British doctor who had served with the Australians at Gallipoli, a man who was not afraid to speak his mind, would become a close military adviser to John Curtin.

In his endeavour to alert Australians to the threat the nation faced, the prime minister made senior newsmen privy to the contents of the defence chiefs' assessment. Unlike many other politicians, Curtin had an affinity with the press. Born and raised in Victoria, he had begun his working life as a copy boy on the Melbourne *Age*, when Melbourne was the seat of national politics. He not only knew many journalists but understood the way they worked and thought. As prime minister, he granted senior political reporters in Canberra unprecedented access to political and military secrets.

The remarkable thing about his secret briefings to these journalists was that he told them almost everything – 'the most hair-raising secrets of the war', as one of them put it. Often senior newsmen knew more about the war than most government members. They were allowed to send copies of these daily briefings to their newspaper proprietors or editors-in-chief, but they were not permitted to quote in any fashion from the briefings, unless cleared by Curtin, as strict censorship was in force.

The Melbourne *Herald*'s parliamentary bureau chief in Canberra was one of those who enjoyed the prime minister's confidence. Joseph Alexander was a short, rotund, God-fearing, conservative man, and a much respected journalist. He was also editor of the annual *Who's Who*. Like Curtin, he was appalled that Australians, especially those in Sydney, continued to live almost as if there was no war. Privately, he hoped that the sudden Japanese thrust southwards would awaken Sydneysiders from their stupor, as he confided to his diary:

> God help us and above all God bless Britain. Went to sleep with a heavy heart tonight mindful of all my sins and oppressed by a sense of disaster. These are terrible times but we must face them. In a flash Sydney has become [more] vulnerable than London or Coventry.

Next night, Alexander was still thinking fearfully about Australia's prospects of survival:

> We are now without effective naval defence in the Pacific and may be raided at any moment. If the Japanese could do what they have done in Pearl Harbor, what could they do to Sydney (the most defenceless great city in the world and probably the most complacent and one of the most materialistic – a place without ideals of any belief in things of the spirit.)

Of all Australia's cities, Sydney – the largest, with a population of 1.3 million – had the worst reputation for complacency. Commentators and civic leaders blamed the harbour city for not adequately supporting the war effort and for being more interested in profit and the good times. Its citizens led the way in enjoying horse races, the trots, and the dogs. At the outbreak of war with Japan, there were few restrictions and little rationing, although the government soon would announce cuts in petrol allocations, use of lighting and late shopping. Hotels overflowed for the nightly six o'clock swill, and all sorts of food was in plentiful supply.

Air raid shelters started to appear and air raid sirens were tested, but blackouts were not considered necessary. Trenches were being dug in parks, prominent city buildings sand-bagged, and evacuation plans drawn up for schools, in case of air raids. But the implementation was slow and half-hearted. An air of false gaiety persisted, even after Japan entered the war and recruitment increased.

It was summer, and Christmas was approaching. Service personnel were out for a good time while they could. Sports and the beaches could still be enjoyed, even if barbed-wire entanglements served as a reminder of conflict. There were gun emplacements along Bondi Beach but they were merely mock-ups with bits of drainage pipe for gun barrels. Still, the Yanks were coming with supplies that they couldn't land in occupied Manila.

With the influx of servicemen into the cities, including the first trickle of American troops, some Australians reassured themselves further. As Curtin put it, even the entry of Japan into the war was met with a subconscious view that 'the Americans will deal with the short-sighted, underfed, and fanatical Japanese'.

Of all the operations at the outbreak of the Pacific war, the Pearl Harbor victory had the most significant impact on the future of the Japanese Imperial Navy and the audacity of its proposed operations. After years of being overshadowed by the army, the navy finally saw itself as a cut above. Better-educated young men chose the navy over the army as a career. The Imperial Navy, with its British background, was regarded by prospective officers as the gentlemen's service, even if in reality it was anything but.

Before the success of the attack on Pearl Harbor, there was a good deal of public grumbling about the navy. Many Japanese had quietly sneered at the 'silent navy', as it was mockingly called. The term *koshinuke bushi* (cowardly warrior) was even bandied about. The war in China had become a military quagmire, but although the army was not going to defeat the Chinese nationalists, and had suffered significant setbacks and a shocking death toll, it could at least point to some significant victories there, unlike the navy. During four gruelling years of fighting, there had been no brilliant naval exploits.

After Pearl Harbor, the Imperial Navy and its fighting spirit had been elevated to new heights, thanks to strident saturation press coverage. Daily Japanese successes on all fronts assured operational planners that the initial phase of the war operations would be completed ahead of schedule. Japan was carving out a massive resource-rich empire for itself.

The formulation of army and navy strategic policy was supposed to be the role of the separate Army and Navy General Staffs ensconced in Tokyo. Yet in the Imperial Navy, the senior sea-going officers of the Combined Fleet command and their smart young staff officers increasingly took the initiative with crucial new war plans. The senior air wing commander of the carrier task force that attacked Pearl Harbor, Captain Mitsuo Fuchida, witnessed the self-importance of the staff men of Yamamoto and Ugaki's Combined Fleet who spent most of their time at anchor at Hashirajima:

> Needless to say, the striking victories won by the Fleet in the first month of hostilities served only to reinforce this influence. Combined Fleet staff officers were filled with elated self-confidence, while the Naval General Staff felt constrained to talk softly in its dealings with the Fleet Headquarters.
>
> It was not surprising, therefore, that the initiative in formulating naval strategy for the second phase of the war was taken by the Combined Fleet rather than by the Naval General Staff.

With operational planning firmly in place for the capture of the Netherlands East Indies, Timor and other points in the south, Admiral Yamamoto began looking even further ahead. Less than 48 hours after the attack on Pearl Harbor, he issued an order to Admiral Ugaki that would bring the question of an invasion of Australia into the Imperial Navy's equation. Yamamoto ordered Ugaki to draw up a plan for the invasion of Hawaii, codenamed *toho sakusen*, or eastern operation. He believed that Japan's only hope against the might of the United States was an audacious strike on Hawaii. The order set in motion the most ambitious and far-reaching Japanese operation of World War II.

If Yamamoto could seize Hawaii, US forces would have to pull back to the American continent, leaving Australia, New Zealand and other parts of Oceania vulnerable. Yamamoto also saw Hawaii in Japanese hands as a safeguard against American carrier strikes aimed at Japan's home islands. The invasion of Hawaii would enable Tokyo to terminate the war on favourable terms before America's superior power could be mobilised.

After Pearl Harbor and the other opening attacks, Yamamoto insisted that Japan must follow through with aggressive action in all directions. This would keep the Americans off balance and allow Japan to expand the new perimeter until Washington sued for peace. But speed was of the essence.

According to Japan's official war history series, *Senshi Sosho*, Yamamoto told his chief of staff that he had three targets in mind: India (incorporating Ceylon), Australia and Hawaii. Of these, he counted Hawaii as the most important, because of the strategic threat posed by the American's Pacific base and its carrier fleet. The American carriers had been absent from Pearl Harbor when the Japanese struck, and so remained unscathed. The capture of Hawaii would allow Japan to take Midway island, closer to Japan, and Yamamoto knew that such an operation would draw out the US Pacific Fleet for the long anticipated 'decisive battle'.

Australia and India were included in Yamamoto's invasion plans because the commander-in-chief wanted a bold strategy which he called *happo yabure*, or 'strike on all sides'. Among other considerations, Australia was seen as the obvious location for an American build-up of forces, in preparation for an all-out American offensive against Japan.

Ugaki had difficulties putting together the blueprint for the eastern operation at such short notice. As he mulled over the fate of Australia, Hawaii and India, he set his staff officers to work on the planning. There were hurdles ahead if Yamamoto's operation was to proceed. Once again, the plan would have to be signed off by the Naval General Staff, who were traditionally conservative about the use of Japan's precious capital ships. More importantly, any such proposal would need to be accepted by the army, and that was a tougher nut to crack, before the emperor could consider approval of a final plan.

As the territory captured by Japan expanded like widening ripples in a pond, in Tokyo Naval General Staff saw the need to make operational changes. Even before the outbreak of war, they had decided to seize the important Australian base at Rabaul, on New Britain, in the first phase of the war. Baron Tomioka had noted that Rabaul, ringed by active volcanoes, offered a natural harbour for a large fleet, and was a strategic point in Japan's artery of communications extending down to Australia: 'The Japanese occupation of Rabaul would afford us an excellent air base for scouting and patrolling the areas to the northeast of Australia, anticipated to be some [areas] of operations of the enemy fleets.'

Tomioka's planners also thought Rabaul would help defend Japan's mandated islands to the north, including the big deep-water naval base at Truk (now Chuuk). Until now an invasion of Australia had been little more than a remote possibility. After Japan's stunning victories, old plans were in need of urgent revision, and remote possibilities were back on the table. Admirals and over-confident staff officers suddenly broadened their sights. As Ugaki wrote in his diary less than a week after Pearl Harbor:

'The way to operations in the southern areas has been paved opportunely. In a military decision, it is everything to catch the tide.'

In parliament, in Canberra, a week after the outbreak of war with Japan, Curtin spoke with evident bravado of the welcome the Japanese could expect from Australians in the event of an invasion: 'Never shall an enemy set foot upon the soil of this country without having at once arrayed against it the whole of the manhood of this nation with such strength and quality that this nation will remain for ever the home of sons of Britishers . . .'

Yet, at times, he must have felt that the forces arrayed against him included his own people. Japan's southward thrust made little difference to the pace of industrial stoppages, which maddened and worried Curtin. For a long time he seemed incapable of preventing the strikes, despite his own union background and personal pleas to union leaders. Strikes were disrupting some vital supplies, especially on the wharves and in the coal mines across New South Wales. Even Sydney's tram and bus drivers staged a 24-hour strike, throwing transport into chaos.

Coalminers, especially in the northern New South Wales fields, sometimes went on strike in defiance of union leaders. Despite the war, they were determined that hard won conditions would not be eroded. Curtin at first was dismissive of their impact, saying there wasn't sufficient shipping to transport all the coal they dug out of the ground. But as time went on, and criticism mounted, the prime minister became frustrated at the coalminers' lack of national spirit.

It was a confused and sometimes alarming period of adjustment to war. The New South Wales government caused great consternation when it announced plans to evacuate children and their guardians from vulnerable areas to the country. Soon Curtin was advised that public morale was not as strong as it could be. A prominent anthropologist, Professor A.P. Elkin of the University of Sydney, gave Curtin the results of his public surveys in Sydney carried out by his anthropology students at his direction:

> The blunt fact is that there are signs that morale may not stand up to the strain sufficiently well. Large numbers of people are feeling that Malaya and Singapore will be lost; some say that Britain is not doing all she could about it, that America is not prepared . . .
> Air raid shelters are inadequate and fire fighting equipment etc are not available; further, the evacuation of children and hospitals adds to the depression . . . anti-British feeling, too, is widespread . . .

Political journalist Joe Alexander noted that the national mood was changing. It was strange to see Melbourne at night partly blacked out, with sand bags around the Herald & Weekly Times building. 'The war is moving very close to us.'

The commander-in-chief of the home forces, Lieutenant General Sir Iven Mackay, had been visiting Perth when the war in the Pacific broke out. He found himself stranded in the west, unable to obtain a flight back to headquarters in Melbourne. When he finally reached Victoria Barracks two days later, Mackay wrote immediately to the army minister, Frank Forde, warning that Japan's extraordinary successes might encourage her into precipitate action, 'including an attack on Australia'. He called for nothing less than full mobilisation of the population.

How much – or how little – to say publicly about the progress of the war and the challenges the nation faced was a question that would continue to exercise the government and the military; often, the message required fine-tuning. Curtin tended to err on the side of caution in releasing military information.

On 17 December, a week after his first letter to the army minister, General Mackay wrote again to Forde, suggesting that the people of Australia should be schooled about what to expect in the event of a Japanese invasion. Civilians, he said, were prone to excitement, exaggeration and rumour. Certainly there would be bombing and shelling of the populous centres with casualties and material losses, but 'we must remember that a nation which suffers even severe losses at the beginning of a war may still win in the end . . . We have the courage and determination to beat off the invaders'.

7

INVASION PLANNING

Winter finally came to the Inland Sea on 16 December 1941, with a strong, icy wind blowing across the ruffled waters, and rain clouds building around the mountains. Sub chasers dashed about the Bay of Hiroshima in quest of enemy submarines that didn't exist. Once again, the Hashirajima anchorage was crowded with the great ships of war.

The chill wind did nothing to dampen the zeal of Combined Fleet staff officers aboard the *Nagato*. They blushed as they gathered around the loudspeaker to hear a speech from Navy Minister Shigataro Shimada to an extraordinary sitting of the National Diet, in which he lauded the Imperial Navy.

The same day, Baron Tomioka climbed the gangway of the *Nagato* again, and made his way to Admiral Ugaki's cabin. He had come to discuss the 'estimated state of war' and the Imperial Navy's next moves. He knew that the boys from Combined Fleet had a few ideas of their own. And sure enough, in his cabin full of charts and maps, Ugaki was working on a plan to invade Australia via the northern port of Darwin. He had given responsibility for plans to take Hawaii – the most important consideration – to a group of his energetic staff officers.

The discussion between the two men seemed to both to be fruitful. Later, Ugaki wrote in his diary that Naval General Staff in Tokyo supported the eastern operation. 'My ideas about this matter have already been handed to the senior staff officer in a paper; what the Naval General Staff thinks about it and what the Combined Fleet does are almost the same.' But while Tomioka had not disagreed with the eastern operation, he misunderstood its implications, and left the *Nagato* unaware that Yamamoto and Ugaki had actually proposed to occupy the Hawaiian islands. This misunderstanding said a great deal about the lack of communication between the two arms of the Imperial Navy.

In conversation with Captain Kameto Kuroshima, Tomioka heard the staff officer discuss the seizure of remote Palmyra island, some 1770 kilometres south-west of Honolulu. If it was intended to hamper communications between the United States and Australia, such an operation was consistent with Naval General Staff thinking. The Naval General Staff had their own less risky plans to occupy Fiji and Samoa, blocking US access to Australia.

Back in Tokyo, Tomioka discussed his conversation with his superior, Admiral Fukudome, and the operations section chief in the Army General Staff, Major General Shinichi Tanaka, a tough fellow with a pleasant face. Tanaka smelt a rat, correctly suspecting that Yamamoto wanted to capture Hawaii. Tanaka wrote in his diary, '. . . a Hawaii invasion could endanger the foundations of war leadership'.

Army General Staff was keen to consolidate its first stage operational gains, and viewed any enlargement of the Pacific perimeter beyond the first-stage goals as unnecessary and dangerous. Tanaka told Tomioka so in blunt terms on 23 December. It seemed that major disagreements between army and navy were on again. Naturally, Ugaki was annoyed when he leaned of the army's opposition. He thought it stemmed from the army's desire to attack Russia, and told his diary: 'What a mean spirit it [the army] has!' But Ugaki didn't plan to drop Yamamoto's eastern operation for one moment.

The Japanese army and navy's strategic thinking were rarely in unison. Despite Japan and the Soviet Union signing a neutrality pact in 1941, strong elements within the Japanese army saw the Russians to the north as their greatest threat in the new world upheaval. Ugaki was told that the army was looking for a chance to attack Russia after the successful end of Japan's first stage operations.

For the plan to proceed, the navy would have to involve the prime minister. There were strong indications that General Tojo initially was not as cautious as Army General Staff. In the Western world, a man of Tojo's standing in the forces would be privy to every major strategy discussion and decision. Not so in Japan, with its independent and politically powerful armed forces. Tojo once admitted that he did not even become aware that the Pearl Harbor carrier strike force had set sail until days after the event. And this despite his well-known hawkishness.

Prince Naruhiko Higashikuni, an uncle to Empress Nagako, had been offered the job of prime minister, but had stood aside for Tojo. The prince had served as a general in China and would be a field marshal before the Pacific war was out. In December 1941, Higashikuni was commander of Defence Command and a member of the Supreme War Council. Despite his own military background, he believed that Japan should sue for peace at an early opportunity.

In his diary, Higashikuni said he told Tojo after the initial successes: 'I think Singapore will fall soon ... Japan should advance negotiations with Chiang Kai-shek's government and start peace overtures with Britain and the United States. We must end this war without further delay.' Tojo was defiant, replying: 'I think we will have few problems occupying not only Java and Sumatra but also Australia if things go on like this. We shouldn't think about peace at this time.'

Prince Higashikuni's diary challenges the often repeated quote in a Sydney newspaper of General Tojo, from an interview by journalist Richard Hughes (who had strong connections with leading warlike figures in Tokyo before and after the war) that Japan at no stage considered a physical invasion of Australia.

On 27 December, Ugaki decided to assume responsibility for all planning of the eastern operation, including Hawaii, because of his concern that his staff officers were not working fast enough. He believed that there was great urgency to invade Hawaii before the Pearl Harbor damage could be repaired.

Until now, Yamamoto's Combined Fleet had demonstrated a more radical approach to war operations than the rest of Japan's military leadership. The Navy General Staff had placed strong emphasis on preserving the Combined Fleet for the anticipated 'decisive battle' with the US Pacific Fleet. Its members were cautious about any proposal that might prematurely jeopardise scarce capital vessels.

This view began to change as their ideas of southern expansion broadened, and more aggressive advocates began to hold sway in operational arguments. Crucially, Tomioka had been won over to Combined Fleet's point of view. In the flush of Japan's victories, amid the military's growing sense of invincibility, the convert would become most passionate for the cause.

The invasion debate accelerated. Arrogant madness began to permeate the corridors and conference rooms of the old navy ministry building in Tokyo. The cry had become, 'Why stop now?'

Of all people, the intelligent and sophisticated Baron Sadatoshi Tomioka should have seen through the swaggering folly of the Combined Fleet radicals off Hashirajima, but he did not. At first, Tomioka opposed the Hawaii operation as beyond Japan's capacity. He thought the Americans probably had three troop divisions deployed on Oahu, and that it would take several divisions to dislodge them. Tomioka knew that the Imperial Army, heavily occupied in southern operations, was not going to divert that many men to the middle of the Pacific.

But as time went on, the influential Tomioka became one of the leading operational radicals within the General Staff. He and his middle-ranking officers realised that if the Americans were to be constrained, Japan would need to ensure that the US could not use Australia as a base. The only answer would be to begin work on a plan to invade key locations in Australia's north as the first step.

Of the major plans under consideration, an attack on Australia was the one most enthusiastically advocated by the operations division of Naval General Staff, according to Yamamoto's biographer and wartime naval spokesman, Hiroyuki Agawa. This was because they saw that any concerted Allied counteroffensive would come from Australia. Even the foreign office recognised this. Radical Foreign Minister Yosuke Matsuoka told the Diet in February 1941 that the white race must cede Oceania (which includes Australia) to the Asiatics. Before the war, both the Imperial Army and Navy had recognised the strategic importance of Australia. In joint planning meetings, they rightly counted on Britain's inability to spare many of her forces for the war against Japan.

Tomioka and his army counterparts believed that if there was not a short, decisive battle after the southern operations, the US and Britain would shift to a war of attrition against Japan: 'At the same time, they will endeavour to secure communications with Australia, India and other remaining strategic areas in the Far East and secure military strength over Japan as quickly as possible.'

Tomioka later told of his own radical answer to counter such action:

> With the outbreak of war, the initial operational successes on all sides brought an opinion that these initial victories should be followed up with more powerful operational activities, and that our strategic formation should be further strengthened in order to forestall all chance of recovery by Great Britain and the United States. India and Australia were the main objectives for attack.
>
> Our plan to attack Australia was made mainly from a strategic viewpoint, but its realisation would also assure us of a political advantage for isolating that continent from the

general currents of the world war, and an economic advantage of having access to such important supplies as wool, wheat and fertilisers.

Tomioka was not just talking about a bombing attack on Australia, or cutting Australia off from the United States. The idea of simply cutting Australia off had existed since the beginning of the war; indeed, Combined Fleet Operations Order No. 1 had alluded to it. In the opening moves of the war, Combined Fleet dispatched several submarines to the Australian region, to cut down US shipments to Australia.

Without doubt then, Tomioka was talking about Japan invading Australia. In early 1942, both in Tokyo and at Hashirajima, this proposition was on the table.

The Japanese occupied the British colony of Hong Kong on Christmas Day 1941. In Malaya, crack Japanese troops under General Tomoyuki Yamashita were making steady progress southwards towards the island fortress of Singapore. John Curtin, who had been in office for 80 days, now gravely feared for his country. On Boxing Day, he tried to motivate Australians, warning in a national broadcast that no part of Australia was invulnerable to invasion and 'a fanatically brave foe':

> We face a very efficient, highly organised enemy armed with mountains of supplies and equipment wrung from people who, for months past, have done without holidays and sport and outings on the beaches . . .
>
> We face, too, an enemy whose fighting men have been nurtured in a tradition that to die for the nation is the highest trait of character and is also, in fact, a national duty fulfilled with much the same outlook as we Australians display in taking a morning shower.

It was a startling situation: in late December 1941, Curtin was still encouraging Australians to go on war footing, even though the nation had been at war since 1939. His government had come to power in October advocating a policy of 'revolutionising the Australian way of life' until a war footing was speedily attained. But changing the 'lackadaisical Australian mind', as Curtin put it, wasn't easy.

When the young submariner Kazuo Sakamaki had woken on the beach at Oahu to see an American soldier with a pistol standing over him, he felt numb and spent. He had committed an unpardonable mistake – capture by the enemy. He was even more devastated later, when, as a prisoner in an American POW camp, he learned that his midget was being toured through the United States on the back of a large truck.

As the Japanese National Diet was heaping praise on the army and navy on 17 December 1941 for their 'sweeping and successive victories', a teleprinter in defence headquarters, Melbourne, churned out an urgent and most secret cablegram from the Australian Legation in Washington. It was a warning about Japan's new midget submarines used at Pearl Harbor. Sydney, the nation's busiest and most important wartime port, could not have expected any better signal of impending danger.

The disastrous midget submarine participation in the Pearl Harbor surprise attack had almost spelled the end to the effective use of the midgets in combat. Yet production of the A-class midget submarines, and experiments with three-man submarines in the Kure area of the Inland Sea, still proceeded, thanks to the support of senior naval officers and the lobbying of more committed crew members.

The subs' proponents assured the navy brass that the A-class midgets were now much improved, faster and more reliable. They also claimed, without proof, that 'considerable results' had been achieved at Pearl Harbor. Three weeks after the Pearl Harbor attack, the skipper of the mother sub *I-16*, Commander Kaoru Yamanda, reported aboard the *Nagato*. With Yamanda was Sub-lieutenant Keiu Matsuo, the young submariner who had taken part in the spy mission to Hawaii in October 1941 and who would go to Sydney. He begged that the midget submarines be given another chance.

Yamanda and Matsuo argued that significant advances had already been made, both in training and in the construction of the vessel. They stressed that the deficiencies of the original two-man midgets were being overcome and the crews were undergoing 'keen and severe training' in the new, improved craft.

According to his diary, Admiral Ugaki was filled with sympathy for the midget sub mission, although recognising that much remained to be done in perfecting techniques. As it turned out, Yamamoto was just as blinded by the bravery, passion and effort of the young submariner proponents as his chief of staff. Despite the failure of any of the Pearl Harbor submariners to return from their mission, Yamamoto allowed the planning of further midget operations.

It would take quite a while for the Imperial Navy to discover that the midget submarine raid on Pearl Harbor was a complete disaster, a huge effort, expense, and loss of life for small, if any, military return. But little time was allowed to elapse between the midget submarine disaster at Pearl Harbor and the decision to launch midget submarine attacks on new targets, including Sydney.

It's August 2007. Susumu Ito bounds energetically up the stairs of his stationery and business equipment firm at Iwakuni, the ferry port for Hashirajima and other islands out in the Bay of Hiroshima. He leads his visitors into the conference room on the third floor. Dressed in a crisp white, short-sleeved shirt, tie, and slacks, the businessman looks 70 years old at the most. Yet here is one Japanese still living who unapologetically remembers the Sydney Harbour operation well.

Ito makes it clear that my interpreter and I are especially

welcome. Australians are 'beautiful people' because of the full military honours granted at the funerals of the four midget-submariners whose bodies were recovered after the Sydney raid. Ito tells us: 'I'm 92 now. I'm very active. I drive myself to work each day. Some tell me it's dangerous. I tell them I'm a good driver – better than you! I'm going on another world cruise again next year. In fact, we've booked for 2009. That is, if my wife's health holds up. We hope to get to Sydney.'

Susumu Ito has been to Sydney before, when he flew over the harbour on a reconnaissance mission just before the midget submarine raid in 1942. As we talk, he holds up a photograph of himself. It is a shot of a young pilot, his face as smooth as a woman's, clad in leather helmet, navy uniform, and high, well polished leather boots.

'You know, I am the only person left alive in Japan who participated in the opening of the war at Pearl Harbor and was on the submarines,' Ito tells us, proudly.

In December 1941, he was off Oahu in the aircraft-carrying submarine *I-21* for the start of Yamamoto's surprise attack on Pearl Harbor. He was scheduled to take off after the air attack to reconnoitre the harbour, but his submarine was called away. The *I-21* was ordered to pursue the old carrier *Enterprise* as it headed back to the US. The sub gave chase across the Pacific, but the carrier escaped. The Japanese craft was then ordered to attack coastal shipping off the west coast of America. Her crew sank two tankers by torpedo and shell fire, but the *I-21* was bombed by US aircraft.

'We were attacked and went down [diving],' he says. 'One of the pipes burst from the pressure and we had no lights. The air was foul and it was difficult to breathe. We started to hyperventilate. We couldn't put the pump on and return air pressure to normal. It took a full 24 hours to return to the surface. We were lucky.'

Ito revels in recalling the past. 'I'm a very capable man,' he comments with a smile, reeling off his exploits, brushes with death, and attributes as a navy man. 'I always had confidence in my own ability.' At that, it dawns on me. Sixty-seven years after the end of Japan's war, here is the personification of Japan's fighting spirit in 1941; of the archetypal young officer turned out by the Imperial Japanese Navy, proud, energetic, and self-assured, almost to the point of nonchalance.

'Whether you die or live in war, there's only a little difference of fate,' Ito tells his Australian guests. 'Luck plays a big part. I could have died in the submarines or in the air. It just depends on the circumstances. You can't help fate.'

8

DAWN OF A FEARFUL YEAR

In late December 1941, John Curtin and his ministers received the disturbing news that Winston Churchill was planning only a limited British defence of Singapore, and in the last resort could even abandon the island to preserve his forces. Some of Curtin's associates didn't hide their anger. 'Doc' Evatt, the minister for external affairs, believed British proposals to evacuate Singapore constituted an 'inexcusable betrayal', and it is thought that he was the author of a cable to Churchill, sent in Curtin's name, containing this accusation. Australian complaints about the inadequacy of British support and leadership began to develop into a significant rift.

Curtin wrote to both Churchill and President Roosevelt on 26 December, 'at this time of great crisis'. Northern Malaya was now in Japanese hands, he said, and fortress Singapore was in grievous danger of becoming another rout, just like the British disasters at Greece and Crete, which were huge reversals for Australian troops.

Reinforcements earmarked by Britain seemed utterly inadequate to the task of staving off the Japanese forces. The fall of

Singapore would mean the isolation of the Philippines, the fall of the Dutch East Indies and would sever Australia's communications.

He pointed out that Australia had three divisions fighting with the British in the Middle East and many airmen fighting in Britain. It had one division in Malaya and was sending more. But if Singapore was to be saved, Britain and the US must act with great urgency. The same day, Evatt received a graphic report from Australia's commissioner in Singapore, Vivian Bowden: 'I feel I must emphasise that deterioration of war position in Malayan defence is assuming landslide collapse of whole defence system.' The situation in Singapore was growing more dangerous day by day.

Australia's relationship with Britain soured dramatically after a feature article under John Curtin's name appeared in the Melbourne *Herald* on 27 December. The prime minister acknowledged the problems that Britain faced with the constant threat of invasion, and the dangers that dispersal of her strength could bring. But he wrote that Australia might fall and Britain could still hang on.

This article signalled a fundamental shift in the Commonwealth's thinking, and was a famous watershed. Curtin wrote: 'Without any inhibition of any kind, I make it quite clear that Australia looks to America, free of any pangs as to our traditional links or kinship with the United Kingdom.' The journalist Joe Alexander, who had asked Curtin to write the feature piece, saw the article cause a sensation, in both Britain and the United States and neither government was impressed: 'It derives from Curtin's feeling that Australia has been deceived or deluded over the Singapore defences – or lack of air defence there.'

Churchill was furious, and showed his displeasure: 'I have been greatly pained in all my labours here by the harsh tone which had characterised your various messages.' He went on:

> I hope you will not mind me saying that you have really not begun to feel the weight of this war, or even begun to experience the danger and suffering under which the people of Great Britain have long been proud to live.

At your wish we arranged for the withdrawal of all Australian forces from Tobruk and the battlefront of Libya and I have myself proposed that you should remove one of your divisions to the Singapore area.

I do not understand the reason for this mood of panic which I am sure is not shared by the people of Australia.

If hostile speeches continue ... I should be quite ready to address a broadcast to the Australian people. I feel confident of their generosity and enduring goodwill.

Churchill was clearly implying that the Australian government simply couldn't take it. He had seen his own nation survive the Battle of Britain, with its mass German bombings of London and other cities at its worst from September 1940 until May 1941. By the time Japan threatened Australia, Churchill was able to feel reasonably safe from a German invasion of Britain.

The Australian troops at Tobruk had been a sore point for some time. The British commander, General Archibald Wavell, opposed General Sir Thomas Blamey's request to relieve the Australians, many of whom had been fighting in the Tobruk enclave non-stop since March 1941, and were in deteriorating health. Eventually, a new British commander, General Claude Auchinleck, agreed to release the 18th Brigade of the Australian 7th Division but resisted relieving the 9th Division. But when Curtin became prime minister, he insisted on the entire 9th Division being relieved as well. Churchill objected.

Former Australian Labor Party leader and prime minister William Hughes further antagonised the relationship between Curtin and Churchill. He privately told Churchill: 'Some of our ministers are extremists and anti-British ... Curtin is at best cool towards Britain.' There was personal history here. Hughes had migrated to Australia from Britain as a boy, in 1884. As prime minister during World War I, the 'little Digger' was the mother country's enthusiastic recruiter, while Curtin, the trade unions' anti-conscription leader, was his strongest opponent.

Churchill later publicly regretted his 'traces of impatience' with Curtin. Somewhat condescendingly, he explained that the Australians 'lacked a true sense of proportion in world strategy':

> They saw themselves exposed to the possibility of direct invasion. No longer did the war mean sending aid across the oceans to the Mother Country in her distress and peril. The new foe could strike at Australian homes.
> The enormous coastlines of their continent could never be defended. All their great cities were on the seaboard. Their only four well-trained divisions of volunteers, the New Zealand Division, and all the best officers were far away across the seas.
> The naval command of the Pacific had passed in a flash and for an indefinite period to Japan. Australasian air power hardly existed. Can we wonder that deep alarm swept Australia, or that the thoughts of their Cabinet were centred upon their own affairs?

It was true that 1942 dawned as a fearful year in Australia. Joe Alexander was among those who apprehended that his country wouldn't escape the horrors of war: 'We begin the new year with great anxiety for the future of Australia. Attack must be very near. Manila is about to fall and Singapore is menaced. This year of Grace 1942 will give us most of the answers.'

On 5 January, Curtin wrote to his wife of his frustrations: 'The war goes very badly and I have a cable fight with Churchill almost daily. He has been in Africa and India and they count before Australia and New Zealand. The truth is that Britain never thought Japan would fight and made no preparations to meet that eventuality.'

Churchill, who was visiting the United States, stayed with the Roosevelts at the White House for three and a half weeks, accompanying the president and the first lady to church on Christmas Day, sharing good meals with them, staying up late at nights talking policy with the president or his advisers, and addressing a joint sitting of congress on Boxing Day. The British PM, still chagrined, continued to spurn Australian requests for reinforcements and for a role on a decision-making body in Washington to help direct the war in the Pacific. But on 9 January, he told Curtin, almost as an aside, that 'the United States would be quite willing, I believe, to reinforce your home defence troops with 40 or 50 thousand Americans. The limiting factor is not so much escort as actual shipping.'

This was surprisingly good news for Curtin, but he worried that the reinforcements would take months to arrive, by which time the Japanese might have landed in Australia. Churchill, now very peeved, thought the Australians unnecessarily 'jumpy' about invasion, and asked Curtin somewhat cynically: 'Do you think you are in immediate danger of invasion in force? It is quite true that you may have air attacks, but we have had a good dose already in England without mortally harmful results.' He assured Curtin, 'I am thinking of your interest at every moment', but he was convinced that Australia would not face anything more serious than air raids.

The next day in Tokyo, the screws were tightened on Australia. Government, army and navy representatives met in view of favourable developments, 'especially in light of the situation in India and Australia', to expedite a swift termination of the war. They decided 'greater pressure shall be brought to bear on Australia through the progress of our southward operations'. The detail was unresolved but the plan included the disruption of Australia's communications in order to break her ties with Britain and the US.

Two days after the Churchill–Curtin exchange, Japanese forces moving southward occupied Menado, Kema and Bangka in the Dutch Celebes, and prepared to occupy Tarakan, a major oil production centre off the east coast of Dutch Borneo. Australia had never been so wide open to an enemy.

*

At Hashirajima, Admiral Ugaki celebrated New Year with a sukiyaki banquet aboard the *Nagato* – complaining later to his diary, as he often did, of his troublesome teeth.

That day, the carrier strike force that had attacked Pearl Harbor had left Hiroshima Bay in preparation for an invasion of Rabaul, on the island of New Britain. Ringed by active volcanoes, Rabaul was a tropical haven with a deep harbour, populated by the prosperous and well-educated Tolai people and by an Australian minority mostly engaged in missionary and plantation work. Mandated to Australia from Germany after World War I, it was defended by a small number of Australian troops and airmen.

Possession of this settlement would give Japan one of her largest sea and air bases in the Pacific, with good access to the mainland of New Guinea and the Solomon islands to the south. Its seizure would safeguard an important Japanese base at tiny Truk, in the Caroline islands 1400 kilometres north. It would also place the Japanese firmly in the neighbourhood of Australia, only 1400 kilometres south-west of Rabaul. The Australian base of Port Moresby, 900 kilometres from Rabaul, would be particularly vulnerable.

Yet, like John Curtin, Admiral Ugaki was experiencing frustration. Combined Fleet's proposals to invade India, Australia and Hawaii were meeting opposition from Army General Staff, as well as from some members of Navy General Staff. Ugaki feared valuable time was slipping away, and demanded of his staff officers that they must establish the navy's second-stage plans by the end of February. Time was of the essence, given the sort of intense planning needed for an invasion:

> We shall be able to finish first-stage operations by the middle of March, as far as an invasion operation is concerned. What are we going to do after that? Advance to Australia, to India, attack Hawaii, or destroy the Soviet Union at an opportune moment according to their actions?

Ugaki was well aware of the risks involved in the invasion scenarios Combined Fleet was now entertaining. He debated the options in his diary, observing cautiously: 'We should limit operations within the scope of capturing and maintaining the resource areas necessary for the country's self-sufficiency.' But then he immediately added an afterthought, possibly referring to Australia and New Zealand:

'It may well be all right to engage in operations that would induce disintegration of the British Empire, if not much fighting strength is needed. But it is most essential to have fighting strength in reserve.' If the theatre of war was extended too far, Japan would lose flexibility in conducting operations. 'The wisdom of invading Hawaii will be another issue, and it can be undertaken only after we have won a decisive sea battle.'

Yet war planners both on Yamamoto's staff and at Navy General Staff were increasingly enthusiastic about invading Australia. Captain Yoshitake Miwa had been his chief's assistant when Yamamoto was Japan's naval attaché in Washington in 1926–1928. Miwa, 42, for years a confidant of Yamamoto, was air fleet officer aboard the *Nagato* before Pearl Harbor and shared Yamamoto's conviction in naval air power. He was one of Yamamoto's closest advisers and would become a rear admiral.

On 6 January 1942, Miwa advocated a huge expansion of Japanese ambitions: capturing Midway island as a prerequisite to landing on the Hawaiian islands and then going even further. 'We must think quickly about invading Australia . . . the United States is now in the middle of reinforcing Australia, Fiji and Samoa.'

Tomioka's men in Naval General Staff were actively working on their own plan for an invasion of Australia. In meetings with the army, they indicated that only key points in Australia would need to be occupied and that a force of just three divisions, or between 45,000 and 60,000 troops, could do the job. The army's planners were taken aback. Far from being an easy objective, they said, Australia would be bitterly defended, and was capable of holding off quite large forces.

On 6 January, on the day of Miwa's outspokenness, the army's chief of staff, General Hajime Sugiyama, went to the Imperial Palace in Tokyo to brief Emperor Hirohito. He set out a progress report on the state of war planning, indicating that the Imperial Navy was examining what could be done about Australia. Sugiyama, a hawk who had pressed for Japan to go to war with the US, nevertheless opposed the invasion of Australia, and avoided describing any action against Australia in those terms: 'Having achieved the completion of stage one of the campaign, operations to blockade the United States and Australia, as well as operations in the Indian Ocean, are being undertaken primarily by the Navy. Investigations by subordinates are continuing in accordance with previously submitted draft proposals to promote the end of the war.'

The army wanted to establish what it called 'a long-term unassailable position'. It proposed a military build-up against a possible Soviet attack in the north, and a defensive strategy only in southern regions. The Imperial Navy had far more aggressive measures in mind. According to Japan's war history, *Senshi Sosho*, the navy's emerging operational planning divided two ways:

> The first concerned launching a direct attack against Australia and as much as possible foiling any counter-attack by blockading the supply route between Australia and the United States, all the while aiming to establish a long-term unassailable position.
>
> The second involved luring the main strength of the US fleet into destruction in a short-term decisive battle through attacks against places like Midway and Hawaii.

On 10 January, the issue was debated at a formal liaison conference between senior representatives of the army, navy, and government in Tokyo. The meeting decided to blockade supply from Britain and the United States to India. The resolution regarding Australia was a compromise with no clear operational plan:

Proceed with the southern operations, all the while blockading supply from Britain and the United States and strengthening the pressure on Australia, ultimately with the aim to force Australia to be freed from the shackles of Britain and the United States.

A contemporary Japanese military historian, Professor Hiromi Tanaka, from Japan's National Defense Academy, argues that the resolution reflected Australia's growing strategic importance in the thinking of both the navy and the army: 'Australia was being taken very seriously and every means of sundering Australia's firm relationship with Britain and the United States was being considered.'

But the wording of the resolution was ambiguous, also reflecting the growing differences in the two forces' view of how to deal with the problem of Australia. It fell well short of speaking about an invasion, owing to army opposition, but the Imperial Navy was actively considering invasion anyhow.

Debilitating antagonism was rapidly building between Japan's army and navy. Imperial General Headquarters, which issued glowing reports for public consumption throughout the war, was a disunited sham, a headquarters in name only. This dysfunctional and self-interested group comprised the chiefs of the Army and Navy General Staffs, army and navy ministers, and selected high ranking officers.

Despite its name, the participants shared no accommodation and no leadership. Occasional Imperial conferences, attended by the emperor, were held in Hirohito's palace chamber. More commonly the group met at liaison conferences, which were woefully bureaucratic and ponderous proceedings that lacked even a permanent chairman.

The adversarial nature of this system fed suspicion and hostility between the two branches of Japan's armed forces, and weakened the war effort. Admiral Nobutake Kondo, who led the southern invasion operations, ran into obstructions from the Japanese army during the initial invasion of Malaya. Most of the airfields being used by navy fighters and bombers on the east coast were soft and muddy and hazardous for his flyers. Kondo said air fields on the west coast of the Malay peninsula were in comparatively good condition, but army air force command there refused to let the navy use them despite questions to army general headquarters.

The ministers for the army and the navy claimed authority to report separately but directly to the emperor without cabinet approval, only informing the prime minister of their actions.

'They [the services] hated each other, almost fought,' an observer officer in the navy ministry, Masataka Chihaya, commented. 'Exchange of secrets and experiences, the common use of airplanes and other instruments, could not even be thought of. The disagreement, lack of understanding and co-operation between the army and the navy are among the most important causes that led to our swift defeat.' Professor Tanaka agrees: 'In a way, that's why Japan couldn't win the war.'

After much discussion, the liaison conference agreed that major air attacks would be launched on Darwin; that air and ground attacks would be made against Port Moresby, which fell within the area defended by Allied air forces based in Australia; and that there would be a midget submarine attack on Sydney Harbour. But this compromise was far from the end of the issue for key staff planners in the Naval General Staff and Combined Fleet. They would soon push for the invasion of Australia at every opportunity.

The army's caution about Australia stemmed partly from the fact that it lacked good intelligence about the country. This was despite an extensive one-man foray into Australia in 1941 by an Imperial Army spy, Major Sei Hashida. He spent over two months in Australia, visiting ports including Sydney, Melbourne and Darwin, pretending to investigate the purchase of Australian wool, wheat, metal and other commodities for the Japanese army.

Japanese diplomats badgered Australian military authorities to allow Hashida on to military bases, but the requests were denied. The spy was apprehended by the Dutch in Batavia (Jakarta); they found him in possession of two notebooks in Japanese. The first contained 60 pages of notes and sketches of Australian harbours and places of military interest. His orders showed that Hashida had been told to discover the strength and topography of Australian army, navy, and air force bases, with emphasis on Darwin, Sydney, and Melbourne.

But this one-man spy mission paled in comparison with the espionage of the Imperial Navy, which had carried out intelligence missions in Australia for years, especially on land and in Australia's northern waters.

Japan was not permitted to establish naval and army attachés in Australia when its legation was established in early 1941, but by mid-year the ambassador in Melbourne, Tatsuo Kawai, had been given substantial funds from Tokyo for intelligence purposes. He retained a naval spy, Mitsumi Yanase, who resided at the Japanese consulate in Sydney. The residence, *Craig-y-Mor*, was located at Point Piper, and had spectacular views of the harbour. Before Japan entered the war, Australian captains and admirals partied as guests on *Craig-y-Mor*'s sweeping lawns. Yanase was able to look out his window and send detailed troopship and warship movements to a grateful German regime.

In the years leading up to the war, the Japanese navy had actively cultivated contacts among Japanese pearl divers in northern Australia. At one stage Australian officials discovered that one 'crewman' aboard a Japanese fishing boat calling at Darwin and other northern centres was in fact a Japanese admiral. The Imperial Navy also had extensive records of Australian ports, including Darwin, which their ships had been visiting for decades.

Partly as a result of the disagreements between Japan's armed forces, it was decided in Tokyo on 15 January that the army mainly would be responsible for India/Ceylon and the navy for Australia, a trend that would heighten the danger to Australia, given the extent of its intelligence. The Imperial Navy was well prepared for a mine-laying operation that was carried out near Darwin by the submarine *I-121*, and for a similar operation just two weeks later involving the *I-123*.

As the Japanese were sowing mines off Darwin, in Melbourne Prime Minister Curtin turned to his defence chiefs, calling for their immediate assessment of the danger of invasion in force. Hong Kong had fallen, the Philippines was a wasting asset, the enemy was within 240 kilometres of Singapore and had made landings in British and Dutch Borneo and the Celebes. A direct move towards Australia from the Japanese bases grew more probable, Curtin was told by his defence chiefs. This was likely to take the form of a progressive southward move securing New Guinea, New Hebrides, and New Caledonia as advanced bases.

A major attack could be launched on Australia from these advanced bases 'if and when the strategic situation in the area of Malaya and Netherlands East Indies is judged to be suitable': 'We therefore consider that the danger of invasion in force will remain until we have clearly stabilised our front along the Malay barrier or until we have secured supremacy over the Japanese fleet.'

Considering the length of the Australian coastline, the joint chiefs of staff added almost despairingly: 'Should Japan secure complete freedom of the seas, the only limit to the forces she could employ against us would be that imposed by the amount of shipping available to her. It is clearly beyond our capacity to meet an attack of the weight that the Japanese could launch.'

They were at a loss to know how they could defend mainland Australia against a Japanese attack, and could only hope that the Imperial Navy would be kept at bay by the US Pacific Fleet. Most of the forces in Australia at this time were untrained citizen's militia. The front line RAAF strength was 65 Hudson bombers, an assortment of flying boats and 98 Australian Wirraways, useless against the modern Japanese Zero fighter.

The Americans were also assessing Australia's situation. Brigadier General Leonard T. Gerow, assistant chief of staff of the war department in Washington, began his own assessment on 17 January with the unsettling words, 'it is not practicable to state how long Australia will remain in friendly hands'. He did not believe that the Japanese would try to conquer Australia entirely, but acknowledged that the enemy could occupy portions of the country, bomb any cities with carrier-based aircraft and, if they seized New Guinea and New Caledonia, bomb northern Australia with long-range bombers.

In Tokyo, General Tojo, his uniform bristling with medals, rose to make an eagerly awaited speech in the House of Peers, the upper house of the National Diet. Imperial forces had crushed all enemies, he said, achieving brilliant victories wherever they went.

> As regards the Netherlands East-Indies and Australia, if they continue as at present their attitude of resisting Japan, we will show no mercy in crushing them. But if their peoples come to understand Japan's real intentions and express willingness to co-operate with us, we will not hesitate to extend them our help with full understanding for their welfare and progress.

As he spoke, the smoke was still rising above Rabaul, which had been attacked by 109 aircraft in a massive raid mounted from the carriers *Akagi, Kaga, Zuikaku,* and *Shokaku*. A convoy of 5000 troops landed at Rabaul on 21 January. After a brief but vigorous Australian resistance, the Japanese South Seas force secured what would become a major air and naval base.

Mitsuo Fuchida led the attack force of 90 bombers on Rabaul. He saw Australian Wirraway aircraft 'promptly disposed of by our fighters'. A further strike on Rabaul was carried out the next day, but Fuchida thought it was superfluous: 'All in all, the employment of the Nagumo Force in this operation struck me as wasteful and extravagant. If ever a sledge hammer had been used to crack an egg, this was the time.'

Imperial General Headquarters on 24 January announced the

successful capture of Rabaul and nearby Kavieng. IGH said it had not only brought the destruction of British and American strategic positions, but had also gained Japan the advantage of establishing an air base in the South Pacific and extending control of the skies from the western Pacific into the South Pacific:

> The capture of this important position, from where it will be possible to spread our influence to the Australian mainland, is extremely significant in terms of our ability to attack and menace Australia.

Baron Tomioka, who would later command the forces at Rabaul, said the occupation of Rabaul afforded an excellent air base for scouting and patrolling areas to the northeast of Australia, 'anticipated to be the zone of operations of the enemy fleets'.

The Curtin government was devastated at the news of Rabaul's loss. It left the door open for a direct assault on northern Australia. This apprehension was shared by the chief of the US Fleet, Admiral Earnest J. King, who reacted by proposing a new US naval command in the waters off the east coast of Australia, extending east to Fiji, and known as the ANZAC area. On 26 January King instructed the commander-in-chief of the US Pacific Fleet, Admiral Chester W. Nimitz, to detach a cruiser and two destroyers to the ANZAC command to join two Australian cruisers as a deterrent to any Japanese moves into waters south of Rabaul.

'Anybody who fails to perceive the immediate menace which this attack constitutes for Australia must be lost to reality,' Curtin told the press.

9

PLOTTING AGAINST AUSTRALIA

The heavy cruiser *Atago*, flagship of Admiral Nobutake Kondo and spearhead of the Malayan invasion, was charging relentlessly across the South China Sea. With Japanese troops fighting their way south down the Malay peninsula to Singapore, Admiral Kondo had turned his attention to other fronts in the south seas operation. His fleet, which included battleships *Haruna* and *Kongo*, and eight destroyers, had headed back to Camranh Bay in Indochina, and then out to the South China Sea to provide 'distant cover' for the invasion of the Philippines.

After standing off the coast of Luzon to cover the Lingayen Gulf landings on 22 December, Kondo shifted his attention to a second invasion two days later at Lamon Bay, southeast of Manila. He oversaw a further landing at Davao. Then Kondo and his staff in the cruiser's operations room began studying the next stage of operations – the capture of Sumatra and Java.

The admiral already had a distinguished naval career. He had been chief of staff of Combined Fleet, chief of Naval General Staff operations division and deputy chief of the General Staff. Probably the only other naval officer of such experience at the time was Yamamoto himself.

Kondo's initial view had been that war against the United States should be avoided by all means. But since early December, much had happened, and very quickly. So he and his staff officers aboard the *Atago* began preparing a proposal for consideration by commander-in-chief Yamamoto on how to force peace on the Allies after the initial southern area invasions. Yamamoto did not especially want his fleet commanders, occupied with combat operations in far-flung theatres, to be bothered by 'other matters'. But the influential admiral had a plan. He believed that the best way to inflict a fatal blow on Japan's enemy was to bring about the collapse of the British empire.

He saw Japan as having two options to achieve this: attacks on India or Australia. Kondo preferred the Australian operation, because the India operation required Germany to penetrate Iraq and Iran, cutting oil resources to the British empire. It would also generate a 'powerful enemy encounter' which would need to be met with sufficient forces, as the admiral later wrote:

> The Australia operation which aimed to cut the American-Australian lifeline was such a threat to the Allied powers that they could not but prevent our operation by all means . . .
>
> Comparing these two operations with each other, the Indian operation involved such disadvantages as part of our main striking forces being withdrawn from the main theatre, the Pacific, which, in other words, would mean our operation would be too widely spread out.
>
> The Australia operation, on the contrary, could be regarded as part of our main operation against America and also would have a rich chance of taking hold of American task forces.
>
> If those operations had proved successful, they would have done much to contribute to weakening the fighting spirit of the enemy, by continuing accumulation of damages upon him.

Other senior naval officers involved in the southern operation also advocated capturing Australia or the task forces that would defend Australia. Vice Admiral Shigeyoshi Inoue was the commander of the Japanese Fourth Fleet based at Truk island. The fleet consisted of three light cruisers, including the flagship *Kashima* and a destroyer squadron. It had taken part in the invasions of Wake island, Guam, Rabaul and neighbouring Kavieng.

Inoue, a much decorated and influential officer, had good credentials as a strategist and, like Kondo, was a moderate. He had opposed army plans to conquer China after the Marco Polo Bridge incident in 1937, and had opposed the signing of the Tripartite Pact with Germany and Italy in 1940. But like the rest, Inoue now could see only prospects of expansion for Japan. His staff officers aboard the *Kashima*, including his chief of staff, Captain Shikazo Yano, worked on offensives that dovetailed with the plans of Baron Tomioka at Naval General Staff. Tomioka espoused Japanese expansion in the Solomons–New Guinea area, as the necessary first step towards landings on the Australian mainland.

As the American naval historian John B. Lundstrom would note, 'Fourth Fleet would have liked nothing more than to knock Australia out of the war.' Inoue and his planners like Yano recognised the danger that the Allies would pour unlimited amounts of men and material into Australia to turn it into an offensive base against Japan's southern perimeter. They noted that US aircraft had already begun to arrive. They foresaw attacks from Australia as directly threatening Japanese holdings in New Guinea, the Bismarck archipelago to the northern Solomons, and the vital Truk naval and air base. In discussions with Yamamoto over Inoue's request for aircraft carrier support for a proposed operation to invade Port Moresby and Tulagi, Inoue took the opportunity to put forward his views about a Japanese invasion of Australia.

In Tokyo, propagandists had been taking notice of the growing Australian dissatisfaction with Britain, as Australian leaders and the public called for urgent war weapons and manpower. CANBERRA IS INDIGNANT, a headline in the *Nichi Nichi* daily reported: '... the war development has made the Australian Government desperate, and public anger against the British

Government is mounting as requests for aid go unheeded ... Australia is now angry at English promises for help that were never carried out.'

AUSTRALIA FEELING UNEASY AS PREMIER ASKS FOR WAR MATERIAL, the *Japan Times* reported on 28 January. The newspaper claimed that John Curtin had left no doubt that Australia felt let down by Britain: 'The Australian people will no longer allow its sons to shed their blood in North Africa nor even Malaya, while the Australian continent itself is bared of every means of defence.'

In Canberra, Curtin, sick and exhausted, departed the national capital for meetings of the Advisory War Council and war cabinet in Melbourne. After that he planned to take the train to Perth for a long-awaited break, while his deputy, Frank Forde, acted as prime minister. He had not been home for many months. At Melbourne, Curtin was informed that major problems in moving materiel had developed on the waterfront at Darwin. The freighter SS *Holbrook*, which had arrived carrying American artillery, had waited three weeks before the precious cargo could be unloaded, because of restrictions on the use of servicemen on waterside duties. Curtin immediately sent a minister to Darwin to negotiate with the waterside workers.

With some sort of attack on Darwin appearing imminent, Curtin's greatest fear now was that Australia still lacked sufficient troops to defend herself in the event of invasion. The return of the three battle-tested Australian divisions in the Middle East would be too late if the Japanese seized the initiative with early landings on mainland Australia. American troops, though promised, were also still light on the ground.

General Iven Mackay, commander-in-chief of the Home Forces, shared Curtin's concerns: 'Although the force available for the defence of Australia was nominally five divisions, in reality the force which could be fully equipped was only half that strength ...' The army's chief of staff, General Vernon Sturdee, was also worried sick by Australia's lack of defence preparedness.

In late January, he received a cable from the British commander of the ABDA command (American-British-Dutch-Australian) based in Java, General Sir Archibald Wavell, calling for Australian assistance at Koepang, in Dutch Timor:

> Threat to Koepang is getting worse. Can you spare a battalion and/or other reinforcements from Darwin?

Sturdee was incensed and sent a snappy reply: 'We have already reduced to an absolute minimum our forces required to protect our vital areas in Australia. Physical difficulties of transportation especially in wet season preclude transference of troops between Darwin and rest of Australia. Desire to impress upon you that our forces lack much essential equipment and are still inadequately trained.'

Wavell was ultimately forced to evacuate Java, and the ABDA command disintegrated, leaving the Dutch to make their final stand.

On 28 January, the *Japan Times* claimed that with the battle at the gates of Singapore, there was now a serious threat to the western flank of Australia which was causing the enemy great consternation: 'A tremendous pincer movement is thus being initiated.' The newspaper wasn't too far from the truth. By the end of the month the operational planners in Combined Fleet were well advanced with invasion planning. They submitted another plan to Navy General Staff listing the following priorities:

> One, invade Ceylon at the end of May/June; establish contact with the German forces; mission accomplished, Combined Fleet will turn toward the east.
> Two, Port Darwin must be taken.
> Three, Fiji and Samoa need not be taken, only destroyed.
> Four, we should like to take Hawaii, if possible.

On 29 January, Imperial Headquarters ordered the Combined Fleet to capture the strategic points of Lae, Salamaua, and the

Australian administrative capital of Port Moresby in Papua. Hirohito's biographer, Herbert P. Bix, later described this action as 'the first step of a plan to isolate and ultimately attack Australia'. On 7 February, Hirohito affixed his seal to the order requiring Combined Fleet to attack the island of Timor north west of Darwin. The emperor was now 'as intoxicated by victory as his senior commanders'.

Only the British prime minister, back in London from his visit to Washington, continued to view Japan's intentions phlegmatically. On 27 January, Churchill told the House of Commons that he was sure everyone sympathised with 'our kith and kin in Australia, now that the shield of British and American sea power has, for the time being, been withdrawn so unexpectedly and so tragically'.

Churchill said hostile bombers might soon be within range of Australian shores, but he thought the Japanese might better occupy themselves securing the rich prizes of the Philippines, Dutch East Indies, and the Malaya archipelago:

> I think they are much more likely to be arranging themselves in those districts which they have taken or are likely to take, than to undertake a serious mass invasion of Australia. That would seem to be a very ambitious overseas operation for Japan to undertake in the precarious and limited interval before the British and American navies regain ... the unquestionable command of the Pacific Ocean.

In hindsight, of course, Churchill was right. But ambitious as it seemed, the Japanese then were seriously considering landing on Australian soil. Churchill's stark qualification of a 'serious mass invasion' should be noted, because by now his own intelligence chiefs were suggesting that a limited invasion of Australia, namely at Darwin, was a distinct possibility: 'Japanese plans at this stage are not thought to embrace major attack on Australia and New Zealand as distinct from raids as set out above. Only exception is attempt to occupy Darwin.'

Britain's joint intelligence committee at this time was expecting a Japanese raid on Darwin or a landing to capture the vital northern port. British intelligence chiefs assessed the military threat to Australia as primarily one of raids, ranging from attacks by midget submarines up to carrier raids on major ports, notably Darwin.

They thought that the preconditions for Japan to invade Australia were Russian neutrality, the capture of Singapore, Java, Sumatra, the Philippines and control of New Guinea, New Caledonia, Fiji, and Samoa. But even then, the British defence chiefs said, Japan would need control of the sea.

While the intelligence committee did not see outright invasion of the mainland of Australia as an immediate option, they thought Japan might well strike Australia or New Zealand before the battle in Malaya was over. The one necessary precondition for this was the seizure of Darwin, as they termed it, an operation far easier than amphibious landings against Brisbane or Sydney. An attack on the port of Darwin was likely in any event, they concluded:

> Before attempting any major operation against Australia and New Zealand, Japanese likely to attempt capture of Darwin, denying to us only possible bases in Northern Australia. Due to its isolated position Darwin is an attractive target for capture before it is strengthened and while our military strength in this area comparatively weak.

The joint British intelligence chiefs went on to point out the ramifications of Darwin as a Japanese base. As soon as the port was captured, Japanese could bring in additional land-based aircraft. Assuming operations in Malaya and Philippines were finished, they might be able to base 400 such planes and 30 long-range flying boats at Darwin. This outcome, they assessed, would depend on the Japanese controlling the East Indies Archipelago, Timor, the New Guinea islands, New Caledonia, Fiji, and Samoa.

In Washington two weeks later, American intelligence chiefs sitting as the Combined Staff Planners considered the British assessments and generally agreed that 'a major invasion' of Australia or New Zealand was unlikely. However, on 13 February, the Americans added the following alarming caution referring to the 'barrier' of Malaya, the Dutch East Indies down to the tip of Cape York peninsula.

> From the barrier, without undertaking a major offensive operation, Japan could deny the use of the Torres Strait by neutralising or occupying key points on the north coast of Australia.
>
> This coast is so inaccessible by land from the settled area of Australia and so accessible by sea from the Netherlands East Indies that it is, strategically, an integral part of the barrier rather than of Australia. From the barrier the Japanese could also raid the ports of Australia and New Zealand...

The Americans thought this landing could occur without the stated British qualification that Samoa, Fiji, and New Caledonia must first be occupied by the Japanese.

Even the Germans knew of the probable invasion of northern Australia, as Grand Admiral Erich Raeder reported to Hitler on 13 February: 'Rangoon, Singapore and most likely Port Darwin will be in Japanese hands within a few weeks.'

In his dismissive responses to Curtin's fears, Churchill never mentioned this Darwin invasion scenario from his own intelligence chiefs. Indeed, the British PM wrote to his chiefs of staff telling them in no uncertain terms that in his view a wholesale invasion of Australia was most unlikely. It was an instance of Churchill's pressure on his chiefs to see his view, and perhaps to downplay Australia's potential plight:

> On this lay-out of Japanese forces it seems very unlikely that an immediate full-scale invasion of Australia could take place. You are now making an appreciation for Australia of her position, and this disposition of Japanese forces might well be the starting-point.

With Churchill's references to 'invasion in force', 'full-scale invasion', and other qualifications, his assessment raises the spectre of a British leader who might have been preparing to abandon Darwin temporarily, if it was invaded, given its distance from Australia's key industrial cities, the difficulties of its defence, and Britain's interests elsewhere. Churchill, it appeared, did not equate the potential loss of remote Darwin with the loss of the whole Australian continent. While he did not express this view, it remains a distinct possibility that he believed a Japanese-controlled Darwin might not be preventable, but that Darwin could be retaken later when the Allies regained control of the Pacific. It is not difficult to imagine the damage Japanese long-range bombers could have done to east coast cities. Yet, as Churchill pointed out, British cities had been through the worst bombings and had survived.

The pathos surrounding the midget submariners ordered to certain death was a constant distraction for the Imperial Navy. Less than six weeks after the Pearl Harbor attack, Yamamoto was persuaded by Ugaki to make an inspection of the 'improved' midget submarines in action. On the morning of 31 January 1942, the admirals clambered down the gangway of the *Nagato* and boarded Yamamoto's launch. They crossed Hiroshima Bay and were piped aboard the submarine tender *Chiyoda*, where they observed the midget submarines being lowered from the stern and launched in gale force conditions.

The young submariners went through their paces. Despite improvements to the subs, the crews knew that combat involving the midgets still represented a one-way ticket. In the brief period available after Pearl Harbor there had been insufficient time to develop and refine the midget sub into a reliable weapon, but Ugaki, at least, was impressed by what he saw: 'Efforts of those concerned in a gale were great and the spirit of the young skippers was really high. It was quite reassuring. Thus we can hope those midget submarines penetrate in to enemy bases and sink major vessels.'

On the same day, Japanese troops captured Johore Bahru at the southern end of the Malay peninsula, and retreating British troops blew a hole in the narrow concrete causeway linking Johore Bahru to the island fortress of Singapore.

By late January, Ugaki had noted that the 'central authorities' in Tokyo were still indecisive about where to attack next, and that army general command had 'matters pending'. Ugaki was impatient for additional offensive action, but even his own staff officers were divided: 'On this occasion we must establish a definite policy promptly, but the staff officers keep on saying they are studying it, and it is getting nowhere.'

A few days later the senior staff officer, Captain Kuroshima, came to Ugaki to explain a scenario he and other staff officers had been studying. It included a decisive battle between the American and Japanese fleets, following a Japanese attempt to invade Hawaii. But Ugaki concluded that his men had failed to discover any good plan for destroying land-based air power on Hawaii. As a result, it was better to operate toward the west at this stage of the war, he believed.

Ugaki had a number of meetings with his staff officers looking at various operational scenarios. In his diary, Yamamoto's chief of staff revealed just how much independence his confident, young staff officers had in proposing and planning major war operations: 'I refrained from giving my decisions, in order to save the face of the staff officers who drafted the idea, or after being forced to give in to their strong one-sided arguments.'

In Japan, the most fundamental future operations were often discussed and planned at a relatively junior level, then sent up to the senior leadership for consideration. This was in stark contrast with Western navies, where decision-making was undertaken on a 'top down' basis, with the most senior officers calling on their resources, meeting to plan future operations, and then issuing orders to their subordinates.

During the 1930s a system had evolved by which junior officers and staff members could and did override the recommendations of admirals and generals. The real decisions were often made by lower-level officials, according to Imperial Navy historian Paul S.

Dull, and if a top official disagreed with them, he might be assassinated. Baron Tomioka and his radical associate Captain Shingo Ishikawa were part of the General Staff's middle echelon 'first committee' on policy who flouted their power in 1941, sometimes overpowering seniors by 'pressure from below' [*gekokujo*].

Ugaki and his staff officers spent the last week of January and the first days of February pulling together Combined Fleet's future operational proposals. An invasion of Australia, via a landing at Darwin, was one of its plans. This scenario was also now being discussed actively in Tokyo by Tomioka's operational planners. But time was running out to persuade all parties.

On 30 January, the head of the operations section of the army department, Colonel Takushiro Hattori, called on the prime minister and war minister, General Tojo, to brief him on the latest discussions between operational staff of the army and navy. Hattori had been Tojo's confidential secretary and was an influential army operative behind the scenes. It appears that he told Tojo that Navy General Staff were pushing for an invasion of Australia as part of the blockade of the country. Hattori said Tojo indicated his assent concerning the FS operation, a plan to invade Fiji, Samoa and New Caledonia generally, with the exception of what to do about Australia, adding: 'There is no consensus on the Australia operation even between high command and the ministers. Agreement has been reached concerning the plans to invade Fiji and Samoa.'

Tojo's initial enthusiasm about the prospect of occupying Australia had waned. He worried about being involved in a protracted operation there when he had major concerns on the Japanese fronts in Burma and China, and also needed to ensure Japan made adequate military provision against the Soviet Union. The Japanese army constantly feared invasion from the Soviets in the north. The Soviet leader Josef Stalin judged that he could not spare troops from the western front.

The following day, the army sought – and was granted – approval for invasions in eastern New Guinea and the Solomon Islands.

10

THE INDEFENSIBLE CONTINENT

John Curtin already knew how vulnerable Western Australia was to attack, with its vast and largely unpopulated coastline. On 19 November 1941, six weeks after he became prime minister, the cruiser HMAS *Sydney* was sunk by the German raider HSK *Kormoran* 112 nautical miles off the Western Australia coast, south west of Carnarvon. Curtin kept the news quiet for 12 days, hoping that survivors would be found, but, in a profound blow to national morale, not a single one was.

Now, on his return home to Cottesloe, John Curtin was appalled to hear from an old friend in the army that troops in Western Australia were drilling with broomsticks. He immediately asked Frank Forde for an explanation, saying he had been told on several occasions that there was a great shortage of rifles in Western Australia for use in protecting the homeland: 'In other words it was contended that a large proportion of the troops would not possess a weapon with which to fight or defend themselves.'

The army minister replied that the shortage of firearms was national. He said 18,000 troops in Australia did not have rifles, but World War I weapons were being reconditioned for their use. So serious was the defence dilemma that Australian defence chiefs wanted to appeal for infantry support from Canada. They warned – correctly, as it turned out – that Australia should prepare for maximum-scale raids, rather than immediate invasion, and commented: 'It is clearly beyond our capacity to meet any attack of the weight that the Japanese could launch either on the mainland or in the islands.'

The army had received intelligence, through the monitoring of Japanese signals, that suggested that air attacks launched from enemy carriers could be expected on the north-east coast of Australia. On 3 February, Brigadier Joseph Lee of headquarters Eastern Command issued a warning to his commanders of 'possible enemy action' in Australia:

> Secret information has been received which shows strong indications of enemy aircraft carrier operations [which] may be expected on the north east coast of Australia. All precautions, concealment, alertness and readiness for action of all AA [anti-aircraft] batteries and AA LMG [light machine gun] units must be ensured. Concentrations of stores and equipment at ports and elsewhere must be avoided as far as possible.

At this time hundreds of important Japanese naval messages were being intercepted and decoded by the Allied Signal Intelligence centres, including an RAAF unit at Darwin, assisted by direction-finding stations around northern Australia. These were collated in Melbourne. They kept track of Japanese aircraft carriers, air squadrons and naval units as they moved freely around the Pacific. In the first week of February, it was discovered that the Japanese appeared to be mobilising a major naval force in Palau, 800 kilometres east of the Philippines and at bases elsewhere, including Truk. A report to the Australian Naval Staff warned of the probability of a major attack in the Java area and in the Torres Strait. The Naval Staff took no action, as they did not consider the evidence conclusive. But the Australian Army did issue its warning.

The same day as the secret intelligence was received, Japanese bombers from Rabaul struck Port Moresby for the first time. Afterwards, the poorly trained, ill-disciplined Australian troops there went on a looting spree of stores, houses, and even churches. Curtin's war cabinet quickly replaced the civil administration with military authority and martial law.

On the island of New Britain, the Australian troops who had put up a fierce fight for Rabaul in late January were now straggling south to escape the Japanese. The men had made their way through rugged jungle and had crossed mountains intersected by rivers. On 2 February, they reached Tol and Waitavalo coconut plantations on Wide Bay, utterly exhausted and without adequate food and supplies. Heavy rain fell. Many of the troops were suffering from malaria, dysentery and tropical ulcers.

When the Japanese landed at Tol by barge, the Australians waved white flags and quietly surrendered. A few days later, about 150 Australian prisoners were lined up and roped together in small groups and led into the bush. Soon, fearful screams echoed through the plantation as the Australian soldiers were shot and bayoneted, some individually and some in small groups.

The waiting men heard the terrible screams as the bayonets were driven home into their mates. The Japanese soldiers returned, wiping blood from the blades. They simply shouted, 'Next!', and pushed their victims forward. Two of the victims, badly bayoneted in the stomach, managed to reach a hut, but Japanese soldiers set fire to it and burnt the Australians to death.

As many as 150 Australian soldiers were slaughtered at Tol and Waitavalo plantations, while about six survived to tell their story. This was one of the first Japanese atrocities against Australians during the war, and the Australian authorities at first could not credit it. Yet the survivors' bayonet wounds provided proof. The chief justice of the Supreme Court of Queensland, Sir William Webb, later conducted an investigation into the atrocities:

'. . . they were outrageously cruel and wicked and carried out with savage brutality. The men were killed one by one, practically in the presence of each other.'

At this time General Iven Mackay set out broad principles of action to be taken in the event of an early invasion of Australia. He was concerned that Japanese aircraft might attempt to destroy the BHP steelworks at Newcastle and metal factories at Port Kembla. The Japanese might invade such localities, he said, which would cripple Australia's war effort, or they might seize localities to disrupt communications with the United States to prevent the development of Australia as a base for future effort against Japan. He put forward an idea that was to have long-term political ramifications and shock the Australian population:

> Considering the extensive coastline to be watched and guarded, and since our forces are so small and distances so great, we must make up our minds that we cannot successfully defend the whole coast of Australia . . . This policy will mean leaving many portions of the Australian coast (even important towns) without troops . . .

On 4 February, Mackay wrote to the army minister seeking the government's agreement about which regions were considered vital to defend. He stressed the importance of holding the Port Kembla–Sydney–Newcastle industrial region, as well as Brisbane, which was earmarked as an important base for US forces. He also recognised the need to defend Melbourne, because of its central military role.

Mackay's assessment began an acrimonious political debate known as the 'Brisbane Line' controversy, a term that Mackay would later say he had never used. The army minister, Frank Forde, was the member for Capricornia, a seat based on Rockhampton in central Queensland. Aghast at the recommendations, recognising political dynamite, he did not even reply to Mackay. Soon after, the Curtin government took the decision to defend northern regions such as Darwin, but while retaining far greater defensive forces in the southern industrialised centres.

In Japan, Admiral Ugaki had now learned that his ambitions to capture Australia had run into stiff army opposition, but he thought he could overcome army objections: 'The high command in Tokyo is against an invasion of Port Darwin. In order to destroy it thoroughly, we are to capture Dili as well as Koupang at the same time. An instruction will be given shortly with regard to the capture of the Andamans. The chief of the Operations Bureau of the General Staff informed us of the above yesterday.'

Combined Fleet would continue to press its own plans, as would Naval General Staff. The following day Ugaki recorded in his diary that one of his staff officers, Fujii, had telephoned from Tokyo: 'He said that they had no concrete plan about the next operation, but he was trying to educate them, using our plan, and was making progress. We have also drafted the principle of directing the operations.'

For Ugaki, time was of the essence. He was desperate for offensive action if the war was to be brought to a quick conclusion. 'A return to negative policies', he wrote, 'involving making time without active operations while our enemies increase their fighting strength, would in effect render futile all our military successes . . .'

As Singapore's inevitable capture drew near, the debates in Tokyo about an Australian invasion became more bitter. To the navy men, the fall of Singapore presented a golden opportunity, with the whole of the southern region thrown open to Japan's bidding. They were scornful of their army counterparts who refused to seize the day, decrying them for their lack of boldness.

On 6 February, at a meeting in the old red and white navy ministry building near the imperial palace, Naval General Staff put up a strong case for invading eastern Australia at the same time as invasions of Fiji, Samoa and New Caledonia were mounted. The

Australian proposal was pushed by one of the firebrands of Naval General Staff, Captain Shingo Ishikawa, who had been naval attaché at Berlin in 1935.

Ishikawa, an extremist soon to become a rear admiral, had been a vigorous supporter of Japan's subjugation of Manchuria and had long argued that Japan had a god-given right to conquest in the South Seas. The following day, at another conference, Ishikawa continued to lecture the army: 'There will be no security for the Greater East Asia Co-Prosperity Sphere unless we make Australia the main target in stage two of our basic war plan, and annihilate it as a base for the American counter-offensive.'

The army disagreed vigorously with Ishikawa's submission, pointing out the need to plan for war against Russia. 'Blinded by victory, our onslaught in the Pacific is getting dangerous. We must realise our limits in the Pacific offensive', the army's operations section chief, Major-General Shinichi Tanaka, wrote in his diary. After the war Tanaka would tell US interrogators: 'The Navy wanted to take Port Darwin in northern Australia. They insisted that we take it, because the American Navy would use it as a base from which to attack Moresby and the Bismarcks... I absolutely refused to agree to the operation.'

In the face of the army's opposition, the navy's desire to capture Darwin had been set back to a major aerial assault, without landings, at the liaison conference of 10 January. On 9 February 1942, Admiral Yamamoto signalled Admiral Nagumo's carrier fleet, describing US, British and Australian forces building at Darwin:

'At an opportune time the carrier task force will conduct mobile warfare, first in the Arafura Sea and next in the Indian Ocean, endeavouring to annihilate the enemy strength in the Port Darwin area and to intercept and destroy enemy naval and transport fleets, while at the same time attacking enemy strength in the Java area from behind.' This rather opaque message was a signal for massive air raids on Darwin, but not an invasion, and, a week later, the Battle of the Java Sea.

But the Imperial Navy had not for a moment abandoned the

idea of capturing Darwin. On 11 February, discussions continued at the Navy Club in Tokyo, with Baron Tomioka's assistant, Commander Yuji Yamamoto, telling his opposite number in the army that energetic offensives were needed against Hawaii, Australia and other Pacific targets. By now, the Japanese leadership was well aware of Australia's defence vulnerabilities, and its dependence on its military allies.

The nation's lack of preparedness to meet an invasion was once again obvious at an advisory war council meeting in Canberra. Arthur Fadden, leader of the opposition Country Party, reported that of the 900 troops detailed to defend the Wide Bay area of central Queensland, only 187 had been issued with rifles. A force of 4000 troops were supposedly defending the coal-producing region on the main road west of Rockhampton. But, Fadden said, the force had only four anti-tank guns between them. Frank Forde promised sufficient Bren and Vickers machine-guns, and said 40 machine-gun carriers were being dispatched to Queensland.

In Parliament, former prime minister Robert Menzies had been outraged by external affairs minister Evatt, who said the defence of Australia had been treated as 'a subordinate and subsidiary part of a distant war'.

Via listening posts, such as one in neutral Lisbon, Japanese newspapers were carefully monitoring statements by Australian officials. The day after the advisory war council meeting in Canberra, the *Japan Times* carried the headline AUSTRALIAN PLIGHT EMBITTERS LEADERS, with a story highlighting disagreements between Curtin and Robert Menzies about responsibility for Australia's precarious situation. 'The immediate danger of Japanese invasion upon the mainland of Australia' had brought about a bitter exchange of criticism in Australia, the newspaper reported.

Two days later the newspaper carried a headline AUSTRALIANS VEER AWAY FROM BRITISH, in which the accompanying story, not entirely inaccurately, reported that

Australia now was looking to her own safety, rather than to fighting for the empire in faraway places.

On 14 February, a day before the fall of Singapore, army and navy chiefs confronted each other again in Tokyo. A navy ministry official suggested that because the war situation was now more advantageous than expected, it was a good chance to make a clean sweep of Australia's forward bases. He asked, 'Has not the time come to take one big leap forward?'

The army was unmoved. Colonel Etsuo Kotani commented: 'It cannot be said that the situation has improved ... It is too difficult. We have no reserves.' Baron Tomioka was adamant: 'But if we take Australia now, we can bring about the defeat of Great Britain. With only a token force we can reach our aim!' A war planner of experience and reported conservatism, Tomioka, like so many of his more radical colleagues, was now under the influence of Japan's endless victories.

At Hashirajima, Admiral Ugaki was prepared to accept as a first step the destruction of Australia's northern port by a massive aerial bombardment; on no account did he abandon the idea of a full-scale invasion. The priorities would simply be rearranged, which was something to be expected in war, and the invasion of Australia could be delayed a little.

The fleet assembled for Darwin was enormously powerful, comprising the carriers *Akagi*, *Kaga*, *Soryu*, and *Hiryu*, the battleships *Hiei* and *Kirishima*, the heavy cruisers *Tone* and *Chikuma*, the light cruiser *Abukuma*, and nine destroyers; two carriers short of the force which attacked Pearl Harbor. It left from Palau island on 15 February. Captain Mitsuo Fuchida, the air wing commander over Pearl Harbor and Rabaul who would also lead the attack on Darwin, explained how the Australian assault came about:

> The Hashirajima headquarters continued to focus its attention exclusively on the southern area, where it was now most concerned over probable Allied use of north-west Australia as a

base from which to impede Japanese seizure of the Dutch East Indies.

Proposals for mounting an amphibious invasion of Port Darwin met a flat rebuff by the Naval General Staff and the Army, so Combined Fleet decided upon the next best alternative, a carrier air strike to completely wreck base installations in the area.

This rebuff from Naval General Staff did not last long. It probably came initially from NGS chief Admiral Nagano, who liked to read the wind before making a firm decision. Certainly, it was not the intention of Baron Tomioka and his operational planning section to block an invasion of northern Australia. Tomioka saw Ugaki's strategy as perfectly logical; he had taken up the cudgels and was fighting strongly for the capture of Australia's north, giving the proposal renewed impetus. It did not take long for the wavering Admiral Nagano to fall in with his aggressive subordinate planners.

'Neither Admiral Nagano, chief of the Naval General Staff, nor his deputy, Vice Admiral Seiichi Ito, was the kind of officer who actively directed the planning of his subordinates,' Fuchida later recalled. 'They allowed the staff to take the initiative and they expressed themselves only when a plan had been drafted and submitted for their approval. It was Tomioka who sparked the Australia-first school of strategy.'

It was the fear of an American counteroffensive mounted from Australia that motivated Tomioka. Such a campaign would be spearheaded by air power to take full advantage of American industrial capacity to produce planes by mass-production. This massive air strength would require land bases in Australia:

Consequently, there would be a weak spot in Japan's defensive armour unless Australia were either placed under Japanese control or effectively cut off from the United States. Following the easy conquest of the Bismarcks in January, the most aggressive proponents of the Australia-first concept started advocating outright occupation of key areas in Australia.

Fuchida's only comment on the invasion plan was that it was an 'extreme proposal'.

Faced with the defence chiefs' warnings of Japanese attacks on the Australian mainland, the Curtin government began to debate another touchy subject, the possible evacuation of essential industry and the civilian population from vulnerable areas. Former army minister Percy Spender told the advisory war council that military authorities should advise which areas should be evacuated 'in the event of an enemy attack and whether it should be done now'.

State premiers were brought in to take part in the evacuation debate in early February. But Curtin's war cabinet was in a quandary. It would be almost impossible to move industry quickly, and to place undue emphasis on evacuation measures would lower morale and the maintenance of essential production.

The war cabinet therefore agreed only to the limited evacuation of children from city areas where there were major targets nearby. But quietly, with Japan making daily advances to the north, a small group of senior public servants and academics began gathering information on how Britain handled her mass civilian evacuations from cities.

No such discretion was possible in regard to the need for air raid shelters. By now, shelters quickly were appearing in city and suburban areas across the nation, in converted basements, subways, and reinforced buildings, and on vacant lots and parkland. The war cabinet approved the expenditure of one million pounds for the erection of more.

In the main cities, office workers gave up their weekends to work on the sandbagging of city buildings. In early 1942, the government removed the 75-metre clock tower on the general post office in Martin Place, Sydney: if it was hit by a Japanese bomb, the impact would probably destroy Australia's biggest communications centre below it.

The Curtin government, at least according to one observer in Canberra, developed a particular fear of Japanese raids on the national capital. Paul Hasluck, who would later become a leading conservative minister and then governor-general, was a young officer in the Department of External Affairs in 1942. He wrote of the atmosphere in the national capital soon after the outbreak of war with Japan:

> There was fear in Canberra of a Japanese invasion. Until the Battle of the Coral Sea in May 1942, the fear was acute even in the highest levels of government and it was not fully relieved until mid-1943 . . . I now record that my personal observation of the Australian ministers, including the Prime Minister at the time of crisis in early 1942, was that they were lacking in fortitude.

In the first half of 1942, the belief that Canberra itself was a war target was very real, according to Hasluck. Typists in the external affairs department spent many hours making copies of important documents and storing them along with code books in steel trunks, in case Canberra should need to be abandoned:

> We were informed of a plan that in case of invasion the government was to be moved southward out of Canberra to a safer place . . . It seemed to be assumed that the enemy would do more harm to the Australian resistance by knocking out Canberra and disorganising the government than by hitting military targets.

For weeks, the navy had been involved in evacuating mostly British citizens from Singapore. Yet when it finally came, the Japanese capture of Singapore was a bitter shock to its defenders and to the remaining one million civilians, including many Chinese and Malays who had fled from the north. The centre of Singapore was bombed into chaos. When the Allies' last desperate counter-attack failed, its commanders ordered their men to lay down their arms and surrender. The Japanese went through a British hospital bayoneting patients, doctors, and nurses. Chinese men of military age were rounded up and systematically murdered in their tens of thousands.

The fall of Singapore brought home to Australians the reality of Japanese invasion. Almost 15,000 Australian soldiers simply disappeared into internment, along with hundreds of remaining British and Australian civilians. While Japan's representative in Australia, Tatsuo Kawai, was enjoying a relaxed form of house arrest in Melbourne, Australia's high commissioner in Singapore, Vivian Bowden, unsuccessfully attempted to escape by boat. While protesting his diplomatic status, he was forced by his Japanese captors to dig his own grave, then bashed and executed.

11

AN ILLUSION OF SUPERIORITY

Winter on the Bay of Hiroshima was cool in the evenings, but the days were often sunny and warm until about noon. On deck, it felt like spring. In his diary, Admiral Ugaki playfully chided himself and his staff officers:

> What's the matter with you people? Fighting,
> Waging war, when flowers are blooming?

He kept close tabs on invasions, battles and skirmishes over a vast distance, ever watchful of threats to his scattered fleets; still, his duties were not excessively onerous in the early months of 1942, when Japan's war was going so well. On 10 February, Ugaki left the *Nagato* early in the morning to go shooting in the nearby islands. When he returned, he saw that the massive new battleship *Yamato* had returned to the Hashirajima anchorage from nearby Kure, where she had undergone repairs after her sea trials. Now she lay just to the west of the *Nagato,* waiting for the commander-in-chief to take possession of his new flagship, named after the Japan race.

The following day, ceremonies were held in the wardroom of the *Nagato* for the 2602nd anniversary of the accession of Japan's first emperor and the sake was broken out. There were frequent celebrations on the *Nagato*, with abundant supplies of good food and drink. Ratings on Japanese warships could draw their ration of rice wine or beer with the evening meal, and there were no restrictions on the amount of sake and beer officers could order. Civilian food rationing began in Japan in April 1941; as the war progressed civilians endured serious shortages. But there was never any shortage of good fare on the Combined Fleet flagship. Menus changed daily, and even the ratings ate generous portions of fish and beef.

On 12 February, Admiral Yamamoto transferred his flag to the *Yamato*. She was a far more comfortable ship than the 23-year-old *Nagato*, and the staff officers were delighted with their new quarters. They now worked from a much larger and better appointed operations room amidships, one level below the main deck. The *Yamato*'s officer accommodation was genteel, befitting one of the most powerful navies in the world. A large antique sideboard and mirror graced one wall in the operations room, which was dominated by a vast timber table.

Soon special guests began arriving to inspect the new flagship, including Prince Nobuhito Takamatsu, bringing congratulations for the Imperial Navy's fine achievements. The thin-faced Takamatsu, the emperor's younger brother, was a commander, soon to be promoted to captain, but was still subordinate to Baron Tomioka in the operations section of Naval General Staff. He had urged his brother not to go to war with the United States, and had privately expressed reservations about the militant Tojo government. But now, like Tomioka, the prince was consumed with the need to win the war.

The *Yamato* was such a stunning ship, it could only add to the sense of self-importance and superiority of her staff officers. But like all battleships at this point of military history, she was already obsolete, given her inability to deal effectively with overwhelming air power.

This was made clear to Ugaki by Rear Admiral Takijiro Onishi, chief of staff, Eleventh Air Fleet. On 1 March, he visited the *Yamato* on his way back to Tokyo from the front. Onishi told Ugaki that the centre of armament was now air power, and the big-ship-and-gun policy was on the way out. Battleships and heavy cruisers were just an armament for surprise attacks, Onishi insisted. Onishi stayed overnight playing chess and discussing the war with Yamamoto. He told Ugaki he itched to get back to the action, fearing that he might be doomed to 'spend the war on a chessboard'.

Onishi's fanaticism and fascination with youths who would sacrifice their lives soon would equal that of Ugaki's. As the war progressed, Onishi conceptualised the idea of the Kamikaze squads, and as the 'father' of the scheme he would send thousands of his brave 'sons' to their doom with some dramatic successes but questionable military gain, given the loss of pilots and aircraft. It was Onishi who would use cherry blossoms and the image of young men as beautiful flowers falling in their prime of life to name the corps, planes and bombs of the 'special attack' forces.

Today the *Yamato* lies partly upside down, broken in two, and rusting, on the bottom of the East China Sea. She was sunk by American aircraft, as Rear Admiral Onishi might have predicted, on her way to the battle of Okinawa in April 1945. In film shot from a modern submersible, the golden imperial chrysanthemum crest can still be seen clearly on her bow.

At the old naval city of Kure, I stand before a recreation of the flagship, in awe of her sleek lines and power, her massive triple gun turrets. The scale model is 26.3 metres in length; the real thing was ten times as long. Even so, the vast grey pagoda bridge towers above me, topped by its revolutionary range finder, once the best and largest in the world. The bulbous bow reduced wave resistance, allowing the battleship speed of 27 knots. But most striking are the low-slung, curvaceous lines of the vessel. The *Yamato* was a truly magnificent and tragic creation.

The model of the great battleship is installed over several levels at the Kure City Naval History & Science Museum, known as the Yamato museum, located on the waterfront within walking distance of the dry dock where the original battleship was built. The display includes the last testaments of crew members, and samples of verse they penned for loved ones. There is also a 'large objects exhibition room' featuring a Zero fighter, different types of naval shells, a submarine, and one of the dreadful *Kaiten* human torpedo craft.

In Kure, reminders of the navy's war are everywhere. On a hill overlooking the port, there's a place the Japanese refer to as the 'old navy graveyard', which is not a cemetery. With its photographs etched in granite of cruisers and battleships, and the Japanese naval ensign prominently displayed, this is a memorial to the ships of the Imperial Navy and the men who served in them. That red and white ensign, with the long rays of sun stretching out across its face, is commonplace all around Kure and these parts, almost as though the flag that led Japan first to victory, then to inglorious defeat, is making a comeback, not only on modern Japan's warships.

The naval museum's director, Kazushige Todaka, a maritime historian of note, tells me he used to work as a senior researcher on military history for the son of Baron Tomioka, Sadahiro Tomioka, who was also a war history researcher. He says he can describe the father, Baron Tomioka, as a very smart man and a 'nice guy', a quiet and more conventional officer, compared with Yamamoto, who was much more outspoken. Baron Tomioka went on after the war to become one of the country's official war historians, setting up his own research unit with other former officers who analysed and edited a vast amount of wartime Naval General Staff documents. Much of this work eventually made its way into the official war history series, *Senshi Sosho*.

Todaka speaks softly and openly. He believes the *Yamato* museum is free from ideology and sentiment. It sheds light on the advanced technology and craftsmanship needed to produced great battleships, he tells me. But will such a fabulous model – the ultimate big toy – encourage today's Japanese youth to glorify war, I ask him. 'I hope not,' Todaka replies easily. 'If you don't know the history of war, you can't understand peace.'

It's a good reply; the same sort that I might expect from curators and guides at the Australian War Memorial at Canberra. Kure is proud of its tragic history and keen to revive interest in the city's shipbuilding industry. Before leaving the museum, Japanese visitors are buying all sorts of memorabilia and souvenirs, including a sticker with the words 'We love *Yamato*' over an outline of the ship, and even toy models of the *Kaiten* human torpedo.

When the British forces at Singapore admitted they were finished, the Japanese commander, General Tomoyuki Yamashita, demanded and received their unconditional surrender. In Japan, the gruff Yamashita was becoming known as the 'Tiger of Malaya' for the speed and daring of his southward advance.

Everyone now had a suggestion about how best to fend off the encroaching Japanese forces. On the day Singapore fell, the outspoken chief of the General Staff, General Sturdee, sat in his office in Victoria Barracks, Melbourne, and worried mightily about the disintegration of Australia's remaining army should troops be sent off in all directions to plug the gaps:

> So far in this war against Japan we have violated the principle of concentration of forces in our efforts to hold numerous small localities with totally inadequate forces which are progressively overwhelmed by vastly superior numbers.

Sturdee bluntly warned that 'considerable risks are at present being taken with the security of this country'. He said Australia was the only practicable base from which an offensive could ultimately be launched and therefore Australian forces overseas, including those en route to Java, must be returned to Australia as soon as possible.

On 16 February, Australians woke to newspaper headlines bringing further frightening news. In addition to the fall of Singapore, Sumatra was now under attack. JAPANESE INVADE ISLAND OF SUMATRA, the *Sydney Morning Herald* reported, revealing how Japanese troops were advancing towards the oil centre of Palembang.

With Singapore, Malaya and Rabaul under Japanese control, Port Moresby under bombardment, and the ABDA command on the brink of collapse in Java, the US Army headquarters in Melbourne reported to Washington that it was 'evident that Japanese seizure of the entire region from Burma to Australia could not be long delayed'.

President Roosevelt now became gravely concerned with the defence of Australia. He informed one of his closest advisers, Harry Hopkins, that the United States should assume responsibility for reinforcing Australia and New Zealand. On the same day, US Army planners performed an astonishing about-face, completely reversing their previous policy towards Australia.

Until now, they had seen Australia as a supply base for the Philippines. According to the American historian John B. Lundstrom, in 1942 the US War Department had planned to send only two troop divisions to the whole South Pacific. Suddenly, the US Army's 41st Division and other troops, numbering 27,000 men in all, were tapped to ship out specifically to Australia.

Roosevelt told Churchill that the US was in the best position to reinforce Australia. He added that the US Navy had already begun operations which would help to safeguard Australia and New Zealand from outright invasion by the Japanese. The Americans faced a race against time to reinforce the southern continent against invasion. Curtin and his defence chiefs nervously waited to see whether Japan would beat the United States to their shores.

The Curtin government now reckoned a Japanese attempt to invade Australia the most likely probability of the Pacific war. The prime minister told the nation:

The fall of Dunkirk initiated the Battle for Britain. The fall of Singapore opens the Battle for Australia. On its issue depends not merely the fate of this Commonwealth, but the frontier of the United States of America, and indeed all the Americas, and therefore, in a large measure, the fate of the British-speaking world . . .

The day after Curtin made this famous statement, General Tojo addressed a special session of the Diet. He called on all nations in East Asia to 'awaken to the real aims of Japan' in order to enjoy Japan's victories. The object of the war was to establish a new order of co-existence and co-prosperity on ethical principle with the Japanese empire as its nucleus.

Tojo said the main body of the American–British fleet had been crushed, Hong Kong had been brought to submission in 18 days, Manila suppressed in 26, and now Singapore had fallen in 70 days. Borneo, the Celebes and New Britain had been occupied. The Dutch in the East Indies would be crushed if they continued to resist. Tojo then urged Australia and New Zealand to 'avoid a useless war' and abandon their reliance on the US and Britain: 'Whether the peoples of these regions will or not enjoy happiness and welfare depends entirely upon whether or not their governments understand the real intentions of Japan and take a fair and just attitude.'

The Japanese prime minister attempted to divide the southern dominions from Britain: 'How Britain has used and treated the officers and men of the Australia and New Zealand forces in Europe, in Hong Kong and again in the Malay peninsula must be fully known to the peoples of Australia and New Zealand themselves.'

Japan's professed ideal of freedom and prosperity for the peoples of Asia was a handy propaganda tool, but it had little influence on the thinking of the Imperial Navy. After the war, Baron Tomioka said the idea hadn't even been discussed among his colleagues: 'We naval planners thought exclusively about self-existence and self-defence. The establishment of the Greater East Asian Co-Prosperity Sphere and the liberation of the Asian colonies were not on their mind.'

Nevertheless, the fall of Singapore was heaven-sent for Japan's propagandists. Government spokesman and naval commentator Kiwao Okumura said the loss of Singapore also meant the loss of Australia and India: 'Now that the world's most important naval base has fallen into our hands, it means that the fate of Australia, India, Burma and the East Indies has also fallen into our hands.'

Japan's foreign office spokesman in Tokyo, Tomokazu Hori, said John Curtin had repeatedly assured his people that war materials from Britain and America were on their way to Australia. Now that he could no longer mislead his people, he had confessed over radio, saying, 'no longer may we depend on external forces and external support'. Hori taunted the Australians, saying British and American aid was destined to end in 'an unhonoured cheque': 'The astonishment and confusion of the Australian authorities are beyond imagination,' he told the Japanese press.

Were all these bellicose statements and dire predictions merely Japanese wartime rhetoric, or was Japan, after the fall of Singapore, really poised to take Australia?

In 1945, when the 'Tiger of Malaya', General Yamashita, was awaiting trial as a war criminal, he opened up to a writer and researcher about his wartime plans for Australia. British newspaperman and author John Deane Potter interviewed Yamashita at the New Bilibid prison, 40 kilometres from Manila. The general appeared clad in a white silk shirt and the remnants of his army uniform, including brightly polished jackboots. He sat on a wooden bench in the sun, outside his cell. He shared a cell block with 16 other Japanese generals and admirals; Potter observed that they sat at a long table, reading and writing.

General Yamashita waved his spectacles toward the 21-page file which contained the indictment against him. His former staff officer, General Akira Muto, was carefully reading the charges. Muto, unmoved and efficient, although he was also held as a war criminal, rapidly covered sheet after sheet with notes as he read, attempting to refute the allegations against his commander-in-chief. According to Potter, Yamashita revealed that he had actively advocated the invasion of Australia:

> He said that after he had taken Singapore, he wanted to discuss with Tojo a plan for the invasion of Australia, and sent him a message: 'Singapore, the great British bastion in the Far East, has fallen into our hands. The Allies are effectively sealed off . . .' Instead of an advance further west into Burma and perhaps India, his plan was to leave a strong garrison in Malaya and Burma and strike down the Pacific to the coast of Australia.
>
> Tojo turned down the plan, making the excuse of lengthened supply lines, which would be precarious and open to enemy attack. But his real reason, apparently, was that he wanted to keep driving west to try to affect a junction with Hitler. In those days when the Axis seemed unbeatable, this meeting was probably scheduled to take place in the Punjab.
>
> Yamashita's plan to conquer Australia was practically identical with his successful campaign in Malaya. He intended to land on each side of the major Australian cities and cut them off, first making a series of dummy landings to draw off the pitifully few Australian troops.
>
> 'Why, there were hardly enough Australians to have organised an effective resistance to the Japanese Army,' Yamashita said. 'All they could ever hope to do was to make a guerrilla resistance in the bush.
>
> 'With even Sydney and Brisbane in my hands, it would have been comparatively simple to subdue Australia. I would never visualise occupying it entirely. It was too large. With its coastline, anyone can always land there exactly as he wants.
>
> 'But it is a long way from anywhere and I could have poured

in enough troops to resist effectively any Anglo-American invasions. Although the Japanese General Staff felt my supply lines would have been too long, so would the American or British lines. They might never have been able to reach the place at all. We could have been safe there forever.'

Potter said that if General Yamashita seemed a little wistful about the invasion of Australia which never came off, he was nonetheless philosophical, as a good Japanese should be, about what he regarded as his inevitable execution. In a highly controversial decision before a court of US generals, Yamashita was convicted for war crimes associated with the Japanese massacre of many thousands of Filipino civilians in Manila in 1945. 'My command was a big as MacArthur's or Lord Louis Mountbatten's. How could I tell if some of my soldiers misbehaved?' he said shortly before his death.

Another American writer, David Bergamini, was able to corroborate Yamashita's intentions regarding Australia when he interviewed Colonel Takushiro Hattori, chief of the operations section of Army General Staff and former confidential secretary to General Tojo. After the fall of Singapore, Bergamini wrote, Yamamoto wanted to land an expeditionary force on the undefended north coast of Australia and at the very least 'terrorise the sub-continent with a division or two'. Bergamini was told that Yamamoto had a prominent accomplice in General Yamashita, who after Malaya was casting around for another stupendous victory:

> General Yamashita, the hero of Singapore, seconded Yamamoto and offered to lead the invasion himself. Despite the vastness of the Australian distances, he felt that it would be feasible to land a division almost immediately at Darwin and thrust hard and fast down the north-south railroad and road links to Adelaide and Melbourne on the south coast.
>
> Later, he supposed, a second division could be put ashore on

the east coast to leapfrog its way from port to port down towards Sydney. Tough as they might be, not even Australian civilians, he felt, would be any match for disciplined troops. Moreover, he thought that the clean, hygiene-conscious Japanese soldier would perform far better in the antiseptic wastes of Australia than in the septic jungles of Burma and New Guinea.

But General Tojo and senior members of the Army General Staff spoke against the Yamamoto–Yamashita plan, according to Bergamini.

John Toland in his Pulitzer Prize winning history, *The Rising Sun*, said the Imperial Navy envisaged invasion of Australia itself with five army divisions:

> This daring operation was drawn up by Captain Sadatoshi Tomioka of the Navy General Staff. At a joint operational meeting his opposite number in the Army, Colonel Takushiro Hattori, ridiculed the idea. Australia was twice the area of occupied China and its conquest would require not only the main body of the Combined Fleet but a dozen infantry divisions as well.

Tomioka suggested that they use the Kwantung Army in Manchuria, which was on garrison duty along the Soviet border. Hattori was against using so many troops on what would essentially be a diversionary effort; every man in uniform would be needed in the protracted struggle with the West.

Historians debate whether Admiral Yamamoto himself pressed for the invasion of Australia. It is unlikely that his Combined Fleet chief-of-staff, Admiral Ugaki, would argue in favour of the Australia invasion if his immediate superior was against it. The Swiss expert on Japan's war, Henry Frei, argues that it was 'middle echelon officers' within Combined Fleet, who did not see eye to eye with Yamamoto, who wanted to sail to Australia and capture Darwin. Admiral Ugaki was not a 'middle echelon' officer.

Japan's war history series *Senshi Sosho* records that the Imperial Navy itself was divided, with Yamamoto's Combined Fleet opting for a decisive short-term victory through battles for Midway or Hawaii while General Staff pressed for the invasion of Australia. The likelihood is that in this fluid situation in early 1942 Yamamoto thought through this range of options, eventually settling on the idea of the Midway invasion and the drawing out of the US Pacific Fleet.

The official war history records that the army chief, General Sugiyama, warned his navy counterpart, Admiral Nagano, to beware that an invasion of Australia could slide out of control if it were allowed to proceed: 'There are grave fears that the operation will gradually expand uncontrollably and slide into a multi-front war. Consequently, because measures to control all of Australia should not be adopted, it is felt necessary to refrain from invasion operations in any part of Australia.'

According to *Senshi Sosho*, Sugiyama believed that it was essential to blockade the supply of troops and materiel to Australia in order to smash enemy counteroffensives. That that was why operations to occupy Fiji, Samoa and New Caledonia were of great importance.

In the final analysis, the evidence from both American and Japanese sources is strong: powerful elements of the Japanese navy, backed by the Japanese army's most prominent field commander, had much-debated proposals to invade northern Australia with various invasion scenarios put forward, although no orders for invasion were ever issued. As Potter wrote, General Yamashita even envisaged moving down the east coast of Australia, and taking Brisbane and Sydney using the same methods he had successfully employed in Malaya. But those pressing for invasion faced concerted opposition from General Tojo and the army's chief of staff, General Sugiyama.

Both the navy and the army could see that Australia was a logical place from which to launch an Allied counteroffensive against Japan. The underlying question was whether it was merely sufficient to blockade Australia and inhibit her transport and communications, or whether it was really necessary to invade and capture the southern continent. The navy, which could swoop and run, and had so far enjoyed spectacular success and light casualties in the war, was optimistic about an invasion. The army, which was already heavily committed on a number of different fronts, was concerned about overextending its operational strength and supply lines. Yamashita thought Tojo himself was more interested in linking up with Hitler's forces in the vicinity of India.

Curtin's fears about an invasion of Australia in the first months of 1942 were thoroughly justified. The question of *goshu o koryaku suru* – whether to capture Australia – was keenly debated in a series of formal and informal meetings in Tokyo. The debate was carried on at the highest levels within Imperial General Headquarters, and was supported by senior naval officers and influential middle echelon rankers.

After Rabaul was occupied, the defence of the South Seas mandated territories became a navy responsibility. Initially, the army wasn't deeply concerned about these islands, and merely co-operated by dispatching the necessary number of army units requested by the navy. Baron Tomioka repeatedly pushed the navy's invasion plan. 'As we were moving to stage two, what I worried about most was Australia,' he said later.

In a heated debate during a joint operational planning meeting, the army's chief of operations at General Staff, Colonel Takushiro Hattori, made it clear to Tomioka he would never condone the navy's plans. 'From early in 1942, the plans for the invasion of Australia were under consideration by a faction in the Navy,' he told the Americans after the war. 'However, this was clearly a reckless operation which would exceed the war strength of Japan, and furnishing the 12 divisions required for land operations, in addition to the tremendous amount of shipping space necessary for the transporting and supplying of this force were considered absolutely impossible.'

Tomioka countered that invasion of Australia was essential:

'The enemy had to be beaten and victory won. In order to win, the enemy had to be denied the use of Australia as a base, no matter what. As long as the enemy had no foothold there, Australia could be taken. But if within the next two years the United States concentrated rapidly on aircraft production and made full use of Australia, Japan would never be able to resist the material onslaught which would follow.'

The naval planner was unconvinced by Hattori's argument. In frustration Hattori picked up a cup and held it out. 'The tea in this cup represents our total naval strength.' Spilling it to the floor he added: 'You see it goes just so far. If your plan is approved I will resign.'

In Australia, Prime Minister Curtin now confronted his countrymen with the Allies' shocking territorial losses. His government took out newspaper advertisements across Australia. A map showed arrows pointing from Japan to all its newly acquired southern territories north of Australia and Curtin's message was blunt:

> The spearhead of the Japanese hordes reaches south – always south. Australia faces the darkest hour in her history...
>
> For many the working pace of peace time has not given place to the pressure appealed for in war production. For many, readiness to provoke strikes or lockouts suggests an ignorance of, or disregard for, national security. Those things cannot continue.

The Department of Home Security also released a booklet on how to behave in the event of an invasion; it warned civilians that they were onlookers who must keep out of the way of the military.

A voluntary observer corps was established around the coast of Australia and others, usually men above military age, volunteered as local air raid wardens. Construction work began on a series of batteries and observation posts along the Australian coast. At Maroubra Beach in Sydney, plans went ahead for a three-storey concrete fort with interconnecting tunnels and a railway linking two six-inch gun emplacements on the pristine southern headland, Boora Point. But when the guns were installed, the first crashing noise of large dumping waves caused great alarm; local residents thought an invasion had begun.

Two days after the Singapore surrender, the Japanese submarine *I-25* surfaced about 185 kilometres off Sydney. Ratings raced on deck, wheeled out major components of a single-engined float plane and began to assemble them. As dawn was about to break, the float plane was launched, heading westward towards Australia's largest city. Pilot Nobuo Fujita circled Sydney at first light, and reported back on a strong naval build-up of warships in Sydney Harbour.

On 18 February, the Australian war cabinet met in the Commonwealth Bank building in Martin Place in Sydney. The meeting was chaired by Curtin's deputy, Frank Forde. The prime minister was in St Vincent's Hospital, Sydney, with a severe bout of gastritis, but he had left written instructions that proposed urgent action.

Curtin had taken precipitous action based on General Sturdee's alarming warning. The prime minister had cabled Churchill the previous day 'owing to the urgency of the matter'. The gist of the cable was that, 'if possible', all Australian forces now under orders to transfer to the Far East from the Middle East should be diverted to Australia. Curtin said Darwin was the first place to be reinforced, despite the need for Australians elsewhere, and that he had also requested 'early consideration' for the recall of the 9th Division of the AIF from the Middle East and the return of two RAAF squadrons from Britain.

War cabinet agreed and also took a number of important measures to improve Australia's defence. The fall of Singapore had given Australia's political leaders a severe shaking. The meeting approved a massive four million pound expenditure item, to buy more bombs for the air force from British manufacturers and to fund new fighter aircraft headquarters at Port Moresby, Townsville, Sydney–Newcastle and Darwin. Approval was also granted for the RAAF Home Defence Force to be built up from 60 to 73 squadrons. War loans would help pay for the significant spending.

Next day, the advisory war council, which comprised senior members of the Curtin government and the Opposition, met in the same room. Before formal proceedings began, they were obliged to undergo an air raid drill, assembling in the building's new shelter. In light of the fact that the Japanese had just begun making their covert reconnaissance flights over the city, it was a timely coincidence.

The war council meeting was told that from his hospital bed, Curtin had cabled Churchill indicating that as the British were abandoning the Dutch East Indies as a base, there was only one destination for the Australian divisions: 'The destination to which they should now proceed is obviously Australia which is in imminent danger of attack which is an essential allied base . . .'

Opposition members of the advisory council baulked at the move, and could not agree with the mass withdrawal of Australian troops from British service, wanting some who were already at sea to be diverted to Burma, 'the most urgent spot at the moment'. While the council, under Forde's chairmanship, debated the pros and cons of the orders, their discussion was overtaken by events in Darwin. The first Japanese attack on the Australian mainland had begun.

Curtin's personal secretary, Gladys Joyce, was at the teleprinter machine in an office a floor or two below the war council meeting. She and the prime minister's press officer, Don Rodgers, watched wide-eyed as news of the Japanese air raids clattered through. There was an alarming number of casualties. 'I was receiving them on the teleprinter, and Don Rodgers was standing behind me,' she recalled later. 'The ships were coming down like that – the list of ships that were sunk in the bay – and his face was getting longer and longer. "Oh God," he said, "oh God."'

Curtin's staff rushed upstairs to inform the advisory war council that Japanese aircraft had bombed Darwin. The head of the department of defence and senior defence adviser, Sir Frederick Shedden, a powerful and highly experienced bureaucrat, later described the response to Paul Hasluck: 'Shedden told me of a pitiful scene in the Cabinet room at Sydney when ministers were told of the bombing of Darwin. He spoke of agitated ministers running about "like a lot of startled chooks".'

The hour of challenge was at hand.

In far north Queensland, women and children quickly were evacuated south. On a cane field outside Innisfail, farmer Charlie Owen-Jones crawled under his broad timber house and began digging. Into the hole went the family's fine china, sent from England, and silverware, all carefully wrapped. It would remain there, safe from Japanese invaders, until the imminent threat had passed.

12

AUSTRALIA ATTACKED

The massive raid that the Japanese mounted on Darwin four days after the fall of Singapore was the first attack on mainland Australia by a foreign power. The enemy had made reconnaissance flights over Darwin, and Japanese submarines had been sighted close to the area before the attack; even so, the town's defence was a shambles.

Warnings went unheeded. Evacuations had been proposed for civilians, but not fully implemented. The few aircraft available to meet the attackers were woefully inadequate to the job, as were the anti-aircraft guns. Air raid precautions, including the provision of slit trenches through the town, were lacking. And on the day of the attack, specific and ample warnings of an impending major Japanese raid were ignored.

At 9.58 a.m., 43 minutes after Japanese aircraft had been confirmed heading for Darwin, the first bombs fell on the port's main wharf and on ships in the harbour. Only then did the air raid warning sirens sound. Eight ships were sunk, including two US transport vessels, a US destroyer, a British tanker, and an Australian coastal trader, the *Zealandia*. An Australian cargo ship carrying explosives, the *Neptuna*, went up in a giant mushroom cloud, killing 45 aboard.

The hospital ship *Manunda* – although clearly marked with red crosses and painted white – was attacked. Twelve people died and 58 were wounded. A bomb crashed through a skylight, exploding at B and C decks, causing great damage. Staff from the *Manunda* had been in the process of rescuing survivors from other bombed ships in the harbour. Despite extensive damage, the ship continued to operate as a hospital with numerous patients on its after end. Two hospitals in the town were also bombed and strafed.

Commander Mitsuo Fuchida had detailed Japanese dive bombers to hit the ships in the harbour and the level bombers to attack harbour installations and oil storage tanks. Zero fighter planes attacked the few Australian aircraft that rose to meet the enemy. As Fuchida noted: 'Anti-aircraft fire was intense but largely ineffectual, and we quickly accomplished our objectives.'

A second Japanese air raid followed at noon. In total, the raids killed 243 people and wounded more than 400, although officially these casualty figures were significantly downplayed. 15 KILLED, 24 HURT IN DARWIN ATTACKS, the *Herald* in Melbourne announced. TWO BIG AIR RAIDS ON DARWIN, the *Sydney Morning Herald* said, but accurate news coverage was largely suppressed.

In the absence of firm leadership in Darwin, panic soon set in with fears of an imminent Japanese invasion. Rumors quickly spread and were readily believed. Houses were abandoned in haste. Justice Charles Lowe, on the scene soon after to conduct a commission of inquiry, witnessed half-consumed drinks and meals standing on tables in the Darwin Hotel. Letters started had not been finished, papers were strewn about, beds were unmade, among signs of a very hasty exit.

The inhabitants of Darwin sought to leave by any means available. Vehicles began streaming southwards. Many people went on foot and others on bicycles. Even municipal sanitary carts were used in the evacuation, leaving the town without a sanitary service. That night, with no proper supervision in the streets, looting broke out in abandoned business houses and continued for days. Civilian and military personnel were involved.

Next day, pale and gaunt, John Curtin left his Sydney hospital bed and was driven to Canberra to attend a special joint meeting of both houses of Parliament. He announced that 93 Japanese bombers had taken part in two raids, and four enemy planes had been brought down. The prime minister warned that every other Australian city now could face a similar attack from Japan. His rhetoric was desperate and fiercely nationalistic: 'We must face with fortitude the first onset and remember that whatever the future holds in store for us, we are Australians and we will fight grimly and victoriously.'

A national security order was issued to prohibit lights at night from any building within the area of 16 kilometres back from the coast, from the South Australian border to the New South Wales–Queensland border. Yet, inexplicably, the order excluded public lighting. Motor vehicles were allowed lights, provided they were screened. Thousands of people began blacking out their windows with heavy curtains or black paint. In reality, most coastal regions remained well illuminated.

Advertisements soon appeared in newspapers telling Australians how to behave if they heard air raid sirens wailing. Gas and lights had to be turned off, windows opened, and bath tubs filled with water. People were urged to dress quickly and take cover in blacked-out rooms or shelters, without rushing, panicking or using the telephone.

In Tokyo, ecstatic newspapers and wireless stations heaped threats on Australia. The *Asahi* said the strategic value of the Japanese occupation of Timor close to Australia would be great: 'Not only is it close to the islands of the Dutch East Indies, but it takes only two and a half hours by air to Port Darwin, pivotal military base of Australia... Thus the fate of Australia has become quite clear now.' The *Yomiuri* quoted Curtin as losing hope of American and British assistance: 'The worst stage is thus confronting

Australia now. It is only natural that they face such a fate since they utterly disregarded our repeated warnings in the past.'

The *Chugai Shogyo* declared that it was time to include Australia in the Greater East Asia Co-Prosperity Sphere: 'If it participates, not only will the disposal of its wool and wheat be settled easily, but its defense can be secured also. From these viewpoints, we can hardly comprehend why Australia is continuing its resistance against Japan.' The *Mikako* spoke openly about an invasion of Australia through Darwin: 'Now the most important strategic point in Australia is about to be captured. It is little wonder that the enemy should now be completely depressed with all hope gone for regaining his lost ground.'

In fact, as the high command in Tokyo had earlier ruled, the attack was not intended as a prelude to invasion. It was a precursor to the Japanese invasion of Portuguese Timor and Java, intended to reduce the build-up of Allied ships, supplies, and facilities at Darwin. On the night of 19–20 February, the town of Dili was shelled by Japanese ships in preparation for invasion. Japanese troops clashed briefly with Australian commandoes, who withdrew into Dili's hinterland. The Japanese paratroopers landed at Koepang the next. Some 84 Australians were killed and 250 escaped inland.

As Japanese army and navy landing parties surged into Dili, 260 miles north west of Darwin, another proposal to invade Australia was being debated aboard the *Yamato* at Hashirajima. The plan was not the idea of middle-echelon officers but came from a close confidant of the commander-in-chief Isoroku Yamamoto, Rear Admiral Tamon Yamaguchi, commander of the second carrier division, including the carriers *Hiryu* and *Soryu*. Yamaguchi took part in the attacks on Pearl Harbor and Darwin and would be in the thick of it at Midway. He was a sleepy-eyed fellow with a friendly, grandfatherly oval face which belied his volatile and audacious disposition. His placid countenance hid an impulsive, brave, 'devil-may-care' character.

Between 20 and 23 February with cold winds sweeping the bay of

Hiroshima, Yamaguchi aboard the *Yamato* took part in war games for an invasion of Ceylon. He distributed copies of a blueprint to others, including Yamamoto, Ugaki, Fukudome and Tomioka, outlining his plans for invasions across the Indian and Pacific oceans. He proposed capture of Ceylon in May, followed by invasions of Fiji, Samoa, New Caledonia, New Zealand and northern Australia in June and July. Midway, Johnston and Palmyra islands would be occupied in November and December while Hawaii would be occupied around December or January 1943. Yamaguchi proposed using three task forces comprising 14 carriers.

The Ceylon table manoeuvres on the *Yamato* were unsuccessful. Visitors including two princes and other senior officers observed the proceedings and in the evenings Yamamoto entertained guests at sukiyaki parties. The 'Yamaguchi plan' caused much discussion. Ugaki and his staff officers had been debating Australia, among the other targets, at length during the exercise, but when the army got wind of the plan, there was immediate opposition.

On top of everything else, the Burma Road, China's lifeline for supplies from the West, was now seriously threatened, as was Burma's capital, Rangoon. To Curtin's irritation, both Churchill and Roosevelt urged assistance in Burma from the two divisions of Australian troops returning home from the Middle East. In a personal note to Curtin, Roosevelt said it was the fall of Burma that would place Australia in extreme peril: 'While I realise the Japs are moving rapidly, I cannot believe that, in view of your geographical position and the forces on their way to you or operating in your neighbourhood, your vital centres are in immediate danger.'

The cable war between Churchill and Curtin over the troop diversion continued unabated. Churchill told Curtin that he was entirely in favour of all Australian troops returning home to defend their native soil, but a vital war emergency could not be ignored and troops travelling through the region must be ready to turn aside and take part in battle. Churchill said the Americans would help Australia: 'Your greatest support in this hour of peril must be drawn from the United States. They alone can bring into Australia the necessary troops and air forces, and they appear ready to do so.'

Supported by his defence chiefs, Curtin resisted attempts from the Opposition and from Churchill to make him change his mind on this issue and divert Australian troops to Burma. But on 21 February, Curtin discovered from overnight cables that Churchill, acting without Curtin's authority, had already diverted the troop ships to Burma. When Curtin sharply protested, Churchill cabled: 'We would not contemplate that you would refuse our request and that of the President of the United States for the diversion of the leading division to save the situation in Burma.'

Curtin's anger was roused. He told Churchill that he had treated the Australian approval as 'merely a matter of form'. It was quite impossible to reverse a decision which had been made by the Australian government with the utmost care: 'Australia's outer defences are quickly vanishing and our vulnerability is completely exposed . . . With AIF troops we sought to save Malaya and Singapore falling back on Netherlands East Indies. All the northern defences are gone or going. Now you contemplate using the AIF to save Burma. All this has been done as in Greece without adequate air support.

'We feel a primary obligation to save Australia not only for itself but to preserve it as a base for the development of the war against Japan.'

Churchill agreed to return the division to Australia after refuelling at Colombo, Ceylon, now Sri Lanka. Clearly miffed by Curtin's refusal to be bullied, Churchill put some blame for the imminent fall of Rangoon on the Australian prime minister. He cabled the Governor of Burma: 'We have made every appeal, reinforced by President, but Australian Government absolutely refuses. Fight on.'

The Japanese took Rangoon on 8 March. The additional

Australian troops requested by Churchill would not have stopped the British defeat in Burma.

Roosevelt soon cabled Curtin saying that he could not agree with the immediate need for the Australian troops to return. But he elevated US concern for Australia saying both Burma and Australia must be held at all costs, and he was convinced that Australia, which he called 'the right flank', could be held. He told Churchill that he was working on additional plans to make the control of islands in the Anzac area more secure and to further disrupt Japanese advances.

The United States Army had diverted, or was in the process of diverting, two infantry divisions, anti-aircraft battalions, one tank battalion and other support battalions to Australia in late February 1942. But at this stage the US presence was not significant, and together with Australia's own available forces, would not have been sufficient to hold out against the Japanese in the event of a fully fledged invasion.

Whatever Roosevelt's intentions, the US Army was strongly considering a much reduced role in the Australian region than contemplated at the outbreak of Japan's war. The security of Australia had just been listed as very low on a secret US Army list of strategic priorities – in fact, behind seven other priorities, beginning with maintaining Britain, keeping Russia in the war as an enemy of Germany, and maintaining the status quo in India, the Middle East, and China.

The defence of Australia had been downgraded. In an appraisal prepared for the US Army's top command in late February, assistant chief of staff Brigadier General Dwight D. Eisenhower wrote that 'the situation involving Australia had changed' for America because Japan now controlled ample sources of oil and tin and practically all the rubber resources of the world: 'Thus, reasons for expanding our forces into the Far Southwest Pacific, are, in this respect, less compelling than they were two months ago,' the future president said.

The Americans appeared to want to have the argument both ways. While Roosevelt thought Australia could afford to divert troops to Burma, General Eisenhower argued that these returning Australian troops, together with the smaller US contingents in or near Australia, could block any Japanese advance into Australia: 'The Australian corps has now been diverted to Australia and it should be able, in conjunction with the forces already in that country, to provide for the land defense of critical areas.'

Eisenhower demanded only a minimum of forces assigned to the Pacific to concentrate maximum forces in Britain ready for an invasion of Europe. 'We've got to go to Europe and fight,' Eisenhower wrote, 'we've got to quit wasting resources all over the world – and still worse – wasting time.'

The arrival in Australia of General Douglas MacArthur would stabilise America's strategic imperatives in favour of Australia and the Pacific. But for the moment, Australia's survival remained towards the bottom of the US Army's list of priorities.

The 6th and 7th Divisions of the AIF returned to Australia and by September were fighting the Japanese on the Kokoda Trail. Curtin would not get the 9th Division home from the Middle East until early 1943.

Throughout the country, Australians were deeply concerned about the Japanese raids, and openly discussed the possibility of attacks on major cities and outright invasion. Commentator on international affairs and diplomat W. MacMahon Ball wrote that the Japanese drive southward made Australians, for the first time in their history, 'think of war not as an expedition in which their soldiers might fight and die ten thousand miles away, but as something that immediately threatened the invasion and occupation of their own country'. But Japan's forays into northern Australia were even more numerous and damaging than they were allowed to learn, and the north's vulnerability in early 1942 was far greater than they were told.

On 4 March, a day after his arrival in Darwin, Justice Lowe cabled his immediate personal assessment to Curtin: 'Absolutely imperative Darwin be strengthened, vulnerable to any major attack.' The Darwin raid devastated the RAAF station, which was mostly abandoned through poor communication. The station commander directed that his men should gather half a mile down the road and half a mile into the bush, but the temporary evacuation descended into farce. Justice Lowe later found that many of the men simply took off into the bush. 'Some were found as far afield as Bachelor, some to Adelaide River, one was found at Daly Waters and another, by an extreme feat, reached Melbourne in 13 days.'

As a result, Australia's forward air base at this crucial time was practically deserted for a time. For days after, men were straggling back. At a parade four days after the attack, the muster showed 278 men missing. Lowe said that as casualties at the station were small, the result could only be regarded as deplorable: 'There is evidence that some of those who took to the bush remarked that they did not know how to use arms and were not going to remain to be massacred in the event of a Japanese landing.'

After the first great attack, Darwin was intermittently targeted in air raids a further 63 times, until the last on 12 November 1943. The Japanese operations against Australia consisted primarily of bombing and strafing attacks by land-based bombers and fighters of the Imperial Japanese Navy. The 19 February attack was the only carrier-based attack on the country.

The vast Indonesian archipelago stretching from west of Malaya down so close to northern Australia, known then as the Dutch East Indies, was being overwhelmed by Japan. On 28 February, the light cruiser HMAS *Perth* was sailing for Tjilatjap, on the southern tip of Java, when she ran into a Japanese invasion force headed for Surabaya, on the eastern end of Java. With three cruisers and nine destroyers in the Japanese fleet, the Australian didn't stand a chance. Four torpedoes struck her, and she heeled over to port and gradually sank. Of the ship's company of 681, some 350 were lost. More than 300 became prisoners of war; about a third of them died in appalling conditions in Japanese POW camps.

1942

The US heavy cruiser *Houston* was also sunk in the Sunda Strait during the Java Sea battle as the Allies attempted to prevent a major Japanese amphibious landing on Java. Nor did the Japanese allow civilian and military evacuees from Java to escape unscathed once they reached the apparent safety of Broome, in Western Australia. Nine Zeros fitted with extra long-range tanks flew in from Koepang, Timor, swooped down and began shooting up the evacuation fleet. An airborne American Liberator carrying 33 sick and wounded servicemen broke in half and crashed into Roebuck Bay.

Flight Lieutenant Gus Winckel had just brought another batch of refugees out of Bandung in west Java and deposited them safely on the airstrip at Broome. The Dutch pilot was tired. Over the course of three months, he had notched up 600 flying hours in his beloved Lockheed Lodestar, a twin-engined transport, to evacuate women and children from the Dutch East Indies.

'I was standing in the doorway looking at the distance. I was just having a stretch you know and I saw some steps on the horizon. And I said to the fellow who was going to refuel the plane, I said, "Listen, is the RAAF flying today?" And he said "No", so I said, "Well, sound the alarm. The Japs are coming!"'

Winckel darted inside his Lodestar and took a Colt machine gun out of its bracket and ran for cover. A low-flying Zero came in, raking Winckel's plane with fire. He could clearly see the pilot and he opened up with the machine gun cradled in his arms. The Zero crashed: 'When I looked at my plane I was very angry ... It was like my mother, my sister, everything. It was a beautiful plane, you know. You get attached to something like that. And he destroyed it just like that.'

Qantas flying boat captain Lester Brain was writing a letter when the Japanese appeared. He had been sick with fever, but was planning to fly refugees out of Broome later that day. Now he could see that three flying boats were in flames on the harbour. He ran down to the beach. As he tried to pull a row-boat down into the water, the airline's representative, Malcolm Millar, turned up to help him.

The bay was a scene of carnage. The Zeros were able to swoop down on the flying boats, some of them crowded with refugees and about to take off, and attack them without opposition. Palls of smoke drifted over the water and the screams of the injured and drowning could be heard. Brain and Millar assisted two Dutch aviators, who were supporting a young woman in the water. They also found another Dutch serviceman swimming on his back, a baby on his chest.

An estimated 70 people were killed in the first raid on Broome and many others injured. The raid destroyed 24 aircraft, including 16 flying boats. A simultaneous raid was also carried out on Wyndham, closer to Darwin.

The raids on Broome and Wyndham had a deep impact on Curtin, who foresaw them as the precursor to attacks on Australian cities in the south:

> As time passes, the enemy comes ever nearer. Darwin, Wyndham and Broome are three important strategical posts in the security of Australia as a whole. I have been impressed by the menace to the populations of our larger capitals which this part of Australia would constitute if the enemy were to use it as a base.
>
> Established in the north, his hitting power at the more larger centres of population and of economic activity becomes all the more inimical . . .
>
> The enemy knows that failure to hold Australia means the ultimate offensive against him becomes more difficult – hence his haste to get in quickly, hence the double urge on us to prevent this happening.

John Curtin was not the only one impressed by the menace of the Japanese overrunning the larger population centres in Australia. Whatever the US Army thought about Australia's defence preparedness, the commander-in-chief of the US Fleet, Admiral Earnest J. King, saw the gravity of the situation. King, who was also US chief of Naval Operations and a key advisor to Roosevelt, warned the US president in early March that the US should be focusing its immediate attention on Australasia. In particular, the approaches to Australia needed to be used actively and continuously by the US Navy 'to hamper the enemy advance and/or consolidation of his advance bases'.

In a secret and somewhat racist memorandum to the president, the admiral rated support for Australasia only just below the holding of Hawaii in strategic importance for the United States in the Pacific: 'Australia – and New Zealand – are "white men's countries" which it is essential that we shall not allow to be overrun by Japan – because of the repercussion among the non-white races of the world.'

The navy's chief planner said the US soon would have strong points at Samoa, Suva, New Caledonia, Bora Bora, Tonga, the Ellice Islands and in the New Hebrides. When those strong points were made reasonably secure, and troops and equipment arrived, the communications link to Australia would be covered and in time 'we can drive northwest'. In line with this thinking, Australia had to be secured as the major base from which an eventual counteroffensive against Japan could be supported.

The commander-in-chief of the US Fleet made the risky but prescient decision to move two American aircraft carriers into the Coral Sea.

Historian Samuel Eliot Morison, friend of President Roosevelt, wrote in his 14-volume work:

Nobody seemed able to stop the Japanese, and in Washington there was even serious talk of abandoning Australia and New Zealand to the enemy. But as King told the President, 'We cannot in honor let Australia and New Zealand down. They are our brothers, and we must not allow them to be overrun by Japan.' And the President agreed.

Admiral King was not the only American to alert his country

to the threat Australia faced. The same month, a *Washington Post* staff correspondent, Richard Oulanhan, visited Australia and wrote a major feature about how the nation was mobilising to resist invasion. It was a jingoistic echo of King's views:

> Facing the blackest peril in their island-continent's history, the people of Australia were mobilised last week to fight for their lives and liberty . . . That the island continent was in imminent danger of attack was evident to every Australian.
>
> All over eastern Asia the yellow plague swept, and its virus reached down into the Indies as far as Timor, only 400 miles away. For the first time in its 150-year history, Australia was actually menaced with a land invasion.

Australia, the newspaper said, had flung an expeditionary force into the last line of defence, Java, to aid the embattled Dutch. The *Post*'s correspondent, like American diplomats in Australia before him, wondered at how Australians could have left their nation so exposed:

> 'Another Australia expeditionary force' is a familiar phrase to the world. Australians have fought on more battlefronts than any other men since the time of Genghis Khan.
>
> The gallantry of Australia on other fronts has weakened her defenses in her hour of need. Today, when she needs them most, more than 170,000 Australians are manning the battle lines in Libya, Burma, Java, Britain and the Middle East.

Later in March, there was another scare. Admiral King feared the invasion of Australia had actually begun when US code breakers discovered that a Japanese force of six carriers and two battleships had left Kendari in the Dutch Celebes. With no American battleships in the vicinity, King scrambled his meagre force of submarines based at Fremantle. Fortunately for Australia, the carriers were actually en route to India.

13

A DAY OF DECISION

John Curtin believed the very future of Australia was now up for grabs, and he was dead right. Australia's fate swung in the balance in Japan when the country was so utterly vulnerable.

He was bitterly frustrated that the threat had arrived, as he always thought it might, and that Australia was so desperately unprepared, despite all his own personal efforts in Opposition to sound the alarm. As early as 1936, Curtin had told parliament: 'It might be that the enemy would consider a major attack on Australia essential to the elimination of British sea power, even if he had no intention of remaining in permanent occupation of the country.'

Now, war cabinet could make all sorts of decisions and spend vast sums of money, but it might be too late. Australia needed aircraft immediately and they were only trickling in from America. Local aircraft production was slow, and would make little difference to the war effort. Curtin privately fumed at the number of Allied bombers flying over Europe; 270 in one flight alone, he discovered. 'By Christ we can't get any here! They're going over places it wouldn't matter if they didn't go over for two months. Four hundred planes here would make a big difference.'

Hurt, disgusted and cynical, the prime minister told his friend biographer Lloyd Ross: 'It's the proper fate of a country which has not built up its own defences. The proper fate of a country which always fights someone else's wars without making its own position safe.'

In early 1942, Curtin was often forlorn as the weight of responsibility bore down on him. The pressure that he was under would contribute to his serious ill-health. On 25 February he wrote to an old friend, unionist Henry Boote, saying 'the strain is very heavy in the present terrible time'.

Curtin's nervous energy was seemingly inexhaustible, but when he slumped, he really came down, according to his press secretary, Don Rodgers. Curtin would pace the floor for nights without sleep, Rodgers said, 'until the Australian divisions coming home from the Middle East to face the Japs in New Guinea had safely crossed the Indian Ocean'.

By mutual agreement, the prime minister's wife, Elsie, remained at home in Perth for long stints, coming to Canberra only occasionally. They had agreed, long before, that while Curtin was in Canberra as a politician, Elsie would continue as mother and carer of her aged mother at the house at Cottesloe. Curtin's personal secretary, Gladys Joyce, knew the pressures and loneliness her boss faced without a family around him in the prime minister's official residence: 'I think he was a very lonely man there . . . his wife didn't come over very often. His daughter came over once and stayed for a short period and then she went back . . . I think he missed his family very much. He was very much a family man.'

Curtin smoked heavily – about 40 cigarettes a day – and with his growing problems, the cigarettes became even more numerous. He rattled around The Lodge alone, apart from a few staff. Sometimes, when he needed a few hours of leisure, he asked his driver, Ray Tracey, to play billiards with him.

Occasionally, he walked across to Government House for a long chat with the governor-general, Lord Gowrie. It was something Curtin had done since his days as Opposition leader. On the surface they seemed to have little in common. Gowrie was British, a former brigadier general and winner of the Victoria Cross. He thought some of Curtin's colleagues, especially Herbert Evatt, disastrous, but he regarded Curtin as a warm personal friend:

> I was filled with admiration for the courage, firmness and patience with which he dealt with these difficulties. And his calmness, foresight and wisdom when the danger of invasion was apparent were a very big factor in maintaining the morale of the people of Australia during the most critical period of her history.

Gowrie, it seems, did not share Churchill's dismissive attitude towards the possibility of a Japanese invasion.

The doors of the shiny brass lift-cage slam shut behind the Australian leader. John Curtin seems oblivious to the clamour and intense activity around him. It's Saturday, 28 February 1942; a day of decision in the debate over the invasion of Australia.

The prime minister, still in poor health after his bout in hospital, is at defence headquarters, in the old bluestone buildings at Victoria Barracks, Melbourne. Through open doorways, there are glimpses of officers deep in conversation, and down the long corridors staff dart from room to room. Female typists clatter away, ratings in sailor suits operate wireless telegraphy machines, and telephones ring incessantly. Outside, there is also a cacophony: soldiers drilling, cars and trucks coming and going, all with a sense of great urgency.

As Curtin strides towards his meeting, his military adviser and cabinet secretary, Frederick Shedden, whispers urgent information into Curtin's ear, and senior officers have a few hurried words. The prime minister nods. He is deeply worried about the safety of thousands of Australian troops now on the high seas passing through Japanese-held waters on their way home from overseas to fight for Australia.

Outside a set of secure double doors, one behind the other, guards bearing rifles snap to salute. Curtin enters the inner sanctum, the war cabinet room. The chamber, about the size of a family living room, is crowded with political leaders and senior officers around a heavy polished oval table. There's barely standing room up the back. Ministers sit in leather chairs around the table, a large blotter and an ornate inkwell before each man. Ornamental cigarette and cigar boxes are liberally distributed around the table as are silver ashtrays. Already the room is heavy with smoke. Heavy brown drapes are pulled over the windows. The walls are hung with military maps that trace the story of Japan's relentless progress southward, and of the Australian situations in Europe and the Middle East. There's also a top-secret map board able to be concealed behind lockable wooden panels.

Curtin opens the meeting, called to consider the defence chiefs' latest assessments. The main task ahead is to confront the unpalatable facts of how a Japanese invasion would probably unfold. Unbeknown to the Australians, a similar meeting is about to convene in Tokyo, as the Imperial Japanese Navy's general staff continues to press for outright invasion of Australia. The Melbourne gathering brings together the Australian War Cabinet, the Australian War Advisory Council, two senior members of the New Zealand government, and the chiefs of staff of the army, navy, and air forces of both countries.

The prime minister is armed with a sheath of papers: the Australian chiefs of staff have completed a new appreciation of the Pacific war situation. Noting Japan's successes in the Dutch East Indies, the appreciation advises that Australia is now virtually at the whim of Japan. Singapore and Sumatra on the west of the so-called Malay barrier have gone, while the eastern end has been cut by the Japanese occupation of Bali and Timor. Java has been isolated.

The defence chiefs, Burnett, Royle and Sturdee, have put forward three possible scenarios for Japan's next moves. The first is to consolidate and exploit territories already gained; the second is to carry out offensive operations on the east coast of India, after the capture of Burma. The third scenario concerns Curtin most:

> An attempt to capture Australia and New Zealand, not so much from the aspect of economic exploitation, as from a desire to deny these territories to us as bases for future Allied counter-offensive action.

The defence chiefs think Japan has the resources to undertake all three scenarios simultaneously if she wants: 'We have, so far, not succeeded in seriously weakening Japanese Naval supremacy with the result that Japan is now at liberty to attempt an invasion of Australia should she so desire.' So vulnerable is Australia, so utterly wide open, that the chiefs list three probable lines of Japanese approach – southward from their mandated territories north of New Guinea, with the aim of taking Port Moresby and New Caledonia; south-east from the captured Dutch East Indies to northern Australia; or southwards from the Dutch East Indies to south-western Australia.

The officers express considerable concern for Fremantle as a potential fleet base for the Japanese. They note that Western Australia will be difficult to reinforce rapidly should Japan invade the west. The defence chiefs recommend, and the meeting approves, that some troops returning from overseas will reinforce Darwin and the west. Otherwise, the vast, remote northern coastline of Australia is left virtually undefended.

The defence chiefs note simply that the east coast of Australia is 'not defended adequately', and if the Newcastle–Port Kembla region is to be held, then it is not possible to reinforce the important northern Australian base of Townsville. 'It is protected by a brigade group, a force not adequate to meet the scale of attack which could be brought against it during a main Japanese southward movement.'

But they recommend that no further army reinforcements should be sent to Townsville, apart from some anti-aircraft defences, as Townsville easily could be cut off from the south. The painful implications of this recommendation will not be visited today. Instead, the advisory war council and the war cabinet approve a landmark paper, entitled 'Future policy and strategy for conduct of the war in the Pacific', drawn up by Curtin in consultation with the defence chiefs, with ancillary input from others including the Opposition's Robert Menzies. The defence chiefs immediately acknowledge the grimness of the situation:

> Japanese successes place Australia and New Zealand in danger of attack. Darwin, Port Moresby, New Caledonia and Fiji are immediately threatened. The Japanese have decisive air superiority and control in the seas in the areas in which they are operating...
>
> The loss of Australia and New Zealand would mean the loss of the only bases for offensive action by the Allied nations against the Japanese from the Anzac area.
>
> The basis of our planning must be not only to ensure the security of Australia and New Zealand but to use them as areas from which offensive action will be launched.

This is a watershed moment in Australian defence policy. The nation's military and political leadership has acknowledged that if Australia is to survive they must actively advocate its use as a major base for a counteroffensive against the Japanese. This decision will help re-energise Australian defence planning. Yet there is more than a hint of hopelessness in the assessment of senior defence personnel. Faced with a Japanese onslaught on Australia shores, they agree that until such time as adequate naval and air forces are available, 'it is estimated that it would require a minimum of 25 divisions to defend Australia against the scale of attack that is possible'. By this account, even with US help, the number of troops needed to hold Australia is impossible.

One of the Australian chiefs of staff advising Curtin is the British officer, Vice Admiral Sir Guy Royle, senior naval officer in

Australia, who had been fifth sea lord in the British Admiralty and chief of British naval air services. His views are out of step with the British prime minister. In Australia Royle reflects genuine attempts to meet Australian national interests, rather than British. He is bitterly denounced by his British colleagues for his determination to reflect Australian national needs, rather than those of Britain.

It will be another month before the army strength in Australia will see any significant increase. By the end of March, about 45,000 fully equipped Australian veterans will have disembarked from overseas. Many will be needed in New Guinea. The number of American servicemen, including airmen, will grow to 33,000. But it will not be until the end of April that additional troops will be battle-ready – 63,000 men of the AIF and 280,000 militiamen, most of them raw soldiers. Military strength in Australia will grow steadily, but given the dispersal problems around Australia and in the islands, the chances of holding off a Japanese invasion is problematic at best, especially during February and March.

On 27 February, an important two-day meeting weighing heavily on the future of Australia begins in the gentlemanly surroundings of the *Suikosha*, the navy officer's club in Tokyo.

The senior officers of the war operations sections of both armed services attend. The participants include the Imperial Army's operations chief, General Shinichi Tanaka, and the equally aggressive General Akira Muto, the Imperial Navy's operations chief, Admiral Shigeru Fukudome, and Admiral Takasumi Oka. Both sides have little respect for the other and suspect each other's motives.

A preliminary meeting among more junior officers on 16 February has failed to reach agreement. The senior leadership also engage in argumentative and lengthy debate about Japan's war aims for the second stage of offensive operations.

Commander Kowashi Sanagi of Baron Tomioka's operations staff takes notes in his duty diary. Unhelpfully, he expounds the army's position in the debate, but not the navy's.

The debate opens with discussion about the invasion of Hawaii, originally instigated by the planners at Combined Fleet, and how difficult a landing operation there will be. The second item on the agenda concerns an invasion of Australia. Navy General Staff, backed by elements of Combined Fleet, insist on invading Australia somewhere along the northern portion of the country's east coast. Army General Staff argue strongly that an invasion of Australia is plain stupid. They argue that it will not bring down Britain and the United States, as Tomioka and others have suggested; instead, it will bog Japan's forces in another war of attrition on the huge Australia land mass, rather like the protracted war Japan is still fighting in China.

The army representatives detail their opposition to the navy's plans for an invasion of Australia:

> This operation is not an absolute imperative for prosecuting the war. It is an effective step, but it will not decide the fate of UK or the US. Neither does it have particularly great value in bringing the [Japanese] empire to a position of self sufficiency and self reliance.
>
> According to investigations into the feasibility of the operation, it will require at least 10 divisions, but these cannot be spared. At present, Australia is judged to have 300,000 (Caucasian) troops, and can mobilise 600,000.
>
> As a comparison with recent operations, there were 130,000 Japanese troops to 70,000 enemy troops in the Malaya campaign; 75,000 Japanese to 100,000 in the Philippines campaign; and 50,000 Japanese to 70,000 in the Netherlands East Indies campaign.
>
> It is not possible to field sufficient troops to face 600,000 Australian troops. If we do field enough troops to Australia, Japan will be threatened to the north. We will also need 2,000,000 tons of shipping. Because of the long distances involved, the operation would probably require more shipping than even this.

This assessment, as it turns out, is egregiously inaccurate, and overly pessimistic. The number of Allied troops in Australia will not reach 460,000 until the end of April, and, despite Australian plans to reinforce Darwin and the west, most of the troops will be based in southern states protecting the big cities and essential war industries. Many will be inexperienced. Furthermore, the wet season severely disrupts road transport in the Northern Territory and north Queensland between November and April; the chance of Australian reinforcements being rushed to meet an invasion of the north is greatly diminished.

Next day, the Japanese leaders reconvene. They call their liaison meeting between the army, navy and government the '90th Communications Conference'. Agenda items include prospects for fuel acquisition from southern occupied territories, isolating Australia and India from America and England, and resources supply, including steel.

Notes of this further conference are taken by General Hajime Sugiyama, the army's chief of staff. The meeting opens with positive reports from both the army and the navy about the resumption of oil production in southern territories captured by the Japanese. Sugiyama then summarises the debate on Australia and India and their relationship with England, as Britain is called:

> Although Australia has traditionally relied on England, since around the First European War it has gradually come to be very close to America, and this tendency can be expected to increasingly become considerably pronounced in this next war.
>
> Its industry consists largely of primitive things, and its defence industry depends entirely on the Americans; it does not have one [a defence industry] of its own.
>
> The relationship of mutual reliance between England and Australia is relatively weak, and even though they both can turn to others, the loss of India and Australia would be a big psychological blow to England.

Finance Minister Okinobu Kaya wants to know the effect of completely isolating Australia. Admiral Takasumi Oka makes it clear that invasion has benefits:

> To the extent of destroying commerce, complete isolation would be quite difficult if we did not completely occupy Australia.

Oka is an influential and aggressive officer who heads the navy ministry's bureau of military affairs. He is one of those who think it's essential to keep the enemy on the defensive. He wants to destroy enemy sea power and any important bases that might be used for a counteroffensive against Japan, including Hawaii and Australia.

But the navy now finds itself fighting a rearguard action on the issue of Australia. Prime Minister General Hideki Tojo turns the debate to discussion about Japan's interests overseas and how they affect the motherland. Tojo favours consolidation of its captured territories.

The conference, typically bureaucratic and wordy, ploughs on discussing the difference between Japan's resource sphere and its co-prosperity sphere. Kaya says there shouldn't be any difference between the national defence sphere, the co-prosperity sphere and the resources sphere. The debate becomes esoteric, but it has deadly implications for Australia. Tojo seems to be attempting to weigh the differences between occupying countries first for the strategic military value, then for the value of having a co-operative and subservient trading partner and finally for the sheer value to Japan of the occupied country's resources. Admiral Oka, becoming frustrated, says that if the three spheres of influence for Japan do not coincide, or if resources in Japan aren't sufficient, 'we will have to make a move'. Oka once again proves himself a hawk and is keen to move on countries like Australia whose geography alone could block Japanese freedom of movement.

The taciturn foreign minister, Shigenori Togo, weighs into the debate, saying it is necessary to determine those territories that will not be invaded under any circumstances and those that will be invaded. He doesn't receive a straight answer.

Major General Akira Muto, the chief of the military affairs bureau of the army ministry seems to be out of step with Tojo when he agrees that decisive action is necessary: 'National defense spheres ought to be clearly decided; once that is done, Australia and India ought to be strategic spheres; and we should make a move when necessary.' Privately, Muto wants to end the war as quickly as possible while Japan has her wealth of new territories and is triumphant. Some weeks earlier he has enjoyed New Year's Day wine with Togo, just as Japanese troops occupy Manila.

Togo writes later: 'After discussing developments of the war in general, he said to me that it was his hope that I would work for a prompt ending of the war, as the sooner it ended the more advantageous for Japan and he added for that purpose it was necessary to replace Tojo as premier.' Togo is indiscreet, and when he hears of the conversation, General Tojo promptly transfers Muto to the southern war front, where he is assigned to General Yamashita's staff. Caution is one thing. Ending the war is another.

Tojo thinks there are too many Japanese invasions going on or being planned. He tells the conference irritably that another invasion should not be necessary every time Japan runs short of a natural resource. He demands, 'What is the purpose of taking Siberia?' An official of the Planning Department replies, 'To extract brown coal.' Tojo is annoyed at all this business of striking out in different directions: 'Rather than saying we will get brown coal because we have a shortage of brown coal, or we will get cotton because we have a shortage in resources we should somehow cover it within the [existing] sphere.'

After a long convoluted meeting, the conference eventually agrees that, as a first step towards determining the national defence and co-prosperity spheres, more research will have to be done into the resources of various countries. Sugiyama curtly notes that the conference agrees to revise the research paper, which currently states: 'The Imperial resources sphere will be Japan, Manchuria, and China and the South Pacific territories, and Australia and India will be supplementary spheres.'

This decision to carry out more research into resources effectively shelves any possibility of imminent invasion threat from Australia (an option that Navy General Staff euphemistically refers to as 'perfect severance of Australia'). The conference ratifies a document entitled 'Consequences of cutting the communication lines between the United States and Australia, and Britain, India, and Australia', that states, among other things, that the total isolation of Australia is the key to Japan's control of the Southwest Pacific. It also envisages the isolation of New Caledonia, Fiji, Samoa and Ceylon.

The liaison conference goes on to discuss Japan's future resource needs. Discussion centres on Japan's steel-making projections, with an estimate that wartime Japan will need 27 million tonnes of steel each year. The meeting is told that occupied Hainan is ready to begin iron ore mining, helping Japan increase steel production by 20 per cent.

The navy minister, Admiral Shigetaro Shimada, who is normally non-committal, suggests that consideration of Australia's raw materials can't be excluded from the discussion. Shimada, seemingly adopting the Navy's aggressive stand, doesn't want the Army to rule out capturing further territories. He says: 'Because the construction of the new order in East Asia starts from the psychology of liberation for the peoples of East Asia, it would not be pertinent to exclude India and Australia; it is not possible to agree to the proposition of excluding territories that we could take into our hands when we cannot see how the war situation will develop.'

The Japanese are acutely aware of Australia's rich iron-ore deposits. Since the late 1930s, Japan looked to Australia for ore for steel-making. From the time of his arrival in Australia in March 1941 until his internment, Ambassador Kawai had made strenuous efforts to gain access to the massive untapped iron ore deposits at Yampi Sound in the remote north of Western Australia. The Australian government has previously blocked a Japanese enterprise, using a British company as a front, from proceeding with mining and exporting iron ore from the Yampi Sound site. In 1938, then prime minister Joseph Lyons had vetoed the operation, even as the mining equipment was being carried by ship from Japan to the project site.

According to Kawai, while Curtin was leader of the Opposition in April 1941, the two privately agreed to consider renewed Japanese access to the Yampi Sound iron ore deposits as a means of keeping the peace between Japan and Australia, provided Japan 'guaranteed Australia's safety'. Japan's subsequent subjugation of Indochina put an end to any such future agreement.

Now the military conference in Tokyo agrees that detailed investigations into steel production should be carried out. The future of Japan's expansionism is also debated. They decide to 'proceed with territories that are currently being captured', including New Caledonia, Fiji, Samoa and Ceylon. As for future invasions, the conference is vague deliberately, agreeing only to insert words: '... and other territories in accordance with developments in circumstances'.

So far as the Imperial Navy is concerned, then, there will be more debate on an invasion of Australia and other territories not yet included in Japan's second stage plans. While the navy might have hoped for clearer and more aggressive outcomes from the conference, on this extraordinary day, the army and navy's top leadership have openly discussed the prospect of taking Australia. General Sugiyama has not agreed to invasion other than to say that the loss of Australia will be a big psychological blow to England.

In what seems to be part of an orchestrated campaign, the *Japan Times* soon intensifies its propaganda about Australia:

> Australia as a member of the British Empire has no tradition of patriotism. The Australian people are devoted to the

nationalistic ideals which run counter to the British economic and political imperialism. Moreover, they still preserve in their subconsciousness the bitter memory of stigma attached to their country as a land of ex-convicts.

14

A CLASH OF PHILOSOPHIES

At Hashirajima, late winter winds brought in thick, ghostly fog. Visibility was so bad that the first battleship division, including the flagship *Yamato*, postponed manoeuvres. The conditions made Admiral Matome Ugaki hope that spring was just around the corner.

Ugaki's ambitions for the Imperial Navy were not diminished by the over-cautious talk of the military bureaucrats in Tokyo. He knew that March would see the conclusion of the first stage operations, and the need for bold new initiatives. He desperately wanted to capture some large enemy warships and merchantmen to aid future invasions: 'Shortage of shipping is a loud cry prevalent now. This is the usual excuse of the central authorities for their hesitation in making operations to the west, to the south, and to the east. The most effective thing, from the national point of view, would be to gain the three hundred thousand tons [of shipping needed] now and shut up these excuses.'

On 3 March, a telegram came for Ugaki, briefly diverting his attention from war-planning. Midget sub *M-13* had sunk during training on the Inland Sea the previous night. The midget, which had a three-man crew, had been located on the sea bottom but there was no answer to divers knocking on the hull. Concerned, Ugaki flew to the scene to assess the incident and report back to Yamamoto. The loss of an 'improved' craft should have spelled the end to use of midget submarines, but once again the program was granted a reprieve.

In Tokyo, debate about the invasion of Australia and other targets was coming to a head, as the Imperial Army and the Imperial Navy attempted during late February and early March to work through their fundamental clash of philosophies. There was more to the navy planners' agenda than bravado and glory-hunting. As the Pacific war developed, with one gain following another but with the United States preparing for a serious fight-back, they had good reason to worry that Australia would become a major base for American offensives against Japanese-occupied territory.

Yet the navy could not dispel the army's genuine concerns about the scale of an operation needed to secure the vastness of Australia, or even parts of the country. The Japanese army readily could imagine protracted warfare sapping the nation's military strength, as Australians resorted to guerrilla and commando tactics.

In Tokyo, on the morning of 4 March, senior operational officers of the army and navy met at the residence of the navy minister, Admiral Shigetaro Shimada. He ushered his guests into a plush sitting room overstuffed with furniture, heavy drapes and ornamentation. General Akira Muto was once again present for the army, while Navy General Staff was represented by admirals Fukudome and Oka. The head of the operations department of Army General Staff, General Shinichi Tanaka, took notes, setting out the position succinctly:

> The positions of the Army and Navy at the meeting were at odds as follows:
> Navy: Offensive strategy against the United States in the

Pacific Ocean (notion of a speedy decisive battle following on from pursuit operations.)

Army: Idea of establishment of an unassailable position in Greater East Asia, and to promote the end of the war through German–Japanese alliance in western Asia.

This disagreement resulted from difficulties in deciding which position should have priority.

The admirals knew they would not convince the army at this meeting to invade the distant areas of Hawaii and Australia, so instead they turned their focus to destroying the enemy's bases of operation to prevent enemy counter-attacks. This was something of a backdown, but left the door well open to revisit their invasion strategy:

The enemy will be able to take a breather and regroup if we do not take this opportunity to completely smash their naval strength. Further, the enemy's base for counter-offensives must be ruined, preventing them from mobilising a counter-attack at any time or place.

This is a heaven-sent opportunity to attack the United States individually... We are determined not to allow the establishment of a defensive posture at this time.

The army, recognising this as navy code for invasions of Australia and Hawaii, expressed opposition:

To seek the enemy main strengths in Australia or Hawaii must be said to be exceedingly dangerous. We cannot dispel misgivings over this expression 'pursuit operations'.

We would like to pay close attention to the extent of this offensive. An operation that exceeds the limits of both military and national strength can have no other fate than failure.

When an enemy is forced into a defensive position, it is natural for us to take hold of the offensive in order to suppress initiation of the inevitable counter-offensive. However, such an offensive must be a tactical offensive. This strategic operation is not a measure that we must take at this time.

In three hours of talks, there was much debate about the wording of a final resolution. Both sides tied themselves in semantic knots as they tried to gain the advantage. In the end, the rival camps agreed to the following set of words to be presented to the emperor about Japan's future direction of war:

> In order for Britain to yield and to force the United States to lose its will to fight, discussions on concrete measures will be undertaken at an appropriate time, while continuing preparations to establish a long-term unassailable position through extending heretofore military victories.
>
> Territories and key transport routes will be secured, the exploitation of vital national raw materials will proceed, and efforts will be made to reach a position of self-sufficiency and to increase national military strength.

General Tanaka thought the army and the navy had reached agreement in the conference. Up to that point, the navy had strongly emphasised the removal of the words 'continuing preparations to establish a long-term unassailable position', which was army-speak for cautious gradualism. The navy saw this as a defensive rather than an offensive posture. But following meetings showed that they were not in complete accord. As usual, the navy representatives simply gave ground while retaining their own plans.

Nevertheless, the outcome was another significant, if temporary, reprieve for Australia. At Hashirajima, the staff officers' planning also began to turn away from the southern continent. The former firebrands aboard Combined Fleet were now busy with far more pressing matters: Admiral Yamamoto's new favoured plan to capture the Midway islands. The tiny islands, some 2000 kilometres north-west of Hawaii, and just east of the International Date Line, were isolated and occupied by a small American force. But they were American territory, and their strategic location in the middle of the Pacific Ocean made them a significant naval berth and a refuelling stop for trans-Pacific flights. After the attack on Pearl Harbor, the US military leadership had placed increasing strategic value on them.

In an interview after the war, Admiral Yamamoto's chief planning officer, Captain Kameto Kuroshima, shed light on his commander-in-chief's change of thinking. He indicated that by February or March 1942 the Combined Fleet had vetoed, at least for the moment, the idea of *Shadan Sakusen*, the cutting-off operation against Australia:

> So long as the U.S. carrier forces were able to move actively, the Combined Fleet thought that Japan's navy could not move into the cut-off operation against Australia. As a preliminary to the *Shadan Sakusen*, the Combined Fleet thought that Japan must defeat the U.S. carrier force. Midway too was the best place to lure out the U.S. carrier forces.

Kuroshima said Combined Fleet wanted the Midway operation carried out first, followed by the invasion of Fiji and Samoa, cutting off Australia. An invasion of Australia then could be next. This was at odds with the thinking of Naval General Staff planners who still favoured a prompt invasion of the southern continent.

The Imperial Navy quickly came to realise that their gains at Pearl Harbor were not so great, given the absence of US carriers in the attack on Hawaii. The desperately anticipated duel at sea with the American fleet over Midway, involving Admiral Nagumo's so-far invincible carrier strike force, quickly assumed more importance for Yamamoto's men than the occupation of the Midway atolls.

Sometime in spring, officers of Naval General Staff, probably Tomioka and an assistant, came aboard the *Yamato* to thrash out differences with Combined Fleet planners. No firm agreement was reached, so further talks between Tomioka and Kuroshima took place in Tokyo. Eventually, Naval General Staff agreed to support the attack on Midway on the condition that Combined Fleet agreed to a simultaneous attack on the American-held Aleutian islands, which ran in an arc in the northern Pacific westwards from Alaska.

This compromise notwithstanding, Naval General Staff continued to use every opportunity to press for an invasion of Australia at formal liaison conferences between the navy, army and government, and in informal discussions. Then the navy proponents of invasion decided to make one last concerted effort to persuade their counterparts to adopt their thinking.

At liaison conference number 92, held on 7 March, Australia was raised in several agenda items. In appraising the global situation, the army and the navy quickly divided along their usual lines. This time, however, the debate turned to the question of the impossibility of winning a protracted war.

An acknowledged moderate, the vice chief of the Naval General Staff, Admiral Seiichi Ito, said that even if current operations looked bright, people should look to the distant future. Foreign Minister Togo hardly sounded confident when he suggested that it would be all right to state in the summary document something to the effect that the defeat of Britain and America was impossible for the short term, but 'something might be able to be done' for the long term.

The prime minister, General Tojo, immediately objected to the very terminology of the agenda item, 'the impossibility of overturning England and America'. At the same time, the prime minister wanted to stop further discussion about more invasions: 'It would be okay to state something to the effect that we have secured bright victories, are steadily occupying our enemies' lands, and that things are going better than was expected at the beginning of the war. Ultimately, we have achieved the initial goals; we have achieved them to an extent much beyond what was anticipated, so from now on there should be no change to the existing plan.'

Open discussion of the long-term chances of victory was too controversial to handle: no participant could agree to an official paper that might suggest that Japan could not defeat the US and Britain in the long term. So the issue was abandoned without decision.

Admiral Ito, a close associate of Baron Tomioka, usually a mild-mannered moderate, now surprised the meeting by showing himself as an aggressive invasion radical:

> At the time at the beginning of the war, there was in some way a feeling we were losing ground, but now not only is there not a feeling of losing ground, there is a feeling of gaining ground, so we must proceed aggressively with operations.

Ito advocated pushing out the boundaries of the operational sphere, regardless of the consequences. It was a demonstration of how radical the intelligent, experienced and 'moderate' planners in Naval General Staff had become.

The army's vice chief of staff, General Moritake Tanabe, took Tojo's line, arguing that the principal objective should be to build a political and military structure capable of withstanding prolonged war. 'Neutralisation forays' into certain areas were practical, but only on a modest scale.

The influential hard-liner Admiral Takasumi Oka vehemently disagreed: 'If we become defensive now, our future strategies will be endangered ... it is therefore vital that we make our enemies take a defensive stance.' Oka was unequivocal about maintaining the offensive:

> ... [We] need to actively move our forces to Australia and Hawaii, annihilate our enemies' marine military force, and decimate our enemies' bases for counterattack ... it is vital that we procure resources within the co-prosperity sphere and ensure that they are not taken by our enemies; further, to that end it is impossible to take an exclusively defensive stance ...

Vice chief of staff General Moritake Tanabe had heard enough about Australia and responded angrily:

> Supreme Command had adequately considered Australia, India, Hawaii and Ceylon. To go to Australia would require a force of ten divisions and 200 to 300 million tons in terms of ships. It is impossible to carry out however you look at it.

Admiral Oka and the navy would not get their way. The liaison conference eventually reached a compromise wording in a new policy document declaring: 'In order to force Britain to submit and the United States to lose its will to fight, we shall continue expanding from the areas we have already gained.' Although this struck an aggressive note, the conference, no doubt at the army's insistence, quickly added what sounded like a compromise; that this expansion should be done 'while working long-term to establish an impregnable strategic position, we shall actively seize whatever opportunities for attack that may occur'.

The obscure, euphemistic language of the resolution left some of those present scratching their heads. The finance minister, Okinobu Kaya, asked: 'What do you mean when you say "expand on the war results we have already obtained"?' General Tanabe, unhelpfully replied that, 'as for capturing Australia, India, Hawaii etc, we understand it as those things other than with respect to as I explain in paragraph 3 . . .' Result: more paper shuffling and head scratching, no doubt.

At times, the debate descended into farce. Admiral Oka said: 'With regard to the meaning of the language "wait for the opportunity and develop proactive measures" at the end of paragraph 1, adjutant general Muto explained to the effect that the meaning of that can be interpreted as also including "measures for even more proactive war guidance" as appears in paragraph 3.' Eventually an exasperated Tojo called this discussion quits, stating: 'Whatever the case, the meaning is not readily understandable'.

The issue of invading Australia was not abandoned but set

aside as 'a future option to demonstrate positive warfare'.

The muddled 7 March conference finally agreed to an 'Outline of war guidance suggested for implementation', but its intentions were far from clear, representing the differences between the army and navy. The convoluted wording would go to Emperor Hirohito, who would take the final decision about Australia and other nations. In his summary of this outcome, army chief of staff General Sugiyama wrote that 'there still was no fundamental concurrence with respect to the discrepancies in the fundamental philosophies of the army and the navy', but nevertheless the resolution had material significance.

He summarised the conflicting lines of argument:

According to the plan at the outbreak of the war, Japan never had any intention to invade Australia or India. But as offensive operations developed, Imperial Headquarters and the government came to take a material interest in measures against Australia and India, and it became a major problem in determining subsequent war guidance.

Put simply, the Navy argued for an aggressive offensive that included attacking Australia, whereas the Army outright opposed attacking Australia, stating that the focus ought to be on firmly establishing the situation so that Japan will be unbeatable in the long-term.

At the time Sugiyama penned this summary, almost three weeks had passed since the first air raids on Darwin; there is no doubt, therefore, that his reference to 'attacking Australia' was meant as a reference to invasion. The day after this conference, Japanese forces occupied the Australian-administered towns of Lae, Salamaua, and Finschhafen, on the north-east coast of New Guinea, giving them control of the Huon peninsula and the entrance to the Bismarck Sea.

Prime Minister Tojo, General Sugiyama and Admiral Nagano met Hirohito on 13 March to finalise the next steps in the war. In relation to Australia and India, the army, no doubt as a compromise forced on it by the navy, had allowed inclusion in the text of a 'temporary invasion of Darwin' as 'a future option to demonstrate positive warfare'.

The military chiefs on 13 March spoke with Hirohito about agreeing to 'new and more positive war guidance', but with stringent conditions attached to the Darwin 'temporary' invasion. This course could only be considered after the most detailed study of everything from the progress of operations to the international situation, especially considering the Soviet Union and China. But the chiefs significantly left the emperor in no doubt what they were talking about: 'By "more positive measures of war guidance", we mean such measures as the invasion of India and Australia.'

On review, Hirohito decided that any invasion of Australia could be postponed until after the conquest of Burma. The army had been forced to agree to an invasion of the big Australian base at Port Moresby, a stepping stone to Australia, which then was being re-enforced. Thus the invasion of Australia formally was shelved for the moment by those in Tokyo and the army hoped that the issue was finished.

But the Imperial Navy planners merely bided their time. When Port Moresby fell, they argued, who and what could prevent an assault on the great land to the near south, within good range of Japanese land bombers? The navy knew they had lost ground leading to the presentation in the Imperial palace. Retaining the possibility of invading Australia and India in the future, in the joint report to the emperor, was important to the navy yet both sides knew the wording was only an elaborate game. One of the key army planners, Colonel Takushiro Hattori, in his own history of four volumes, later observed:

> Thus, the Navy's insistence on invading Australia was blocked, but the Army yielded to the Navy's positive stand, agreeing to carrying out limited offensives.

Hattori added: 'although it was made to appear as if an agreement had been reached by rephrasing various measures and decisions, actually, the Army's and the Navy's basic concepts remained unchanged.'

On 14 March, a Combined Fleet staff officer, Shigeru Fujii, who had been in the capital, briefed Ugaki about the unfolding events in Tokyo. In his diary, Ugaki summarised the recent agreements between the navy and the army with some contempt: 'They only wanted to enlarge the war results and didn't decide on any practical plan that meant a positive operation.' Ugaki said the army as usual refused his plans. They argued there was no reserve army strength. It was difficult for them to extend the scope of the war because of considerations of the threat from the Soviet Union.

Ugaki also noted that General Tojo, with an election coming in April, wanted to use available shipping to pacify an atmosphere of discontent in Japan, a nation experiencing a fair amount of shortages: 'This sounds reasonable to a certain degree and I have nothing against the purport. But I think they will follow us without fail if we keep on pressing persistently, taking in to account that it will be delayed about six months from the time of our initial idea. In the meantime, we had better show them what the navy or Combined Fleet can do.'

On 23 March, Ugaki noted that General Douglas MacArthur, his wife, and his staff officers, had escaped the Bataan peninsula for Australia, where he was appointed supreme head of the Allied command in the south-west Pacific. Ugaki's overconfidence was brimming:

He has become the anti-Axis nations' idol and has been assigned as commander of Allied forces in southeast Asia. He stressed the urgency of American support in fighting strength and materials for the defense of Australia. Is he a great general or a crazy one?

Yamamoto's right-hand man knew that the Japanese had made a landing on New Guinea; he was waiting confidently for the conquest of the remainder of New Guinea before Fiji and Samoa would be taken in time. After that would come Australia and New Zealand. But for now the two small atolls at Midway would occupy his every waking moment.

In Melbourne, Curtin and his ministers now received a first-hand account of the efficiency of the Japanese fighting machine. The officer commanding the AIF at Malaya, General Gordon Bennett, controversially had escaped from Singapore after the surrender. For abandoning his men, he was shown the cold shoulder by senior Military Board officers back at Victoria Barracks. But he told the war cabinet that 'there had been a general under-estimation of the enemy. Our men were better individually, but the Japanese leadership was remarkably good'.

After the fall of Singapore, defeatism was creeping into the Australian outlook. On 5 March, Professor A.P. Elkin in Sydney wrote to the prime minister about a critical failure of morale in the country. Unless positive measures were taken, he said, resistance to Japan would fade away. He warned that Australian authorities were engaging in crude and ineffectual propaganda: 'Posters displaying gorilla-type hands or faces and representing apparent monsters about to pounce on or grab Australia, will only have the desired effect in a very few cases. Generally speaking it will terrify or worry people or cause them to act in some adverse emotional way.'

An even greater problem, Elkin told Curtin, was a growing sense of futility and a serious 'make peace' mentality in Australia:

> There is much unhappiness amongst people of different groups in our society because of a belief, which some say is based on fact, that numbers of our leading business and financial folk would sell out to Japan and make peace in the hope of preserving their business and profits.

Associated with this is the statement which is made by some of these folk that we just cannot prevent Japan landing if it wants to and therefore we should not waste blood and money over it, but come to terms.

Curtin immediately put himself in charge of a new campaign to improve public morale.

The American military leadership in Australia had an even more critical view of the state of the locals' fighting spirit. The chief of staff of US army forces in Australia (USAFIA), Brigadier General F.S. Clark, feared morale would collapse if the Japanese landed: 'Strong, forceful leadership is required to maintain morale in the event of an invasion. The people need to be continuously spurred on to an effectual war effort.'

In a confidential intelligence memo, Clark told US General George H. Brett, who was about to become MacArthur's deputy, that the Australians appeared too willing to lay the burden of responsibility on someone else, like the US: 'The indicated weaknesses of the Australian people and their Government, faced with Japanese invasion, appear to be, first, a deep-rooted complacency and a feeling "it can't happen here". Second, a lack of realism and a tendency to avoid unpleasant issues. Third, some tendency to panic when suddenly faced with reality.'

The American military leadership noted with concern that the combined US and Australian forces were obviously insufficient for the protection of the whole of the vast Australian continent which was 'almost equal in size to the United States and with a coastline 12,000 miles in length': 'Concentration in any area to oppose Japanese landings was exceedingly difficult because of the great distances to be covered and the inadequate transportation facilities.' The road and rail network of Australia was of limited capacity and of varying gauges and did not permit the rapid movement of troops. Principal routes frequently paralleled the coast and were vulnerable to amphibious attack.

American officers in Australia told Washington that the

Australians had disposed the bulk of their forces in the general coastal region around Brisbane south to Melbourne where most industries were located. The vast east coast area was all important to Australia's war effort and thus was given the country's prime defence consideration. Yet this strategy exposed the rest of Australia to attack. Small forces were stationed in Tasmania and Western Australia and at Darwin, Townsville, Thursday Island and Port Moresby.

By now, the Australian defence chiefs had just about given away the idea of holding Darwin, which they expected to be invaded by the Japanese at any moment. In early March the defence chiefs had made dire predictions about a Japanese invasion of Australia, and Curtin forwarded the appreciation to the Australian minister in London, Sir Earle Page, on 12 March, for discussion with British chiefs.

Perhaps no other archival document points so powerfully to the hopelessness of the Australian situation by March 1942, and to the nation's extreme vulnerability if the Japanese decided to move further southward. The defence chiefs noted that with Malaya and Singapore gone, the Japanese invading Burma, occupying Borneo, the Celebes, Sumatra, Ambon and Timor, and with Java being overrun, an attempt to occupy Darwin and Broome 'is not unlikely'. Further, Port Moresby, New Caledonia, and Fiji were immediately threatened:

> Australia and New Zealand are therefore in danger of attack. This loss would mean the loss of the only bases for offensive action by the Allied Nations against the Japanese from the south east.

The Australian defence chiefs suggested that the Japanese could occupy Darwin in early April with only two divisions of infantry, if they were supported by at least four aircraft carriers carrying some 200 aircraft. The chiefs further predicted that even an attack on a much smaller scale would be effective, because of the inadequacy of the forces available to defend Darwin.

These forces included US submarines based at Fremantle, about two-thirds of one army division and a pathetically weak air force comprising two under-strength RAAF squadrons of Hudson bombers and one squadron of already obsolete Wirraway aircraft badly in need of major reconditioning. Two squadrons of US Dauntless A-24 Banshee dive bombers had been diverted from Manila to Australia, but these were plagued with mechanical problems and very few could fly.

Curtin relayed his defence chiefs' plea that the minimum forces needed to defend Darwin were at least three carriers and their aircraft, escorted by cruisers, destroyers and submarines; an additional army division; and ten squadrons of planes, mostly fighters and bombers. Port Moresby was expected to fall in one week's time; its defence would require three aircraft carriers, 13 squadrons of planes and a brigade of infantry.

The chiefs also thought the east coast of Australia was vulnerable, but they correctly assumed the Japanese first intended to remove Moresby and New Caledonia from the equation: 'It is likely that Moresby and New Caledonia will be occupied by the enemy before an invasion of the East Coast [of Australia] is attempted. Such an attempt may be made in May if the attacks on Moresby and New Caledonia are successful . . .'

The chiefs said the area of Australia vital for continuing the war effort was on the east and south coast, generally between Brisbane and Melbourne. But the Japanese, with air and sea superiority, could now attack from a number of quarters. They worried that Fremantle could be captured in an invasion launched from the former Dutch East Indies. Current defences in Fremantle included one light cruiser, destroyers and submarines, one squadron of Hudson bombers and another of Wirraways. A squadron of US P-40 fighters was not due until the end of March.

The Australian base at Port Moresby now was being hammered by Japanese bombers. When 75 Squadron of the RAAF flew their new Kittyhawks to the town on 21 March only four of their 21 pilots had any combat experience. Over the next 44 days, only three Kittyhawks would survive and most of the pilots would die, be wounded or stricken with disease.

Australia's position in March 1942 appeared hopeless to the three service chiefs: 'Until such time as adequate naval and air forces are available, it is estimated that it would require a minimum of 25 divisions to defend Australia against the scale of attack that is possible.'

The huge, complex burden of reinventing Australia's defence policy, while fighting a losing battle to save Allied territory in the region, sometimes manifested itself in bizarre political bi-plays. In March, the US consul-general in Melbourne, Earle R. Dickover, reported to Washington an extraordinary conversation he had with former prime minister Robert Menzies. Over lunch at the Australian Club, Menzies, a supporter of Britain through and through, told Dickover that the Labor prime minister was at heart an isolationist and wanted to defend Australia only, 'letting the rest of the British empire go'. Thanks to the Labor Party and British blundering, Menzies reportedly said, half of Australia now was anti-British, according to Dickover:

> Mr Menzies proceeded to state that he would not be surprised, if the Japanese invaded a part of Australia, to see the Labor Government revolt against Britain, declare their independence, and try to make Australia a second United States.

15

SCORCHING AUSTRALIA

The genuine fear of a Japanese invasion in early 1942 can be seen in the minutes of the Australian war cabinet, and the massive war expenditures it approved under John Curtin's chairmanship.

On 2 March, the cabinet increased funding for the continuing construction of the graving dock at Garden Island, Sydney, from three to 4.6 million pounds, an immense sum. A decision was also made to equip Australian merchant ships with deck guns. The war cabinet also approved the purchase of three million respirators for civilians and 450,000 respirator helmets for babies and children to be issued free of charge. Clearly it thought the nation must be prepared for gas attacks.

Such was the concern about resources production, that the White Australia Policy was temporarily overlooked. Cabinet approved a recommendation by the supply minister, Jack Beasley, to allow some 580 Chinese miners and mechanics from Nauru to mine tungsten in central Australia.

Soon war cabinet members were startled to hear that a million pounds worth of radar equipment, intended for the US forces who were beginning to arrive in Australia, was sitting in cases on

Melbourne wharves as waterside workers took industrial action over pay and conditions. The war cabinet gave the issue 'one of the highest degrees of urgency'. Industrial disputes in wartime Australia, on the wharves, in mines, public transport and in factories, were an ongoing burden for Curtin.

The prime minister even worried about the work of government being disrupted by Japanese bombing attacks on the national capital. He demanded security for the navy's wireless transmission stations in Canberra to guard against sabotage and suggested anti-aircraft batteries to protect the stations from air raids.

The fear of Japanese attack was personal for Curtin and his ministers. They even debated what might happen if the cabinet war room at Victoria Barracks was bombed. Authority was given for the bricking up of windows on the lower floor so that cabinet could meet there during air raids.

In his darkest hours, Curtin could vividly imagine the Japanese taking control. He worried about his family's safety and even his own survival, as his daughter Elsie Macleod testified: 'He probably could even imagine what the Japanese would do to him if they won the war and he was taken prisoner.'

Despite the PM's thundering speeches on work, austerity and sacrifice, only a portion of the Australian population cooperated. The moderator of the Presbyterian Church, the Reverend Dr C.N. Button, wrote an appeal to Curtin to 'save Australia' by outlawing strikes and extravagances: '. . . on the streets of our great cities scenes of drunkenness and disorder the likes of which have not been known before, are being witnessed daily, to the utter disgust of every respectable person. Money and petrol badly needed for the country's defence are being wasted on amusement, much of it of a degrading kind; your appeals in regard to these matters have fallen on deaf ears'.

As the Japanese forces moving southward captured major centres in Java after the loss of Singapore and the initial attacks on Darwin, talk of 'making peace with Japan' became more prevalent in Australia. The *Herald*'s senior political correspondent,

Joe Alexander, began to record in his diary signs of people, especially in Sydney, wanting to make peace with Japan. He even suspected two of Curtin's own ministers, Evatt and Beasley, of being involved, although he offered no proof.

Alexander himself expected the Japanese to offer Australia a separate peace based on the abrogation of the White Australia Policy; he thought there were many Australians who would accept. On 9 March, Alexander had the rumours confirmed, as he told his diary:

> Curtin said an alarming thing today. He said he was depressed because he had heard that a number of people in Sydney were prepared to make peace to save Sydney. So he has dragged into the open what I have felt myself for so long.
>
> Sydney, the incredibly selfish, callous, pleasure living, without faith in God or man, is semi-defeated, and might want to save itself as Paris was saved. It may want to be declared an open town. Unless we are psychologically reborn, with the first shock of attack we are doomed.

Around this time, Alexander began building a small air raid shelter in his backyard.

Curtin had also confirmed to him privately that stories of Japanese atrocities in the capture of Hong Kong, which they had been hearing from the start of March, were 'all too true'. On Christmas Day when Hong Kong surrendered, the Japanese had come through Saint Stephen's College, which was being used as a Red Cross hospital, and had bayoneted wounded British and Canadian soldiers in their beds. Doctors and nurses who tried to stop the massacre were themselves bayoneted or shot. A group of British nurses were taken away by troops, raped and shot. In his diary, Alexander was aghast: 'It is too terrible to conceive seeing that we are in such terrible danger. British women exposed to Japanese lust.'

Curtin relentlessly agonised over the prospect of Japanese

troops landing on Australian soil, overrunning brave but pitiful defences. In his mind's eye, he could see the devastation in ports, cities and towns as Japanese aircraft blasted Australian forces and fleeing civilians alike. It was horrible to contemplate, but Curtin felt obliged to face the facts squarely. In March, 1942, under Curtin's direction, the war cabinet began putting in place a 'scorched earth policy' to deny the Japanese Australian resources in the event of an invasion.

An order that authorised the Australian Navy to immobilise vessels by whatever means at a given signal was implemented on 10 March. Other orders under national security regulations were secretly put into effect without public knowledge. They included tunnelling under airstrips and placing explosives, especially in northern Australia, so that strips could be destroyed if the Japanese tried to land. The aerodrome at Mackay, in central Queensland, was one of the first to be readied for demolition. Key bridges in northern Australia were prepared for destruction. Priority was given to the destruction of vital facilities in coastal areas which could not be adequately protected by troops.

A major plank of the scorched earth policy was the proposed destruction of power stations, in the event of invasion. Navy, army and air force installations and facilities were also high on the demolition list. Wireless, cable, telegraph stations and telephone exchanges were the next priority. Petrol and oil installations and refineries were marked for early destruction, as were harbour facilities, water supplies, stocks of food and alcohol and stocks of coal and raw materials. It was a massive undertaking.

Initially, the military and some federal government departments worked on the complex details of preparing for Curtin's scorched earth. Curtin wrote to state premiers and local government leaders revealing 'the great importance of the scored earth policy of territory invaded by the enemy'.

The recipients of these letters must have been shocked. Curtin, who personally signed the secret correspondence, was quick to point out that it did not signify a lack of fighting spirit: 'You will realise that such preparations are part of the general defence scheme and are not in any way inconsistent with the government's resolve to defend Australia to the limit of our capacity.'

Cities and towns where the civilian population had withdrawn and the military was about to withdraw were given first priority for destruction. In those situations, Curtin sought 'the complete and total denial, removal or destruction of everything likely to maintain or assist the enemy'. In places where the civilians had been instructed to remain during enemy attack or occupation, a partial demolition policy would be implemented, leaving essential services to enable the population to live. 'All other services, utilities, vehicles, materials, and everything likely to be of assistance to the enemy in his operations will be removed to a safe area or [will be] totally destroyed.'

Meanwhile, the military campaign to save Australia was about to be ratcheted up. General Douglas MacArthur stepped from his battered B-17 at Bachelor Field, south of Darwin, on 17 March. He told waiting reporters that President Roosevelt had ordered him to escape the Corregidor fortress in Manila Bay and to come to Australia to organise the American offensive against Japan. 'I came through and I shall return,' he promised. Ten minutes after the Supreme Allied Commander of the South-West Pacific took off for Alice Springs, the airfield was attacked by Japanese fighters and bombers.

In another welcome development, the AIF troops from the Middle East began arriving home. General Sir Thomas Blamey, commander of the AIF forces in the Middle East, was on the deck of his troopship, the converted liner, the *Queen Mary*, when it dropped anchor in the Fremantle roadstead on 23 March. The local commanding officer came aboard with a letter from the prime minister. It told Blamey that he had been appointed to the new post of commander-in-chief, Australian Military Forces.

Soon after setting up his headquarters in Melbourne, General

MacArthur drove to Canberra to meet Curtin for the first time. The two leaders cooperated from the start, but the American found Australia in a sorry state:

> The immediate and imperative problem which confronted me was the defence of Australia itself. Its actual military situation had become desperate.
>
> The bulk of its ground troops were in the Middle East, while the United States had only one division present, and that but partially trained. Its air force was equipped with almost obsolete planes and was lacking not only in engines and spare parts, but in personnel. The navy had no carriers or battleships. The outlook was bleak.

So far, his assessment was much the same as the official Australian one. MacArthur set out to change Australia's war policy: 'The concept was purely one of passive defence, and I felt that it only would result in eventual defeat . . .'

MacArthur expresses a view of deep Australian pessimism, which was partly true, as evidenced by Curtin's scorched earth policy. Yet, even before MacArthur's arrival, it was the Curtin government's view that Australia must become the Allies' base for offensive action against Japan.

Ill and frequently depressed, Curtin despatched his foreign minister, Herbert Evatt, to Washington and London to seek greater support for Australia. On 15 March, Curtin made a rather desperate shortwave broadcast, primarily to the people of the United States: 'Australia is the last bastion between the west coast of America and the Japanese. If Australia goes, the Americas are wide open . . . I say to you that the saving of Australia is the saving of America's west coast.'

The Australian leader sounded aggressive, keen to demonstrate an Australian fighting spirit. 'This war may see the end of much that we have painfully and slowly built in our 150 years of existence. But even though all of it go, there will still be Australians fighting on Australian soil until the turning point be reached, and we will advance over blackened ruins, through blasted and fireswept cities, across scorched plains, until we drive the enemy into the sea.'

MacArthur personally doubted that there would be a full-scale invasion of all of Australia, but the US general did not rule it out, according to a briefing Curtin gave the advisory war council on 26 March, quoting MacArthur: 'It would be a dramatic blunder for the Japanese to undertake an invasion of Australia. He did not consider that there was sufficient spoil here to warrant the risk. The Japanese, however, have a peculiar outlook. They like to create the impression in the Oriental mind that they are superior to the white man and, for that reason they might try to overrun Australia. They are always likely to do the unexpected. There were many "anti-white man" natives who would be impressed by such a fest such as the conquest of Australia.'

Nevertheless, MacArthur thought piecemeal invasions of certain areas of Australia – possibly in Australia's north – were indeed likely: 'He thought that the Japanese would also attempt to secure air bases in Australia.'

Churchill gave Curtin an assurance on 30 March, and again on 1 April, that Britain would support Australia in the event of an invasion in force. Curtin saw this as Australia's right, the nation having contributed so much to Britain under threat. Churchill promised Curtin the assistance of the 2nd British Infantry Division, which was rounding the Cape of Good Hope en route to the Far East in late April or early May: 'If, by that time, Australia is being heavily invaded, I should certainly divert it to your aid. This would not apply in the case of localised attacks in the north or mere raids elsewhere. But I wish to let you know that you could count on this help should invasion by, say, eight or ten Japanese divisions occur.'

Churchill's use of the strong qualifying words 'heavily invaded' and 'localised attacks in the north' should be noted; they had ominous implications for the future of Darwin, which the Japanese leadership had now marked for 'temporary invasion' some time in the future, if the right circumstances arose. The British prime minister might well have regarded the capture of Darwin and other northern Australian outposts as 'localised attacks' that would not result in reinforcements being sent, as long as the major population centres in the south remained safe.

Both Curtin and MacArthur were desperate to take the offensive against the Japanese, but London and Washington had higher priorities. Churchill still insisted that the Japanese probably were not planning to invade Australia in force. The British PM thought there was a grave risk in overcommitting forces and weapons which would be more use if sent to the Middle East and India.

While the chiefs of Britain's three armed services tended to agree in part with their prime minister, they were much more circumspect than Churchill on the crucial issue affecting Australia's very survival. They made their own assessment in response to the assessment of 12 March prepared by Australia's defence chiefs. The British military leaders spoke directly of the likelihood of a Japanese invasion of parts of Australia. In fact, they went so far as to assess that Japan might capture one or two key Australian cities – Darwin and Fremantle were mentioned.

'It seems clear that Japan intends to capture Port Moresby and probably Darwin also,' the most senior British officers wrote, in words that Churchill never used in his public utterances or correspondence with the Australian government. In saying this, the British defence chiefs were agreeing with their Australian counterparts and with Curtin's assessment of likely Japanese action. The British chiefs said there were four major operations which Japan might consider or face: invasion of India; invasion of the Pacific islands; invasion of Australia; or war with Russia.

They said 'a genuine invasion of Australia' – that is, presumably, capturing the whole Australian continent or southern capitals – did not form part of Japanese plans. There were three reasons for this assessment: it would be more profitable to attack India and China from Burma; there was an ever-present risk that the Soviet Union, which had not yet declared war on Japan, would decide to do so; and finally, the fact that it would be easier to neutralise Australia by blockade 'than by attempting to control the whole of the continent'. But occupying parts of Australia was on the cards.

The British defence chiefs thought that Japan could probably consolidate her Asiatic co-prosperity sphere more easily and cheaply by placing herself astride the eastern and western reinforcement routes to Australia than by taking 'the whole of Australia', adding: 'This could subsequently be achieved by occupation of Samoa, Fiji and Caledonia on the one hand, and Fremantle on the other. Admittedly this would not isolate Australia, but we think that it would suffice for Japan's purpose.'

The defence chiefs said that if Japan did invade Australia, the scale of the initial assault was not likely to exceed a total of four divisions, which would be directed at not more than two points simultaneously: 'The capture of Fremantle would deprive us of a base on the South Eastern sea board of the Indian Ocean. Neither we or the United States can afford to lock [up] such important naval units for [the] local defence of Western Australia and the sea approaches to that area.'

They thought that invading parts of Western Australia would be safer for Japan than any objective on the east coast of Australia: 'For these reasons we consider the defence of Fremantle just as urgent a commitment as the defence of eastern Australia, although the area is intrinsically less important . . . we estimate that the scale of the attack might be two to three divisions.'

This report was part of Curtin's Easter reading. In his capacity as Member for Fremantle, he would have found the words deeply foreboding. General Blamey had shared similar sentiments with him, advising Curtin that the Japanese attack on Australia would come via the west – Fremantle and Albany. Awaiting a transcontinental flight to Melbourne after his landing in Fremantle, Blamey had two days to ponder the remoteness and vulnerability of the enormous state of Western Australia. He later told his biographer:

Had the Japanese wished to seize it, Western Australia, with its vast potential wealth might have fallen an easy prey to them in 1942. While it would have extended their commitment to a tremendous degree, it would have given them great advantages. At that time it could probably have been captured and controlled by a force no greater than that used to capture Malaya.

Its capture would have cut off Australia from all the British areas to the west. Its communications with the remainder of Australia depended almost entirely on the sea and on the tenuous single-track overland railway inadequately provided with rolling stock; and therefore very difficult to reinforce rapidly.

The commander of US forces in Australia, General George Brett, also prepared an estimation of Australia's grim position, in conjunction with Australia's three defence chiefs. It was rather blandly entitled 'Probable immediate Japanese moves in the Proposed New Anzac Area'. Brett and the Australians said that their best forecast was that major Japanese attacks might occur at Darwin in early April, Port Moresby in the middle of March, New Caledonia in the middle of April and on the east coast of Australia in May: 'We visualise that, should New Caledonia be occupied, the next step of the Japanese might well be to attack the east coast of Australia.'

The officers declined to make further forecasts about the east coast, other than to say that with the fall of Java, Japan could reinforce her attacks on Australia. Rather than mere raids, the chiefs were actually talking about Japanese troops landing at points in Australia and the islands. They said, for example, a minimum Japanese force of one division would be sufficient to secure Darwin, 'but we think that the Japanese would probably use two or more divisions for such a purpose, as up to date, their policy has been to run no risk . . .'

Under the heading 'Forces Available for the Defence of Darwin' they inserted the signal line: 'No Naval forces are available at present.' They noted that army forces consisted of about two thirds of one division of largely untrained and inexperienced men, while Darwin's air defences consisted of two under-strength squadrons of lumbering Hudson bombers, one squadron of hopelessly inadequate Wirraways, and various training aircraft.

So this was how Australia found herself in April of 1942. The position was so grave that General MacArthur's senior staffers believed that the Australian military forces were prepared to abandon much of Australia to the Japanese if necessary, reporting: 'The Australian Chiefs of Staff would be virtually compelled to yield the northern part of the continent to the Japanese should they attempt an invasion.'

In a report prepared in Tokyo soon after Japan's surrender, officers from MacArthur's general staff said the Australians would have made their defence against the Japanese at Brisbane. Defence by major units north of Townsville was not even contemplated and sufficient forces to secure Fremantle and Darwin against determined enemy assault simply were not available, they said. This estimate was very close to the truth. Minimal or no reinforcements were planned for the more remote outposts, which were expected to fight to the last should the Japanese try to land. Withdrawal of forces altogether was considered to be bad for morale. The vast majority of the thinly spread Australian forces were to protect the southern manufacturing capitals.

On 27 March, Curtin announced that General Thomas Blamey had been appointed commander-in-chief of Allied Land Forces under MacArthur. Blamey had done more research into the vulnerability of Curtin's home state and that day he privately told Curtin of his fears. He was sure that the Japanese attack on Australia would come via the west – Fremantle and Albany.

Faced with this ominous accumulation of expert defence opinion, Curtin needed no further proof of probable disaster. He immediately sent the latest forecast from General Brett and the Australian chiefs to his foreign minister in Washington, for dissemination to President Roosevelt, and also sent a copy to Churchill.

On 8 April, Curtin told the advisory war council that General MacArthur 'was in entire agreement' with the defence appreciation by General Brett and the Australian chiefs. Further, MacArthur was sending the report to the US Army chief of staff, General George C. Marshall, 'urging the provision of the Naval Forces and aircraft recommended in the appreciation as being the minimum essential . . .'

Curtin felt gutted. Angry and glum, he sat down in his Parliament House office with Gavin Long, a senior journalist from the *Sydney Morning Herald* who would later become an official war historian. In a private briefing, the prime minister quickly revealed that he had put forward a major offensive proposal developed by the chief of the Australian Navy Staff, Admiral Royle, that called for a bold, large-scale naval and air offensive, chiefly involving cruisers, aircraft carriers and torpedo craft from Britain and the US. The plan had the approval of General MacArthur. 'The time to carry out this offensive, according to Royle, MacArthur and myself is now, while there is stability in Europe and this would give us time to push Japan out of her conquered territories,' Curtin said.

'Churchill opposes this plan,' he went on. 'He does not believe that Australia is seriously threatened, though he is very much alive to the threat to India. He offers Australia, in place of [our] plan, an assurance that, if Australia is seriously attacked, a British infantry division and a British armed division which will be going round the Cape in June and July will be diverted to Australia. My reply is that the Australian army leaders consider that 25 divisions would be needed to hold Australia against attack if she lacked naval and air superiority . . . thus, at best, Churchill is offering too little too late, as he did at Singapore. On the other hand a sea–air offensive now would stun Japan.'

Curtin's sourness at Churchill giving priority to India over Australia was based on fact. In February, Churchill had written to the chief of his personal defence staff: 'The reinforcement of India has become more urgent. I am deeply concerned with the reactions from Japanese victories throughout Asia. It will be necessary to have an additional number of British troops in India.'

16

AUSTRALIA'S REPRIEVE

In Canberra, stifling summer heat has given way to autumn; the leaves are turning. On 14 April, the governor-general, Lord Gowrie, is working at his desk at Government House, Yarralumla. 'We are, as you will gather, having rather an anxious time out here at the present moment,' he writes to George VI, in a tone of calm understatement:

> The fall of Singapore and Java created a serious situation in this part of the world and we were really anxious for some time. But a great deal has happened in the last month or two, and provided we can have another month or so immune from serious attack, we ought to be secure, but this next month will be critical and I shall be glad when it is safely over.

Gowrie has been impressed by Curtin, if not some of his ministers, and he now detects some change in the lackadaisical attitude of Australians towards the war effort: 'The people here, of course, in the early stages of the war . . . were inclined to adopt the attitude "it cannot happen here", but there is a very different outlook now. They realise that we may be invaded at any moment, parts of Australia are already being bombed and it is pretty certain that a good deal more bombing will take place before very long. Australians, when once they realise the possibility of real trouble, do get down to the job, and men and women are all in it up to the neck now.'

Curtin doesn't entirely agree and worries about the attitude of some Australians. On the same evening, he issues a statement showing that 800,000 tons of coal production have been lost in three months by strikes in New South Wales coalmines, mostly for trivial reasons. Only one in five stoppages is employer-related. To add to his frustrations, there is a strike of 400 men in the tool room at a small arms factory in Lithgow where the Bren gun is produced. In his diary, Joe Alexander dubs it 'a fearful crime against the nation, and a monstrous irrelevancy'.

Curtin's vision of Australia as the redoubt for a staunch Allied counteroffensive is just starting to become a reality as American servicemen and weapons arrive; meanwhile, his compatriots are still dragging their feet. A report compiled by a new advisory committee on civilian morale has reached him. It suggests that the rapid approach of physical danger 'has tended to thrust idealism into the background and displace it with a crude physical self-preservation. People are concentrating on personal safety, rather than that of the nation or the Allied cause'.

In Canberra, senior political reporters gather around Curtin's desk for another secret briefing. News has reached the PM that the destroyer HMAS *Vampire* has been hit and sunk while escorting the British light aircraft carrier *Hermes* off Ceylon. Joe Alexander records Curtin's renewed anger with the British prime minister:

> Curtin very bitter about Churchill today. Says he will not take advice of his chiefs of staff. He refused to concentrate naval strength in the Indian Ocean and then the Americans refused also. Result is British and Australian fleets being destroyed

piecemeal. We have just lost the *Vampire*. Curtin says it is wonderful how Churchill gets absolution for every mistake.

Curtin is also angry about Churchill's offer to divert two British divisions to Australia if the need arose, telling Churchill 'our advisers observe that, should Japan be able to launch an invasion on the scale mentioned by you, she would have such command of the sea that it would probably be impossible to reinforce Australia to any great extent by seaborne forces'.

Curtin's defence advisers are right. Churchill has been taking a gamble, and the British troops are highly unlikely to be available if Australia is subjected to a major invasion. Churchill originally made his offer in late March, saying the divisions would be going around the Cape of Good Hope in late April or early May. He immediately corrects this on 1 April to say that only one infantry division would be rounding the Cape at this time and an armoured division would follow one month later. As time goes on, the projected 'rounding the Cape' stretches out to 'June or July' – by which time the immediate crisis is over. The point is, these British troops would not have been available at the critical time of Australia's need, despite the promises and Australia's traditional expectations of assistance in times of threat in return for the nation's significant sacrifices for the British empire.

At the Hashirajima anchorage on the Inland Sea, the spring rains come, and the cherry blossoms begin to make their long-awaited appearance on surrounding islands.

The commander-in-chief of the Combined Fleet, Admiral Yamamoto, is keen to meet the young submariners who will soon depart for operations against Sydney and Madagascar. Seven officers and seven petty officers from the midget submarines come on board the *Yamato* with their senior officers, including Vice Admiral Teruhisa Komatsu of the Sixth Fleet.

Yamamoto wishes the men of the midget subs well in their

forthcoming missions across two vastly separated oceans. Before drinking formal farewell cups of sake, he makes a special plea to the young submariners to do everything to ensure their safe return. His chief of staff, Admiral Ugaki, is moved by the spirit of the submariners, but in his diary he has already consigned them to death:

> I wanted to give them a hearty send-off and wish them a brilliant success and the best of luck. Especially to those young sub-lieutenants and ensigns of the midget sub crews, being confident of their skill and with firm determination to die for their country, which I could sense, must be called noble and exalted. With this spirit the foundation of the empire can be considered safe. Again I wish them the best of luck in the war.

At Keiu Matsuo's request, his mother Matsue, father Tsuruhiko, sister Fujie, and older brother Jikyo arrive by train on 29 March, knowing that he is going away on a mission and is unlikely to return. 'When we arrived we couldn't see him for tears,' sister Fujie says. Meeting in a navy *ryokan* or inn, Keiu assures his parents of his love and respect. Mrs Matsuo at the inn notices that Keiu's eyes are watery and his skin pale. She asks him if he has been drinking too much and he says 'no'. He goes out drinking with Jikyo. In one of Kure's many drinking establishments, Keiu asks his brother to tell his fiancée, Toshiko Kinoshita, the beautiful daughter of a naval officer, that their engagement must be broken. He will not be returning.

After the formalities on the *Yamato*, the surface ships and mother submarines with their midgets leave the anchorage. One force heads for the southern Indian Ocean via Penang. The other force sails in the direction of the east coast of Australia, via the Japanese Pacific island of Truk. Watching them depart, Ugaki notes mournfully: 'Spring rain was falling gently as if it was lamenting over their departure.'

Japan is well advanced on a plan to terrorise Australia's largest city. Four midget submarines are designated to attack Sydney Harbour. But one of the large support submarines has been damaged in an enemy attack and cannot make it to the rendezvous at Truk island, leaving three large submarines carrying midget subs to Sydney.

Because their midget submarine is not available, Katsuhisa Ban and his navigator, Mamoru Ashibe, are ruled out of the Sydney attack. After all their training and dedication, they are devastated. Ban's friend Jikyo Ishino, a crewman aboard the support ship *Chiyoda*, sees Ban's reaction. 'He said to me, "Oh my God, I've missed out."'

With the shelving of his strategy for an invasion of Australia, Baron Tomioka of Naval General Staff moved on to more immediate concerns. In time, he would be forced to accept that the proposal might well have been foolhardy. But after the war, he indicated that at the time he hadn't abandoned his dream of invasion:

> Speaking with the army, I was told it was not possible to occupy Australia. The army was set up in the north and could not spare another five or six divisions. Given Japan's military strength, such a strategy would be foolhardy. I see, I thought. There is logic in that. It would be foolhardy. But the war has started. We must win. We must destroy the enemy.

For now, he merely put the Australian plan aside, and travelled down to the *Yamato* to initiate discussions about future operations. Knowing of Yamamoto's plan to invade Midway, which was opposed at General Staff headquarters, he tried to construct a compromise. In talks with Yamamoto's senior planner, Captain Kameto Kuroshima – now dubbed the navy's 'god of operations' – Tomioka agreed that Midway could be supported, if the Aleutians to the cold north were included. They also agreed that after Midway and the Aleutians, the invasion of Fiji and Samoa would follow.

Having evicted the British from the Indian Ocean, the commander-in-chief of Combined Fleet was now concentrating on 'eastern operations'. The invasion of the Midway Islands would expand Japan's defence line 3700 kilometres to the east, within striking distance of Pearl Harbor. Yamamoto reasoned correctly that such an attack would draw out the American fleet. At last the commander-in-chief saw the opportunity of smashing the US navy in the much-touted 'decisive battle'.

Naval General Staff eventually came around to the view that Australia should be isolated first before any invasion. In Tomioka's view, once Hawaii had been occupied the invasion of Australia should quickly follow:

> No matter what happens, in order to win we simply cannot allow the enemy to use Australia. If the enemy is not able to prepare themselves yet, then we can take Australia. If things continue as they are and two years slip by . . . and then it starts to fully utilise Australia, Japan will most likely be unable to oppose such a force.

But this was a point Tomioka still could not win: 'With that in mind I discussed and negotiated the matter, but to no success. Anywhere but Australia; there was simply nothing the navy alone could do. Resigned to that fact, we set off for Guadalcanal and Port Moresby . . . Discrepancies in strategic thinking began to emerge between the Combined Fleet headquarters and Army Command. Headquarters were worried that if we didn't take Midway, America would attack mainland Japan . . . The Army wanted to isolate Australia from America by stretching out to the southeast and setting up submarine bases and some air bases . . . It was at this point that the argument became particularly heated. And thinking back on it, I realise that that was the argument that decided the fate of the Japanese navy.'

Although the army strongly opposed the Midway plan, it was unable to prevent it proceeding; Yamamoto threatened that the navy would go it alone if the army didn't cooperate. The conclusion was that the Imperial Navy would first take tiny Midway, and once that had been done, it would turn its attention back to isolating Australia from America.

Naval General Staff began work on plans to cut the entire Australian continent off from US supplies by occupying Fiji, Samoa, and New Caledonia, known as operation FS. But this plan was not a small or easy task, as it would still greatly extend Japan's original operations in the south-west Pacific. The United States was well aware of the importance of these islands for the protection of their new staging post, Australia, and quickly beat the Japanese to the punch by moving strong forces into the islands.

Admiral Yamamoto also wanted to take Port Moresby by 10 May, to strengthen Japan's strategic hold on the New Guinea islands and in part to help protect its huge new base at Rabaul, captured from the Australians. The establishment of a major Japanese air base at Port Moresby would threaten the northern and north-eastern regions of Australia.

Port Moresby was the key to Papua and it had to be secured in order to bring Australia within range of Japanese warships and bombers. High Command had agreed before the war to the 'seizure of important points in the Australia area' in its Basic War Plan. The American historian Samuel Eliot Morison wrote that the 'Australia area' presumably meant 'ports and airfields of Northern Queensland down to Townsville'. But as things developed, he said, the Japanese decided it was easier to acquire Moresby and places such as the New Hebrides and New Caledonia, serving equally to control the Coral Sea and force Australia out of the war.

Australians had heard stories of Japanese brutality for some years, especially in China, but there remained an element of doubt. Now they began hearing them from their own people, as survivors of the Japanese atrocities on New Britain reached Port Moresby. On 7 April, the *Sydney Morning Herald* carried 'almost incredible revelations' from three servicemen who had escaped the island.

One told of the massacre at Tol plantation near Rabaul, where the men were tied together in small groups and each party was taken into the jungle in different directions:

> My party was stopped after going a short distance. A Japanese officer drew his sword and ordered his men to fix bayonets. One Australian after another was detached from the party and sent into the bush with a Japanese soldier armed with a bayonet. Soon after we heard screams and wondered what was happening . . .
>
> One of our men asked to be shot, and this was done by the officer himself. Another of our fellows got loose some way and dashed into the bush, but the officer caught up with him and then ran his sword through his back and then shot him.
>
> After that several men were bayoneted only a few yards from me without being taken into the undergrowth.

Australians found it extremely difficult to come to terms with such atrocities. Curtin at first said they were not proven. The *Herald*'s Joe Alexander also thought the horror stories unlikely, as he wrote in his diary: 'There is an overwhelming weight of circumstantial evidence against the atrocity charges against the Japanese since they entered the war.'

Curtin was hoping that the allegations were untrue. The government was concerned for the relatives of the victims of atrocities, and worried about the effect such news might have on the well-being of Australian POWs still being held. Its ministers couldn't know that thousands of Australian prisoners of the Japanese, especially those captured in Malaya and Singapore, would soon suffer the most appalling and prolonged atrocities and ill-treatment on the Thai–Burma railway.

There are indications that in late April Curtin received word which suggested that Japanese attention had turned towards an invasion of India, rather than Australia. The intelligence was not definitive and Curtin appears to have chosen to ignore it. US 'Magic' intelligence intercepts of Japanese diplomatic traffic on 18 April had reported a conversation between Hitler's ambassador in Tokyo, General Eugen Ott, and Japan's foreign minister, Shigenori Togo. According to the 'Magic' summary:

> Ott said that he would like to ask whether Japan's future attacks were to be centred in India or Australia... Judging from these Japanese operations he said he was thinking that probably it was the former. In reply to this the Minister [Togo] said, although Japan had opened attacks on Ceylon and ports north of that, gradually they would extend operations to Western Indian Seas, and he presumed this would no doubt coincide with Germany's wishes.

Togo apparently didn't mention Australia or the word invasion. For his part, Togo and his Foreign Office had no doubt where Japan would attack next.

In late April, General MacArthur gave Curtin advance warning that there would be a Japanese invasion of Port Moresby in early May. He had received the news through highly secret Magic intercepts of the Japanese navy, in which Australian code-breakers played a significant part in a joint Allied operation. Curtin confided in Alexander, who wrote in his diary: 'Today Curtin told me what I have been long expecting to hear. He said there were signs of heavy Japanese concentrations in the Bismarck Archipelago [north of New Britain in the New Guinea islands]. He added that the newspapers were treating the war against Japan far too optimistically. It seems from his manner that he expects an early heavy attack.'

Parliament met the following day, 29 April, and the prime minister publicly revealed his renewed concerns about a Japanese invasion. Journalist Joe Alexander recalled the air of presentiment that hung over the House:

Curtin gave a review of the war in which he said the Government regarded an outright Japanese attack on Australia as a constant and undiminished. He declared: 'We will yield no part of Australia to the enemy.'

Although the Japanese have lost 130 planes in the New Guinea fighting zones in recent weeks, and more than 100 are damaged, the Japanese position is not materially weakened, Curtin said.

Curtin's concerns are fully justified. Aboard the flagship in the Inland Sea, Admiral Ugaki is brimming with confidence. The islands all around are fresh and green in the warming spring air 'floating on the sea', as Ugaki joyfully puts it in verse. Full-scale war games are being held over four days on the covered fore mess deck of the *Yamato*. Numerous senior officers visit the battleship, putting their views. But Ugaki is a poor referee. He will only listen to those who agree with his radical plans. He clashes with Admiral Kondo, who thinks the Midway invasion is fraught with danger. Ugaki is superintendant, chief judge and commander in chief of one of the forces on the war games table. Taking Midway is centre of attention, but Ugaki has demanded of his planners that they look ahead: '... we made all speed to bring the scene up to an invasion of Hawaii', after the capture of Midway and the Aleutian islands, Ugaki tells his diary. Ugaki plans that the carrier strike fleet of Admiral Nagumo will return to Truk from Midway, replenish and then sail south for attacks on New Caledonia and Fiji. As the doyen of US naval historians, Gorden W. Prange, describes it, the Nagumo fleet then will turn southwest:

> ... Nagumo's carrier force would launch air attacks against Sydney and other key points of southeast Australia.

At the conclusion of the study conferences for the war games, Admiral Yamamoto tells his commanders in chief: '... we must keep on striking offensively at the enemy's weak points one after another. This will be the central aim of our second phase operations.'

This new carrier-based attack plan on Australia would be followed by the occupation of Hawaii. But the Imperial Navy is getting ahead of itself. Imperial orders soon will come in approving merely the first stage – the invasion of Midway and the Aleutians only.

Now Curtin is told by MacArthur that there has been a great deal more happening in the Coral Sea. Curtin is worried, testy and irritable. The press sense big developments. Nerves are on edge.

Reporters ask if there are important movements occurring. Curtin replies:

> Great things are in train. I'll soon be known whether Australia is to be invaded or not. Within 48 hours we will know.

Saturday, 8 May, was the last scheduled day of the House of Representatives' sittings. Late in the day, the prime minister rose in the chamber. Members – distracted and anxious to return home – thought he would move to adjourn, but as soon as Curtin began talking, it was clear that he was speaking off the cuff and with great emotion. Journalists, hearing the prime minister's tone, ran from their rooms to the press gallery. This would be one of his shortest speeches but at the end of it, tears would fill the eyes of many present, including the reporters.

Curtin had just received a communiqué from MacArthur. A great naval battle was now in progress. Events were now taking place he said, that were of crucial importance to the conduct of the war:

> If it should go advantageously, we shall have cause for great gratitude and our position will then be a little clearer. But if we should not have the advantages from this battle for which we hope, all that confronts us is a sterner ordeal, a greater and graver responsibility.

> ... As I speak, those who are participating in the engagement are conforming to the sternest discipline and are subjecting themselves with all that they have – it may be for many of them the 'last full measure of their devotion' – to accomplish the increased safety and security of this territory.

The fate of Port Moresby, Australia's base, was suddenly on a knife's edge and, in turn, the terrible reality of an invasion on mainland Australia loomed before the national parliament. If Moresby fell, it was not hard to see that mainland Australia could follow.

Within a few hours, radio broadcasts in Tokyo claimed a great naval victory in the Coral Sea to the north-east of Australia. Several Allied ships had been sunk, including the US aircraft carriers *Yorktown* and *Saratoga*, and a battleship of the California class. The Japanese claimed that a British battleship and cruiser of the Canberra class had also been damaged.

Curtin, shocked, made a broadcast to the nation:

> Invasion is a menace capable hourly of becoming an actuality. I tell you bluntly that the whole world may very well shake within the next few weeks under the blows that full-scale warfare will strike – and Australia cannot escape a blow. We face vital, perilous weeks fraught with exceedingly important happenings for Australia.

Yet Australians woke to victorious newspaper headlines next day: GREAT NAVAL BATTLE IN CORAL SEA. TEN JAPANESE VESSELS SUNK, the *Sydney Morning Herald* proclaimed.

Although it was achieved at considerable cost, the Allies had forced the Japanese to abandon their seaborne invasion of Port Moresby. The Japanese had two invasion forces, a minor one involved in the invasion of Tulagi in the Solomons, and a larger force steaming towards Papua. They were supported by aircraft from bases to the north, and by two naval forces containing a small aircraft carrier, the *Shoho*, sailing with 14 heavily loaded transport ships and several cruisers. The heavy aircraft carriers *Shokaku* and *Zuikaku*, together with escorting cruisers and destroyers, provided additional air cover.

Admiral Chester Nimitz, commander-in-chief of the US Pacific Fleet, deployed two carrier groups. As well, an Allied naval squadron known as Anzac force was deployed from the south, commanded by an Australian-born officer, Rear Admiral John Crace, of the Royal Navy. It consisted of the cruiser HMAS *Australia*, the flagship HMAS *Hobart*, and the heavy cruiser USS *Chicago*, supported by destroyers.

The Battle of the Coral Sea was a new form of naval engagement. For two days, aircraft launched from opposing carriers which never sighted each other hunted and destroyed enemy forces. The Americans lost the carrier USS *Lexington*, a destroyer, and a fleet oiler; the carrier USS *Yorktown* was damaged, but not sunk as the Japanese had claimed. The Japanese lost the *Shoho*, a destroyer, and some smaller ships. *Shoho* was the first carrier the Japanese navy had lost since the war started. As well, the carrier *Shokaku* received major bomb damage, and many of *Zuikaku*'s aircraft were destroyed. Both carriers were put out of action long enough to miss the crucial engagement at Midway.

Disgusted by his side's failure to capture Port Moresby, Admiral Ugaki recorded the event with sarcasm: 'This evening Imperial Headquarters made public the war result since yesterday and made it out to be the most significant gift to the nation . . .' Japan could claim a tactical victory in the Coral Sea, since it had inflicted more damage on the enemy, but it was also a strategic defeat, the Japanese navy's first since the war opened. The troopships in the invasion fleet regrouped at Rabaul; that was the end of a Japanese amphibious landing at Port Moresby. In a change of strategy, the Japanese would plan to take the Australian base by landing their troops on the north coast of Papua and marching them south west over the Kokoda Trail.

But the threat to Australia remained very real. Not even President Roosevelt could guess if Australia was safe in May 1942. In a signal to MacArthur, Roosevelt said: 'I wish you would let me have your personal guess on whether Japan will continue large operations against India and Ceylon or will stop at approximately the Calcutta line. Also, as to whether an all out attack will be launched against Australia.'

In Melbourne, General MacArthur thought that, for the time being at least, the Japanese had probably abandoned any attempt to occupy Port Moresby or obtain a foothold on mainland Australia. But he did not discount the threat to Australia, calling on President Roosevelt to send aircraft carriers and an additional 500 aircraft:

> At this time there are present all the elements to produce another disaster. If serious pressure were applied against Australia prior to the development of adequate and balanced land, sea and air forces, the situation would be extremely precarious . . . the enemy, moving freely by water, has a preponderant advantage.

MacArthur's request, backed up by Admiral King, created a furore in Washington's military planning circles, which now were preparing for a major offensive against Germany. Roosevelt decided that US forces in the Pacific were sufficient to prevent a large-scale Japanese offensive against Australia or New Zealand. American war supplies and reinforcements to Australia continued as previously planned, and were not increased on the scale envisaged by MacArthur and King.

At this time, Australia's governor-general (2003–2008) Mike Jeffery clearly remembers the construction and provisioning of an air raid shelter in his family's backyard in outer suburban Perth when he was a boy.

These were the most perilous months in the history of Australia, and the people who lived through it, still remember how exposed they felt. We feared invasion of our undermanned and ill-prepared island continent.

General Jeffery sees the Battle of the Coral Sea as the indispensable prelude to success at Midway, meaning the end of Japanese expansion southward and having made it largely impossible for Japan adequately to sustain its existing forces in the Pacific. 'Japan could never again threaten Australia and New Zealand with blockade or invasion.'

17

BOLD, NEW TARGETS

In the early hours of 13 May, the large Japanese submarine *I-29* reconnoitres off Sydney. As day breaks, the crew scan the coast through powerful binoculars, looking out for warships. Early next morning ratings rush on deck in the dark. A float plane is taken out of a sealed hangar on the deck. Its wings and floats are fitted quickly, then the plane is catapulted from the deck of the submarine.

This is the first of at least three reconnaissance flights the Japanese make over Sydney in the days before launching their midget submarine raid. On 23 May, the reconnaissance plane is again launched from the *I-29*, this time after daybreak. The pilot reports a number of good targets, including a large cruiser or battleship at Cockatoo Island, apparently being repaired under bright lights. At least four destroyers and several merchant ships also are sighted.

Despite the brazenness of these missions, Australia's civil and military authorities appear blind to evidence warning of a Japanese attack on the major port of Sydney. The city's distance from the vulnerable north of Australia mitigates against the highest levels of preparedness.

In Canberra, the prime minister is preoccupied by continuing strike action, and the failure of the left-wing minister for labour and national service, Eddie Ward, to ameliorate it. Joe Alexander tells his diary: 'There is great anxiety among ministers about the coal stoppages. All the mines out yesterday were at work today but two other mines have stopped . . . Ward is impudently thwarting Curtin's efforts to deal firmly with the disaffected miners.'

The prime minister, frustrated, pleads in parliament: 'In the name of Australia . . . I call upon the miners to go back tomorrow to work . . . if they do not go back, the Government will invoke all its authority to compel them to do so.' The miners do not respond, and the government serves a statutory order on them. Curtin begins a series of meetings with unionists and mine owners to secure a temporary agreement on how future disputes can be handled.

Wartime living conditions in Australia are changing rapidly. The federal government has already announced that it is restricting liquor trading to seven hours per day. Liquor is in short supply and the shortages will only grow more severe. In the cities, panic shopping to purchase clothes has broken out, following Curtin's announcement that the sale of clothing will be limited, with an enforced 25 per cent reduction in retail stock. The government's aim is to reduce non-essential manufacturing, but the sale of clothes rationed by coupon comes as a rude shock to many civilians. Curtin urges Australians to avoid buying new clothes if old ones will do; he is largely ignored, of course. The scene in major stores all over Australia is like a pre-war bargain hunt on sale day.

In Melbourne, several department stores and smaller clothing outlets close their doors by 11 a.m. Joe Alexander writes with disgust: 'Chaotic scenes continue in the cities . . . Australia is about to feel the pinch of war and this spoiled, pampered and censorious people will not take kindly to the ordeal. They are more concerned with buying unnecessary clothes than with the powerful enemy concentrations in the north.'

Suddenly, Japan's war moves much closer to Australia's more populated shores. Having completed her aerial reconnaissance, the *I-29* heads north from Sydney watching for a tempting target. She attacks a Russian steamer, the *Wellen*, only 50 kilometres east of Newcastle. The steamer's crew return the submarine's gunfire and the merchantman escapes, only slightly damaged.

The naval officer in charge at Sydney, Rear Admiral Gerard Muirhead-Gould, suspends merchant ship departures from the ports of Sydney and Newcastle. An air and surface search is conducted; nothing is found, so the admiral prematurely lifts the suspension of sailings within 24 hours. The searches are also called off. The attack on the *Wellen* should have instigated the highest level alert, but authorities have other priorities, including the protection of convoys sailing with Australian troops to New Guinea.

Meanwhile, the mother ship *I-28* had missed her rendezvous at Truk island with the other craft involved in the Sydney operation.

On 17 May, she was spotted by an American submarine, the *Tautog*, on the surface and en route to Fremantle. The American fired a torpedo. The Japanese crewmen fired shells in return, but with a second torpedo, the *Tautog* blew the *I-28* apart. All hands were lost, and the organisers of the Sydney midget submarine raid were down one ship. Fate had taken a hand in the lives of the young men set to pilot the midget submarines.

At remote Truk, well to the north of Rabaul, the midget sub crew of Katsuhisa Ban and Mamoru Ashibe anxiously awaited the arrival of the mother sub, not knowing her fate. Ashibe wrote a final letter to his sister Mikiyo in Japan. It revealed a fun-loving, yet fatalistic, young man who felt he was already dead:

It is so hot here that I cannot sleep for more than three hours at night. But I am having fun with all the other young men here. I am part of the honorable special attack unit now, so I will adhere to what I have learned and fight with everything I have until the very end.

Coming back alive is of course not possible, I know. So I want you alone to please know, even if you have not yet received notice from the navy yet, that if you have received this letter, your brother has accomplished his military goal by at least destroying the enemy's ship and dying gracefully.

Our mother is old now, and all alone at home, so please don't say anything until you receive notice. There is no greater wish a man may for so long cherish than to be given the most honorable place for a soldier to die, as I have been . . . Mamoru Ashibe, First Petty Officer.

When the *I-28*'s destruction was confirmed, Ban and Ashibe especially felt devastated by the news. On 18 May, the surviving mother submarines, *I-22*, *I-24*, and *I-27*, took delivery of their midget subs from the *Chiyoda*, but, like an orphan, Ban and Ashibe's sub was left behind on the deck of the ship.

The submarine fleet sailed for Sydney, but disaster soon struck again. Sub-lieutenant Teiji Yamaki and his engineer-navigator, Shizuka Masumoto, were doing routine work on their midget *M-24* when a gas leak caused an explosion. Yamaki remembered Masumoto going over into the sea. The *M-24* searched for Masumoto for six hours without success. 'He was standing near the hatch and was blown up out through it and overboard. We never saw him again.'

Teiji Yamaki suffered burns to his feet and the midget aboard the *M-24* was damaged, so the mother sub returned to the Truk base to collect a new midget and a new crew. As Yamaki was carried to the hospital on the *Chiyoda*, he encountered Katsuhisa Ban, who was replacing him: 'We were already close friends at naval training school and during our training to become midget submarine commanders at Ourasaki beach we became like brothers.'

Ban and Ashibe's midget submarine was lifted aboard the *M-24*, and they set off for Sydney. Before departing Truk,

Katsuhisa Ban wrote a mournful letter to one of his brothers back in Japan:

> I hear that father passed away... and it took me quite by surprise. But now it has become a reality, it grieves me unspeakably to think that I have been unable to fulfil my duties as a son and that at this time of war I could not pay my final respects.
>
> It would make me very happy if father is still secretly watching my efforts [as] today, it was decided that Mr OOOO [referring to himself] will be sent to the front. Of course, I myself am not anticipating that I will return safely from this war, but I do have hopes for a successful outcome.
>
> Deep down in my heart I am filled with the gravity of my duty to my country, and because of this even the grief I feel following the news of father's death has gone beyond grief to increasingly give me the presence of mind to devote my efforts single-mindedly to the cause, to the extent that I feel this is my last act of filial duty to my lost father.

Ban told his brother that he might be asked to travel from his home to the Kure naval base. The proposed journey was almost certainly to collect Ban's final letters, photographs and hair and nail clippings, mementos of a young life for a grieving family. 'I pray that you will always stay in good health. And I want mother, too, who has been weak with sickness, to be strong. Please, my brother, ensure mother takes care of herself.'

In Japan, many years later, Teiji Yamaki, with tears in his eyes, recalled his friend Ban:

> The day before his departure [for Sydney] about 10 of the younger crew members, including myself and Ban, went to a restaurant on the Truk Islands. We had a farewell dinner for him... there must have been a bit of sake drunk and sashimi eaten, and a few songs sung. During dinner he said to me about

his orders, 'I am the only one able to do the job.' He said it bravely, but I really don't know what his true heart was.

One of Ban's brothers, Iwao, later recalled Katsuhisa's determination: 'After he left Japan on the way to undertake his duties in the south, my brother sent a letter written in beautiful calligraphy to our mother. It was clearly meant to be his last letter. The letter said: "At the time of crisis of our nation I am resolved to steer 000 [code for his craft] and drive it into the heart of an enemy battleship."'

Lieutenant Kenshi Chuman had been selected to be the commander of the Sydney operation. Friends, quoted in wartime Japanese newspapers, described his departure from Truk: 'He had completed all arrangements which had to be made. "Everything is all right. I pray that Providence may be with us." So saying, he walked into his room. Two hours later a friend, a lieutenant, went to wake him. He found him sleeping with a low snore. He felt like crying as he looked a hero in a peaceful slumber.'

Chuman had the face of a child. Friends remembered that he was always smiling and that he would stroll along the beach after training singing nursery songs.

'Be sure of catching big game,' one of the well-wishers at his farewell said. 'All right,' came the reply. There was a faint smile on his face. Afterwards, Chuman reportedly gave his lieutenant friend his bankbook. It contained 700 yen. 'If the worst happens,' Chuman said, 'please see to it that 500 yen will go to the surviving family of petty officer Takeshi Omori. As for the remainder it shall be used to pay for the school expenses of my younger brother.'

The friend was in tears, imploring him to return from the attack, reminding Chuman that dying for the emperor was not the only way of being loyal. The young commander reportedly replied: 'I shall not die until I have no doubt about the fate of the men under me.'

*

On a warm Monday evening in late May, after a staff conference to study future operations, the *Yamato*'s stewards delivered a picnic basket of food to the upper deck of the mighty battleship, still anchored at Hashirajima. Ugaki and his fellow officers quietly celebrated the start of the new second stage offensive operations with special treats. Sake arrived, a gift from the emperor, and a toast to his majesty was drunk.

Despite the gentleness of the evening, Ugaki's sharp mind was active. He mulled over the Coral Sea battle, not understanding what had gone wrong in the invasion attempt on Port Moresby. He noted that both sides were claiming victory. He thought maybe a poor relationship between the naval fleet and the air fleet was to blame.

On Wednesday, Emperor Hirohito entered the House of Representatives' chamber, wearing the uniform of commander-in-chief. He stood before a throne set in an alcove above and behind the speaker, and overlooking the assembled members of both houses of the Diet. As one, members in their frock coats and uniforms bowed deeply. Hirohito took his seat.

The emperor was in an ebullient mood over the progress of the Greater East Asia War, despite the setback in the Coral Sea. Hirohito's language was aggressive: 'Our expeditionary forces enhanced national dignity at home and abroad by smashing enemy forces everywhere and reducing their strongholds, while the ties with Our allies and friendly powers have been growingly tightened. We are deeply satisfied with this. We in confidence of the bravery and loyalty of Our subjects expect speedy achievements of the objective of the war.'

In a stirring address to the Diet, the prime minister, General Tojo, said the Japanese empire had been consolidated and its wartime economy strengthened to cope with depleted supplies. All the important resources for national defence in the southern regions, such as oil, rubber and tin, had fallen into Japanese hands. The empire had grown two and a half times in size.

Tojo, who was aware of the planned midget submarine attacks, had special words of warning for the Australian people:

Now that the Southwest Pacific has completely been brought under our control through the concerted operations of the invincible Imperial Army and Navy, Australia has become the so-called orphan of the Pacific.

As the result of the Battle of the Coral Sea which recently took place in the vicinity of Australia, the naval forces in defense of that country have disappeared with nothing standing now to defend her before the onslaught of the Imperial Forces.

I wish, therefore, to remind the leaders of Australia at this juncture of my sincere desire that they will ponder what I had previously stated in this House, perceiving the international situation and considering Australia's geographical environments, and then courageously and speedily decide upon her most important step.

Tojo told the Diet that the naval forces of Britain and the United States had been 'virtually exterminated' in the Pacific and Indian oceans. As the prime minister spoke, most of the Combined Fleet was either already at sea, or about to sail for Midway or the Aleutian islands. Aboard the *Yamato*, Admiral Yamamoto was preparing to go to sea – not that his flagship would venture even close to the action.

He brushed a letter to his mistress and great love, Chiyoko Kawai, the former geisha with whom he had just spent four nights at a traditional inn at Kure: 'I will devote all my energy to fulfilling my duty to my country to the very end – and then I want us to abandon everything and escape from the world to be really alone together.' Yamamoto signed off with a little verse: 'Today too I ache for you/ Calling your name/ Again and again/ And pressing kisses/ Upon your picture.'

The risks that Admiral Yamamoto and his colleagues now faced were great: nothing less than Japan's naval power and prestige was at stake. A massive fleet was being deployed, far larger than the one that had attacked Pearl Harbor six months earlier, and even stronger than the entire US Pacific Fleet. As ships began departing on the afternoon of Thursday, 28 May, senior officers of some of those destined for the Midway invasion came on board the *Yamato* to say farewell. The carrier force of Admiral Chuichi Nagumo included the aircraft carriers *Akagi*, *Kaga*, *Hiryu* and *Soryu*.

Twelve transports carrying some 5000 troops to capture Midway left Saipan on 28 May. A further 16 vessels, including two battleships and the carrier *Zuiho*, sailed from Hashirajima anchorage on 29 May. In all, 11 battleships, eight carriers, 23 cruisers, 65 destroyers, and 90 auxiliary ships left Japanese ports for the Midway and Aleutian islands operations.

18

THE BOY WHO SAW THE JAPANESE

In Canberra, Prime Minister Curtin is handed a cable from London marked 'Most Secret. For Curtin Alone'. It's Thursday, 28 May. The Midway fleet is leaving the Inland Sea of Japan. In three days, the Japanese submarines will attack Sydney Harbour.

Curtin is about to receive crushing news. Bert Evatt has been sent to London and Washington to plead Australia's case to help prevent a Japanese invasion. In briefing the external affairs minister, Curtin told him that if an invasion occurred, Britain would be 'greatly indicted', considering Australia's sacrifice of 60,000 men in World War I. But, in London, Evatt has discovered that both the US and Britain regard the war in the Pacific as nothing but a holding or defensive operation.

At this crucial time, Churchill and Roosevelt have agreed jointly that regardless of Japan's entry into the war, Germany remains the primary enemy. Evatt reports to Curtin bitterly: 'In a phrase it was "beat Hitler first". The existence of this written agreement came as a great surprise to myself and I have no doubt you. We were not consulted on the matter.'

The minister has also uncovered an Allied aide-memoire of

recent origin that asserts, 'for a number of reasons, some very unconvincing', that a full-scale invasion of Australia is unlikely. The British paper gives six reasons why Australia is not about to face invasion. These include the enormous additional Japanese commitment needed, which rules out a land invasion of northern Australia, plus the great risks presented by the US Pacific Fleet.

The document suggests that Australia would be given 'all practicable help' to defend the country as a base for the future offensive against Japan. But this promise is nullified by a warning that the 'utmost care should be taken remembering the overall war strategy' of Britain and the United States.

According to Evatt, this means that Britain will not divert large land forces to Australia until it is 'reasonably clear that Japan will strike heavily'. The minister, who is meeting regularly with Churchill and his defence chiefs, has added a rather curious note which runs counter to Churchill's known position: 'I should add that the Prime Minister and Chiefs of Staff adhere to the view that a full-scale invasion of Australia is still highly probable.' But this opinion is not explained further.

Curtin does not overreact to the 'beat Hitler first' policy. He thanks Churchill for his promises of support, as reported by Evatt, including an offer of several squadrons of Spitfires – an offer which, once again, is quickly whittled down by the British. The Australian prime minister is stuck between a rock and a hard place; his government's more dire pleas for British help have already played into the hands of the Japanese propagandists, who repeatedly seek to convince Australians that their position is hopeless.

After General Tojo's threatening address to the Diet, the Japanese army begins to examine ways to step up its psychological warfare. The generals are trying to force Australia into 'neutrality'. They pursue a strategy 'to accurately illustrate Japan's true intention to Australia's leaders, namely to respect the sovereignty of Australia's territories in return for Australia promising to maintain neutrality'. The ultimate aim is to incorporate Australia politically into the Japanese fold; in the short term, the strategy would remove Australia from the war.

The Japanese chief of the operations, Bureau of Army General Staff, General Shinichi Tanaka, investigates the feasibility of several methods of coercion, including the despatch of special emissaries to Australia. He also considers political manoeuvres, using the Australian government representative in New Caledonia and the undersea telegraph cable between Sydney and Noumea.

Tanaka argues that if Australia does not respond, Japan should step up attacks on her territory in order to disrupt her contact with other governments. The Imperial Army high command favours the FS operation: the Japanese invasion of key areas in the islands of New Guinea and Papua, and of Fiji, New Caledonia, and Samoa, that will seriously jolt the Australian leadership. Suddenly, another invasion attempt on Port Moresby is firmly back on the agenda.

On Friday, 29 May, one hour and 11 minutes before sunset, a Yokusuka E14Y-4s, or 'Glen' to the US, seaplane takes off from a Japanese submarine and heads west to Sydney Harbour. There are two of these subs operating off Sydney late in May. The *I-29* has been in the region for some time and the *I-21* has just arrived, making the dash from Auckland.

Ian Spring is a seven-year-old Sydneysider with an intense interest in aircraft. Like many boys of his age, he wants to be a fighter pilot, an ambition he will later fulfil. He is playing on a patch of lawn in front of the block of flats where his family lives in Addison Road, Manly, on the northern side of Sydney Harbour.

Manly, like many other suburbs and towns on the coast, is in a state of anxiety. Some residents are selling their homes, or temporarily abandoning them to move to the mountains. Large areas of the Manly peninsula, including North Head, have been requisitioned for defence purposes. Some of the iconic Norfolk pines behind the beach have been cut down to afford a better field of fire for the machineguns installed at the girls' grammar school.

The boy senses the war coming closer: 'As I played there I heard a very strange aeroplane noise coming from the north-east, looked up and saw a very unusual-looking float plane – the low height at which the aeroplane was flying, its unusual noise, and the unfamiliar appearance of the aeroplane from the front drew my sharp attention.'

It is a low-wing float plane, with a radial engine, bottle green in colour. The location where the boy is playing is elevated, and he can see the plane close up: 'As the aeroplane flew across in front of me... at about 150 to 250 metres, something struck me as being quite strange about it, and I conceived the idea it was Japanese.'

The aircraft flies past in a general south-west direction and is quickly out of sight. Spring rushes inside to tell his mother, yelling out that he has seen a Japanese plane. She believes him, and goes next door to the home of an army sergeant, to report her son's sighting.

Amazingly, a small boy appears to have seen what Sydney's defenders can neither detect nor even comprehend. A Japanese flight over Sydney is utterly implausible in May 1942. Enemy aircraft would require a Japanese occupied airstrip – and there are none anywhere in range – or an aircraft carrier, which Sydney's defenders are confident they would detect.

As dust settles, lights are blazing, except for the lighthouse at Barrenjoey Headland, at the end of Sydney's northern beaches. The harbour is strung with navigation lights. Australian defence chiefs think that a full blackout is unnecessary. At the war cabinet, they have vetoed the introduction of a blackout policy for coastal Australia: '... a good "brownout" is all that is necessary, except in factories, which should be blacked out.'

The Japanese pilot flying over the harbour at dusk reports back that there is an American 'battleship' 400 metres east of Garden Island, with some large cruisers and a big troopship nearby. As the result of the reconnaissance flight, the date of the attack on the harbour is set for Sunday, 31 May. The participating submarines receive the following message from their commanding officer: 'I firmly believe [in] the victory by this golden opportunity, and I hope you could press the enemy with cool minds and annihilate the great enemy at a single stroke.'

Aboard the *I-21*, reconnaissance pilot Susumu Ito had become an expert on the geography of Sydney Harbour. Aided by Admiralty charts and aerial photographs of the harbour taken from Australian periodicals and books, he studied every anchorage, especially the naval base at Garden Island.

Early in the morning of 30 May, he took off from the deck of the *I-21*. It was a tricky manoeuvre. If his float plane was launched when the sub's bow was up, it would not reach flying speed by the time it left the ship, and could crash. Ito pressed the launch button as the sub pitched downwards in rough seas, catapulting his plane into a strong headwind. It was 2.45 a.m. when Ito turned west, climbing to 500 metres.

Encountering cloud, he descended over Sydney to 150 metres and lower. He saw his biggest worry as obstacles like electric cables across the harbour. 'I could see the lights of Sydney flashing ahead of me. We flew over South Head and I saw the lights from the houses. They were beautiful. Then there was the city and the Harbour Bridge, the symbol of Sydney.

'We were desperate to find a target, otherwise the midget-sub pilots would die for nothing. We circled around and came over Garden Island again, and there we saw two large-sized boats. "Looks like battleships to me," I yelled to my co-pilot Iwasaki. We were overjoyed.' The pair made sketches of the anchorage before returning over the harbour, heading east.

Phil Dulhunty, 18, an anti-aircraft gunner from Kempsey in northern New South Wales, was on duty on Sydney Harbour foreshore, and heard the Japanese plane's engine: 'The enemy was way away up in the Coral Sea. We'd just stand there bored stiff.

And I thought it was a big truck coming up the hill, and I thought, "That's funny." And then I saw this aeroplane fly by – a little seaplane. Naturally I thought it was off one of the American ships. We had the *Chicago* and quite a few other battleships in port, and I thought it was obviously one of the things off them.'

Not for one moment did gunner Phil Dulhunty seriously suspect that the aircraft he saw was an enemy one: 'I thought, "How could a Japanese plane come all the way down and be down here?" That was impossible.'

The submarine-launched reconnaissance missions were dangerous. When Ito flew back to the sub later, his plane could not land in the treacherous conditions. The old pilot smiles as recounts his narrow escape from drowning:

> The waves were very high and I crashed. The captain of the submarine called 'The plane's going to tip over'. I wasn't hurt. I have confidence in my own abilities. But I had a pistol and three cases of bullets so when you get into the water with your life jacket you don't float, even though I used to swim 20 kilometres a day ... I was choking on the seawater ... and splashing about when I was pulled out.

The crew on the submarine used large hammers to bash the plane's floats, until the floats finally filled with water, and the aircraft sank. Ito apologised to the captain for losing his plane. But he felt good about finding a target for the midget subs.

Two months after the reconnaissance flights and the midget sub attack, an official Navy Office report confirmed that enemy reconnaissance aircraft had been sighted and had been active over the Sydney area during the period 29–31 May.

The army artillery battery at Georges Heights, Middle Head, thought the reconnaissance plane was American, according to the Navy Office. The duty intelligence officer at Garden Island, Lieutenant Commander Percy Wilson received the report of the sighting by telephone, but was told 'there is no cause for alarm as it's an American Curtiss Falcon float plane'. Wilson was quite aware that the float planes on the *Chicago* were still on the cruiser's deck. He went over to the *Chicago* and 'frightened the wits out of the deck officer'.

The Navy Office summary also revealed that a passing New Zealand forces aircraft had detected a submarine off Sydney two days before the raid on the harbour:

> On 29th May, a signal was received from the New Zealand Naval Board reporting that D/F [direction finding] indications placed an enemy unit (probably a submarine) ... approximately 40 miles East South East of Sydney.

The Navy Office appears to have justified the appalling lack of defensive action over the New Zealand sighting by saying: 'There had, however, been no reported enemy submarine activity on the East Coast of Australia since 2020 16th May, when the Soviet vessel *Wellen* was gunned by a submarine ... 31 miles from Nobby's Light, Newcastle.'

It seems inconceivable that an enemy submarine can surface and attack a small freighter with its deck gun, and then be dismissed after a search of only 24 hours. It is even more astounding when an Allied aircraft reports a submarine just east south-east of the most important harbour in the region, and, again, little action is taken.

Apart from one 24-hour period of patrols after the *Wellen* attack, no special action had been taken off the coast to protect Sydney from attack.

Far away across the Indian Ocean, a midget submarine operation was in progress off the island of Madagascar, off the east coast of the African continent.

The Vichy French had controlled the port on Diego Suarez Bay, at the northern tip of the great island, until 7 May 1942; then, the old battleship HMS *Ramillies* began a bombardment, and soon after occupied the port with little opposition. On 29 May, a Japanese float plane took off from the *I-10*, near Diego Suarez. The aircraft returned reporting a battleship and other British warships in the harbour. The British identified the enemy aircraft and responded quickly. The *Ramillies* anchored in a new location in the harbour, while British aircraft mounted anti-submarine patrols.

There were five large submarines off the port, three carrying two-man midget submarines on their decks. One midget had mechanical trouble and was left out of the attack. Two were launched off the bay on 30 May, a clear, moonlit evening. The harbour was difficult to negotiate at night with treacherous reefs and strong currents. One midget made it safely into the main anchorage of Antisirane, while the other apparently struck a reef.

The *Ramillies* was discovered, and the first torpedo was fired by the operational midget sub. The battleship exploded. Only quick work by all hands kept her afloat. An hour later a torpedo hit a British tanker and she settled on the shallow harbour bottom, her upper works still visible. Both ships were later recovered.

None of the submariners involved in the Diego Suarez attack made it back to their waiting mother subs. The British reported finding two Japanese on the island several days later. Both men were shot. According to Japanese propaganda sources, one of them died while rushing a machinegun post brandishing a pistol.

The Japanese reconnaissance flight over Diego Suarez Bay, in which the British accurately identified the aircraft circling as an enemy plane, came almost two days before the attack on Sydney Harbour. Unfortunately, no one informed Australia.

It felt good to be at sea again. Combined Fleet's commander-in-chief Admiral Yamamoto stood on the high bridge of the battleship *Yamato* as she slipped out of the Inland Sea in clear weather, closely patrolled by destroyers.

1942

The largest and most powerful battleship in the world had spent too much time at her buoy. But now the great *Yamato* was part of the vast supporting force for the Midway invasion. The flagship and the battleships that sailed with her, though, would remain hundreds of kilometres from the attacking carrier fleet.

Yamamoto's chief of staff, Admiral Ugaki, was concerned about submarines as the ship lifted her speed to 18 knots under a bright full moon. The fleet soon ran into high winds and rough seas. Ugaki worried about the inadequate screen provided by the destroyers as the fleet zigzagged, and he ordered the *Yamato* to increase speed.

Heavy seas and rain continued the following day, Sunday, 31 May. A radio intercept indicated that enemy aircraft and submarines in the Aleutian islands, Hawaiian islands and the mid-Pacific were up to something. Despite his immediate worries about the Midway invasion and the expected crucial battle with the American fleet, Ugaki took time to reflect on the midget submarine operations far away. He wrote in his diary:

> The east detachment of the Eighth Sub Squadron is scheduled to converge upon Sydney and attack *Warspite* and two heavy cruisers in that harbour with midget submarines, taking advantage of tonight's moonlight. Can they successfully knock out the remnant left from the Coral Sea battle?

On the eve of the Battle of Midway, as the *Yamato* sails from Hashirajima well behind the carrier strike force, Ugaki fretted that the midget subs should not miss 'big game' by sticking too closely to detailed operational plans. That Ugaki should spend time worrying about the midget submarine attacks, at a time when Japan is risking her most powerful fleet, defies comprehension. In fact, the five *I*-class mother submarines now lay silently and secretly underwater in position, about 55 kilometres north-east of Sydney Heads, about to unleash war on Sydney's doorstep.

19

ROWBOAT RECONNAISSANCE

Sunday, 31 May, dawned fine and warm in Canberra. Joe Alexander, who had feared so much for Australia's future, was in the brightest of moods. A former minister had assured the *Herald*'s bureau chief that if Australia could hold out until the end of May the country should be safe. Now, on the last day of the critical month, Alexander recorded in his diary his 'profound thanks' that Australia was still free:

> There has been no active invasion attempt though had we lost the Battle of the Coral Sea, an attempt would have been made before this. Yesterday Brett, Chief of the US Air Forces, says he has no fear for Australia. *Deo Gratia!*

But the threat has not passed. The future of the Pacific region hinges on the massive fleet heading towards Midway. If the remote atoll is taken by Japan, Australia and Hawaii are certain to be in line for occupation.

Sydney had now been monitored by the Japanese since 13 May. Off Sydney, five large Japanese submarines – the aircraft carrying subs *I-29* and *I-21* and the midget sub carriers *I-22, I-24* and *I-27* – begin moving underwater from a position off Port Hacking, south of Botany Bay, to the north until they are about four to six kilometres east of the Sydney Heads. During Sunday afternoon six young crewmen make their final preparations, checking and re-checking their midget subs until nothing more can be done. They write final farewell letters, placing locks of hair and fingernail clippings in envelopes. The letters are gathered to be taken back to Kure for copying and posting. Some make small gifts of money to colleagues aboard the big submarines who have assisted them. Others, like Lieutenant Keiu Matsuo, have their heads ceremoniously shaven like warriors of old.

Their letters are generally couched in the honourable warrior bravado tradition of the Samurai. The *M-24*'s commander, Katsuhisa Ban, writes: 'Nations that fear death will surely be destroyed – it is necessary for the youth of Japan to take notice of this.' At 22, his own youth has been short-lived.

Petty Officer Masao Tsuzuku, 24, writes stoically: 'I have nothing to regret – take care of my parents and sisters.' Tsuzuku, the son of a farmer from Minowa, Chiba, has been personally selected for the mission by Matsuo, the naval agent who spied on Honolulu before Pearl Harbor. They will sail into Sydney Harbour together aboard the *M-22*.

At 4.54 p.m., the sun sets behind the clouds over Sydney. Below the sea, Matsuo and Tsuzuku climb up through the mother sub and enter a tight hatch located in the floor of the midget. The midget hatch is only 45 centimetres wide, but the thin young crew have no trouble. Squeezing through the chute above it, the submariners have access to five extremely cramped compartments, each watertight in case the sub is flooded. Settling into the tiny control room, both Matsuo and Tsuzuku are in a high state of excitement and anxiety.

The *M-22*'s telephone cable to the mother vessel is cut and clamps are mechanically removed. As the mother sub gently dives, compressed air is released, sending the midget floating away on its own until its electric motor cuts in at 5.25 p.m. A few minutes later, slightly to the south, Chuman and Omori's *M-27* parts from its mother sub. Twelve minutes later, at 5.40 p.m., Ban and Ashibe's *M-24* is running free from a point 11 kilometres north-east of the harbour entrance, Sydney Heads; ironically, not very far from where they will finish.

Chuman and Omori enter the harbour just after 8.00 p.m. and turn south initially, intending to reach the anchorage of the largest warships. The *M-27* follows a large fishing boat heading for the eastern gate of a long boom stretched across the harbour.

But Chuman suddenly changes course, perhaps because of a shipping hazard or a mechanical defect. His midget sub rams the boom net, and partially mounts it, sticking out of the water. The engines race but the *M-27* is stuck fast, her propellers tangled in the sturdy metal rings of the net. Inside the sub, panic mounts as desperate attempts to free the sub are made.

Outside, from where Able Seaman Horrie Doyle stands, it's a hell of a cold, boring night far from the action. He feels the chill come in from the open waters beyond the Heads. Lucky, he thinks, that he put on his heavy coat. The 22-year-old is on watch aboard the *Yarroma*, an erstwhile pleasure cruiser now pressed into wartime service in the Channel Patrol Flotilla. The 'Hollywood Fleet' is the disparaging name Sydney folk have given the patrol. People can't take these former pleasure craft seriously. As they zip busily around the harbour they have become something of a joke, especially among the deep sea navy men.

But Horrie Doyle knows the *Yarroma* is special. As far as he is aware, she is the only member of the patrol fitted with 'hush-hush' submarine-detection gear. The sonar equipment is a bit of a nuisance, being located in the crew's living space. And it doesn't always work that well, especially on a Sunday with so much boat traffic around and re-echoes coming from the shore.

Sydney Harbour is also protected from submarines by the defence boom net across the harbour from Georges Head, near Obelisk Bay, to Green Point, on the northern end of Watsons Bay, close to the harbour mouth. More than five months after the start of war with Japan, construction of the net below the boom, made from large interlocking circles of steel, has not yet been completed. There are long gaps at both ends of the middle section.

Warning of submarine crossings is meant to come from indicator loops, cables on the harbour floor that detect metal passing over them. When a vessel passes, they record the event as 'signatures', rather like a seismic recording. The signatures can be read at the indicator loop station at the harbour entrance on South Head, but tonight two of the six indicator loops down harbour are not working.

Around 8.00 p.m., the loops record a vessel about half the length of a Manly ferry passing down harbour. But those on duty at the indicator loop station do not report the signature. The significance of the warning being scratched out on the roll of paper is not recognised.

Navy Office headquarters in Melbourne will later absolve the men who either don't notice the warning or misinterpret it. Its official report into the attack says: 'Although loop crossings (four in all) were registered, it was not until after the attack was over that they were connected with the Midget Submarines. They had been marked down as – (1) ferry, (2) tug, with barge, etc. There was a good deal of traffic on the night of the attack, and the confusion was this, to some extent, understandable.'

The *Yarroma* is inside the anti-submarine boom net covering the west channel. Horrie Doyle is also trying to keep a watch on the east channel, but in the dark it's hard, if not impossible. His boat rocks on the swells coming in from the Tasman Sea. His thoughts are interrupted by the sudden splashing of oars. Through the dark, he makes out a rowboat heading directly for him. 'Do you hear there?' Doyle shouts. 'What's your business?'

'I'm a watchman from the pontoon,' comes the reply. 'There's something at the net.' It is 8.15 p.m. War has come to Sydney Harbour, and the Royal Australian Navy receives the news via a civilian watchman in a rowboat. 'What is it,' Doyle calls, 'a fisherman in a

Starting point. Pictured is the harbour entrance at Hashirajima, the island off which the great ships of the Imperial Navy anchored before their forays into the Pacific. Here aboard the flagships, Combined Fleet officers debated an invasion of Australia.

Navy heartland. The officer candidate school at Etajima naval academy in the Bay of Hiroshima was built from a British design and bricks brought from England in 1893. It is almost the same today as when it produced officers for the Imperial Navy. Baron Sadatoshi Tomioka was born and graduated from the academy at Etajima.

Targeting Australia. These officers in the operations section of Naval General Staff used the maps and charts around them to plan and argue for an invasion of Australia. They include in the front row (left to right) bureau chief (then Captain) Sadatoshi Tomioka, Commander Prince Nobuhito Takamatsu, Emperor Hirohito's younger brother, and Tomioka's superior, Rear Admiral Shigeru Fukudome.

Sakamaki's disgrace. The midget submarine of Lieutenant Kazuo Sakamaki and Petty Officer Kiyoshi Inagaki washed up on a beach at Oahu after the attack on Pearl Harbor. Sakamaki surrendered, becoming the first POW for the United States. Inagaki's body was recovered from the sea.

Without hope. Lieutenant Keiu Matsuo, who shot himself in the midget submarine raid on Sydney Harbour in 1942, in formal summer uniform at his graduation at the Etajima naval academy, around 1941. He is pictured with his proud family: brother Jikyo, father Tsuruhiko and mother Matsue.

Zealous advocate. Chief of the operations section of Naval General Staff Baron Sadatoshi Tomioka famously said 'we can take Australia.' Tomioka pictured as a rear admiral, was a most enthusiastic proponent of invasion.

Plotting war. Commander-in-chief of the Combined Fleet, Admiral Isoroku Yamamoto, aboard the flagship IJNS *Nagato* at the start of the war.

Expansionist. Admiral Matome Ugaki, chief of staff to Admiral Yamamoto. Ugaki's wartime diary asked 'Advance to Australia, to India, attack Hawaii?' The diary recorded his preoccupation with death and the young men of the midget submarines.

Saving Australia. Colonel Takushiro Hattori was chief of the Imperial Army's operations planning staff and one-time secretary to Premier Tojo. Hattori fought successfully against the Imperial Navy's proposals in early 1942 to invade Australia.

Provocateur. General Hideki Tojo, Japan's premier at the outbreak of war, initially said, 'I think we will have few problems occupying not only Java and Sumatra but also Australia if things go on like this.' Later he denied interest in invading Australia.

Help arrives. Prime Minister John Curtin escorts General Douglas MacArthur into Parliament House, Canberra, during the critical stage of the Japanese threat to Australia in 1942. MacArthur would later say that Curtin saved Australia.

Curtin's friend. Japan's first ambassador to Australia, Tatsuo Kawai, in the garden of 'Carn Brea' at Auburn, Melbourne. He and John Curtin discussed iron ore as a way of preventing war. Kawai was placed under house arrest when war broke out. This photograph was presented to his American private secretary, Tamaye Tsutsumida.

Dire predictions. General Sir Thomas Blamey in Sydney before sailing to the United States with Elsie and John Curtin in 1944. Blamey earlier warned that had the Japanese wished to seize Curtin's home state of Western Australia in 1942, it could have fallen 'easy prey' to Japan.

Fishing mates. These happy anglers near their base in the Bay of Hiroshima include the commanders of two of the three midget submarines destroyed in the attack on Sydney in 1942. The two are Lieutenant Keiu Matsuo, front left, skipper of the *M-22*, who spied on Pearl Harbor, and Lieutenant Kenshi Chuman, rear left, who ran his midget, the *M-27*, onto the Sydney Harbour boom net. Both were killed.

Below: Fatal ride. A Japanese two-man midget submarine being carried on the deck of a mother sub. In advanced models, submariners entered the midget from the mother sub while under water. Midget operations largely ended in disaster and they kept large submarines from their primary task – sinking ships.

Death awaits. Prior to his departure for the midget submarine attack on Sydney and the death that he knows awaits him, Lieutenant Keiu Matsuo aboard the mother sub *I-22* has just had his head shaven by a friend, Lieutenant Muneaki Fujisawa (in the background), torpedo officer for the mother sub.

Tokyo's view. The midget submarine raid on Sydney Harbour was played up as a significant victory in Japanese newspapers, including the *Japan Times and Advertiser*. The news was suppressed for days after the raid while the Imperial Navy awaited the fate of the crewmen.

War of words. Bitter debate raged between prime ministers John Curtin and Winston Churchill over the Japanese threat to Australia in 1942. Curtin momentarily expected invasion. The British leader thought Curtin was 'panicky'. They later met amicably in London at the Dominion Prime Ministers' conference.

Below: Family grief. Small white caskets containing the ashes of four of the six submariners killed in the Sydney Harbour raid are carried by naval colleagues and followed by family members on the wharf at Yokohama in October 1942 after arriving from Australia with Ambassador Tatsuo Kawai.

Susumu Ito, a businessman from Iwakuni on the Bay of Hiroshima, displays a photograph of himself as a brash young Imperial Navy flying officer during the war. Ito flew over Sydney on reconnaissance missions and stood on the deck of a Japanese submarine as it shelled Newcastle and was in turn shelled.

Below: Selective memory. The entrance hall of the war memorial museum attached to the Yasukuni Shrine at Kudankita, Tokyo. The C56 steam locomotive is hailed as the engine used at the opening ceremony of the great feat of the Japanese Thai-Burma railway. No mention is made of the 160,000 Asian and Allied POWs who died building the railway.

Bob Wurth collection. (Photo, Willie Phua)

Bob Wurth collection

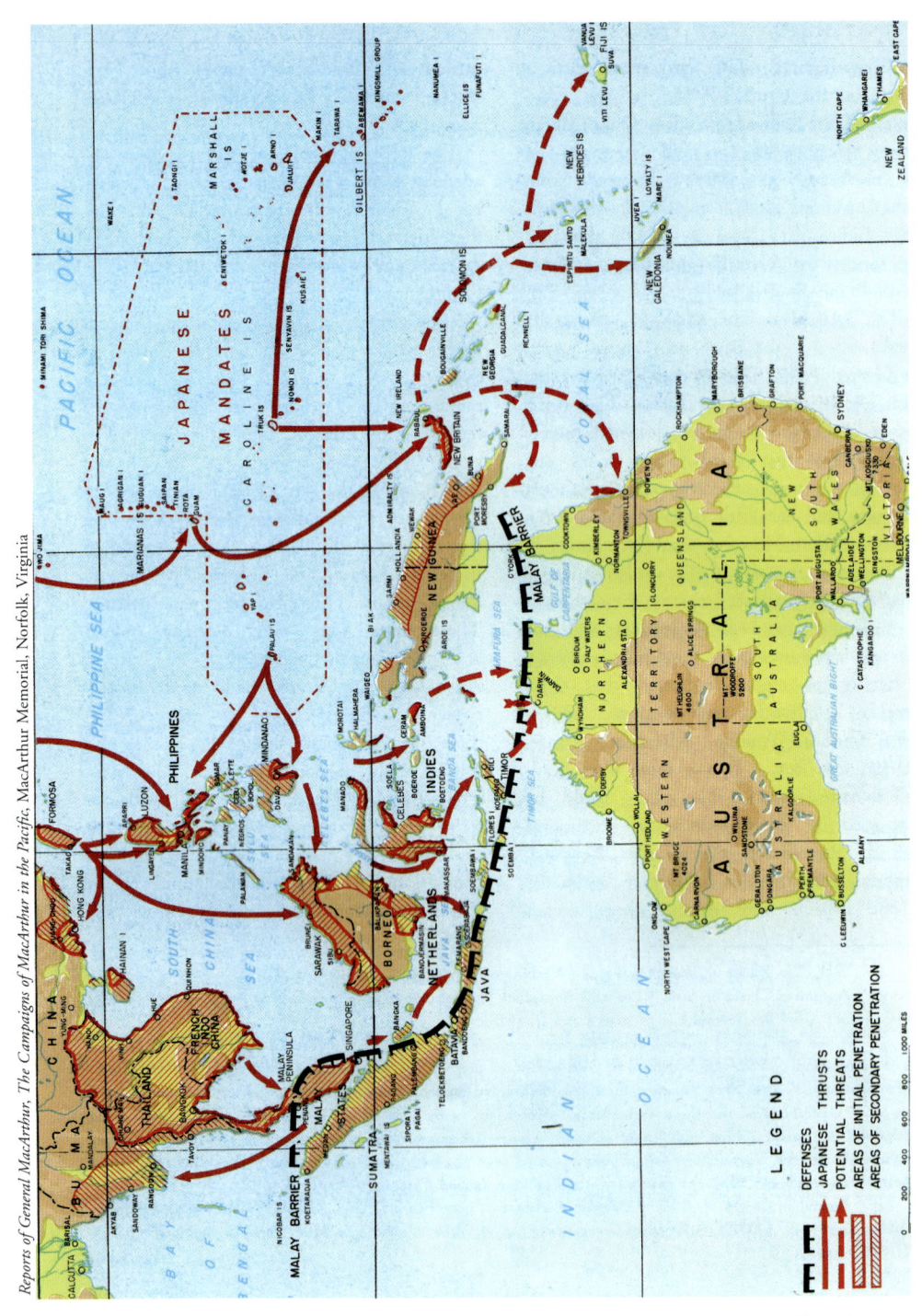

Disintegrating defences. The collapse of the 'Malay barrier' and the threat to Australia in early 1942, as mapped by General MacArthur's headquarters. 'The Japanese directly menaced the security of Australia,' MacArthur's senior officers wrote. The emphasis in this post-war map on the menace to Darwin and Townsville is shown.

The Campaign Plan: The 2nd Phase (February - April 1942)

Invasion scenario. Japan's second phase operations between February and April 1942, according to this map in the Yasukuni shrine museum in Tokyo. The dotted line around northern Australia refers to 'Australia invasion manoeuvres' [or 'operations']. The vertical words off the east coast of Australia refer to the Pacific theatre war zone. The line around New Caledonia, Fiji and Samoa indicates a blockade between the US and Australia. The line encircling southern Australia is a shipping route.

Taking Australia. Admiral Nobutake Kondo, one of Japan's most experienced naval officers, in 1942 drew up a plan for an 'Australia operation' which he said would have 'a rich chance of taking hold of American task forces'. But Admiral Yamamoto had other priorities.

Simple to subdue. General Tomoyuki Yamashita pictured during his trial in Manila in 1945 as an A-class war criminal, for which he was executed. Yamashita was quoted as saying it would have been 'simple to subdue Australia'.

Toxic parent. Vice Admiral Takijiru Onishi, the 'father of the Kamikazes', who conceived the plan to send thousands of young men to their deaths in suicide attacks. His memory and photograph are venerated today in the naval academy at Etajima.

Invasion activist. Rear Admiral Tamon Yamaguchi who proposed a crash ship and aircraft building campaign so that Japan could undertake widespread invasions in the Indian and Pacific oceans, including Australia, beginning in May 1942. He chose to die at sea.

Combined Fleet. The men who strongly influenced the destiny of the Imperial Navy and Japan in 1942 aboard their new flagship, the super battleship IJNS *Yamato*. The two officers in the centre of the front row are chief of staff Admiral Ugaki and, on his right, his commander-in-chief, Admiral Yamamoto.

Tragic giant. The super battleship IJNS *Yamato* during trials in late 1941. Called the world's largest battleship, but branded the *'Yamato Hotel'* by her Japanese detractors, she was the flagship for commander-in-chief Admiral Yamamoto and his chief of staff, Admiral Ugaki, when Australia was being discussed for possible invasion.

Bizarre mission. The super battleship IJNS *Yamato* – which had seen little fighting during the war – blows up on her idiotic suicide mission following massive attacks by US Navy carrier planes north of Okinawa on 7 April 1945. An escorting Japanese destroyer is at left.

Hiroshima Peace Memorial Museum

The cataclysm. Downtown Hiroshima in 1945 after the US atomic bomb blast. The city's exhibition building, now known as the 'peace dome', is in the foreground. After Hiroshima, President Truman warned the Japanese to surrender or face 'a rain of ruin from the air, the like of which has never been seen on this earth.' Nagasaki was next.

Naval Historical Center, Washington

Final assault. New midget submarines readied for the expected US invasion of Japan in dry dock at the Kure naval base in October 1945. There are at least four different types of midget submarines here. The majority are of the five-man 'Koryu' model. Japan concentrated on the production of suicide weapons towards the end of the war.

Fond tribute. General Douglas MacArthur gave this photograph to John Curtin in March 1944 inscribed with the words: 'To the Prime Minister who saved Australia in her hour of deadly peril. With the admiration and affection of Douglas MacArthur.'

US Army Signal Corps. Photographs collected by John Curtin family, John Curtin Prime Ministerial Library

Naval Historical Center, Washington

Final indignity. The chief advocate for capturing Australia, Rear Admiral Baron Sadatoshi Tomioka, in the Japanese surrender party aboard the USS *Missouri* in Tokyo Bay on 2 September 1945. He's in the middle of the second row between two Foreign Ministry officials in top hats. Tomioka was awed at the lack of apparent contempt demonstrated by the Americans on the day.

boat or a mine?' The watchman, James Cargill, employed by the Maritime Services Board, says he doesn't know, but he thought he ought to report it immediately.

Cargill later recalls the story slightly differently:

> He asked me what I thought it was and I told him I thought it was a submarine or a mine and I suggested he send a man with me and I would take him to it in the rowing boat. I then rowed almost alongside the obstacle, which had by this time come higher out of the water, and he said it was a submarine and asked me to put him back aboard the patrol boat as quickly as possible, which I did.

Despite the gaps in the boom net, Kenshi Chuman and Takeshi Omori have steered their craft straight on to the net. Perhaps their steering has gone haywire, as with the midgets at Pearl Harbor. After the disastrous Pearl Harbor midget raid, a large metal cutting device like a giant pair of scissors has been fitted to the front of the new midgets, but it proves useless.

Chuman and Omori are beginning the most excruciating two and a half hours of their lives; their last hours alive. Inside the tight, sweltering confines of their steel compartment, they desperately work to free their sub, which is becoming more and more exposed to the enemy. The submariners know the Australians soon will find them and will open fire. It is a harrowing time, too, for the harbour defenders. The *Yarroma*'s commander, Sublieutenant Harry Eyers, 21, in peacetime a shipping clerk from Melbourne, is desperately trying to contact naval headquarters to report their strange object on the boom net, but no wireless stations reply. The *Yarroma* tries to send a message using an Aldis lamp, but to no avail. Lack of effective communications between shore bases, ships and the port war signal office proves to be a major hindrance on this dramatic night. 'This went on for a very long period,' Doyle recalls.

Horrie Doyle shines a small searchlight on the boom, but the light is poor and the night is very dark. He can see a large object on the net, maybe a very large mine. Yet it is too big but not big enough for a submarine. It is a steel structure with steel objects running out from the pointed top. 'Should we open fire on the object?' he asks. Doyle is afraid that machine-gun fire will cause casualties ashore. Eyers orders the *Yarroma* across the harbour to Georges Head where there's a searchlight station. Its light is swung onto the net, but at such a distance, the object still remains a mystery.

The *Yarroma* returns to Cargill in his rowboat and asks him to take a stoker to the object on the net. The rowboat returns from the boom net as fast as possible to report a small sub. The *Yarroma* is in an impossible position. The chart indicates there is only 10 feet of water – too shallow for depth charges.

At 9.48 p.m. another strong signature is recorded at the indicator loop station on the hillside at South Head, but it too is ignored. The *M-24* crewed by Katsuhisa Ban and Mamoru Ashibe has made it safely over the cables near the harbour entrance and soon gains access to the inner harbour by the simple act of following a vessel, probably a ferry, through the boom net opening. The midget sub is on course for Garden Island, the busiest hub of Allied shipping in Australia.

Inside the *M-27*, Chuman and Omori work desperately, shifting the lead ballast weights by hand, but their sub remains stuck fast. Fumes from the overworked batteries and motors fill their craft. Another of the 'Hollywood Fleet', the *Lolita*, motors up, and promptly drops three depth charges. There are no explosions as the water is too shallow to exert sufficient pressure to explode them.

It takes Lieutenant Eyers an hour and a half after the watchman's first discovery of the mystery object before contact is made with naval operations at Garden Island.

Sydney's naval officer-in-charge, Rear Admiral Gerard Muirhead-Gould, is entertaining at *Tresco*, his official residence, a two-storey colonial mansion at Elizabeth Bay, when he receives word that enemy submarines are in the harbour. Muirhead-Guild has come to Sydney in 1940 with his wife, their three children and a nurse; he is 'on loan' from the Royal Navy. The admiral's guest tonight is the commander of the US heavy cruiser *Chicago*, Captain H.D. Bode. The *Chicago* is berthed in Sydney for minor repairs following the Battle of the Coral Sea.

At 10.27 p.m., more than two hours after the *M-27* becomes entangled in the boom net, Muirhead-Gould gives the order to sound the general alarm within the harbour. All ships are instructed to take anti-submarine precautions. As Bode leaves *Tresco*, the admiral suggests that he should take the *Chicago* to sea accompanied by her destroyer escort, USS *Perkins*.

At around 10.30 p.m. Lieutenant Eyers sends a signal to the admiral's headquarters: 'Object is submarine. Request permission to open fire.' Presumably Eyers plans to open fire with the machine-gun mounted on the *Yarroma*'s bow, which would have been useless. Why he seeks permission to fire in wartime is a question only he could answer, but five minutes later, his request becomes irrelevant. Sensing the hopelessness of their plight, and wanting to avoid capture at all costs, the young commander of the *M-27* takes his pistol out of its holster.

Chuman, the boy with the child's face who would skip along the beach singing nursery songs at the midget sub base at Ourasaki, fires a single shot into his crewmate's head. Then he turns the gun on himself and presses the trigger again, simultaneously exploding the sub's demolition charges.

A huge ball of flame rises, lifting the *M-27*'s carcass off the net. Her bow is severed from the rest of the submarine just forward of the conning tower, and both sections immediately sink to the harbour floor. First blood flows in Sydney Harbour. The bodies of Chuman and Omori are later recovered in the wreckage, together with various objects including a tobacco pipe and a Nambu type 14.8 mm pistol, bullet and lanyard belonging to Chuman. The officer's name tag is recovered from clothing.

Although the Navy Office report into the midget submarine raid will not mention a shooting aboard the *M-27*, it is discussed in

1942

the private correspondence of the governor-general. Lord Gowrie relates to King George VI how two of the submariners died:

> The officer had obviously shot his mate then pressed the button to blow up the submarine and then shot himself. Though why it was necessary that they should shoot each other when they would have been killed by the explosion a few seconds after, it is hard to see. It is probably some fanatical ideal of the Japanese that when they have failed in their object, they commit suicide.

Soon after the *M-27* explodes, showering the *Lolita* with hot debris, Rear Admiral Muirhead-Gould's barge arrives alongside the *Yarroma*. The *Lolita* also comes alongside. Muirhead-Gould steps aboard, addressing the *Lolita*'s skipper, Warrant Officer Herbert Anderson: 'What are you fellows playing at? What's all this nonsense about a submarine?'

The admiral wants to know why the object has been identified as a submarine. Able Seaman James Nelson replies that he has sighted submarines in the Mediterranean, and another crewman had been a submariner in the last war. Muirhead-Gould remains sceptical: 'Did you see the Japanese captain of the submarine? Did he have a black beard?' He goes into the wheelhouse to talk with the skippers. Able Seaman Doyle is stunned at the events. 'I thought, could there be more submarines, how could they get this far, [with] no bases? We are in for a very busy night.'

As the admiral is preparing to leave *Yarroma*, another large explosion is heard up harbour. Muirhead-Gould races on deck: 'What was that?' 'An underwater explosion, sir,' Doyle replies. 'How would you know what an underwater explosion would sound like?' the admiral scoffs. Doyle, annoyed but unfazed, replies: 'I have just returned from overseas. I served on the HMS *Wild Swan* shortly after Dunkirk ... we did nightly runs up and down the east coast to cover any German sea attacks ...'

As the commotion continues, Herbert Anderson, wryly comments to his admiral: 'If you proceed up harbour, sir, you might find your Japanese captain with a black beard.' Muirhead-Gould replies, 'Thank you', and quickly departs on his barge.

Using her Asdic submarine-detection gear, the *Yarroma* now moves up harbour taking underwater soundings. Near the entrance to Rose Bay, an echo confirms a submarine; it makes an evasive move by slipping under a large freighter at the buoy for ammunition ships in mid-harbour.

Horrie Doyle remembers the American captain of the freighter asking what's happening: 'C.O. called "we are under attack by subs and there is one lying on the bottom directly under you". His voice was very loud and agitated. "For goodness sake, get it away from us, as we are full of all the most modern explosives and if we go off half of Sydney will be damaged."'

At 10.45 p.m. – somewhat belatedly – the navy alerts the air force to the Japanese presence at Sydney: 'MIDGET SUBMARINES NUMBER UNKNOWN AT ENTRANCE TO PORT JACKSON APPROXIMATELY 2245K [local time] /31. POSSIBILITY OF SOME BEING IN HARBOUR.'

Able Seaman Ernie Jamieson, 19, is a homesick and broke Melbourne lad who has spent a boring day on shore. At Circular Quay, he joins other ratings boarding a navy workboat for the quick trip around the point to the Garden Island naval base, to rejoin his ship, the HMAS *Bingera*. The workboat has just deposited them on the ferry pontoon at Garden Island, when suddenly, 50 metres out, the USS *Chicago* switches on a searchlight, and opens fire along its path with red tracers. 'The workboat had taken off and the skipper found himself in the outer beam of the searchlight,' Jamieson recalled later. 'He reversed hard, very hard, and hit the pontoon and bounced out against into the light with tracers zooming past him! We had a ringside view of all this and it was very spectacular.' The *Chicago* has spotted the conning tower of Ban and Ashibe's *M-24*, now located about 200 metres off the ferry pontoon.

The heavy cruiser HMAS *Canberra*, a three-stacker, is moored close to the Man O'War steps, a short walk from Bennelong Point. Its officer on watch is Lieutenant Mackenzie Gregory, who joined the service in 1939 as a 17-year-old cadet midshipman. Later, he recalls 'absolute mayhem that night'. At first, the crew of *Canberra* have no idea what is going on, except that guns are being fired and searchlights illuminate the water. Then, they spot the *M-24*, before the sub fires on the *Chicago*. The *Canberra* is close enough to the midget to see that its crew is having trouble maintaining depth. It keeps bobbing up to the surface and then down again, just as Kazuo Sakamaki's midget had done off Pearl Harbor.

'She was that close they [the gunners on the *Chicago*] couldn't depress the guns close enough, down enough without knocking off their own guardrails,' Gregory says. 'Then she [the *M-24*] got down... Ban got it under control again and lined up *Chicago* but ran it too deep, and eventually *Chicago* got fed up and went to sea.'

The minesweeper HMAS *Whyalla* also opens fire on the midget sub with a machine-gun. On shore, anti-aircraft gunner Phil Dulhunty witnesses Sydney under attack:

'Bullets were ricocheting, and one actually ricocheted off Fort Denison. We could see a cloud of sandstone going into all sorts of pieces. I think those pockmarks were on Fort Denison for quite a long time.' Known as 'Pinchgut' to Sydneysiders, Fort Denison is a minute 19th-century stone fort with a small tower in middle of the harbour. It is struck a glancing blow by one of the *Chicago*'s five-inch shells. Some of the *Chicago*'s shots finish up in the northern harbour suburbs of Cremorne and Mosman.

With bullets pinging off the *M-24*'s hull, Katsuhisa Ban pilots the vessel on the surface towards the Sydney Harbour Bridge. Perhaps he has trouble diving, because west of Garden Island he almost collides with the dockyard motor boat *Nestor*, which has to swerve to avoid a collision as the *Chicago*'s gunfire falls all around the *M-24*.

Meanwhile, Ernie Jamieson has managed to get a boat from Garden Island to the *Bingera*, which moves off around the north side of the harbour: 'Soon after we saw and then heard a mighty explosion alongside Garden Island. It turned out that a midget fired its two torpedoes at the *Chicago*, missed, and one "fish" [torpedo] porpoised ashore, a "dud", and the other hit the bottom and exploded under the *Kuttabul* . . . it caused a lot of casualties and we could hear a lot of screaming, an awful sound.'

At 30 minutes after midnight, over an hour and a half after the initial sighting, Ban and Ashibe have controlled their unstable craft sufficiently to launch two torpedoes at the American cruiser. Only then do the floodlights at Garden Island go out.

Ban has fired from the direction of Bradleys Head on the northern side of the harbour, just as the cruiser *Chicago* is about to slip her buoy and head to sea. The *Kuttabul*, an old ferry, has been requisitioned as a depot ship, anchored near Garden Island, and used as accommodation by the RAN. The torpedo that hits her misses the *Chicago* then passes under the Dutch submarine *K9*, before exploding under the old boat. The second torpedo runs aground on rocks on the eastern side of Garden Island and fails to explode.

Ban and Ashibe now proceed down harbour and succeed in escaping. Their *M-24* is not seen again in Sydney Harbour; for 64 years, her whereabouts will be one of Australia's great maritime mysteries.

Able Seaman Neil Roberts has finished his sentry duty and returns to the *Kuttabul* to get some sleep. On reaching the upper deck, he wearily climbs into his hammock, fully clothed. 'I lay down and went off to sleep and there was this terrible explosion . . . in the panic I went down the steps to get out and by this time the vessel was sinking and a wave of water came up the stairs and the thing was starting to settle on me; so I had the option then of just diving underwater and swimming underwater out through the side of the ship and swam across eventually to a sea wall.'

Roberts climbs the sea wall and is told there is an unexploded torpedo underneath the nearby wharf.

Another able seaman, Colin Whitfield, an 18-year-old New

Zealander, has just returned to duty from weeks of wild leave. Reporting to his superiors, he is ordered to spend the night on the *Kuttabul*. He wakes in the middle of the night to face his next shift: 'I was standing on the deck, getting ready to lash and stow my hammock, when there was this almighty bang. There was just something terribly wrong. I saw a table and got under for a while, heard terrible noises out in the harbour, so said to myself: "I've got to get out of here." But when I tried to stand up I couldn't. Every bone was broken in both ankles. My feet were just hanging by the skin.'

Whitfield slides on his backside down the gangway. Then something hits him on the head, knocking him out. He is found floating unconscious in the harbour, and comes to in Sydney Hospital two days later.

An unnamed seaman who wouldn't give his name to the press watched events unfold while on watch on the deck of a steamer moored near the *Kuttabul*. His story reveals the terror which Ban and Ashibe must have suffered inside the *M-24*: 'Bright moonlight was flooding the water and the periscope and conning tower were clearly visible only 50 yards away from where I stood. I thought I must be dreaming ... For a moment I thought it must be one of our own submarines but I was quickly disillusioned.'

There was a terrific explosion and the *Kuttabul*, berthed a short distance away, shook violently and began to sink: 'Almost simultaneously there was a rattle of gunfire. It was the smartest bit of work I have ever seen. Machine-gun bursts of .5 inch calibre were spitting all round us, with tracer bullets like shooting stars as the gunners tried to get in the range ... The submarine remained visible for a few minutes but in that time the conning tower must have been riddled with bullets. Searchlights were now playing on it ... There was some mighty pretty shooting.'

Rear Admiral Muirhead-Gould has ordered the duty intelligence officer at Garden Island, Lieutenant Commander Percy

Wilson, to extinguish the floodlights at Garden Island, where major construction work was proceeding on the graving dock. The floodlights were on tall masts, illuminating the whole area. Unable to raise anyone at dockyard by telephone, Wilson runs at full pelt across the rough and rocky road through the dock and the work sheds:

> Paul Revere had a more comfortable trip than I did... as I went through I shouted to all and sundry, 'Get out fast, the port is under attack.' Some delay occurred finding the engineer responsible, and with authority to put the lights out. When I found him, he found it hard to believe, and spoke of the difficulty with hundreds of men in the dock, many below sea level. I left him in no doubt of the admiral's requirements...

To add to the confusion, at 10.54 p.m., only two minutes after Ban's midget was sighted near the *Chicago*, another midget sub, the *M-22*, is sighted between the outer and inner submarine detection loops down harbour by the anti-submarine vessel *Yandra* and the patrol boat *Lauriana*. The *Yandra* attempts to ram the sub and drops six depth charges, confident that its attack is successful, but the *M-22* escapes.

Forty minutes after the *Kuttabul* is hit, Rear Admiral Muirhead-Gould orders a message to all ships: 'Enemy submarine is present in the harbour and *Kuttabul* has been torpedoed.'

Fishermen on a trawler off Cronulla also detect one of the five mother submarines lying in wait for the potential recovery of the midgets. The mother subs are positioned in a line stretching seawards from a point about six kilometres off Port Hacking, just south of Sydney. Muirhead-Gould flashes a message to the Naval Board in Melbourne which should be taken as the tip for major aerial searches close offshore from Sydney's southern beaches: 'TRAWLER SAN MICHELE REPORTS SIGHTING SUBMARINE 4.5 MILES OFF CRONULLA AT 0106K/1 STEAMING SOUTH AT 2 TO 3 KNOTS. SUBMARINE

CLEARLY OBSERVED IN MOONLIGHT APPEARED TO BE ABOUT 200 FEET IN LENGTH . . .'

At about 2.50 a.m. on Monday, 1 June, the USS *Chicago* is cruising at speed out of Sydney Heads when she spots a midget submarine; her crew alert Garden Island. A detection loop recording later indicates that a submarine has crossed the inner loop at around this time. This is Keiu Matsuo and Masao Tsuzuku passing through the west gate and heading up harbour in the midget *M-22*.

By now, thousands of Sydneysiders have realised that all the noise and commotion on the harbour is no exercise. News of a raid is getting out by word of mouth. But nothing official is broadcast during the night or the next morning, adding to rumour and tension. One boy from Bondi vividly recalls the raid. Jim Mair, then aged nine, lived with his family in Hastings Parade, near the tram terminus at Ben Buckler on the northern end of Bondi Beach.

It was an exciting place for an adventurous youngster. The beach had been covered with barbed-wire entanglements erected by soldiers soon after the Pearl Harbor raid. So desperate was the Australian supply situation at the time that dummy gun pits had been erected with four-inch-diameter green painted downpipes stuck through the netting to represent gun barrels.

Late on the night of the 31st, Jim and his siblings were hauled out of bed by their mother, who told them, 'The Japanese have invaded!' Mrs Sylvia Mair had just received a telephone call from her husband, Bill, a veteran who had been medically discharged from the AIF and was now a taxi-driver. She shoved Jim and his five siblings under the billiard table that served as the family dining table.

'Father had been driving his cab in the city and had phoned to tell us of the Japanese attacking Sydney with bombs going off in the Harbour, cannon firing and all,' Mair recalled. 'Mother took this to be a Japanese invasion, although it had no urgency for us kids.' Bill Mair called later to say there was no invasion, but not before Mrs Mair had packed her bags ready to take the children to Aunty Belle's farm at Yass. Next day, Jim and his brother Billie helped their father dig out the collapsed air raid shelter in the backyard, which had filled with sand.

Many Sydney residents watched the attack on the harbour in awe and relative safety. Patricia Black, a WRAN, of McLeod Street, Mosman, would walk to work at the naval facility HMAS *Penguin* at Balmoral, with its extensive views from Middle Head. She described the 31st as 'the most exciting night of my life'. Her sister, Helen, who was then 14, also remembered it well:

> We were woken up at night with the noise of gunfire. We lived in a lovely old house looking across the harbour. There were flares going up – lights flashing and guns roaring from the direction of Garden Island, which was the centre of everything.
>
> I ran into my parent's bedroom and got into bed with them. I knew Australia was at war but it didn't affect us, being so far away. I used to hang towels out the window to farewell the *Queen Mary* taking troops overseas.
>
> Then we all got out of bed to have a look because we had such a good view of the harbour. Noise and flashes went off for quite a while. The sky lit up. Then a warden fellow like something out of *Dad's Army* came along and yelled at us: "Put that light out!"'

Some of the military witnesses to the events on Sydney Harbour were scathing about the Australian response. Lieutenant Gregory of the *Canberra* said Sydney's defenders somehow muddled through, but Rear Admiral Muirhead-Gould made 'an absolute bog of it':

> The poor Japs were very unlucky not to get the *Chicago*. I think probably, the *Chicago* was a heavy cruiser but she was very top

heavy – she looked like a battleship and I suspect that they [Ban and Ashibe] set the torpedoes too deep and passed underneath her.

We were totally inept that night. The dockyard lights didn't go off until about 11.00 p.m. Captain Cook Dock was ablaze. The ships were just silhouetted.

20

FROM CHAOS TO CONFIDENCE

The ferry service timetable around Sydney Harbour on Sunday night and Monday morning was not greatly altered despite the open warfare occurring in the harbour around them. The boats chugged from wharf to wharf, dodging bullets and shells.

Admiral Muirhead-Gould had given the order to keep Sydney's ferries running, and at daybreak the order stood: 'This was done by my direct order as I felt that once there was a submarine, or more than one submarine in the Harbour, the more boats that were moving about at high speed the better chances of keeping the submarines down until daylight.'

Passengers on one ferry that left Circular Quay as Ban and Ashibe moved up harbour off Garden Island witnessed most of the fire fight against the *M-24*. There were 27 passengers on board when the guns began to blaze not far away. They presumed the navy was practising with blank shells – until the captain suddenly received orders to go hard astern as he was running into the fighting. By that time, searchlights flooded the waves, guns blazed, red tracers streaked across the water, and water spouts marked where shells had fallen in the harbour. Bright moonlight lit the scene.

1942

The governor-general, Lord Gowrie, and his wife, Lady Zara, had been relaxing at their official Sydney residence, Admiralty House, at Kirribilli Point, just under the northern end of the Harbour Bridge:

> ... the guns began to go off and the Admiral rang me up to say there were submarines inside Sydney Harbour. Zara and I took up our positions on the balcony and had a good view of the proceedings. We couldn't actually see the submarines, but we could see the small craft buzzing about dropping depth charges and searchlights moving all over the surface of the water.

Gowrie, writing to George VI from Admiralty House, added: 'The hunt was pretty successful and eventually we got four [sic] submarines which I think were all that actually got inside the Harbour. They are now being dragged up and examined and it is most interesting ... two of them were badly damaged and one had evidently been blown up by the crew when they found that we are after them.' Gowrie described the midgets as 'nasty, suicidal contrivances' which were launched from large submarines, 'with very little prospect of return'.

There were numerous sightings of midget submarines during the night into the early hours as patrol boats, minesweepers and anti-submarine vessels ploughed the harbour. First light on Sydney Harbour brought more signs of war. City workers took ferries from Manly and other harbourside suburbs to Circular Quay, just as they would on any other day. At one stage, a naval vessel had to fire a machine-gun across the bows of a ferry to divert the skipper from entering a fighting zone.

The patrol boat *Sea Mist*, skippered by Lieutenant Reg Andrew, was sent to investigate a submarine sighting in Taylor Bay, Mosman, just north of Bradleys Head. Around 5.00 a.m. the patrol boat spotted a midget submarine in the bay and went after her. The sub crash-dived. The *Sea Mist* fired a flare over the spot and dropped a depth charge before roaring off as a huge geyser of water erupted. The depth charge made the midget rise slowly to the surface, according to naval historian Steven Carruthers. As the sub rose, revolving propellers could be seen in their metal cage. The sub began to turn over. Andrew reportedly saw a conning tower boiling with escaping air. The craft slipped below the surface.

The patrol boats *Steady Hour* and *Yarroma* saw *Sea Mist*'s flare and sped over. They too began dropping depth charges in Taylor Bay. At 6.25 a.m. the *Yarroma* started a depth charge run at top speed. Able Seaman Horrie Doyle said that by using the boat's Asdic, they could see that the sub was 'very slow in moving forward [in] shallow waters'. Suddenly an early morning Manly ferry on its way to Circular Quay came up on *Sea Mist*'s port side just as Doyle prepared to fire his depth charge. The ferry crew and passengers got a ringside view of the *Sea Mist* going into action. As Doyle said: 'She would feel nothing but what a sight for them!'

Horrie Doyle dropped one charge, and the tremendous explosion nearly wrecked the *Yarroma*, which couldn't get away fast enough on the five-second fuse: 'Both our engines lifted off their housing. We stopped and could not replace them [as they were] far too heavy.' The *Yarroma* limped slowly back to base for repairs.

It was also the end for Keiu Matsuo and his navigator, Masao Tsuzuku. The *M-22* and her crew could go no further. They had endured a frightful pounding that seemed never to end. The explosions had damaged the sub and dented her hull plates.

Matsuo had summoned up all his experience to try to shake off the patrol boats overhead, but he knew that he was cornered. His sub was damaged. He had failed to fire his torpedoes. Six weeks earlier he had written to his parents: 'Please forgive me for dying before you . . . with my own blood I will serve the Emperor . . . My dear parents, take care of yourselves.'

Now, with Tsuzuku looking on grimly, he reached for his revolver hanging on the bulkhead near him. He had failed to fire his torpedoes and the midget sub's mission was a failure. For these boys, there was no tomorrow, as they had anticipated from the beginning at their training island off Kure on the Inland Sea.

*

Bill Bullard knew his way around Sydney Harbour. A Sydney boy from Ashfield, he joined the navy at the age of 15 during World War I. Bullard, now 40 and a leading seaman diver, was called to the wreck of the *Kuttabul*:

> I will never forget the scene when we arrived on the sleeping deck of the sunken ship. The sun was shining through a gaping hole in the deck head, giving a green glow to the still water. Blankets and clothing were scattered round the deck. Hammocks were still slung with their occupants as if asleep. There were two men sitting on a locker leaning towards each other as if they had been having a yarn before turning in. The blast from the explosion must have killed them instantly.

Bullard's team recovered 17 bodies before the divers were called down harbour to Taylor Bay. They arrived at about 7.30 a.m. to investigate an oil slick and bubbles coming to the surface.

The tide was running out. Lieutenant George Whittle anchored about 45 metres upstream from the bubbles. One of the divers, Ray Coote, donned a heavy diving suit and was lowered over the side. In about 26 metres of water, Coote made a big sweep trailing his lines. Finding nothing, he resurfaced. The dive boat moved upstream and Bill Bullard, waiting in his suit, dropped down: 'While descending, I heard a continual throbbing noise in my helmet, but assumed it was caused by some boat on the surface. On the bottom I walked out to the full extent of my lines and started to sweep. The bottom was about six inches of mud on hard sand.'

Bullard found it hard going, with the stirred up mud obscuring his visibility. The water was freezing cold. Suddenly Bullard saw a large object. It turned out to be the *M-22*:

> I walked towards it and saw a submarine lying practically on an even keel and apparently undamaged. I put my hand on the hull, which was quite warm. Suddenly I realised that the sound

I had heard from the time I entered the water was coming from the sub and was quite loud.

I thought she might take off at any minute and I hated the thought of tangling up with her if she did. I reported by phone to the boat and Lieutenant Whittle asked me to hang on for a while and he would send Ray Coote down my lines with a buoy rope...

I had a good look at the bow and was surprised to see the doors of the torpedo tubes, one on top of the other, were partly open with the noses of the torpedoes protruding...

It seems that the mechanism allowing the doors to drop had failed and the operator had fired both torpedoes with the result that neither had left on their journey to the target... Evidently she had been depth charged and her hull damaged, putting her out of action before she could do any damage.

The Navy Office's summary report on the raid raised unanswered questions about the manner in which Matsuo and Tsuzuku died. While it was clear that both had been shot in the head, some of the circumstances were puzzling:

Both men were found to have died as a result of self-inflicted revolver shots in the head. It is possible that the junior member of the crew [Tsuzuku] had attempted to escape as his boots had been removed. The Captain was wearing boots. A ceremonial sword, bearing the name of the Lieutenant, was found hanging in the control room.

When the conning tower hatch was subsequently opened, the bodies of Matsuo and Tsuzuku were seen in the control room. Strangely, though, the commander, Matsuo, was slumped in the navigator's seat while the navigator, Tsuzuku, was crumpled on the floor.

The probability is that Matsuo shot Tsuzuku in the head before turning his handgun on himself. It is possible that both men sustained their fatal wounds while the *M-22* was forced to the surface, taking water, just before sinking. If this was the case, and Tsuzuku intended to swim for it, did Matsuo murder his partner, as was also suggested in the case of Kazuo Sakamaki and his junior, Kiyoshi Inagaki, at Pearl Harbor? Matsuo and Tsuzuku had graduated together in 1938 and were good friends.

Important documents were recovered from the *M-22*. They included call sign lists, operational orders and code words. Japanese copies of British Admiralty charts included photographs of important targets. There were shots of Garden Island and its graving dock, the shipyards at Cockatoo Island and Walsh Island, the Hawkesbury River railway bridge and the big BHP steelworks at Newcastle.

At 6.35 a.m., eight Australian bombers had taken off from Sydney to search for a possible submarine 'parent ship'. Their huge search area extended more than 300 kilometres off the coast, but the aircraft found nothing. In a flurry of signals, the Navy Office at Victoria Barracks in Melbourne recommended immediate counter measures around Australia's ports, including patrols by the maximum number of surface craft. All important vessels including merchant vessels were to be located as far up harbour as possible.

This order to move ships up harbour for maximum protection had first been given on 21 December 1941, five months earlier, after the Pearl Harbor attack: 'It is considered that separate action should be taken to instruct the Rear-Admiral in Charge, Sydney, to make the necessary arrangements for cruisers and other important Naval units to be berthed above the Harbour Bridge.'

Muirhead-Gould was in charge of the Sydney naval station on 21 December 1941. The fact that the order was never implemented appears not to have attracted any criticism of his actions. Had Ban and Ashibe's torpedo hit the *Chicago* rather than the insignificant *Kuttabul*, the story might have been different. Later, the admiral apportioned blame for the attack in a report to the Navy Office. He deplored the fact that 'the human element' had failed at the loop indicator station at South Head: 'There was a regrettable failure on the part of the watchkeepers to identify the unusual crossings at 2001 and 2148 [hours].'

The admiral seemed reluctant to share any of the blame himself. Had he acted on warnings received more than 12 months earlier, Sydney might have been better secured. On 4 May 1941, Australia's military operations and intelligence office in Melbourne had told all commands that attacks against harbours overseas had been made by one-man motor boats or midget submarines. The information came directly from the Admiralty in London. The warning recommended 'great vigilance in patrolling boom defences and side gaps or gaps in boom nets' and the use of small depth charges by patrol craft at harbour mouths. The intelligence office also recommended 'patrols within harbour mouths and also as far seaward in approaches to important harbours', and the posting of lookouts and machine gun posts, where conditions were favourable.

By the time of the Sydney raid a submarine boom net had been constructed, but not finished. Sea patrols outside the harbour were notably lacking, even when Japanese submarines were known to be off the east coast of Australia.

Even though Sydneysiders could hear and see the military fireworks on their harbour, there was precious little in the way of official explanation. The Australian government, on navy advice, tried to hush it up.

The official obsession with censorship and secrecy contributed to the unease and the spread of rumour. Most morning newspaper editions appeared containing little mention of the unprecedented action on the harbour overnight. Even the duty censor in Sydney was stunned at being told to suppress the newspapers' stories. It was a censorship blunder as serious as that after the first Darwin raid. As they had already experienced the news blackout that followed that devastating raid ten weeks earlier, the people of Sydney had reason for anxiety. As the day wore on, radio stations began broadcasting the barest of details in a few clipped, dismissive sentences.

That same morning, John Curtin learned that in strategic terms, the raid on Sydney was a relatively unimportant skirmish compared with the gravity of events in the mid-Pacific. In a little-reported meeting, the prime minister was told one of the greatest secrets of the war, as well as a few home truths about Australia's relationship with the United States.

Curtin had travelled by train from Canberra to Melbourne to meet General MacArthur. He went straight to the war cabinet room at Victoria Barracks, St Kilda Road. Only the previous month MacArthur had commandeered the Trustees Executive and Agency building at 401 Collins Street. The prime minister and his defence secretary, Frederick Shedden, had met MacArthur three times in April in formal meetings termed the Prime Minister's War Conference.

Curtin had established the war conference as the key strategic decision-making body in Australia. He privately admitted that he had surrendered part of Australia's sovereignty to a foreign military leader in Australia's interests. MacArthur later wrote of his relationship with the PM: 'We promptly came to a sense of mutual trust, co-operation, and regard that was never once breached by word, thought, or deed. He was the kind of man the Australians called "far dinkum".'

Curtin and Shedden were greeted warmly by MacArthur and his chief of staff, Major-General R.K. Sutherland. The two leaders were opposite types with an unwavering common goal. MacArthur was a flamboyant showman prone to dramatic statements. Curtin was a homespun leader who disliked the trappings of office. Both were known to speak frankly.

Today, the Supreme Allied Commander of the South-West Pacific Area had significant news to impart. But first, the two leaders discussed the Sydney raid. When Curtin explained the navy's concerns about going public about the attack, MacArthur said he understood, but in view of the fact that the attack was known to the whole population of Sydney, he believed a statement should be issued. Curtin agreed.

MacArthur's bland and belated statement said that in an attempted raid on Sydney overnight, three enemy midget submarines were believed destroyed – one by gunfire and two by depth charges. The communiqué added: 'The enemy's attack was completely unsuccessful and damage was confirmed to one small harbour vessel of no military value.'

The Sydney raid took up little of their meeting. Curtin and Shedden were there to discuss a report from MacArthur which set out American strategic policy in the south-west Pacific, regarding both the war with Japan and the relationship between the USA and Australia. The American firstly goaded Curtin to do more to obtain major defence commitments from Britain. Despite requests, the general said a little testily, Britain had sent 'no additional ship, soldier or squadron' to Australia's aid.

You must 'hammer' the British government to release two aircraft carriers for the south-west Pacific, MacArthur told the Australian leader. If he were prime minister, he'd insist on the return of the 9th Division of the AIF from the Middle East. 'In Australia's hour of peril she is entitled at least to use all of the forces she can raise herself,' Curtin later recalled the general advising him. While Australian troops were returning from overseas, the 9th Division was still in the Middle East and Churchill was resisting their release.

MacArthur then told Curtin some truths about the relationship between Australia and the United States. He said Curtin must realise the distinct difference between British and American responsibilities towards Australia, as Curtin related it:

> The United States was an ally whose aim was to win the war, and it had no sovereign interest in the integrity of Australia. The interest in Australia was from the strategical aspect of the utility of Australia as a base from which to attack [and] defeat the Japanese.

This was a rebuke to Curtin, who had put so much faith in the new relationship with the US. Now he was reminded that Australia was part of the British empire and related to Britain and the other dominions by ties of blood, sentiment and allegiance to the Crown, MacArthur insisted.

The American assumed that a principle of the British Commonwealth of Nations was jointly to protect any part of the British empire that might be threatened. Curtin should consider this when talking about the failure of the British and US governments to support Australia.

MacArthur added that although the American people were 'animated by warm friendship for Australia', the purpose of building up US forces in Australia 'was not so much from an interest in Australia, but rather from its utility as a base from which to hit Japan.' In case Curtin did not understand, MacArthur added: 'In view of the strategical importance of Australia in a war with Japan this course of military action would probably be followed irrespective of the American relationship to the people who might be occupying Australia.'

MacArthur's sober assessment appeared to be correcting, if not undermining, Curtin's historical declaration of December 1941 that 'without any inhibition of any kind, I make it quite clear that Australia looks to America, free of any pangs as to our traditional links or kinship with the United Kingdom'. Australia was merely a future US base of operations, MacArthur was saying.

As MacArthur and Curtin were meeting, the commander-in-chief of Combined Fleet, Admiral Yamamoto, was on the bridge of the *Yamato* as she punched through heavy seas in fog and rain. The mighty battleship led the so-called 'Main Force', yet this was a euphemistic misnomer. The actual commander-in-chief of the Midway occupation force was Admiral Nobutake Kondo, the spearhead of the Malaya and Philippines invasions. Kondo, who had been so keen to invade Australia only a few months earlier, would direct the carrier-based operations from his own flagship, the cruiser *Atago*.

The *Yamato* was accompanied by the battleships *Nagato* and *Mutsu*, cruisers and destroyers, and the light carrier *Hosho*, which during the battle would only launch her aircraft for reconnaissance flights. As usual, great caution surrounded Yamamoto's battleship group. It was located safely about 1000 kilometres to the rear of Kondo's powerful strike force now bound for Midway in the mid-Pacific.

Yamamoto's chief of staff, Admiral Ugaki, was tense and worried about the forthcoming operation. The weather was worsening and there was enemy activity in the region. An enemy submarine had been spotted by a Japanese flying boat. Then the oiler *Naruto* blundered in signalling its position to the *Yamato*. Ugaki sensed that the enemy were preparing to meet them. He was almost certain that they had deployed subs in the vicinity of Midway Island and had intensified their watch with planes.

Because of difficulties in distributing new codebooks, Japanese naval operators had been forced to continue using their existing naval codes until 25 May, by which time the Allies were decoding over 100 messages each day. The breaking of the Japanese codes by the Allies had been one of the greatest secrets of the war and although there were Japanese suspicions from time to time, the secret was never revealed. Working in complete secrecy, American, British and Australian code-breakers in Hawaii, Colombo and Melbourne were now receiving a great deal of intelligence flooding in from the previously impenetrable Japanese naval code JN25b.

Now MacArthur revealed news of the looming and decisive Battle of Midway, as Curtin describes it:

> In the opinion of the Commander-in-Chief, there will be a decisive naval action in June and this will be fraught with the gravest consequences for Australia. If it is successful it will relieve the pressure on Australia. If it results in a draw it will

decrease the pressure, but if it results in a Japanese success, it will be followed up by mopping up operations against the islands on the line of communications between Australia and Hawaii, in order to isolate Australia from America.

The Battle of Midway, crucial to the whole course of the war, would erupt in less than three days. Out in the mid-Pacific, night settled over the huge, strung-out Japanese fleet as the weather deteriorated. Admiral Ugaki told of being handed an urgent telegram from Tokyo:

> ... according to broadcasts from Sydney and San Francisco, three Japanese midget subs attacked Sydney Harbor last Sunday [the previous night]. As they attacked, it is supposed that they must have inflicted considerable damage on the enemy. Pray to God for the safe recovery of their crews!

When detailed reports of the Sydney raid finally broke in Australian morning newspapers on Tuesday, 2 June, Allied leaders united in praising the defenders of Sydney for their vigilance and skill. Luck, in fact, had a good deal more to do with it.

ENEMY SUBMARINES ENTER SYDNEY HARBOUR. THREE MIDGET RAIDERS BELIEVED DESTROYED. FORMER FERRY BOAT HIT BY TORPEDO, the *Sydney Morning Herald* dramatically announced. The newspaper confirmed that excited rumours 'had been circulating in Sydney since residents had seen and heard guns firing on the harbour the previous night'. The *Herald* was now able to report the attack in detail.

The newspaper had to make some guesses. The thought of reconnaissance aircraft being carried by Japanese submarines wasn't being considered: 'The fact that the submarines appeared soon after the succession of stand-by warnings to Sydney ARP [Air Raid Post] personnel has led to a suggestion that the two might be related and that an enemy ship, standing well out to sea, might have been employing reconnaissance aircraft.'

Sydney had learned of the attack with astonishment, the paper said, but it could have been worse: 'Sydney may well feel grateful that its first experience of a Japanese attack, one made across the very threshold of our front door, was not more serious. Certainly as an attempt at terrorism by night, it was a dismal failure . . .' *The Age* in Melbourne ventured: 'Midget two-men submarines of the type captured at Pearl Harbor have a range of about 300 miles, and are launched by crane from the deck of a parent ship.'

All sorts of theories sprang into life. In federal parliament, a Country Party member from Queensland, Bernard Corser, suggested that a mother ship might have lurked in a sheltered part of the coast and made contact with enemy agents in Australia. The federal minister for the navy, Norman Makin, lavished unwarranted praise on Australia's defence preparedness to meet the Sydney raid:

> That the attempt by such midget craft to enter Sydney Harbour in the middle of the night was instantly detected, and that the counter measures were so prompt and effective, reflect credit on those responsible for the harbour defences, and should prove both a disappointment and a deterrent to the enemy.

Makin had just returned from a hurried visit to Sydney where he consulted Rear Admiral Muirhead-Gould. Unashamedly ignoring the facts, Makin went on:

> Long before Japan entered the war, and at a time when Australia seemed remote from the possibility of attack, steps had been taken to safeguard the defences of our ports. Fortunately, therefore, with Japan's entry into hostilities we were well prepared for any eventuality.

Nevertheless, *The Age* thought the Japanese threat had intensified: 'Air attacks, submarine forays and ventures by surface ships, even attempts at landings and invasion are all possibilities which must be reckoned with at any time in the future.'

On 2 June, Curtin spoke at a huge meeting at the Melbourne town hall to promote Australia's second liberty war loan. He told the animated crowd: 'The thrusts the enemy made on our soil have been repulsed. He has been driven off with loss. He has sought to come here with immense naval strength and establish a spearhead, but, with the aid of our gallant Allies across the Pacific, making common cause, the enemy found his most southerly venture a venture beyond his capacity to execute.'

His cheering audience might have been forgiven for thinking that Curtin was referring to the midget raid. In fact, he was talking about the Coral Sea battle, which had turned back the invasion of Port Moresby. Emboldened, Curtin added, 'Today I speak to you with a spirit of confidence born in the knowledge of how the war is proceeding. I defy the enemy to land a large force in Australia . . .'

It was the spirit that Australians wanted to hear, but the shocks were far from over.

21

A SCENE OF DREADFUL CARNAGE

In the early hours of Wednesday, 3 June, thick fog enveloped the huge Japanese battle fleet crashing through the seas towards Midway. The cover was so heavy that searchlights were turned on and fog beacons were towed behind the ships to prevent collisions. When the fog cleared away before dawn, rain began falling.

Ugaki, still worried that the Americans had detected the invasion fleet, received more bad news: 'It is learned from an unidentified station in Australia that three Japanese midget subs attacked only harbor vessels and two of them were sunk by depth charges, the remaining one by bombardment.'

No major targets had been destroyed. The news was especially disappointing after the failure of the midget submarines at Pearl Harbor. Ugaki's depression was only just beginning. A new message followed overnight and, again, the news was not good, as he wrote in his diary:

'None of the midget sub crews who made the surprise attack upon Sydney were recovered, and the mother sub suspended its search.' Ugaki was about to enter Japan's greatest battle, but his thoughts amazingly were with the men of the midget submarines who attacked Sydney. He tried to console himself that the young submariners had done their duty.

In Sydney, on 3 June, six of the men killed aboard the *Kuttabul* were buried with full military honours. Three volleys from a firing party rang out and the 'Last Post' was played. In parliament, the navy minister, Norman Makin, said no sign had been found of the third submarine in the raid on Sydney, referring to Ban and Ashibe's *M-24*. However, he said, naval authorities were sure it had been destroyed.

A select group of senior parliamentary reporters assembled in Curtin's timber panelled office in Parliament House, for a portentous briefing. They found the prime minister in a buoyant mood, according to Joe Alexander: 'Today Curtin said he had never been so sure of ultimate victory but there were still unpleasant surprises and unexpected reverses before us. Reviewing our own position he said we had now 12 well equipped divisions in Australia.' Alexander revealed that Curtin had an insight into the future: 'His [Japan's] main naval forces might be heavily engaged at this hour. All his important Naval Squadrons were now north of Truk.'

Curtin made no mention of the impending Battle of Midway, but five days later he let his trusted press contacts in on a major Allied secret: the Americans could intercept and decode Japanese naval traffic, and that was how the Japanese fleet build-up had been detected. 'The Nip Naval concentration was discovered ten days ago by means of *an intercepted signal*,' Alexander confided to his diary. American and British political and military leaders would have been aghast at the sharing of this most secret intelligence with civilian newsmen. Alexander went on that Curtin thought that 'now was the time for us to open an offensive of limited targets'. Evatt was discussing this with Roosevelt now. 'It might mean an attack on Rabaul or some similar objective.'

At sea aboard the *Yamato*, Ugaki received more messages about the Sydney operation, and pondered in his diary the fate of the six submariners:

None of the midget sub crew who made a surprise attack on Sydney were recovered, and the mother sub suspended their search. As one of our subs staying south-by-southeast of the harbor noticed at 2200 [on 31 May] to the left of the harbor entrance light a big water spout almost three times as big as the light, which seconds later went down, it seems certain that our midget subs made a daring attack.

On the other hand, the Australian defence headquarters announced that a torpedo hit a naval auxiliary vessel and another one exploded in her vicinity with a result that she was sunk ... two sunken midget subs are possible to be salvaged, as their positions are ascertained. Searches are being made for another midget sub and their mother subs. Although they claimed that our attack was unsuccessful, their shock received from our attack must have been tremendous.

When it was clear that the midget submariners were not returning to the mother subs, orders were issued for the *I*-class submarine fleet off Sydney to sink commercial shipping. The Japanese began a new, intense campaign to wreak as much destruction as possible along the east coast of Australia. Some of the attacks were so close to shore that people living along the coast would see and hear the explosions.

The *I-29* was ordered to patrol north and remain off the coast near Brisbane, *I-21* and *I-24* were to remain off the Sydney area, *I-27* was to sail south to Melbourne while the *I-22* was to sail for New Zealand. The first attack came on the night of 3 June. The *I-24* was 56 kilometres off Sydney when an approaching ship was spotted. The big sub surfaced. At 10.18 p.m., using its deck gun, the submarine began to shell the coastal steamer, the *Age*, heading to Newcastle from Melbourne. The *Age* sent out a distress message and immediately put on maximum speed. Somehow, she managed to flee at top speed in heavy seas, reaching Newcastle the next morning without damage.

But the Japanese subs soon claimed a substantial victim. Sydney

Radio received a signal from the Australian bulk carrier *Iron Chieftain*, owned by the steelmaker BHP, and carrying coke and ship-building materials south to Whyalla in South Australia. The ship had been torpedoed and sank quickly, killing 12, including Captain L. Haddelsey, who was last seen standing on the bridge with another officer as the ship went down.

Able Seaman Ernie Jamieson, the 19-year-old who had witnessed the midget attack in Sydney Harbour, was aboard the small anti-submarine training vessel *Bingera* sent out into the high seas to look for survivors: 'We found and rescued only one survivor. He was floating on a wooden door in the midst of a lot of wreckage. He was very lucky. As we hauled him aboard we saw a very large triangular shaped fin circling around the flotsam.' Lifeboats containing 37 survivors landed on beaches around Lakes Entrance, north of Sydney. Aerial searches were immediately carried out.

In Sydney Harbour, the crews of the 'Hollywood Fleet' channel patrol boats were jumpy, with numerous sub 'sightings' inside the harbour and along the coast and in Sydney estuaries.

Before first light on 4 June, Rear Admiral Muirhead-Gould sent the following signal to the Navy Board in Melbourne: 'TWO SMALL SUBMARINES REPORTED IN VAUCLUSE BAY AT 0410/K/4 ATTACK CARRIED OUT BY CPB WITH DEPTH CHARGES ON A.S. CONTACT. SUBMARINES NOT SINCE SIGHTED.' The raids were false alarms, but the sounds of further explosions in Sydney Harbour did nothing to calm waterfront residents.

As survivors were coming ashore on the central coast of New South Wales, the *I-27* struck off southern Australia in the early morning of 4 June. The steamer *Barwon* was travelling towards Tasmania when she was attacked by both gunfire and torpedo off Gabo Island in Bass Strait. The torpedo exploded prematurely close to the *Barwon* without hitting her. The steamer, carrying interstate freight, managed to escape at high speed.

That afternoon, an RAAF Hudson bomber spotted a submarine on the surface near the *Barwon* incident. It was lurking in the vicinity of three merchant ships. The Hudson dropped two bombs, which missed the sub. As the pilot came around to drop two more, the *Iron Crown*, carrying manganese ore from Whyalla to Newcastle, blew up before his crew's eyes. The *I-29* managed to dive before being hit. The heavily laden *Iron Crown* sank before any boats could be lowered, taking with her 37 of the 42 men aboard.

The same day, the *Echunga*, a coal carrier from Newcastle, was chased by a submarine on the surface off Wollongong, but her crew fired her deck gun at her pursuer, and she was able to escape. A few hours later, off Cape Moreton, near Brisbane, the *I-29* fired a torpedo at a large passenger ship, the *Canberra*, but as the Japanese report on the incident said, 'the torpedo exploded itself on the way and had no effect'. Disgusted by torpedo failures and a lack of targets, the master of the *I-29* headed for Noumea.

Just before dawn on Friday 5 June a naval campaign of far greater moment had reached its critical point. The Americans, having broken the Japanese naval codes, knew that Yamamoto was planning a battle in the vicinity of Midway, allowing the Americans to ambush the Japanese carrier strike force. Admiral Chuichi Nagumo, aboard the carrier *Akagi*, launched his planes against the US air base on Midway. His scout planes had failed to find a US carrier fleet that was lurking. Japanese reconnaissance efforts before the battle had been grossly inadequate, and the huge area of engagement complicated the operation for both sides. Nevertheless the US Navy was out in force, and while US ground forces at Midway inflicted major damage on the Japanese aircraft attacking the base and airstrip, the American carrier force launched waves of aircraft against Nagumo's fleet.

Admiral Yamamoto and his chief of staff, Admiral Ugaki, aboard the *Yamato*, were some 900 kilometres to the rear of Admiral Nagumo's fleet. Ugaki wrote of devastating reports coming in: 'As a result of enemy carrier-borne bombers and land-based bomber attacks, *Kaga*, *Soryu* and *Akagi* were set ablaze. *Hiryu* continued her attacks upon enemy carriers, while the task force is going to withdraw to the north for a while to regroup. This report immediately changed the prevailing atmosphere in the operations room into one of deepest gloom . . .' Nagumo managed to escape from the burning *Akagi*, and transferred his headquarters to the light cruiser *Nagara*.

Yamamoto, on the combat bridge, merely compressed his lips and gave a grunt at the turn of events. The *Yamato* and her escorts sailed towards the scene to give assistance, but as usual they were too far from the action to do any good. The flagship soon would return to Hashirajima. 'The Hashirajima Fleet', or 'the *Yamato Hotel*', was now a term of increasingly bitter derision and the butt of contemptuous jokes, especially among the naval pilots, who had sustained great losses among their ranks. They also privately jeered the 'battleship admirals' for their anachronistic views and their notions, only now beginning to change, of battleship supremacy.

The commander of the second Japanese carrier division in the Battle of Midway was Admiral Tamon Yamaguchi, a bellicose officer who in February had tabled a blueprint to invade Australia, Midway and Hawaii and who had attacked Pearl Harbor and Darwin, among others. His plan had been dismissed by Yamamoto in favour of the Battle of Midway. Now, American aircraft had fatally damaged three of four carriers in the battle, and only Yamaguchi's flagship, the carrier *Hiryu*, was still afloat, although she had been hit by an estimated 26 torpedoes and 70 bombs.

Dive bombers eventually found the *Hiryu* again and she was hit by more heavy bombs, setting numerous loaded aircraft on fire. The blaze raged out of control until the carrier was a burning wreck with an increasing list. All officers and crew were summoned to the flight deck, and Yamaguchi addressed them: 'As commanding officer of this carrier division, I am fully and solely responsible for the loss of *Hiryu* and *Soryu*. I shall remain on board to the end. I command all of you to leave the ship and continue your loyal service to his majesty, the emperor.'

A SCENE OF DREADFUL CARNAGE

Yamaguchi then led his men in three Banzai cheers for the emperor. He turned to *Hiryu*'s master, Captain Tomeo Kaku, and said: 'There is such a beautiful moon tonight, shall we watch it as we sink?' Yamaguchi's staff begged to stay with them but were refused. Yamaguchi and Kaku were last seen on the bridge waving to the crew who were abandoning ship. Two Japanese destroyers delivered the coup de grace with torpedoes and the big carrier exploded violently. Soon the *Hiryu* – one of the carriers that had launched planes in the first devastating attack on Darwin – slid beneath the waves. She was the fourth Japanese carrier to sink near Midway.

The Americans lost the carrier *Yorktown*, hit by aircraft, and finished off by torpedoes from a Japanese submarine. Ugaki wrote in his diary: 'Thus the distressing day of 5 June came to an end. Don't let another day like this come to us during the course of this war! Let this day be the only one of the greatest failure of my life!'

The Americans, now in the third year of massive warship production, were able to recover quickly from their loss. The Japanese were never able to replace the four lost carriers and the Imperial Navy had suffered a fundamental and permanent blow to their war plans. Midway, on the other hand, spurred US planners to go on the offensive.

For days, the Imperial Navy in Tokyo remained silent on the Midway battle. Instead, the navy made Japan's first announcement of the submarine attacks on Sydney and Madagascar on 5 June, in a radio broadcast by the chief of the navy press section, Captain Hideo Hiraide: 'Our special submarines penetrated deep into the Port of Sydney, the port of first importance in Australia, and terrified the whole of Australia by sinking a large-size warship supposed to have been an American vessel.'

Hiraide said the port of Sydney had been thrown into 'utter disorder' by the midget sub attack. He referred, in a roundabout way, to the loss of 'a handful of Japanese heroes with the special submarines', and restated General Tojo's warnings to Australia: 'If Australia ignores Japan's repeated warnings and wastes away the grace of a few months granted to it without showing any signs of reflection on its part, a great and serious disaster will befall the peaceful land of Australia and the Commonwealth will be turned into a scene of dreadful carnage, of which it can never hope to rid itself.'

The Japanese press desperately played up the midget submarine attacks. SPECIAL SUBMARINES STRIKE MADAGASCAR AND SYDNEY, screamed the *Japan Times* in a banner headline on 6 June: 'The mighty Imperial Navy has scored again. And in this latest blow to the Anglo-American combine, Japan's Special Submarines carried out similar attacks to those at Pearl Harbor at the outset of the war.'

The newspaper repeated Hiraide's specious claim that the special submarines 'penetrating deep into the inner harbor of Sydney, the greatest and most important city of Australia, sank one enemy warship'. By the evening edition, the newspaper had whipped itself into greater frenzy: SYDNEY REPORTED TERROR-STRICKEN OVER JAPANESE SUBMARINE ATTACK.

Its front page report claimed that the 'entire city of Sydney was thrown into a state of turmoil and confusion upon the announcement that Japanese submarines had attacked Sydney, reminding the citizens of the devastating Japanese attack upon Pearl Harbor . . .' The *Nichi Nichi* newspaper editorialised that the result of the Coral Sea battle had caused great uneasiness throughout Australia and the attack on Sydney intensified the Australians' terror: 'No matter what the propaganda of Britain and America may be, the control of the ocean east of Australia has now fallen into our hands.'

On 8 June in Tokyo, the chief of the Navy General Staff, Admiral Nagano, appeared before Emperor Hirohito to explain events at Midway. Hirohito's chief aide, the Marquis Koichi Kido, lord keeper of the privy seal, was present: 'I had supposed that the news of the terrible damage would have caused him untold anxieties, yet his countenance did not show the least bit of change. He said that the setback was severe and regrettable, yet notwithstanding that, he told Nagano to make certain that the morale of the navy did not deteriorate and that the future policy of the navy did not become inactive and passive.'

Soon the Japanese submarine campaign against merchant shipping switched back to Sydney. On 6 June, HMAS *Wilcannia* dropped depth charges on a submarine just eight kilometres off the Sydney Heads. No sub was hit, but the *I-24* continued to lurk offshore, perhaps with the forlorn hope of recovering the midget submarine crew of Ban and Ashibe.

Less than a week after the midget sub raid on Sydney, Australians listening to their wireless sets received another rude shock. Although Curtin had by now privately spoken to the press about his certainty of ultimate victory, the deputy prime minister and army minister, Frank Forde, during a national broadcast, said that Australia was in 'grave and imminent peril'. His attempts at morale building were crude and clumsy. Speaking in support of the liberty loan drive, Forde unleashed an apocalyptic vision:

> An enemy invader – strong, efficient, ruthless and cruel – is massing on our northern gates. At any hour his hordes may be loosed upon us, to deluge this country in fire, bloodshed and destruction. Whether we can stave off that peril rests primarily upon ourselves.

The deputy prime minister was still experiencing difficulty fine-tuning his message. He also said the entry of enemy submarines into Sydney Harbour 'marked the beginning of an attack on the industrial heart of Australia'. It didn't.

Life continued much as normal. Coalminers went about their regular business of striking on a whim, despite the urgent need for coal. Four New South Wales mines were idle, and two partially idle, as the result of strikes on 8 June. Even the Miners'

Federation was appalled. 'The whips are cracking now and it is the duty of miners to pull their weight,' the union's central executive said.

At Admiralty House, the governor-general reflected on how lucky Australia had been:

> If the Japanese had really pushed hard against Australia three months ago, they would have had a very good chance of success, but the situation is very different today. A lot of stuff has been coming in from America; men, munitions, aeroplanes, and many of our own troops have got back from the Middle East, and an invasion of Australia would be a very different proposition today . . .

Lord Gowrie on 9 June told King George that Australians were elated at the success at Midway. With great foresight he added: 'If it is as good as it looks at the moment, it will alter the whole situation in the Pacific.'

22

THE SUBMARINERS' REVENGE

The men of the mother sub *I-24* had waited in vain off southern Sydney for the return of their two comrades. Now, spurred on by frustration, anger and revenge, the big sub surfaced, and in the chill winter air crewmen leapt to the still dripping 5.5 inch deck gun, and began rapidly to fire shells towards the city. While the *I-24* was ordered to destroy merchant ships, its crew was also encouraged to instil additional terror into the hearts of Sydney people. Off Newcastle, the *I-21* received a similar order – fire your deck gun at civilian shore targets.

At five minutes past midnight on 8 June, thousands of Sydney people near the harbour and along the city's coastline were awakened by the boom of guns and the whoosh of shells passing overhead. Flashes lit up the sky. Many ran into shelters constructed in backyards, schools and parks.

This time, for nine-year-old Jim Mair and his family at Bondi, it just had to be the dreaded Japanese invasion. Once again he and his siblings were put under the billiard table to shelter from the bombardment. 'We distinctly heard the shells going overhead and the air raid sirens. It was pretty scary.'

1942

The sound of shells from the sea seemed loudest in Bondi, Bellevue Hill, Rose Bay, Bronte, Coogee and Randwick. Despite the midget submarine attack on Sydney a week earlier, Sydney still was not fully blacked out when the shelling began. Someone in authority quickly threw the switches, and the city was plunged in blackness. Air raid sirens began wailing.

The *I-24* fired ten rounds that night, but only four of the shells exploded. Three caused minor damage and one blew up harmlessly. Other shells splashed into the harbour. Sydney coast watchers saw gun flashes at sea and soon coastal batteries responded loudly. But the *I-24* quickly disappeared beneath the waves.

Shells fell in Rose Bay, Woollahra, Bellevue Hill and Bondi. One that failed to explode tore through flats in Manion Avenue, Woollahra. In one of the upstairs flats lived the Hirschs, a family who had fled from Nazi Germany. A friend, Miss Lanham, was staying with the family: 'I heard some whistling sounds overhead. I tried to be calm and tell myself it was only practice. Then I felt the building shake and saw some debris. I took the baby and went out to a shelter room. I felt very nervous as I passed the shell on the stairs on my way down.'

The Hirschs themselves – an electrical engineer and his elderly mother – were lucky to escape. The dud shell hit the outer wall of the flat, tearing a hole through two thicknesses of brick above Mrs Hirsch's bed, then skidded along the wall flanking the bed, smashed through another wall, and finished up on the staircase. Mrs Hirsch was showered with bricks and her bed was broken by falling debris, but she escaped unscathed. Her son, sleeping in the adjoining sitting room, was hit by bricks.

Other shells partly demolished the rear of two cottages in Bellevue Hill, one exploded outside a grocery shop at Woollahra causing minor damage, and another buried into the ground before exploding harmlessly. In Kings Cross, crowds gathered in the street when the shelling began and refused to disperse when air raid wardens tried to move them on. Buses and trams continued to operate and wardens had difficulty in getting the few motorists on the streets to shade their headlights.

Joan Hamilton of Chamberlain Avenue, Rose Bay, was startled by an explosion. Then came the sound of shells shrieking overhead and exploding nearby. The young mother was at home with three children; Jim, aged six, Kyran, three, and Dominic, two. She quickly rounded up her sleepy children and crammed the lot of them into the linen closet with her, a tight fit. The explosions soon ceased, but Mrs Hamilton was determined to follow instructions from her husband, Walter, to stay put. When the phone started ringing and persisted over several hours, she wouldn't budge.

The caller was her husband wanting to tell her that the all clear had been sounded. Soon afterwards, Joan Hamilton, like many Sydney parents, decided to take her children to the countryside. They went to Trangie, 500 kilometres north-west of the capital. But after a fortnight, the family returned. 'Never was one for the country life, my mother,' her son Walter later wryly recalled.

Less than two hours after the Sydney shelling, the *I-21*, which had carried Susumu Ito's float plane before the aircraft was destroyed, surfaced in Stockton Bight, north-east of Newcastle. Gunners raced to the sub's 5.5-inch deck gun and fired 34 rounds on the city, aiming at the shipyards at Carrington and at the steelworks at Kooragang Island.

About 24 shells fell in the area of Newcastle's power station and customs house, causing minor damage. Many of the submarine's shells were faulty and failed to explode. One unexploded shell damaged a storage shed at the steelworks. Another shell landed on an elevated park near the Parnell Place air raid shelter, sending jagged shrapnel in all directions. Two small boys were in a house and saw the gun flashes at sea from their bedroom window. Their mother raced upstairs and brought the boys to safety just before a shell exploded, wrecking their bedroom. Young Peter Wilson was photographed by the *Newcastle Morning Herald* beaming from the scattered window, and was called 'the luckiest boy in town'.

After a delay of 13 minutes, the gunners at Fort Scratchley

opened fire on the enemy vessel with four rounds. Gunners in the fort could not spot the sub even though they could see the flashes. Pilot Susumu Ito was on the conning tower of the *I-21* watching all the action:

> They fired shells at us and they came pretty close. We knew it [our gunfire] wouldn't be very effective but we wanted to cause concern for the people and make them feel uncomfortable. I was on the bridge watching the gunfire. The enemy shells hit the water with a splash. That was scary. If they hit us we were dead. Even one would sink us. Usually if a sub comes up to fire guns, you don't expect return fire. Captain Matsumura Kanji was the most courageous of all the submarine captains. We did not dive and kept firing for a time. But I was thinking ... we should get out of there.

After the Newcastle shelling, one mother, Catherine Hitchcock, of Wallsend, slept with a carving knife under her pillow, determined to protect her clan should the worst occur. Her husband was away in the air force and Mrs Hitchcock had responsibility for her grandmother, Kate, 83, her great Aunt Maud, aged in her sixties, and her two sons, Phil, aged ten, and John, born at home just ten days earlier.

The national home security minister, H.P. Lazzarini, now issued a civil defence pamphlet for parents and teachers: 'Now that Australia is directly threatened we need to understand the reaction of children to air raids and similar dangers ... The fear or courage of children is greatly influenced by the example set by their elders.'

During the shelling, Lord and Lady Gowrie and their staff spent an hour in their air raid shelter at Kirribilli. But Gowrie, writing to King George, noted dryly that shells were dropped 'in the fashionable resident area of Bellevue Hill, Sydney, where all the "best people" reside, but the slums of Kirribilli, where Admiralty House is located, were left undisturbed'. After the midget raid and the shelling, the value of houses in harbourside suburbs suddenly declined sharply, and waterfront houses became much more affordable.

Gowrie said John Curtin was 'a very sound, well balanced, sane and able man'. Yet despite Australia's 'magnificent war effort', he thought Australians could do more:

> In spite of the fact that the war has actually come to these shores, there are still sections of the community who do not seem to realise what is happening. But I hope the events of this last week will produce a different atmosphere.
>
> One miner's wife was heard to remark that 'if the Japs come, they will still have to have their coal'. She had to be reminded that they would still have to have their coal, but they were not likely to pay her husband ten pounds a week to get it for them!
>
> Another lady is said to have suggested that if the Japs come, there will be plenty of good servants in Australia at last. Apparently she had omitted to consider the question as to who would be the servants and who would be the masters!

Lord Gowrie had toned down an earlier version of his thoughts. In a draft letter to George VI, prepared but not sent, the governor-general was slightly more critical:

> These two actions have had a stimulating affect and one had long hoped that something of the kind would occur in order to bring home to the people of Australia the reality of the dangers with which they are faced.

Japan now celebrated the six-month anniversary of the emperor's declaration of war. In that time, the Japanese military had occupied an area of 3,836,000 square kilometres, and more than 136 million people had been 'liberated' from the shackles of Anglo-Saxon imperialism. Japanese newspapers were proclaiming 'unparalleled war results.' For such gains, Japan's losses were small, they said, with only 9000 war dead and 20,000 wounded. There was no mention of the disastrous Midway battle. The leadership of Japan now had access to almost unlimited supplies to help construct its Co-Prosperity Sphere and carry on the war to its conclusion. But after Midway the Imperial Navy was woefully diminished, particularly in regard to aircraft and skilled pilots. Worst, its carrier fleet was irreparably reduced.

On 8 June, Canberra newsmen found Prime Minister Curtin in an unusually happy mood when they met him for yet another private briefing. Joe Alexander wrote in his diary:

> Curtin told us today that the battle of Midway Island removed the danger of large scale effect on Australia for the time being. The Nip Fleet which included many transports is retreated... He said in view of this the submarine campaign along our coast – which had proved very expensive for the Nips – should not be taken seriously. Today's shellings were childish in execution and results and were merely face savers.

A few days later, Curtin's mood darkened when told that, with less than five days to go, the government's second liberty loan was only one third of the 35-million pound subscription sought from the public. One million pounds per day was needed to run the war. 'A soldier who leaves his unit and his mates without authority is branded and dealt with as a deserter,' he said angrily, 'a civilian who selfishly deserts his fellow Australians and his country is no less a traitor.' Two weeks later, Curtin was pleased to report that the loan was oversubscribed.

On 10 June, Imperial General Headquarters in Tokyo belatedly mentioned the Battle of Midway. But it did so in dishonest terms, claiming that Japan had 'at last secured Supreme power in the Pacific', with two American carriers sunk for the loss of one Japanese carrier and another badly damaged. Street celebrations were held in Tokyo; injured Japanese survivors of the battle were

THE SUBMARINERS' REVENGE

isolated in remote hospitals and sworn to secrecy to prevent the truth leaking out.

The navy planners had feared that their attacking force wouldn't be given the opportunity to clash with US carriers. Before the ships strike force had departed Hashirajima, Baron Tomioka went as far as saying: 'What we fear most in this operation is that the enemy will avoid our fleet and will not launch attacks.'

Later, Tomioka particularly would lament the loss of highly skilled Japanese pilots and their aircraft: 'It was a shattering defeat. What was more important than anything else was crew members ... it ended in that resounding defeat and almost all of our experienced men were killed ... a lethal loss.'

Japan estimated that 332 aircraft were lost in the Battle of Midway, including some 280 aircraft lost with carriers when they sank. No battle would have a greater impact on the outcome of the Pacific war. Vice Admiral Fukudome was aghast: 'The losses are massive,' he told his subordinates, instructing them to conceal the extent from Japan's political leaders.

After the initial attacks on coastal shipping, protective security was ramped up. The Navy Board introduced a convoy system linking most ports between Adelaide and Brisbane. On 9 June, a small British freighter, the *Orestes*, was fired on by two Japanese submarines south east of Jervis Bay. The ship escaped with slight damage.

RAAF aircraft continued to report submarine sightings. On the night of 11 June, the residents of Wamberal on the central coast north of Sydney reported seeing flashes at sea and heard noise. The Panamanian freighter, the *Guatemala*, had been torpedoed and sunk, although all aboard managed to get away in lifeboats. The freighter had fallen behind in a convoy.

General MacArthur attended the advisory war council meeting of government and opposition leaders in Melbourne on 17 June, and reported that Australia, after the Coral Sea and the Midway engagements, was fortunate. Had the Battle of the Coral Sea been lost, Australia 'would have been placed on the defensive indefinitely or even worse'. 'Australia was in grave danger up to the time of the Coral Sea action,' he said. 'The results of that action and the successes gained at Midway Island had assured the defensive position of Australia.'

But he warned that Japan had shown great resiliency and notwithstanding these two major defeats, 'she has not been thrown on the defensive'. The American general spoke glowingly about the building up of the Australian defence forces and the Australian war effort. But he did not rule out the chance of a future invasion.

The loss of the Coral Sea battle could have seen Australian east coast cities, at the very least, bombed from carriers and shelled. It might even have spelled invasion. A Japanese victory at Midway would have made invasion a certainty, in MacArthur's opinion.

Despite the recent Allied naval victories, invasion still worried Curtin. Less than two weeks after MacArthur's Melbourne briefing, in the privacy of his office and speaking with journalists sworn to secrecy, Curtin lashed out at Churchill and Roosevelt: 'Two men thousands of miles from here are inclined to think that Australia is in no danger.'

When General MacArthur visited Curtin in Canberra in July, he had an even more positive view of the war. In his own 'off-the-record' chat with senior parliamentary reporters, MacArthur said that in the last six months Australia's position had strengthened immeasurably. He could envisage half a million servicemen, with a little more training, as a powerful fighting force. Equipment was coming to Australia in considerable quantity, he said. There were no major units of the Japanese fleet south of the Caroline Islands, but there was evidence that the Japanese were 'working like beavers' to consolidate their positions to the islands north of Australia.

MacArthur repeated that if not for the Allies' successes in the Coral Sea and Midway battles, Australians by now 'would have been fighting the enemy on our own soil'. He reassured reporters that the much anticipated offensives to be launched from Australia would occur soon.

By now Curtin, partially reassured, thought it unlikely that Australia faced imminent invasion, although he wouldn't rule it out. He knew there would be a torturous effort ahead to stem the Japanese tide with costly, bloody battles to reclaim systematically the Pacific islands. Recent shipping losses were beyond the nation's annual replacement capacity, and shortages would increase, he said. In a national broadcast, he also said:

> In the past fortnight, we Australians have had a taste of submarine warfare. Australian steamers have gone to the bottom. Our forces struck back successfully. But, who can foretell the future?

Nevertheless, it was vital to the grand strategy of the Allied cause that Japan should not take Australia:

> I say flatly it is possible that Australia can be lost. And if that happens, then Hawaii and the whole North American coast, from Alaska to Canada down to Mexico, will be open to Japanese attack free of any threat from any base in the Japanese rear. Had the outcome of the Coral Sea battle been adverse who could give guarantees as to the consequences for Australia? That battle was crucial with fate.
>
> The combined effect of the Coral Sea, Midway Island and Aleutians battles, while frustrating from Japan's point of view, are far from decisive in the struggle through which we must pass if we are to reach our men locked up in Singapore... and if we are to strike at the very heart of Japan.

On 20 July, after a lull in coastal activity, the Japanese submarine campaign was renewed in earnest. On a clear, moonlit night, a Greek freighter, the *George S. Livanos*, was hit by a torpedo

30 kilometres off Jervis Bay. Fishing boats picked up the crew, some injured.

The following morning, the Nowra observation station reported a boatload of survivors heading for the coast, and wreckage floating on the sea. As the location was close to the sinking of the Greek freighter, it was assumed that it was not a new sinking. But the same Japanese sub had put a torpedo into a US supply ship, the *Coast Farmer*, which was abandoned. Of its crew, 41 were saved, but one could not be located. By now, the navy and air force were mounting heavy patrols on the east coast of Australia, but with its massive coastline, and so many Australian warships and aircraft overseas, the exercise was close to futile.

On 22 July, Curtin received a tremendous shock when he was told that the Japanese had landed an invasion force on the northern side of Papua. The enemy had begun fighting their way inland against a small Australian militia force. The Japanese were headed towards the massive Owen Stanley Range, the great natural mountain barrier which protected the Australian base of Port Moresby on the other side in the south. After failing in their earlier bid to capture Moresby from the sea, the Japanese had decided to take the base from the rear, by climbing over the Kokoda track, a narrow walking trail linking mountainous villages.

Curtin had every right to be worried. The Imperial Army wanted to capture Port Moresby, so close to Australia's Cape York Peninsula, the second time around to prevent the expected American counterattack. Moresby's planned capture was 'a prelude to a Japanese occupation of northern Australia', according to naval historian Professor Paul S. Dull, a former marine corp officer, interpreting Japan's *Senshi Sosho* official war history series.

The Australian prime minister was now desperate for superior sea and air power in order to wrest the initiative from Japan, and to assure the essential defensive position of the south-west Pacific. Guided by General MacArthur, Curtin was hammering Washington and London about the urgent necessity to strike Japan hard.

At the end of July, Curtin received an appreciation of the war situation from British defence chiefs and was appalled to discover that it did not even mention the Pacific. Since the outbreak of war British chiefs had never fully realised the possibilities in the Pacific, Curtin complained to Churchill:

> Japan ... has made a landing in Papua which threatens our important advanced base at Port Moresby, which is vital to the defence of the north-eastern coast against enemy landings and the maintenance of the passage through Torres Strait for the supply of Darwin.

A further Allied war of words about the defence of Australia was underway. As Japanese troops were pouring on to the northern beaches of Papua, another US cargo vessel, the *William Dawes*, was attacked and sunk, this time 24 kilometres off Tathra Head, on the far south coast of New South Wales. Fifty-six survivors were landed at Merimbula, including five wounded. The ship's four-man gun crew were among those killed.

Next morning, La Perouse radio station in Sydney received the distress message 'S.S.S.S.' and a vessel's position near Newcastle. A cargo vessel, the *Allara*, had been hit by a torpedo and was going down by the stern. Despite her serious damage, she was towed into Newcastle harbour by a tug. Five crew had been killed and five wounded.

That was four ships sunk in four days. There was an immediate rush to establish more observation and communication posts along the south coast, in particular. Local postmasters and clergy were among those who signed up for voluntary duty at new posts at Cobargo, Bega, Bombala, Bemboka, and Nerrigundah, among others.

In the early hours of 26 July, a submarine surfaced 40 kilometres off Eden on the far south coast, and began shelling the small British steamship, the *Coolana*. The ship was undamaged and made it to the nearest port. Soon there was a particularly vicious attack against a big deep sea fishing trawler, the *Durreenbee* off the south coast. When survivors came ashore at Batemans Bay they reported: 'Sub was 200 feet long and shelled ship from 80 to 100 yards, circled ship two or three times and fired 12 shells and fired with machineguns. Ship not holed from waterline and still afloat.'

A pilot flying overhead radioed: 'Damaged ship identified as *Durreenbee* – funnel knocked towards stern, four shell holes in bridge which is burnt out, bad list to port, nine miles out.' A message soon came from the volunteer air observers' corps at Moruya: 'Damaged vessel is fishing trawler ... casualties two killed, four injured, one seriously. All injured in Moruya Hospital. Sub attacked at 0045/K/3 which shelled and machinegun fire when within hailing distance.'

According to Japan's war history series volume on submarines, *Senshi Sosho, Sensuikanshi*, the *I*-class subs that took part in the Sydney raid sank five ships totalling 25,413 tons and 'destroyed' another three ships [presumably meaning badly damaged] totalling 17,122 tons. The *I-21* reported that of ten torpedoes fired, two hit their targets, two self-detonated, two were presumed to have sunk on launch and one deviated from its intended trajectory. The others missed. Four torpedoes from the *I-24* self-detonated, as did one from the *I-27*.

The original Sydney raiders were relieved by other subs, continuing their warfare off the Australian east coast for many months. In January 1943, more ships were sunk off Sydney Heads, with survivors actually coming through the Heads in lifeboats. The toll of sunken and damaged ships would have been far less had the RAN and the RAAF developed effective anti-submarine techniques. None of the submarines being hunted immediately after the Sydney raid in 1942 or off the east coast in 1943 were sunk or damaged by Australian forces.

23

RETURN OF THE HERO GODS

Ambassador Tatsuo Kawai, under house arrest in Melbourne, stood motionless as he read the multiple headlines of the *Age* newspaper, tears welling in his eyes. RAID BY SUBMARINES ON SYDNEY HARBOUR. THREE JAPANESE MIDGETS DESTROYED. ONE SMALL HARBOUR BOAT SUNK. It was his first news of the midget attack on Sydney.

On the afternoon of 5 June, the midget submarine *M-27*, containing the remains of Chuman and Omori, was raised by crane from the floor of Sydney Harbour. The sub had been severely damaged by depth charges. About five or six metres of the vessel's stern was missing, the result of the suicide demolition charge. On 8 June, the Japanese ambassador was informed by the navy that all four bodies found so far – Matsuo, Tsuzuku, Chuman and Omori – would be cremated the following day, unless Kawai had any objection.

The ambassador expressed deep appreciation for Rear Admiral Muirhead-Gould's courtesy and kindly thought, and asked if he could take the ashes of the dead men back with him to Japan as part of an exchange of diplomats and other civilian nationals that was in the process of arrangement.

When news of the planned service with full military honours appeared in newspapers, many Sydneysiders were aghast. One prominent Rose Bay resident, Mr H. R. Redding, protested: 'The proposal is abhorrent to Australians who heard with regret of the tragic loss of life on the depot ship which was sunk at the hands of these persons.' Muirhead-Gould felt obliged to defend his actions publicly, which had been approved by Foreign Minister Evatt: 'It must take courage of the very highest order to go out in a thing like that steel coffin... How many of us are really prepared to make one thousandth of the sacrifice that these men made?' the admiral asked.

The RAN proceeded with its funeral honours anyway. Those present at the service included Muirhead-Gould and the consul general of Switzerland, Hans Hedinger, who gave Kawai a full account of the service:

> The coffins, which were of good quality, were placed in the chapel at the Crematorium and were each draped with a Japanese flag. While the remains were being placed in the crematorium furnace, the naval escort, which included a firing party, bearers and bugler, stood at attention outside the Crematorium, the firing party with arms reversed. As the last coffin disappeared from view, three volleys were fired by the naval party, after which the party presented arms with fixed bayonets while the bugler sounded 'The Last Post.'

The *Nippon Times*, a rabid wartime propaganda sheet, gave an excitable account of Tatsuo Kawai's reaction on reading of the Sydney raid: 'We gripped the paper tightly and were moved to tears by the news. Who would have thought that the brave men of the Imperial Navy would make such a thrust at the very heart of the enemy. The dauntless, invincible spirit of the Japanese Navy threw the 7,000,000 inhabitants of Australia into the depths of fear and despair.'

Kawai may have made such a statement after his return to

Japan, but at *Carn Brea* in June 1942, his personal reaction was quite different. He called the Japanese operation 'clumsy' in a memorial poem he penned at the time as a private remembrance:

> Whether they achieve or not, in the end they come to know, it is a one-way path to death.
>
> Deep under the water, they cannot come up; they die there, regrettable – more good men.
>
> This clumsy surprise attack failed: they died, fighting with the enemy; astonishing . . .
>
> Bullets and blades, bloodshed and death: now I know exactly how easy it is to die.
>
> Mid-winter, know not of what it is to kill, deep in the sea is where you should die.

Kawai, the ardent expansionist, had not changed his views about Japan's just rights as the leader of Asia, but he had moderated his views about the need for war.

The former ambassador had been under house arrest at *Carn Brea* since 8 December 1941, along with some 20 of his staffers. The residence was a comfortable place to sit out the war. It was set on a rise, within expansive wooded grounds that boasted a tennis court and formal rose gardens. The married couples on Kawai's staff had their own rooms. At the rear of the residence, linked to the main house by an ornate wood-panelled hallway, was a large two-storey ballroom where the single male diplomatic and consular staff had bunks. The ballroom was overlooked by galleries. In this genteel atmosphere, Kawai and his young American-born hostess and private secretary, Tamaye Tsutsumida, had entertained the elite of Australia's business, government, legal and newspaper world.

Kawai still kept his staff fully employed during the week. Weekends included tennis parties at *Carn Brea*. There were special birthday and anniversary Japanese dinners, games of chess called *shogi*, at which Kawai would always emerge victorious, and walks with the legation's giant hound through the charming grounds.

Curtin's foreign minister, Herbert Evatt, who was in charge of the Japanese diplomats, maintained correspondence with Kawai, praising him in parliament just before the outbreak of war, and telling him in March 1942 he was 'above suspicion'.

Australia's military authorities suspected that this trust in the Japanese was misplaced, and they were right. Kawai had put his staff to work gathering intelligence of military value, adding to a detailed study started before the war, and employing a collaborator to pass it on to Japan. They had open access to the Swiss Consulate library in Melbourne.

On 13 August, just before his departure for Japan as part of the diplomatic exchange, the legation's staff saw a hearse come winding up the drive. The Swiss consul in Melbourne delivered four small white boxes which were carried inside to a special room where Kawai had prepared an altar: 'I gazed every morning and night at the coffers containing the ashes of the heroes, the thought of their loyalty and bravery, transcending life and death, invariably overwhelming me with gripping emotion.'

Kawai was deeply touched over the chivalry displayed by Rear Admiral Muirhead-Gould:

> Enemies they may be, but admirable they are, for which I offer my praise and gratitude, for the flag at half mast,
> Admirable Gould, though enemy he may be, is a warrior who knows the pathos of things,
> The ashes of the four brave soldiers were welcomed home, a sakaki tree put in place,
> And festivities were held. Bless us,
> Under Japan's national flag, young men and enemy scared: shocking.

Kawai sent thank-you messages to the Australian navy and to Evatt, which said the return of the ashes would be 'deeply appreciated not only by the relatives of the deceased but also, I am sure, by the whole of my fellow countrymen'.

On the evening of Sunday, 16 August, the ambassador was escorted to Station Pier at Port Melbourne, where the Japanese official party boarded the *City of Canterbury*, an old British cargo-passenger steamer converted into a troopship. The ship had the words 'DIPLOMAT' painted down both sides in large letters, together with the British flag. She would be illuminated throughout the voyage to guarantee passage free from attack.

The Australian press was not allowed to report the ship's departure, although there was no similar restriction on foreign correspondents. Two weeks later, the *Times* of London ran an extraordinary interview with the Japanese diplomat, in which he regretted the outbreak of war. The story would ruin his career back in Japan:

> I have failed in my mission and return to Japan bitterly disappointed. I came to Australia in high hope of creating a better understanding, even though the war clouds were already gathering on the Pacific.
>
> The outbreak of war was the greatest blow I have received in my life. Australians who know how I struggled to avert war in the Pacific will understand when I say that my spirit has been broken.
>
> The gods decreed that Japan and Australia should go to war, but there is no bitterness in my heart towards Australia. Every patriotic Australian and Japanese must offer his life to his country, but we can see this horrible thing through like gentlemen.
>
> It will be a stern and bitter struggle, but it cannot last forever, and when peace comes Australia and Japan must resume normal trading. I believe that the world will be a better place for all after this war. The old order has gone, no matter which side wins.

The *City of Canterbury* sailed for Lourenco Marques (now Maputo, the capital of Mozambique). The crowded ship carried 948 Japanese passengers and an Australian Army guard unit.

Kawai's officials would include known military spies, including an Imperial Navy agent formerly attached to Singapore, Mitsumi Yanase. The spies and agents could take their intelligence back to Japan. The luggage of the Japanese officials was not searched, nor their cameras and film checked.

Kawai's regrets at leaving Australia under the cloud of war appeared to be genuine. After the war he would write about his friend John Curtin's elevation to the prime ministership in October 1941: 'I thought things would now start to happen, but unfortunately in little more than a month war was declared between our two countries. After being detained for seven months and without even an opportunity to bid him farewell, I made my departure from Australia, silently praying for his good health and a brave fight.'

After an appalling voyage through mountainous seas in the Great Australian Bight, the *City of Canterbury* crossed the Indian Ocean and reached the coast of Africa safely; on 9 September, the Japanese transferred to the *Kamakura Maru*. The luxury passenger liner, so different from the overcrowded old steamer that had carried them on the first leg of their voyage, bore the Rising Sun on each side, together with two large white crosses. She left port on the homeward journey with 870 passengers.

The *Asahi* newspaper correspondent, Seishi Kurozumi, was aboard the ship, and had ample opportunity on the voyage to Japan to interview Kawai. Before leaving Lourenco Marques, Kurozumi filed a long feature on Australia's progress in the war which appeared in many Japanese newspapers. AUSTRALIA IS RIPE FOR LIQUIDATING DEPENDENCE ON UNRELIABLE BRITAIN, its headline ran in the *Japan Times* on 16 September.

The story documented how Japan's military successes had driven 'the whole of Australia into a fearful state of confusion' and had prompted appeals to Britain to send help. But the British did not reply promptly, forcing Australia to turn towards the United States for assistance. At this time, John Curtin and Winston Churchill were still locked in bitter disagreement about support for the Australian and south-west Pacific theatres of war.

On 25 August, the Japanese launched the second phase of their attempt to capture Port Moresby. Their forces began shelling Milne Bay, at the very south-eastern tip of the New Guinea island 'tail' in preparation to landing. The Japanese expected that the port and its three airfields would become a major base and give them air cover for the invasion of Port Moresby and also allow them to bomb northern Australia from a land base.

The Japanese military were astounded by the ferocity of the Australians' defence. Milne Bay was protected by two brigades of Australian troops, covered by two RAAF fighter squadrons. The over-confident Japanese had neglected air cover and their ships and troops immediately came under intense fire from the air. Bitter fighting occurred in rough terrain, amid appalling heat and humidity.

Further north on the eastern side of the 'tail' of New Guinea, the number of Japanese troops landed at Gona and Buna had increased to more than 13,000 by late August. The invaders were pushing the Australians back, fighting their way forward over the torturous Kokoda track towards their eventual goal of Port Moresby.

At the same time, the Japanese occupied the Micronesian Ocean and Nauru islands well east of New Guinea. Nauru, administered by Australia, New Zealand, and Britain, was a major phosphate producer.

You listen, and the noise increases, pressing closer. Birds, insects, rustling trees and bushes. The dank jungle is seething with life, and you crouch, listening, watching, and waiting. The trees overhead form a dark, dripping canopy. An exotic bug crawls over your hand; something scratches in the undergrowth just out of sight. You wait some more, sweating, breathing heavily; the most beautiful, ridiculously coloured butterfly makes a jerky flight across the track.

With your mates, you have dashed across moss-covered logs tied together with vine over a dangerous cascading stream, crashing its way over boulders downstream. Then an hour spent dragging yourself ever upwards through a steeply sloping, slippery track of mud, using branches, vines and stumps to pull yourself higher. Two steps forward, one back.

You're bathed in perspiration, yet the air is cool as you crouch in the firing pit, a cube dug into the track with a clear field of fire down the slope. The pungent smell of the earth mixes with the whiff of smoke from a distant cooking fire. Your glasses constantly fog up; take them off and the sweat stings your eyes. Suddenly, it starts to rain again. Torrentially. The socks in your mud-caked boots are wet with your own blood where you have pulled swelling leeches from your feet. Your bones ache. You try not to breathe too heavily, all the while keeping a constant lookout. The heart pounds. Surely it can be heard?

You twitch at every sound, eyes darting this way and that, fearful. They are still coming, and you never see the bastards. But they are everywhere, fanatical, experienced and willing to die. The mind plays tricks. You sense them.

Yet, you have no rifle and ammunition and your pack is not that heavy, 12 kilograms, nothing compared with what Australian troops carried in the war years when they were being chased over the Owen Stanley Range. No one is chasing you, cutting you off from your mates, and shooting at you. The firing pits are still there, and vestiges of the war – a clip of bullets, rusting scraps of metal, even a mortar bomb in the stream – are still to be found. But the war ended many decades ago, and you are just an Australian trekker on the remnants of the Kokoda track.

When they came from Rabaul and landed in August 1942, the Japanese army's knowledge of what lay ahead was almost as poor as that of the newly arrived Australian officers. They thought the good walking tracks across the mountains might readily be made into roads. The Australian officers in Moresby thought exactly the same. How mistaken both sides were. The roads still don't exist.

The Japanese were led by the tubby little general Tomitaro Horii, who had invaded Rabaul, and had been with the first invasion force turned back before reaching Port Moresby. Now, the invaders had little problem against the under-strength Australian 39th Militia Battalion. At Kokoda, the fighting became even more desperate; the government centre was retaken by the Australians, then lost again. Behind them stood the awesome black massif and the path to escape.

Like Japan, Australia had sent youths off to war. It was in contravention of Curtin's war cabinet, which had decided that Australian militiamen under 20 who had not completed six months basic training were not to be sent to the front line. But the army's chief of the General Staff, General Sturdee, pleaded that the youths not be withdrawn as this would disintegrate their units. The advisory war council and war cabinet agreed and 18 year olds fought on the Kokoda track. The civil defence force militiamen eventually were reinforced by elements of the 7th Division of the AIF.

The Japanese thought they would reach Port Moresby in a couple of weeks, but they soon realised the nature of the track. The inexperienced Australian militia fought a desperate battle, gradually retreating over the mountains. Horii established his headquarters at Kokoda on 24 August, and by 12 September, with reinforcements quickly coming up from the beaches, he had 5000 men under his command.

On the track, the Australians were continually forced back from ridge to ridge, with bloody battles in between each retreat. Malaria and other diseases struck down both sides. Sustaining their supply lines became a nightmare for both the Australians and the Japanese, despite the efforts of thousands of overworked and frightened local bearers on both sides.

There was increasing discontent in Australia with the situation in New Guinea. The war cabinet had decided that two senior ministers, Arthur Drakeford, minister for air, and Frank Forde, minister for the army, should visit New Guinea. They stayed only a few days. Forde flew up to New Guinea with Brigadier

C.E.M. ('Gaffer') Lloyd, and during the flight, Forde reportedly said to Lloyd: 'Gaffer, you don't think they'll get Moresby, do you?'

'No', said Lloyd. A bit later Forde asked, 'Are you really confident?' 'Yes.' 'You don't know what would happen if the Japs got Moresby!' exclaimed Forde. 'Don't I?' said Lloyd. 'No', said Forde, 'I'd lose my seat in Capricornia.'

On 16 and 17 September, the Australians were forced to withdraw from Ioribaiwa ridge to Imita ridge, only some 50 kilometres from Port Moresby, or little more than a day's march from the edge of the Sogeri plateau, overlooking the coastal plain with Moresby and the sea in the distance.

At Ioribaiwa a Japanese officer scribbled desperate notes in his diary:

> 19 September: Inspected tents and noticed the scarcity of food. Entire company turned out to forage for food. Thirteen malaria, six diarrhoea and five other patients are getting worse. No medicines have arrived. Went to battalion headquarters to report the food situation and requisition supplies. Returned empty-handed. Wonder what General Headquarters is doing. Patients will die, and we will soon starve. How can we fight against this?

General Douglas MacArthur, not knowing the condition of the Japanese, was deeply disturbed at the gradual Australian withdrawal. In a secure phone conference with Curtin, he questioned why the Australians once again were withdrawing 'although no casualties are reported'. The American leader questioned the efficiency of the Australian troops, and said he had no confidence in the Australian command. He insisted that the Australian Military Forces commander-in-chief, General Blamey, go to Port Moresby to 'take personal command and energise the situation'.

So Curtin sent Blamey to Moresby, where Blamey sacked the fiery commander of the New Guinea Force, General Sydney

Rowell after a row. Rowell took Blamey's presence as a lack of confidence. Blamey's trip to Moresby was the result of agitation from a worried MacArthur. In fact, with reinforcements coming over the Kokoda track from Moresby, Australian commanders had been confident of holding the Japanese, who by now were experiencing appalling difficulties of supply, including the most basic food, leading to starvation.

Back in Canberra, fears of a Japanese invasion of cities such as Sydney and Melbourne were on Curtin's mind. By 11 September, the Australian prime minister was losing his battle to persuade the US and Britain to amend the 'beat Hitler first' policy to make a priority of beating the Japanese in New Guinea and the Solomon islands. He told President Roosevelt that should the Allies suffer naval losses in the Pacific, and be unable to prevent an invasion of Australia, the result would be catastrophic: 'The Japanese would probably by-pass our isolated northern concentrations and attack nearer to the main centres of population in the south.'

Curtin said General Blamey considered that the forces at Australia's disposal were too thinly spread to meet such a contingency. Blamey and Curtin placed the minimum strength required at three divisions more than Australia actually possessed, even counting the two American divisions in Australia. Curtin said the Japanese were offering determined resistance in New Guinea: 'There is every reason to believe that they will attempt to oust our forces from Milne Bay and Port Moresby.'

The US president wasn't convinced. On 16 September, Roosevelt replied that that the US Pacific Fleet could not provide a superior naval force solely for the defence of Australia and New Zealand. But increased ground and air forces were being considered for Australia. Roosevelt agreed with his military chiefs who thought that the current forces in Australia, when fully equipped and effectively trained, were adequate for the task:

[They] are sufficient to defeat the present Japanese force in New Guinea and to provide for the security of Australia against invasion on the scale that the Japanese are capable of launching at this time or in the immediate future.

Roosevelt estimated that available Japanese shipping could support an invasion force of about 200,000 troops. Curtin knew that Australia at this time had about 560,000 troops scattered throughout the continent. Many were still under training and would have to travel vast distances to engage an enemy in combat.

Curtin's representative in London, the former Australian prime minister Stanley Bruce, found Churchill even more immovable: 'He personally, however, could not feel that there was an immediate danger of a full scale operation by the Japanese against Australia and this being the case it was vital we should proceed with our plans against the primary enemy – Germany.'

As this was going on, Australians were startled by a newspaper report from Washington that quoted Prime Minister General Tojo boasting that Japan would occupy the city of Perth by next January.

24

SAVAGERY AND DISHONOUR

Night is rapidly settling over an idyllic beach in the tropics. The sky turns pink, and then it's suddenly dark. A gentle surf rolls on the black sand beach with its fringe of coconut palms. This is the tiny village of Gona, a key location in the Kokoda campaign. A tall timber cross marking the site of the original Gona mission is riddled with bullet holes. The mast of the troopship *Ayatozan Maru* can still be seen off the beach where it was sunk by an Allied bomber while landing troops.

It's 1977. A local Papuan, Eric Damai, a small old man, still strong, sits on the beach staring out to sea, smoking tobacco wrapped in newspaper, telling me his story: 'The big ships were off the beach and at first we were told they were American, but then we realised they were Japanese. We could see the natives [conscripted Tolais from Rabaul] doing a dance on the deck of the ship. They were shouting and banging their bamboo on the deck. It sounded like great drums.'

As the Japanese neared the shore, Eric Damai ran into the bush and was lucky to escape. He feels no malice. He willingly takes parties of Japanese through the bush to find overgrown memorials to their war dead.

We drop our backpacks and dive into the water, washing off the day's grime and sweat after a trek from the town of Popondetta. Tiny, phosphorescent sea creatures cling to us, and our bodies sparkle in the dark.

Next day, friendly local villagers and children with flowers in their hair guide us past wrecked bombers and a rusting Japanese landing barge. We wade through a deep estuarine creek, our packs on our heads, and walk onwards along the black sand to another idyllic village, Buna, where we pitch our tents on the beach.

Gona to Buna: no walk could be as pleasant or easy. Yet this beautiful and serene place inevitably evokes reflections about the enormous and almost incalculable death, pain, and suffering inflicted by the Japanese armed forces on innocent villagers during the Kokoda campaign, and the bloody retribution the Japanese would receive at campaign's end.

Buna beach, with its swaying palms and dugout canoes drawn up on the black sand; in July 1942, this was a wicked, hideous place. It was both the starting and finishing point of the flawed Japanese attempt to take Port Moresby. Here, a few days after the initial landing, a Japanese lieutenant hacked and murdered nine people, mostly with his sword. Six were captured Australians, and three were villagers. The Australians included a militia lieutenant and two Anglican missionary sisters.

The Japanese officer dealt his summary justice in the most hideous manner. As the blood spilled, the lieutenant had difficulty beheading a terrified teenaged Papuan girl and screaming, she had to be held down by soldiers until, with difficulty, her head could be hacked off by the officer. A little boy of six, the son of a Papuan mission worker, was the last to be brutally murdered. Terrified and screaming, the child clung to his mother and was shot.

Within days of the landings at Gona and Buna, General Tojo told a meeting in Tokyo that Japan was determined to destroy the United States and Britain. Japanese forces, he said, continued to hold the initiative from Sydney to Madagascar. The peaceful construction of the New Order had not been neglected, Tojo said. The peoples of the southern regions already had 'grasped Japan's true intentions and had joyfully cooperated in the great task'.

On the Kokoda track, the tide had turned. Australian reinforcements and supply, now far closer to their own base at Port Moresby, quickly increased. Even 25-pounders were dragged up the track in order to hammer the enemy's positions. The Japanese, enduring a hopelessly inadequate supply line, fell back along the track and were on the defensive. There would be many bloody battles along the track and especially on the coast, but the Japanese threat to Port Moresby was diminishing by the day.

Half starved and with significant casualties, the Japanese finally fought a gruesome series of battles at one of their starting points, the once serene beach at Buna. The heaped bodies of their dead would serve as breastworks protection for the coconut log bunkers of the defenders.

With strong American and Australian air cover, Australian forces also repelled the Japanese landings at Milne Bay in southern Papua. It was a notable Australian victory. For the first time in the Pacific, a Japanese amphibious invasion force had been defeated on land and forced to withdraw. On 5 September, over 1100 Japanese were evacuated, leaving over 300 troops dead and another 700 missing. The Australians suffered 373 casualities, including 161 missing or dead.

It is argued by revisionists today that Australian troops in New Guinea and on the Kokoda track did not help save Australia as the war was decided elsewhere. Yet General Douglas MacArthur had no doubts that the loss of Port Moresby would have meant the loss of Australia. He wrote in his memoirs:

> ... I decided to abandon the [Australian defensive] plan completely, to move the thousand miles forward into eastern Papua, and to stop the Japanese on the rough mountains of

the Owen Stanley Range of New Guinea – to make the fight for Australia beyond its own borders. If successful, this would save Australia from invasion and give me an opportunity to pass from defence to offence, to seize the initiative, move forward, and attack.

Japanese war historian Professor Hiromi Tanaka believes there's a tendency to downplay both the significance to the war of the fighting in New Guinea and the actual role of Australia in the war. Tanaka says, 'The role of Australian forces in these battles far exceeds the general Japanese understanding of the events.' He explains New Guinea's importance:

The Japanese army wished to prevent Allied counter-offensives from Australia, and also felt the necessity of expelling any Allied military force from New Guinea in preparation for a possible advance to Australia. The failure of the overland and seaborne campaigns to capture Port Moresby signalled the end of these operations and the end of the first stage of the war.

Curtin felt the same about the battle for the Kokoda trail, telling newsmen in a long private briefing on 21 September: 'We are not defending New Guinea of course, we are defending Australia.'

In September 1942, the Australian leader was 'profoundly disturbed' that America and Britain had rejected his government's further appeals for aid; he thought the nation would have to manage with what it had for the next six months. 'The Japs may discover that they could make an attempt to take Australia from Timor and Java, instead of New Guinea. That would bring them down the west coast ... that would make the Indian Ocean as unsafe as the Pacific.'

But Curtin felt that Port Moresby was now secure and would not fall to the Japanese advancing over the Kokoda track, because of the enemy's supply difficulties. 'Until they take it [Moresby] we have an anchor a long way from an effective invasion point.

Moresby is vitally related to the strength of the attack they can bring against Darwin...'

In the calm seas of the Indian Ocean, five days out of Lourenco Marques, the luxury liner *Kamakura Maru* sliced through the ocean en route to Japan. Ambassador Tatsuo Kawai attended a shipboard memorial service for the submariners killed at Sydney.

Hundreds of passengers crowded the wide promenade deck outside the ship's first class smoking saloon, where the urns containing the ashes of four of the submariners had been placed on a high altar backed by a huge Rising Sun flag. During the service Kawai and the ship's master placed offerings of raw chestnuts, fish, rice and sake on the altar. Then as one the assembled crowd bowed deeply toward the submariners' remains and then toward Tokyo in honour of the emperor.

Newspapers across Japan began splashing front page stories about the deeds of the Japanese submarines at Sydney two days before the *Kamakura Maru* docked at Yokahama. SYDNEY BASE COMMANDER LAUDS BRAVE ACTION OF NAVAL HEROES, the Japanese newspapers proclaimed. The press quoted Rear Admiral Muirhead-Gould in a broadcast from Sydney giving 'unqualified praise for the courage displayed by the four Japanese naval men on the night of 31 May'.

Domei newsagency reported in lurid terms the confusion and fear on the night of the attack on Sydney Harbour. 'Calling the scene a regular corner of hell, [Sydney] newspapers describing the situation said that men thrown into the water by the force of the explosions floated helplessly around and ships of all sizes tied up in the harbour were battered about like toy sailboats by giant tidal waves... When at last word spread that the attack was made by Japanese Special Submarines, the entire city fell into a coma of fear not knowing whether to expect a subsequent bombing from hundreds of airplanes or not.'

The *Japan Times* misquoted Curtin speaking in 'a shivering voice', saying: 'The war has finally reached a stage most disadvantageous to Australia as has been expected. The Japanese submarines have perpetrated a piercing thrust deep into the heart of Australia, and this does not mean that such attack has been brought to a conclusion.'

The *Chugai Shogyo* said in welcoming the ashes of the submariners back to Japan that the nation was filled with 'indescribable emotion': 'The action of the Australian Government in conveying the ashes of these heroes in the *Kamakura Maru* to be carried home is a beau geste compatible with the ways of a warrior.'

The nation's attention was turned to Yokohama harbour as the *Kamakura Maru* arrived just after dawn on a grey Friday morning, 9 October. At 7.15 a.m., a launch carrying 12 relatives of the deceased submariners left the pier. Offerings of bouquets and sakaki branches were carried aboard. One after the other, the families paid homage at the altar in the first-class smoking room, before being invited to a saloon downstairs where Tatsuo Kawai addressed the gathering, which included members of the press and young comrades of the dead. 'Pray be seated. Let me recount the scene of their heroic end,' Kawai began, his face reportedly aglow with emotion.

'Glorious indeed was their end. Look at this photograph. It is of the naval funeral held by the Australian Navy,' he said. Kawai showed the photograph to the assembly. 'Even the enemy was moved by the daring of the heroes.' The relatives listened attentively with deep nods.

Kawai met the parents of Masao Tsuzuku aboard the *Kamakura Maru*:

> The first words to be uttered by them was, 'Did our son use all the shots he had?' Such words! When Chief Warrant Officer Tsuzuku's parents came to see him before his departure and learned that their son was determined to make the supreme sacrifice in this war, they gave up their plans of finding a bride for their beloved son and spent the last night with him in the small boarding house room. Such father! Such mother!

The ashes of the dead submariners were borne from the ship in the arms of submariner comrades; they were greeted by a sombre crowd of more relatives and friends, and an honour guard of naval cadets. A procession slowly moved along the dock with several thousand Japanese bowing as it passed. Led by Kawai, the whole assembly gave three banzai cheers for the emperor.

In late November, Curtin wrote to President Roosevelt urging him to provide shipping for the immediate return of the Australian 9th Division from the Middle East. Roosevelt replied that the 9th could be shipped home in early 1943, but he wanted the division to stay where they were until the forces of General Rommel had been defeated, an outcome he expected soon.

Roosevelt said that with the inflow of US troops to Australia, and the eventual return of the 9th Division, Australia would be safe: '... I feel that you can be reassured as to the adequacy of troops available to drive the Japanese away from Australia to such a distance as to make an invasion impossible.' Curtin, responding, reiterated the need for the 9th Division in the south-west Pacific, pointing out that Australia's wastage through disease and battle in Papua had been considerable: 'The two together may soon place us in what may be a very precarious position.'

Japanese submarine attacks off the east coast of Australia continued into 1943. Four submarines operated off the coast, including one carrying a new reconnaissance aircraft for Susumu Ito, the pilot who flew over Sydney before the midget attack. The Japanese had heard that Sydney Harbour had many British and American warships at anchor.

On 19 February 1943 Ito took off in his float plane, bouncing over the sea in moonlight:

I took off in the middle of the night. I can't remember the time. Our submarine had been in action against shipping in the Solomons and at Bougainville. I was trying to be careful to make sure no one knew it was a Japanese plane. I thought people wouldn't know its nationality. It was nearly a full moon. Sydney Harbour was very illuminated. I could see very well. When I got to South Head they began shooting at me, but couldn't reach me. I was up about 2000 metres and far out off the coast. So there was not a chance of them hitting me. I knew they wouldn't hit me and so I wasn't scared at all.

The suspected large fleet of British and American ships was never found.

Once again, Jim Mair, the boy from Bondi, was about to encounter the enemy. On the ground just south of the South Head battery, a group of boys were out late playing on the Bondi golf links, kicking a football around. Jim Mair remembers a clear, warm night: 'We were watching with fascination a small plane caught in searchlights flying in an arc over Bondi. It had just suddenly appeared there, seemingly out of nowhere, heading north towards us over the bay. It was a float plane of some sort. We leapt up and fled as fast as our legs would carry us. I raced into the house all breathless and my mother yelled something like, "Where have you been? The Japanese are invading!" We were all shoved under the billiard table again. This was the scariest because we thought "this is it" – the invasion was on for sure.'

Out through the back window, the boy plainly saw the same float plane caught like a moth in a number of searchlights: 'It made a peaceful circuit of Bondi and Rose Bay and then flew off north unmolested.' Ito flew around for about two hours attracting the attention of anti-aircraft and searchlight crews. No aircraft challenged him. He was hoping to find large British and US warships in Sydney Harbour, but there were none. Eventually, he headed up the coast and landed on the water near an island well north of Newcastle, as Ito described it. The mother submarine quickly surfaced, recovering Ito and his float plane.

In Japan in 2007, Susumu Ito, still the proud warrior, has no apologies to make: 'I had a definite purpose for my reconnaissance flights. My role was to find warships... We in Japan have the warrior spirit. If I tell you my feelings it is respect towards the Royal Australian Navy handling of the situation [for the submariners who were killed]. All of us who participated in some way are extremely grateful. Because of that my feelings about Australians are that they are beautiful people. I appreciate what they did. You don't see that very often at all.'

Ito does not mention the Australian occupiers who landed a wing of Mustangs at the Iwakuni air base in his home town in 1946.

Tatsuo Kawai realised that he would have to leave the foreign office. He had become too close to the Australians and his statements had not supported the war. With a heavy heart, he lunched with Emperor Hirohito at the Imperial Palace on 18 March 1943, then returned to resign on the spot.

He escaped the politics of war by taking the train south to his beloved retreat overlooking the sea at Manazuru, on Sagami Bay, where he grew vegetables and tangerines and was at one with nature. But he was not altogether alone. His young friend and hostess in Australia, the bright American–Japanese woman Tamaye Tsutsumida, was now working as a translator in Tokyo, and often joined him at his exquisite house overlooking the bay.

Kawai had another public duty to perform. The occasion was the awarding of a citation to ten dead submariners, in recognition of especially meritorious service. The citation had been recommended to the emperor by the commander-in-chief of the Combined Fleet, Admiral Yamamoto. The imperial sanction not only officially recognised the men's bravery, but in practical terms it meant that the submariners were posthumously promoted two ranks, increasing navy benefits to their families.

In making the commendation to the men who had participated in the midget attacks at Diego Suez Bay and Sydney Harbour, Yamamoto spoke of the effect on the navy:

> There are no means of knowing details of war results secured by the Second Special Submarine Attack Flotilla at Sydney naval station, but [they] achieved great war results, thereby demonstrating to the world the loyalty and valour of the officers and men of the Imperial Japanese Navy and enhancing the morale of the entire Japanese Naval Forces.

Newspapers began a renewed orgy of lamentation and hero worship. The young submariners who had given their lives were now 'hero gods'. Newspapermen converged on Kawai's house to ask him, yet again, about the Sydney attack, and he readily responded: 'So impressed were the Australian people that in spite of the fact that Australia recognises herself as the 49th State of America, they responded with the courtesy and honour of a naval funeral . . . The unannounced and unheralded action of the heroes performing their duty in mute silence had found a responding chord in the hearts of the Australian people.'

Just as Japanese propagandists did their utmost to exploit the return to Japan of the four submariners from the Sydney raid, so did Australians also attempt to win the minds of the Japanese. One bizarre operation, long kept secret, stemmed directly from the Japanese public reaction to the return of the ashes of the young men. Like the Japanese raid on Sydney, this operation was an unmitigated disaster.

An intelligence group based in Brisbane devised the scheme, to gather the remains of Japanese from the battlefield, cremate them, and return the ashes in urns to be dropped over Japanese-occupied areas of New Guinea. The idea came from a top secret branch of the Allied Intelligence Bureau, which operated under the name of the Far Eastern Liaison Office (FELO). The office prepared propaganda material that was intended to lower the morale of the Japanese forces.

FELO's director, Commander John Proud, had been smarting

over the perceived success of Japanese propaganda in allowing POWs to send censored messages home in broadcasts and in postcards. He was concerned this might create a favourable impression of the Japanese among some Australians and he wanted to counter the impact. Why not raise the esteem of Australians in Japanese eyes? He proposed that:

> The ashes will be in separate 'urns' and will be dropped by parachute, each 'urn' being labelled with the name, rank, etc. of the remains. At the same time we will drop leaflets drawing attention to our 'chivalrous' act, and deploring the unnecessary wastage of life.
>
> This scheme may seem fantastic at first, but it has been inspired by the somewhat spectacular reaction in Japan to the action of the R.A.N. in cremating the bodies of the Japanese who were killed in the submarine in Sydney Harbour, and returning the ashes to Japan...
>
> The cremating would, of course, be done on a comparatively small scale and, 'off the record', there would be no guarantee that the ashes were those of the person named on the label, but I do not suppose that even the Japanese have got to the stage of being able to identify ashes.

Proud told his men in Moresby to investigate how they might cremate dead Japanese. 'You might also start collecting any enemy identity tags you can get hold of, particularly those of airmen and officers.' In a 'secret and personal' response to Proud a few days later, his representative in Moresby said cremation there would be difficult as 'most of the bodies are very far gone'. He asked Proud: 'Is it necessary to use genuine Japanese bodies. Would not ashes of cremated animals be just as effective? I think there would be no difference in the chemical composition. These could be readily obtained in Australia.' But there was no evidence to suggest that Australian authorities ever substituted animal ashes for human remains.

In early January 1943, Commander Proud gave details of his plan to G2, General MacArthur's intelligence office: 'The great importance attached by the Japanese to the return of the ashes [of the midget submariners] to Japan appears to me to give us a method by which we can get under their skin in the same way as their prisoners-of war-broadcasts have done.'

Proud also proposed a leaflet informing the enemy that Australians respected their traditions: 'It would impress upon the Japanese soldier that he is fighting "gentlemen" and therefore offset Japanese propaganda which has been to the effect that Europeans have no sense of tradition and are rather brute beasts . . . In this case it is likely to be that "the other fellow is not so bad after all".'

Eventually, ashes were gathered in urns, identities and details of where the bodies were recovered were attached and a propaganda leaflet was approved and translated into Japanese. An American B-24 bomber piloted by US Air Force Lieutenant William B. Cox, was allocated the task of dropping the ashes over occupied Lae. Flying with Cox on 'Little Beaver' was a crew of ten US Air Force men of the 403 Bomber squadron. One Australian was aboard as an observer, Flying Officer Gerard Michael Keogh.

The remains of 50 Japanese soldiers were loaded into the B-24, which took off from Jackson's airstrip in Port Moresby just before 4 a.m. on 30 August 1943. The bomber thundered down the dark strip and clawed into the still morning air. Cox and crew began to gain height ever so slowly in the climb over the massive Owen Stanley Range, which loomed as a dark mass ahead, with Lae on the other side of the range. The nearest hurdle was known to the locals as Dark Mountain.

Intrigued, I sat in the reading room of the National Archives in Canberra, flicking through the file that had just been declassified at my request. Towards the end of the file was a brief cable, transcribed from code. As I read it, I could feel the hairs on the back of my neck standing on end. A cable from Port Moresby to Proud in Brisbane read: 'IMPORTANT. FOR FELO. AEROPLANE WITH F/O KEOGH AND ASHES OVERDUE FEARED

LOST. BELIEVED NOT TO HAVE REACHED LAE, SUGGEST SEND MORE ASHES AND LEAFLETS.'

US Sergeant Stephen Dubinsky was part of the small team sent to search for 'Little Beaver'. No trace of the aircraft could be seen from the air over the rugged terrain. Dubinsky and team, aided by local villagers, walked three days before finding the wreck:

> To all appearances the airplane, flying at an altitude of approximately 4,000 feet failed to clear the summit of the mountain and crashed into the face of a solid rock cliff. Apparently the fuel ignited and exploded immediately and was followed seconds later by the explosion of three 500-pound bombs. Wreckage is scattered for 100 yards in all directions from the face of the cliff.

Dubinsky said three bodies were found as were scattered parts of other bodies. Identification mostly was impossible and all remains found were buried at the scene. But Flying Officer Gerard Keogh was identified by his dog tag and an RAAF sweater. Keogh's roll of honour card at the Australian War Memorial simply reads: 'Cause of death, flying battle'; his date of death is given as 30 August 1943.

The group chaplain for the American 43 Bombardment group in Port Moresby, Major Thomas F. Shea, who was with the team that found the wreckage, wrote to Keogh's widow, Justina, at East Maitland on 22 September. He described the flight as an early morning reconnaissance and supply mission: 'Everyone in the plane died as all airmen wish, if to die is God's Will, in a moment. There was no prolonged suffering. I was never more convinced of anything.'

Parts of the wreck of the 'Little Beaver' remain visible today on a rugged slope of what is now the Varirata National Park near Sogeri to the north of Port Moresby. No attempt has been made to remove the remains of the broken wreck as it is scattered down a difficult cliff face and hillside.

In 1946, John Proud was awarded the Order of the British Empire for services as director of FELO. No other attempt to drop ashes was made.

25

TURNING THE TIDE

In July, 1942, General Douglas MacArthur was issued with an order from Washington to begin a gradual offensive against Japan. Going on the front foot took time. Despite the reverses the Japanese had suffered, massive concentrations of Japanese troops built up around Australia's northern approaches as the enemy frenetically constructed new airstrips.

MacArthur and the Australian Army chief, General Thomas Blamey, laid plans to drive the Japanese out of Salamaua and Lae in north eastern New Guinea in the initial stages of the Allied offensive. The US Navy was ordered to occupy Santa Cruz and Tulagi in the Solomons. MacArthur moved his headquarters from Melbourne to Brisbane on 20 July.

From August 1942, the Americans sought to deny the Japanese a base at Guadalcanal in the Solomons. The Japanese had landed there and had begun constructing an airstrip. In the early hours of 9 August, seven Japanese cruisers attacked American and Australian ships participating in the invasion of Guadalcanal and Tulagi. The Japanese turned searchlights on the Allied warships and immediately began firing, taking the Americans and Australians by surprise.

Two heavy cruisers that had survived the midget submarine attack on Sydney were hit. USS *Chicago* was struck in the bow by a torpedo, but managed to stay afloat and escape. HMAS *Canberra* was struck by two torpedoes and about 20 eight-inch shells. Fires raged on board, and the ship developed a heavy list. American ships took off the survivors, and next day the cruiser was scuttled. There were 193 Australian casualties.

One of the peaks of the battle for Guadalcanal came in October 1942 when the Japanese made a number of desperate attempts to capture airfields and the island. The Japanese failed in their efforts, with terrible loss. Japanese battle commanders made constant pleas to the Imperial Navy for battleships to bombard American shore defences. On 14 October, the *Haruna* and *Kongo* briefly laid down a massive and accurate bombardment, but it was a rare intervention, and soon they were gone.

While the struggle for Guadalcanal raged, the super battleships *Yamato* and *Musashi* lay peacefully at anchor in Truk lagoon, north of Rabaul, as they had done for many months. Since the start of the war, Truk was something of a haven for the self-assured Japanese.

The new *Musashi* had sailed from Hashirajima in January 1943 to join her sister-ship in the lagoon at Truk to await operations. But Naval General Staff refused to risk the prized vessels on minor sorties. Occasionally the two ships would move from their anchorage for practice drill, but would remain inside the reef.

Months would pass in the lagoon as the giant warships, often accompanied by a carrier, cruisers and destroyers, floated peacefully, the thoughts of the crew far from preoccupied with war. The boredom was broken for the *Musashi*'s crew on 11 February, when Admiral Yamamoto's barge arrived alongside as the ship's band played. Yamamoto was transferring his commander-in-chief's flag to the new battleship, specially fitted out for the purpose. The crew occasionally saw their deeply tanned chief on the *Musashi*'s deck in his crisp whites playing quoits with his staff officers, betting beer on the outcome.

A German naval attaché in Japan during the war, Vice Admiral Paul Weneker, experienced the lax, over-confident Japanese attitude early in the war during a visit through Japan's southern island outposts:

> I was astounded in the South Seas. The Japanese there were thoroughly enjoying the lush life. They had parties continually and were drinking all the liquor they had captured. I asked them why they did not prepare fortifications and do something to make these places stronger, but they said that the Americans would never come...

The desperate pleas of the Japanese battlefield commanders on Guadalcanal fell on deaf ears at naval high command, who were keeping the big ships for the long-awaited 'decisive battle' with the American fleet, and did not wish to risk them. Some 25,000 Japanese were killed there before a withdrawal was ordered in February 1943.

On the Kokoda track in Papua, the Japanese were eventually pushed back to the coastal lowlands. The Imperial Navy in Rabaul made a number of attempts to reinforce the army, but without air cover Japanese ships were regularly strafed and bombed. On 12 December 1942, five destroyers took on troops at Rabaul and sailed for Buna, without air cover. They managed to land almost 600 men, but because of the heavy air attacks, which were taking their toll on Japanese destroyers, it would be the last reinforcement and supply convoy. From then on Buna and Gona received only a trickle of supplies from barges and submarines operating mostly at night.

A few days earlier John Curtin privately had told newsmen in Canberra that the delay in capturing Gona and Buna was due to the Americans' commitments in the Solomons, as journalist Fred Smith of Australian United Press wrote in his diary: 'Curtin said that the delay at Gona–Buna, where the Japs are holding a strip of coastal swamp 500 yards by 200 yards, was due to the fact that the Americans could not fight. He said the US had suffered more naval losses in the Solomons, although nothing so serious as those of the Japs.'

Japan's military leadership effectively abandoned the men who had fought bravely and under appalling conditions across the Owen Stanley Range and back to beaches that had been their starting points. The Japanese defenders made long and desperate last-ditch stands on the coastal strip of Papua, especially at Buna, against both US and Australian forces. But annihilation was their only option; they simply would not surrender. The last Japanese at Buna were killed on 3 January 1943. Japan's dead for the entire misguided Kokoda campaign numbered 12,000. The Australians lost 5700 men, and the Americans 2800.

MacArthur did not plan to attack every Japanese strongpoint. The massively defended Australian base at Rabaul on New Britain island would be isolated, continually bombed, and allowed to 'wither on the vine'. John Curtin now knew Port Moresby was safe once again, at least temporarily, but still there would be horrors and reversals ahead. He addressed parliament on 10 December 1942 in a gratified mood:

> Australia has much to be thankful for. We have felt the impact of enemy bombs on a number of our northern towns and Sydney has been attacked, but we have been spared the horror of the devastation of war on our own soil.
>
> The victories won at Coral Sea, Midway Island and in the Solomons were of crucial importance to us. There should be throughout the whole continent a universal feeling of deep gratitude and thanksgiving for what we have so far been spared.

1942 had been the most momentous year in John Curtin's life. Against every strongly held conviction he had ever expressed, Curtin – the pacifist and trade unions' leader of the anti-conscription movement during World War I – had introduced legislation authorising the government to send Australian conscripts to war overseas. This was an agonising decision that rocked him personally. In 1918, the Australian Labor Party had almost foundered on the question of conscription, but this time around, the party backed its leader's judgement, such was the magnitude of the threat. Curtin felt that he could not ask American troops to fight the Japanese while keeping Australian conscripts at home.

By the end of that momentous year, John Curtin was spent. On Christmas Eve 1942, feeling exhausted and alone at the Lodge, Curtin penned a generous season's greetings to his political nemesis, Bob Menzies:

Mrs Curtin and [daughter] Elsie are at Perth, [son] Jack is at Adelaide and I am at Canberra. Tough!

You know well how I regard you. May this stress end and all of us have a chance to live like decent human beings. For myself I would like a spell in the pavilion watching a new generation.

As to my health – it is only fair. The rashes have gone but I've got a skin bother which is not nice. At times I think I am Job II. Anyhow may your New Year be happy for all of you. John Curtin.

Curtin would not get that much-needed spell; his health would continue to deteriorate. The Japanese threat, despite the victories at Midway and on the Kokoda track, was ever present. Darwin was still being bombed intermittently. But in January 1943, Curtin at least had the satisfaction of knowing that the experienced 9th Division was finally coming back from the Middle East. He told journalists: 'We would be in a pretty pickle if the AIF had not come back. If they had gone to Burma or to some other places that were mentioned, this country could well have been lost.'

On 16 March 1943, after a major raid on Darwin destroyed oil storage facilities, Curtin and MacArthur shared their concerns. At this time the Japanese were developing 67 airfields in the arc of islands around Australia's north, that would be capable of handling up to 2000 planes, although the aircraft had not yet arrived.

There was evidence of heavy concentrations of ground troops in the region, including at least eight first-class shock divisions. Australia was still woefully exposed, as Curtin discovered in his conversation with MacArthur, who was trying to get three cruisers and nine destroyers and at least 1000 additional American troops to protect the western end of the Torres Strait. As Curtin noted: '... General MacArthur said there was no doubt that the enemy was trying to infiltrate and shove his position nearer to Torres Strait and in the greatest strength he can. This is clear evidence of the enemy's ambitions.'

In mid-March 1943, MacArthur told Curtin that the enemy was no longer attempting to cut Australia's communication with the United States, but the danger was not yet over:

> His [the enemy's] concern is to deal with the Australian base and to concentrate the whole of his power on this weak country... We can as things stand hold now, but we could not hold against a greatly increased strength unless we were able to build up greater strength.
>
> The enemy has diagnosed the situation pretty well the same as we have. He knows the correct thing in war is to concentrate superior strength against a weak position. The southwest Pacific [specifically, the Hawaii region] is no longer menaced but the northwest approach to the Pacific area and North Australia is.

Some have argued that by now, Curtin well knew that the threat of invasion to Australia had passed. MacArthur's advice of 16 March 1943 throws a different light on the subject.

Two days after the meeting between MacArthur and Curtin, newspaper correspondents at MacArthur's headquarters were informed that it was General MacArthur who abandoned the 'Brisbane Line' concept: 'When General MacArthur first came to

Australia the defence plan for the safety of this continent involved North Australia being taken by the enemy . . . It had been drawn up on the fundamental that the littoral of islands to the north of Australia would be taken by the enemy and that Northern Queensland and Darwin area would be overrun by the Japanese.'

In a letter to Curtin, MacArthur wrote: 'It was never my intention to defend Australia on the mainland of Australia. That was the plan when I arrived, but to which I never subscribed and which I immediately changed to a plan to defend Australia in New Guinea.'

Australia's official historian on the first year of the war in the Pacific, Dudley McCarthy, has subsequently thrown doubt on this claim. He wrote that Curtin and MacArthur debated this point, with Blamey telling Curtin that if MacArthur had had a radical change of policy in mind when he arrived in Australia, Blamey was not made aware of it.

On the warm morning of 4 April, Admiral Yamamoto and several of his staff officers motored from the *Musashi* to shore and took off in two land-based attack planes. The aircraft took a southward route and his remaining staff officers and the captain of the *Musashi* waved them off from the deck of the new flagship. Yamamoto was headed for an inspection of Rabaul and Bougainville at a time when the fortunes of the Imperial Navy were in decline.

The navy was rapidly losing both operational freedom and striking power, due to its limited carrier-based air strength. US shipyards were working at a frenetic pace building a new fleet, especially aircraft carriers. In less than a year, the US would have sufficient carriers for clear-cut superiority in the air. The US Navy was also rapidly adding to its fleet sufficient modern heavy ships to offer reasonable protection against the biggest Japanese vessels.

Japan had a big shipbuilding program but her industrial potential was about 10 per cent of that of the US. She could not build sufficient ships or escort vessels to keep up and was hampered once again by a shortage of oil.

Isoroku Yamamoto was sitting upright still in his aircraft seat in his neatly pressed admiral's uniform, when they found his body on 18 April 1943, in a jungle clearing in Bougainville. His medals were pinned to his tunic, and the three cherry blossoms on each of his gold epaulettes sparkled. He was still wearing his white gloves. In the jungle clearing in Bougainville, his left hand held his sword and his right hand rested lightly on it.

Yamamoto's head lolled forward and his eyes were closed as though in thought. A small bullet wound had pierced his lower jaw. The commander-in-chief of the Combined Fleet was dead, and the bodies of his pilot and other officers lay all about him amid the smouldering ruin in the jungle.

Yamamoto had been on his way to tour the front when his plane was ambushed by a squadron of American P-38s, which were fitted with extra fuel tanks for their secret long-range operation. Magic, the Americans' secret code-breaking system, had revealed Yamamoto's movements; the Americans had to dispose of this high-profile target.

His chief of staff, Ugaki, had been keen to visit the front and thought it would be good for Yamamoto to be seen by the troops. Yamamoto wondered if it was necessary for the commander-in-chief to take such risks, but went along with the visit to the forward regions of Rabaul and nearby islands.

Ugaki had been enjoying the pleasant flight over Bougainville. He would later confide to his diary that he thought he 'looked gallant' going to the front in his rarely worn neat khaki uniform. Suddenly, Ugaki's medium torpedo bomber started to dive, following the first plane. 'What's the matter?' Ugaki asked. 'Maybe some mistake . . .' someone muttered. The co-pilot of Ugaki's bomber, Petty Officer Tanimoto, suddenly screamed 'Enemy aircraft!' and a P-38 roared past overhead, firing. Ugaki yelled 'Follow plane number 1! Follow plane number 1!' He later recalled his plane making a high-speed dive down to treetop level as bullets tore into it:

> What I saw then was astounding. Lo! The first plane [Yamamoto's] was staggering southward, just brushing the jungle top with reduced speed, emitting black smoke and flame. It was about four thousand metres away from us. I just said to myself 'My God!' I could think of nothing else. I grabbed the shoulder of Air Staff officer Muroi, pointed to the first aircraft, and said, 'Look at the commander in chief's plane!' This became my parting with him forever.

Soon Yamamoto's plane disappeared, and a tall column of black smoke rose out of the jungle. Ugaki's bomber swung out to sea skipping the waves at full throttle with P-38s in hot pursuit. The bomber was hit and plunged into the sea, ripping one of the engines off.

Ugaki opened his eyes to find himself floating on the sea. He and his chief pilot, Hayashi, began swimming for shore some 200 metres away. Ugaki tired quickly and found a box on which to float. Hayashi made it to shore, despite friendly fire from the beach. Ugaki was injured, with a severed radial artery and a compound fracture of the right arm, but under medical care he recovered, flying back to Rabaul with the ashes of Yamamoto.

In February 1943, the war planner Baron Sadatoshi Tomioka had left Naval General Staff in Tokyo to command the new light cruiser *Oyodo* being completed at the Kure yards. The cruiser, complete with float planes, was a new type of ship primarily designed for an anti-submarine role. The *Oyodo* initially spent a good deal of time at anchor at Hashirajima and at the Truk and Rabaul bases. She did not fire her big guns in anger under Tomioka's brief command, although her anti-aircraft gunners would be kept busy.

In April, soon after Yamamoto's death, Sadatoshi Tomioka was seconded to Rabaul as chief of staff to Vice Admiral Jinichi Kusaka, the quietly spoken naval chief who commanded the South-East Area Fleet and the Eleventh Air Fleet. In little time, Tomioka took over Kusaka's position as overall naval commander in the region, and was promoted to rear admiral.

The Rabaul command was a poisoned chalice in those days. Increasingly, Tomioka had to shelter in his command bunker below ground, as Allied bombers blasted the town, port and airfields and Allied fighter-pilots engaged the Japanese air aces. The Japanese air fleet suffered serious losses under the onslaught, and shipping in Rabaul's beautiful Simpson Harbour was routinely forced to scatter as Australian and American bombers raided the base.

The Japanese made local Tolai natives dig extensive tunnel networks into the volcanic hills surrounding Rabaul, where they established factories, workshops, warehouses and hospitals. The tunnels even stored supply barges that ran down to the harbour's edge on railway tracks at night.

Tomioka was now far from the grand navy ministry building in Tokyo and the salubrious surrounds of the navy officers club. He worked at the disintegrating base from a large bunker with private sleeping accommodation and cupboards on one side. There was a large desk covered in a heavy floral cloth, on which sat two black telephones as well as a heavy vase of tropical blooms that were replenished daily.

Today one of the Japanese bunkers survives in the centre of Rabaul town, the Imperial Navy anchor still etched in concrete over the doorway. The bunker is regularly filled with ash. What war could not destroy, continuing volcanic eruptions in the devastated and once idyllic Rabaul are gradually finishing. The ash falls constantly from the Tavurvur volcano. The town of Rabaul has been smashed and largely abandoned, although a few businesses and residents defiantly remain.

Rabaul's prime role as a massive naval and air base was rapidly fading in 1943. The Allies had island-hopped all the way up the Solomons and were now at New Britain's doorstep, a little over 160 kilometres to the east. There was the usual lack of co-operation between the army and the navy, even on the front line. Tomioka witnessed the army, with its own priorities in New Guinea, pulling out its aircraft and transferring them to Lae and Wewak.

The navy Zero pilots remaining were outnumbered and outclassed by the growing numbers of American Corsairs, Hellcats and Lightnings. Rabaul became the scene of terrible air battles in which the Japanese pilots, many apparently young enough still to be in high school, engaged in daily dogfights, with a soaring death toll.

Despite these difficulties at the front, the Hashirajima anchorage in the Bay of Hiroshima remained the tranquil headquarters of the Combined Fleet when it was not at Truk. As the war turned against Japan, Hashirajima was a refuge from strife. Here, giant battleships waited at anchor after taking mostly token roles in major sea battles.

It's a peaceful scene on 8 June 1943 with the early summer fog over the water hiding the extent of the fleet. The old battleship *Mutsu*, displacing 43,000 tons and with eight 16-inch guns, is attached to the flagship buoy. The flagship *Musashi* has just delivered the ashes of Admiral Yamamoto to Tokyo Bay. She can't be seen from nearby Hashirajima by the islanders working their rice paddies. The crew readies to move the *Mutsu*, launched in 1920, to make way for the battleship *Nagato*, which is leaving the dry dock at nearby Kure.

Suddenly, farmers and fishermen on Hashirajima are almost bowled over by a massive explosion coming from the flagship buoy. The *Mutsu* is consumed by an enormous white cloud. As the smoke clears, the great battleship is broken into two sections. The large forward section sinks quickly. As the fog lifts, the islanders ignore stiff penalties and strain to see what has happened. They are shocked to see just a small stern section of the great battleship emerge, upside down and slowly sinking.

Nearby destroyers race to pluck survivors from the debris. Only some 350 men are saved from a complement of almost 1500. A secret investigation reveals that the explosion has been caused by 'human interference'. The principal suspect, who has been charged with theft, does not survive. The loss of the *Mutsu* – like so many Imperial Navy disasters – is hushed up. The people of Hashirajima know what has happened, but they dare not discuss it openly.

Further south, on the front line, the Americans begin a punitive daylight bombing campaign against Rabaul in the first massed aerial strike on 12 October 1943. Tomioka and his men can do little but sit in their bunkers hearing and feeling the effects of 300 tons of bombs dropped from 350 aircraft. A similar raid occurs six days later. Rabaul, once the great base and threat to New Guinea and Australia, is becoming untenable.

Tomioka is spared the worst. Before daybreak, a bomber rumbles down one of the patched-up airfields and takes off, flying low over Simpson Harbour. The Americans have just landed on nearby Bougainville, but Admiral Tomioka is needed back in Tokyo. He departs leaving 90,000 men in and around the besieged Rabaul base, now only to be supplied by submarine and occasional aircraft. Most will remain there, beleaguered and short of supplies and weapons until the end of the war.

In November 1943, Baron Tomioka was appointed overall chief of the operations department in Naval General Staff, where he had earlier been chief of the first operations planning bureau. As the navy's senior planning staff officer, Tomioka probably had a major part in the decision virtually to abandon Rabaul.

Saturation bombing now gutted the port and downtown areas. Ninety-six Zeros were destroyed in one bombing raid alone in January 1944, and soon after the order came to fly out to safety all the base's remaining combat aircraft.

The suffering in Rabaul was great. Staff air officer with the Second Air Fleet, Commander Masatake Okumiya, had been absent from Rabaul for six months. When he returned he noticed stark differences in the once cheerful defenders: 'Now they were quick tempered and harsh, their faces grimly set. The fighting spirit . . . was gone. The men lacked confidence; they appeared dull and apathetic. No longer were they the familiar well-functioning team.'

The Japanese were driven back by the Allies island by island. Australians played a major role in pushing the Japanese back from New Guinea. In time the Allies, mostly US troops, took Guadalcanal, Choiseul, Bougainville, New Britain, Kavieng, Truk, the Marianas and many others. The US Air Force General Curtis Le May once said, 'If the Japs had a goose left, it was cooked the day of the first mission from the Marianas.'

The Japanese called it the Battle of the Marianas. The Americans called it the Battle of the Philippine Sea. But to American seamen and airmen who participated in June 1944, it was 'The Great Marianas Turkey Shoot'. Japan lost three heavy carriers, two oil tankers and an estimated 330 of 430 carrier planes, after which Japan's naval air power was no longer a major factor in the war. The US lost 123 planes but no ships.

The super battleship *Yamato*, now chosen to sail under the flag of a new commander-in-chief, Admiral Soemu Toyoda, was some 185 kilometres from the carriers during the Marianas battle. She fired her main 18-inch guns, armed with anti-aircraft star shells. The only planes they hit were Japanese. *Yamato* was not damaged.

Ugaki was now commanding officer of the Fifth Air Fleet, which was decimated in the Marianas battle. He knew it would be extremely difficult for the Imperial Navy to recover, as he wrote in his diary: 'When I think the prospect of a victory is fading out gradually, it's only natural that my heart becomes as gloomy as the sky of the rainy season.'

He composed this mournful verse:

Utterly awakened from the dream of victory,
Found the sky rainy and gloomy.

Rainy clouds will not clear up,
My heart is the same
When the time for the battle's up.

The Marianas represented a strategic part of the Japanese system of island fortresses and had formed one of the main barriers defending the seas between Japan and the Philippines. The Japanese losses in this battle paved the way for American marines to storm Saipan, the main island in the Marianas group. On 18 June, Emperor Hirohito had warned his prime minister and war minister, General Tojo: 'If we ever lose Saipan, repeated air attacks on Tokyo will follow. No matter what it takes, we have to hold there.'

Baron Tomioka also knew the significance of the fall of Saipan, believing its capture gave the Americans military supremacy in Japanese eyes: 'In the south theatre there was no suitable place where we had sufficient tactical reason to make a stand for a showdown. Saipan, however, was such a place. From there you could bomb the Homeland.'

With the occupation of Saipan, US B-29s began firebombing one city after another on the Japanese mainland islands, including the capital, Tokyo on Honshu. Hirohito urged the army and navy to overcome all obstacles and retake the island. In February 1944, as Japan's war grew more desperate, Tojo amalgamated the posts of army and navy chiefs, and sacked Admiral Osami Nagano from his old job as chief of Naval General Staff. Navy minister Admiral Shigetaro Shimada replaced Nagano, under orders to recapture Saipan. But it was too late. The disaster was complete.

Vice Admiral Takijiro Onishi was 17 when he had entered the Etajima naval academy. He quickly earned a reputation as a tough little know-it-all, full of self-confidence and always outspoken. He frequented brothels and geisha houses. As a young man he was punished by the navy as 'conduct unbecoming an officer' after slapping a geisha.

Onishi was ardent in everything he did. An accomplished aviator, he became one of the navy's foremost aviation officers and then chief of staff of the Eleventh Air Fleet. At the start of the war, he built up land based bombers on Formosa (Taiwan) and worked to extend their range.

He enthusiastically supported Yamamoto's attack on Pearl Harbor, but was highly critical of expenditure on giant battleships. It was he who came aboard the newly completed *Yamato* in 1941, and in no uncertain terms set Admiral Ugaki right about the fact that aircraft carriers were the way of the future.

Baron Tomioka disliked Onishi intensely and they disagreed about most things, but as usual Tomioka's insights about his opponent were perceptive. He regarded himself as a rationalist, and Onishi as a spiritualist: 'He was the type who believed that nothing was impossible if one went forward with great spiritual determination. I felt that there was a limit to which this could go no matter how strong the spirit, but Onishi felt that one could accomplish anything if he believed in it and worked hard enough for it.'

On 14 October, General MacArthur waded ashore at Leyte in the southern Philippines, fulfilling his famous promise, 'I shall return.' While MacArthur consolidated his position in the southern Philippines, Admiral Onishi arrived in Manila as commander-in-chief of the Japanese Air Fleet in the Philippine islands.

Japanese aircraft production was still high, but the design of fighters and bombers coming off numerous production lines was generally inferior to new models of American aircraft. The Americans were gaining the ascendency in the air war.

As the war was turning against Japan by the day, Onishi brought with him the inhuman proposal of a fanatic, which he explained to his assembled commanders: 'There is only one way of channelling our meagre strength into maximum efficiency, and that is to organise suicide attack units composed of Zero fighters equipped with 250-kilogram bombs, with each plane to crash-dive into an enemy carrier.'

The beginning of the wasteful and wilful slaughter of pilots and innocent boys began within days, and was to grow to a well organised death roster on an industrial scale. Onishi organised the Kamikaze suicide attack corps just before the American landing at Leyte. His proposal was explained to the first batch of young flyers in a dimly lit room and 'their eyes shone feverishly', according to a witness.

At 6.30 next morning, the first Kamikaze attack group, comprising six suicide planes and four escorts, took off from Mindanao and headed north. Two of the young pilots crashed their Zeros into transport ships, damaging them. While the Kamikazes would wreak havoc, causing considerable Allied deaths and injury and loss of shipping, they would never save the Imperial Navy from its inevitable fate.

Four great naval battles, known collectively today as the Battle for Leyte Gulf, raged around the southern Philippines in October 1944. The United States lost one light carrier, two escort carriers and three destroyers. The Japanese losses were crippling: four carriers, three battleships, six heavy cruisers, three light cruisers and ten destroyers. Within a short period Japan lost some 300,000 tons of combat shipping.

One of the doomed carriers was the *Zuikaku*, whose crew were famously photographed crowding the high tip of the steeply sloping flight deck, saluting the lowering of the flag and then giving banzai cheers to the emperor. Fourteen minutes later many hundreds of seamen tumbled overboard and drowned. The carrier's officers had been too busy with ceremonial traditions to concentrate on quickly evacuating the crew to a destroyer which was waiting to one side.

On 21 October, after taking part in bombardments in the Leyte Gulf, the heavy cruiser HMAS *Australia* was hit by a Kamikaze in one of the first of the suicide attacks initiated by Admiral Onishi. Six Australian officers and 23 ratings were killed, including her commanding officer, Captain E.F. Dechaineaux. More than 60 men were injured.

During this month, John Curtin took a rare 13-day rest break at home in Western Australia, but frequently visited his Perth office for work. One day, a visiting Labor Party official found Curtin head down at his desk. When the prime minister raised his head, the official saw that he had been crying. 'Here, read this,' Curtin said. 'I've just received a communication of the Japanese Kamikaze pilots who made an attack on one of our warships and killed a lot of good men . . .'

At the end of October, on arriving in Melbourne from Perth, Curtin suffered a heart attack and was taken by ambulance to hospital, where he spent the next two months.

26

DEATH OF AN EMPIRE

Since January, 1943, the Imperial Navy has been experimenting with a new secret weapon at top-secret Base P on an island just south of Kure. Manufacture of the human torpedoes, known as the *Kaiten* (*Turning of the Heavens*), is rushed, and the end product is a crude improvisation and is grossly unreliable.

The craft is the fusing together of two enlarged torpedoes, the most forward part of one filled with explosives. A mid section with the pilot's seat, controls and periscope is attached. Behind the pilot is another torpedo containing the propulsion system.

The weapons are launched by mother submarines with a volunteer aboard who is expected to guide his craft into a warship. Should something go wrong and an enemy ship is not found or hit, the young man in the metal coffin has few options: detonate the high explosives in the nose, or suffocate from lack of oxygen on the bottom. It's also possible that the torpedo craft could be blown up by the enemy.

Naoji Kozu was in his second year at higher school when the war broke out. In 1943 he joined the navy, eventually enlisting in the *Kaiten* Corps based at Kawatana. On three separate occasions the teenager crawled into his *Kaiten* aboard a mother submarine about to be launched. While others launched alongside him, and no *Kaiten* pilot ever came back, Kozu's turn simply never came. If they returned from a mission, some young pilots were beaten more often than usual and called a 'disgrace' by their superiors.

On 16 January 1945, as Curtin is about to resume his duties in Canberra, Lieutenant Commander Mochitsura Hashimoto guides his mother submarine *I-58* towards the American-held island of Guam. His sub once carried a reconnaissance float plane, but has been converted to transport six *Kaiten*s instead.

Four boys squeeze into separate torpedo casings. Hashimoto, who has already encountered serious mechanical problems with the human torpedoes, is struck again by the youthfulness of the *Kaiten* crewmen. They inevitably have an air of fanaticism about them that chills the seasoned submarine commander. He thinks these youths are 'intoxicated with their patriotism'. Just before squirming into his coffin, one of the boys hands Hashimoto a farewell note. Hashimoto quickly reads it: 'Hereafter, no matter, there will be thousands and tens of thousands of boys, and we now offer ourselves as a sacrifice for our country.'

Sometime after the launch, smoke is seen rising from the harbour and a victory is assumed. But no American accounts confirm the attack. Four boys die in their death machines this time and the submariners aboard the *I-58* pray for them. Commander Hashimoto launches another two boys in their *Kaiten*s off Palau in July, and yet another two off Okinawa in August. For all the *Kaiten*s launched by Japan, the Americans confirm just a few ships damaged or maybe sunk; the torpedoes are desperate, futile, sacrificial killing machines.

On 19 February 1945, US marines storm the small island of Iwojima, 1000 kilometres north of Saipan and 1060 kilometres south of Tokyo. The Japanese capital is now within reach of American bombers. The Stars and Stripes are raised over Iwojima on 14 March. The ferocious battle for the island has claimed the lives of more than 4500 US marines and over 360 naval men. The

Japanese dead exceed 18,000. Only some 200 surrender. Tokyo is now even closer for US bombers.

Emperor Hirohito took comfort in the proportionately greater losses of the defenders. From his underground bunker in the Imperial Palace he expressed satisfaction at the spirit of the Japanese on the island: '... they fought ferociously against much greater forces and contributed to the entire operation.'

Having received a vote of no confidence from the privy council of elders, both General Tojo and Admiral Shimada are forced to resign. It is clear to all in Japan that Japan's Axis partner, Nazi Germany, soon will be defeated. Closer to home the Japanese army in Burma has been destroyed. Japan's slide is gathering momentum.

The desperation shows in the increased reliance on Kamikaze tactics. After Leyte, there is an all-out effort to increase the number of planes and pilots. The suicide missions are given priority in weapons manufacture. The high command is beginning to stockpile aircraft and suicide weapons and to organise new troop divisions for the defence of the home islands.

Okinawa is the last stepping stone to mainland Japan.

The tide is rushing out for Japan. A massive US fleet moves towards Okinawa.

The Americans want the island as an air base and staging post for their invasion of Japan's home islands. After intense bombardment from the huge fleet, 60,000 Americans storm ashore on 1 April to begin a horrendous battle which will last almost three months.

On 29 March 1945, the giant *Yamato* takes aboard a full supply of ammunition, including more than 1000 shells for her 18-inch guns. On 2 April, she slips out of Kure with hundreds looking on, including the men who had built her at the nearby yard. The onlookers seemed to sense that it might be her last voyage. Depending on their point of view, her mission represents either the nadir of the insanity of the Imperial Japanese Navy, or the zenith of its glorious traditions and bravery.

The *Yamato* passes the scattered remnants of the Imperial fleet – a few carriers, battleships, cruisers and destroyers, many battle-damaged, some now on the scrap heap, furtively hiding among the islands. The carriers mostly have no planes or flight crew, and none of the warships have fuel. They serve as anti-aircraft platforms, and are increasingly under attack by American aircraft.

War has come to Kure with a vengeance. US bombers begin to plaster the shipbuilding yards and steelworks. The great shipbuilding dock in which the *Yamato* was constructed is now desperately turning out midget submarines for use against the final assault on Japan. They will never be launched.

On 3 April, the *Yamato* and her escorting ships, the light cruiser *Yahagi* and eight destroyers, arrive at Mitajima, an isolated spot west of Hashirajima. The mighty *Yamato* is in hiding. The old Combined Fleet anchorage is too well known to the Americans, who daily fly their bombers over the Inland Sea, bombing, dropping mines, and keeping tabs on the biggest battleship of them all.

In Tokyo, the expansive navy ministry building near the palace in Tokyo is caked in dust and ash. The building that has seen the planning of war cannot withstand the enemy's bombs much longer. The bombing of Tokyo has been going on since November 1944.

A little over three weeks earlier, more than 330 American bombers dropped flaming napalm incendiaries on the capital. Most of the humble houses are made of timber. Massive fires, worse than all previous bombing, kill an estimated 72,000 people in the one raid alone. The charred remains of great mounds of civilian bodies can be seen in parks, under railway viaducts, in gutted buildings, in ditches along roadways, anywhere the people think they can seek protection. Thousands drown or even boil to death in Tokyo's Sumida River.

Regular massed bombing raids continue. Sometimes more than 500 B-29s take part in the one raid, all aimed at eliminating Japan's capacity and will to fight on. Tokyo is now a place of mayhem. Industries have ground to a halt. Food shortages are critical, transport is in chaos, the surviving hospitals can no longer cope, frightened residents are fleeing to the provinces. The government and the military, mainly through broadcasting stations, continue to exhort the population to work harder for the victory that is just around the corner.

The military fanatics delude themselves. The army asserts that the closer the Americans come to Japan, the easier it will be to eliminate them. But it is not difficult for the average Tokyo citizen to gauge that the country is on her knees. They keep their views to themselves and their close friends, lest the officially designated 'thought police' beat them and throw them into prison.

Thick-set and round-faced, still wearing a chest full of medals, Admiral Soemu Toyoda toils at his big desk on the first floor of the navy ministry, which is about to be evacuated. He has been appointed by the prime minister as chief of the Navy General Staff and jointly commander-in-chief of the Combined Fleet. Even now Toyoda still expresses hopes of the fabled final decisive battle and victory at sea.

But the Imperial Navy is mostly on the bottom or badly damaged. It is out of fuel oil. Toyoda is in command of many men and bases, but Japan's seagoing capacity on his appointment in April 1945 includes only two serviceable battleships, two carriers without planes, three cruisers and a motley fleet of destroyers. The *Yamato*, the super battleship on the Inland Sea, is still in good condition among the remnants of a once great fleet, having taken part in precious few battles, although attacked by American aircraft and submarines on several occasions.

Through his window in the ministry building, where so many grand Imperial Navy plans have been concocted, Toyoda sees a blackened, devastated capital. He and his ilk have brought this disaster on the people of Tokyo. Emaciated survivors in bandages and rags wander the ruins seeking shelter and food in between bombings. Toyoda can smell defeat in the air, but won't admit it. He is intent on continuing the fight against all odds. It is a matter of honour in the Samurai tradition, regardless of the mass destruction of his own people, who have never mattered.

Toyoda and his senior staff officers, including Rear Admiral Sadatoshi Tomioka, now one of Toyoda's most senior deputies, debate the options, as though there were options. Toyoda insists on a bizarre operational plan that will come to be a hallmark of Imperial Navy insanity: Operation *Ten-Ichi-Go* (*Heaven Number One*.) His order typifies the navy's irrationality. Victory is no longer the issue. The men who have contributed to the slaughter of millions and the subjugation of much of Asia and the Pacific are concerned how they will be perceived by future generations.

Toyoda drafts a new order. It is transmitted to the *Yamato* and the few remaining ships afloat; it is more about glory and 'self' than anything else:

> The fate of our empire truly rests upon this one action. I have called for the organisation of a surface special attack unit for a breakthrough operation of unrivalled bravery so that the power of the Imperial Navy may be felt in this one action in order that the brilliant tradition of the Imperial Navy's surface forces may be exalted and our glory handed down to posterity.
>
> Each unit, regardless of whether or not it is a special attack unit, will harden its resolve to fight gloriously to the death to completely destroy the enemy fleet, thereby establishing firmly an eternal foundation for the empire.

There it is again! Toyoda isn't the only one who has lost his grip on rationality. Call it the Western mind not understanding the East but call it what you may, there is no logic in it. Baron Tomioka, too, has seen this same unfathomable and irrational thinking permeating the Imperial Navy ever since Japan plunged recklessly into the war against the United States of America. Indeed, with his rash schemes, such as the invasion of Australia, Tomioka has been an active player in the game of delusion. When it is all over he will begin to bemoan the reality: 'Such optimistic predictions it is clear, were not really based on rational or reliable calculations.' This is even more perverse coming from so zealous an advocate of war.

Toyoda's plan is bizarre. The *Yamato* is expected to carve through the US invasion fleet, sink as many ships as possible, and beach herself on Okinawa, halfway between the Japanese mainland island of Kyushu and Formosa (Taiwan). She will then use her 18-inch guns as a shore battery and anti-aircraft platform. In the meantime, the scratch fleet will have drawn American carriers, and these will be destroyed by massed waves of Kamikaze attacks in a glorious victory that no one for one moment believes possible.

In effect, Toyoda is telling the men of the *Yamato* and their escort ships to commit suicide; to go down in a blaze of glory. There is no chance of survival because Toyoda has not been able to guarantee air cover. The refuellers at Kure are told that *Yamato* is to be given fuel only for a one-way journey.

The *Yamato* and her escort ships now are designated the 'first special attack force'. 'Special attack' has become synonymous for 'suicide'. The man selected by Toyoda as commander of the small force is a moderate, in comparison with many of his colleagues, Vice Admiral Seiichi Ito, Baron Tomioka's superior back in those heady days of 1942. Tomioka remembers Ito as 'not a man of great decisions and by nature very cautious. He was not the type to commit bold and rash acts'. Yet Ito, during debate on the invasion of Australia in March 1942, did state: '... we must proceed aggressively with operations'. According to Tomioka, Ito has a reputation as an officer with an even temper who rarely gets angry. Not now.

The judicious Admiral Ito simply is not committed to the rashest of acts; he thinks the Okinawa mission for the *Yamato* is idiotic. Ito has already demonstrated his outspoken distaste for the Imperial Navy's suicide tactics in the use of Kamikaze pilots. When the latest plan is revealed in all its detail in the operations room of his flagship, Ito speaks bluntly to his incredulous officers: 'I must state in all honesty that I have doubts about this plan. Still, if those are the orders, we will naturally do our best.'

The evening before sailing the order goes out aboard the *Yamato* and her escorts to open ships' stores and distribute sake. There is a period of quiet while final letters are written in time to catch the last mail boats; then the sounds of intoxicated men singing, reminiscing and shouting 'banzai!' can be heard across the still waters of the Inland Sea.

Ensign Mitsuru Yoshida, an assistant radar officer in his twenties, goes up on the main deck of the *Yamato* with his young shipmates after a drinking party below. They sit on mats on the deck, forming circles:

> Most of us sing traditional folk songs from our home districts. Pouring cold sake with a splash into an enormous cup, we drink it off in one draught. I do the honours for each of the sixteen men under my command. The mission is upon us. Should we deny ourselves even oceans of sake? Of course not.

Senior officers are drinking heavily too. Some laughing, some crying, some yelling out passionately. In rowdy scenes, youthful crew members even pat the bald heads of senior officers.

Early next morning the *Yamato* quietly heads south under distant but watchful American reconnaissance eyes. The inevitable US bombing and torpedo attacks on the super battleship begin less than halfway from the mainland of Japan to Okinawa. The cruiser *Yahagi* is attacked and quickly sinks. One of the destroyers goes down.

The *Yamato* is also hit early in the attack. A torpedo penetrates the stern. Power fails and turrets jam. The rudder is jammed hard left, her port side awash. The officers on the bridge are thrown into a heap. Vice Admiral Ito slowly regains his feet as the giant ship begins circling helplessly. Still wearing his white gloves, he salutes his staff and shakes hands. 'Save yourself,' he says sadly, 'I shall stay with the ship.' He makes his way one deck below to his sea cabin, goes inside, and locks the door.

The world's biggest battleship is hit by ten torpedoes and several bombs, and begins to capsize to port. Water is rushing through the ship with catastrophic results. The operations room, one deck below the main deck, is deserted. Seawater surges across the room. Admiral Yamamoto's globe of the world, a gift originally to the *Nagato*, is knocked into the water. Charts where Admiral Ugaki and his staffers plotted their extended conquest of half the world, including Hawaii and Australia, surge around the blackened room in a sodden mess.

On the bridge, the ship's captain, Rear Admiral Kosaku Ariga, ties himself to the brass binnacle. Two navigation officers do likewise at their post and, transfixed, watch the water rise. Ensign Yoshida waits for death as the water rises: 'Bodies flying in all directions. It is not simply a matter of being swallowed by the waves. The pressure of the water boiling up sends bodies flying like projectiles . . .'

Yoshida is in a whirlpool: 'Tossed up, thrown down, beaten, torn limb from limb, I think: O world, seen with half an eye at the last moment. Even twisted and upended, how alluring your form! How exquisite your colours! . . . At an instant *Yamato*, rolling over, turns belly up and plunges beneath the waves, she emits one great flash of light and sends a gigantic pillar of flame high into the dark sky.'

That massive blast, with a soaring mushroom smoke column that can be seen scores of kilometres away, hurls Ensign Yoshida to the surface. Remarkably, he survives. So do a few hundred other hands from the *Yamato*. Close to 2500 men from the battleship are lost, plus more than 1000 from the cruiser *Yahagi* and the escorting destroyers, most of which are sunk.

Admiral Toyoda and his officers at Naval General Staff receive the news in silence. They have sent thousands of men and boys, most of them in their prime, to the bottom for their own glory.

On 7 April, after the crucial loss of Okinawa, Prime Minister Kuniaki Koiso resigns and Admiral Kantaro Suzuki, 77, is appointed by Hirohito. There are three other old admirals in the new cabinet, prompting a disillusioned Admiral Ugaki to call it mockingly a 'Naval Cabinet'. Ugaki is now sending hundreds of young Kamikaze naval pilots off to their deaths. His diary shows touches of hysteria:

> Now that the good natured navy is going to take charge of the state at this time of agony, I hope they'll govern forcefully, because it was the unanimous voice of the people at present. The navy, now without ships, is going to fight at the critical time by forming a cabinet with its predecessors. Ha! Ha!

President Franklin D. Roosevelt dies on 12 April 1945 and is replaced by Harry. S. Truman. In his Berlin bunker, 18 days later, Adolf Hitler kills himself.

John Curtin is in the last months of his life. He knows that it is only a matter of time before the fall of Japan. But no one doubts that the victory will be an immensely costly exercise in terms of human life.

On 12 March, the prime minister, suffering frequent intervals of illness, settles before a microphone in Parliament House. In an appeal for another victory loan, Curtin tells a national radio audience that 'the grim days of 1942 for us have become the anxious days of 1945' for the Japanese enemy:

> For almost three years, Japan was squatting in bloated strength on the Pacific. Today, bombs rain on Tokyo.
>
> Less than three years ago, the Japanese were within a few miles of Port Moresby. Today, Australian fighting men are completing the task of wiping out the enemy from territory for which Australia is responsible.
>
> Unhappily, the picture I have briefly drawn for you has

caused many people to pull on a cloak of complacency and to regard the ultimate defeat of Japan as just a matter of time calling for no sustaining of past efforts or energetic prosecution of new tasks.

I can think of no better answer to that attitude than the words of General MacArthur in his communiqué only a few weeks ago when he found that the Japanese grip on the Philippines had been broken. General MacArthur said: 'We do not count anything done as long as anything remains to be done.'

On 21 April, the prime minister enters hospital again with suspected 'congestion of the lungs'. The *Courier Mail* in Brisbane suggests that Curtin might consider his health and strength, for Australia needs 'vigorous and active national leadership'. But Curtin's sense of duty prevents him from resigning.

He arrives back at the Lodge in Canberra and is photographed with wife Elsie smiling in the garden of the prime minister's official residence. Elsie senses that her husband is taking his last opportunity to enjoy the view. Curtin is too weak to climb the stairs to his bedroom and ambulancemen carry him up on a stretcher. His condition deteriorates, as Elsie later writes:

Late on July 4 I had a cup of tea with 'Dad.' 'You'd better get some sleep,' he said. The nurse brought him a sedative. 'Just wait a minute,' he said. He was quiet for a moment, then, 'I'm ready now.' I kissed him goodnight and went off to my room.

Three or four hours later, when the sister in charge, Sister Shirl, came to my room, I knew before she spoke that it was all over. We rang Elsie [daughter in Perth], just a few hours before the bomber was to take off, and told her not to come. It was too late.

John Curtin dies, aged 60, just before General Douglas MacArthur announces the liberation of the Philippines. The general sends the following message to the Australian people: 'He was one of the greatest wartime statesmen, and the preservation of Australia from invasion will be his immemorial monument. I mourn him deeply.' The Curtin family would treasure a photograph MacArthur sent of himself in March 1944 with the inscription: 'To the Prime Minister who saved Australia in her hour of deadly peril. With the admiration and affection of Douglas MacArthur.'

Shortly before the war with Japan began, Curtin, already weary from political battles and the threat of Japan, had reflected on life in a birthday greeting to his wife in Cottesloe:

You have given me a deep well of content and met the urges of my nature completely. I have had supreme happiness in your love and loveliness. And no man has ever had more than that . . .

All my love and all my heart and all my gratitude for all you have been and are, the wife – the stout hearted, sweet natured wife – of my manhood and the beloved of my soul.

Even Curtin's political opponents, the conservatives whose infighting led to Curtin's ascendancy in 1941, acknowledge that an exceptional leader had passed. Arthur Fadden, the man Curtin defeated on the floor of the house to become prime minister, is frank in his memoirs: 'I do not care who knows it but, in my opinion, there was no greater figure in Australian public life in my lifetime than Curtin.'

Opposition Leader Robert Menzies pays an emotional tribute in the House of Representatives, praising the late prime minister's clear-sightedness, and his correct view of politics as a contest of ideas and 'not as a sordid battle of personal hostilities and ignoble ambitions': 'Of John Curtin, I can say, as I believe we all can say, with a full heart, "he was my friend, faithful and just to me".'

On 17 May, the remnant Imperial Navy has its last sea battle. The heavy cruiser *Haguro* is sunk by Royal Navy destroyers off

Penang, Malaya. The Japanese Imperial Navy is finished, and the warmongers have nothing but their visions of glory to hand down to posterity.

On 24 May, Tokyo is firebombed in a raid by 562 American B-29s. The urban and industrial area of the city south of the Imperial Palace is gutted. Two days later, 502 Superfortress bombers hit Tokyo again, causing widespread destruction of the financial, commercial and government district of the capital.

There is now no distinguishing between military and civilian targets. US air chiefs order 3262 tons of incendiaries dropped on the capital, and massive firestorms sear huge areas of Tokyo and nearby Yokohama. Civilian deaths are so great that services break down, hospitals which haven't been destroyed overflow and charred bodies pile up, uncollected, in streets, in ruins and in rivers.

Burning debris crosses the moat of the Imperial Palace; the flames spread to several buildings, and then to the palace itself, which is destroyed. Twenty-eight staff members die fighting the fires. Hirohito and his empress remain safe in their *obunko* annexe, an underground shelter.

27

SURRENDER

On 6 June, the Supreme Council for the Direction of War meets in Tokyo. The army and the navy argue strongly for continuing the war. The dour, expressionless foreign minister, Shigenori Togo, opposes them, later commenting: 'The high command's theory was that the nearer the battlefields to Japan, the more advantageous for us; but this could not be conceded when we had no supremacy in the air.'

The few surviving Japanese warships can no longer go to sea. Many are in port, badly damaged and in need of repair work that will never happen. Oil is the essential problem; it is in critically short supply. American bombers and even fighters now operate over Japan with impunity. Available Japanese aircraft are being kept in readiness for the final American assault on the homeland and they rarely take off to meet everyday enemy attacks.

The *Nagato* is moored at the Yokosuka naval base in Tokyo Bay, partly covered by a massive ring of anti-aircraft gun positions in the mountains behind. The former flagship of Admiral Yamamoto is now a parody, festooned with big potted palms, and with netting hanging from the pagoda tower to the main mast.

Planks cover her 16-inch guns at different angles, and a third of her smoke stack has been removed. To obscure the vision of enemy aviators further, barges have been brought alongside; with the pier, they are painted in dazzling uniform colour in stripes.

The mountains make attack by torpedo bombers difficult, so the Americans decide to abandon torpedoes and drop bombs instead. The first 500-pound bomb crashes into the bridge of the battleship, smashing the pilot house and ripping a massive hole in the deck. Several levels of the pagoda are in ruin, and the ship's captain and 11 others are dead. The symbolism is not lost on the Americans. This is the bridge where commander-in-chief Yamamoto stood, at the height of his authority, as he planned the Pearl Harbor attack.

The next 500-pound bomb tears into the officers' mess on the port side, blowing a massive hole in the deckhead. Another 22 men are killed instantly. The officers' mess: one of the places where the gentlemen of war sipped sake in the heady days of 1942, passionately discussing whether to invade Hawaii, India, or land troops on the beaches of northern or western Australia.

The *Nagato* continues to float, and despite the damage it has sustained can still operate as an anti-aircraft platform. The former flagship will meet a bizarre and inglorious end – smashed and sunk by a towering 100-metre tidal wave at Bikini Atoll in the Marshall islands, during one of many American nuclear tests after the war.

The Kure naval dockyard is bombed relentlessly through June and July. Shipbuilding and repair facilities, wharves, warehouses and residential and commercial districts are destroyed. The heartland of the Imperial Navy becomes a wasteland. On 28 July, US carrier-based aircraft attack the old battleship *Haruna*, which is lying off the port. Anti-aircraft fire is intense. Two B-24 bombers flying away from Kure over Hiroshima are hit and most of the crew bail out, to be quickly rounded up on the outskirts of the doomed city. It is the second day of the latest operation to destroy the ageing battleship; finally, she is hit by nine bombs, some as large as 2000 pounds. The *Haruna* lists to port and sinks.

The old battleships IJNS *Ise* and *Hyuga* are hugging land and island on the Inland Sea and are being used as anti-aircraft platforms. The *Ise* is off Kure and the *Hyuga* is off Nasakejima, near Hashirajima. They are attacked by unrelenting swarms of US aircraft. Both battleships are smashed and sink, their hulls resting on the bottom, with waves washing their decks.

On the same day, US bombers attack the light cruiser *Oyodo*, once under Admiral Tomioka's command. The *Oyodo* is alongside Etajima, Tomioka's birthplace. It is the second time she is hit by large bombs in four days. Student officers at the Imperial Navy academy are given a harrowing lesson about air power more potent than any of their text books. Before their eyes, the cruiser capsizes in the shallow waters off the academy, killing 300 of her crew and officers, most of the latter Etajima graduates. She, too, rests on the bottom, partly visible above the waterline.

Hisashi Inoue, 23, a graduate of the Otake naval training corps in Kure, and a sub-lieutenant on the *Oyodo*, was told in his training to 'cut off any love or attachment for our blood relations'. It is an order disobeyed, as his diary reveals: 'I hope that I too will never forget about my mother's tender love until that final moment when I perish in some southern sea.' He perishes off Etajima, bosom of the Imperial Navy.

On 26 July, the Potsdam Proclamation is issued by the leaders of the United States, Nationalist China and Britain, warning Japan that she faces either unconditional surrender or utter destruction. It is intended by President Harry S. Truman, who replaced Roosevelt, to be the final warning to Japan before atomic bombs are used. There is no mention of the new weapons of mass destruction. There is no mention, either, of the intended fate of the emperor. The Japanese high command hears of the proclamation via American radio.

A meeting of the Supreme Council for the Direction of War is called on 27 July. The chief of the Navy General Staff, Admiral

Soemu Toyoda, who sent the men of the *Yamato* and her escorts on their suicide mission, now wants more bloodshed to leave a lasting memorial to the Imperial Navy.

Toyoda rejects the proclamation as absurd. Foreign Minister Togo argues against such a response. As a result, it is agreed by the group, including the new prime minister, Admiral Kantaro Suzuki, that no response will be made while there remains a chance of the Soviet Union agreeing to mediate in talks. Japan is desperately trying to get the Soviets to mediate in a settlement.

But next morning the newspapers are filled with the news of the Japanese government's rejection of the Potsdam Proclamation, and word quickly gets back to Washington. According to foreign minister Togo, the army and the navy took over the dissemination of the news, misrepresenting the supreme council's decision.

Japan's military fanatics demand a fight to the death and are backed by new, decrepit leaders. The fanatics are calling for 100 million Japanese to die in repelling the American invaders. Already soldiers are teaching housewives, girls, and old women how to kill invading US troops with sharpened bamboo poles.

Admiral Toyoda is one of the most rigorous opponents of a Japanese surrender, urging greater suicide attacks by young men. He forms an alliance with the hardliners, war minister, General Korechika Anami, and chief of the army, General Staff General Yoshijiro Umezu. The prime minister, Admiral Suzuki, tries to persuade the hardliners to agree to the proclamation for surrender, without success. In the end, he takes the unprecedented step of going directly to the emperor for a decision.

A short distance north of Kure, at Hiroshima, air raid sirens wail. It seems nothing unusual; reconnaissance planes and bombers go over all the time. Anti-aircraft gunners on the surrounding mountains are at their posts. Over 8400 schoolchildren are not at their desks; they have been mobilised to demolish timber houses in Hiroshima city to create firebreaks in case of further massed bombing.

The day is already growing warm. It is 8.15 on the morning of

6 August, and the people of the Bay of Hiroshima, from Kure to Iwakuni and even out across the sea to the little isle of Hashirajima, are going about their business. Suddenly, there is a terrific and unprecedented blast. Gradually, a great, bubbling maelstrom of a mushroom cloud spreads above Hiroshima city.

It's a massive, evil, soaring black cloud with a purplish tint. At the base, as seen by the awe-struck American aviators aboard the bomber *Enola Gay*, the mushroom is boiling with flame. Flame and smoke are whirling out into the foothills of the mountains behind Hiroshima. Fires are springing up across the city, too numerous to count. Now the hills are disappearing under smoke and flame.

Toyofumi Ogura, a history professor at Hiroshima University, is outside the Fukuya department store when he sees the incredible mushroom cloud rising: 'I glanced at my watch. It was just past 8.15 am. Just then there was a dull but tremendous roar as a crushing blast of air pressure assailed me. I kept still, stretched out flat on the ground. At the moment of the roar and blast, I had heard tremendous ripping, slamming and crashing sounds as houses and buildings were torn apart.' Ogura passes out. When he comes to he walks the burning, decimated city searching in vain for his wife and youngest son.

In an instant, Hiroshima becomes Dante's inferno. In a city of 320,000 civilians and soldiers, 80,000 are killed or mortally wounded. Thousands of survivors stagger naked, blackened and bewildered, skin dripping off their bodies like molten plastic. Of the 8400 conscripted schoolchildren working in the open, 6300 are dead. The rest are suffering. By the end of 1945, an estimated 140,000 people will have died from burns and the effects of radiation.

In 2006, in Hiroshima city, I stand looking at a beautiful curved ornamental stone bridge over a tranquil lake in the Shukkeien gardens, less than one and a half kilometres from the bomb's hypocentre. In wartime, the gardens were a tranquil resort and a rare haven for lovers. Immediately after the atomic explosion, survivors took refuge here in the gardens. Most died before receiving medical attention. A sign by the lake shows a photo of the devastated gardens and the stone bridge intact soon after the devastation in 1945.

I ask some Japanese women meeting in a quaint tea house over the lake whether the stone bridge was the original one photographed after the gardens were ripped apart in the blast. They bring out an older woman. 'Yes, the original bridge,' she says simply. Then she turns to face me squarely. She is horribly disfigured, and I am caught off-guard and somewhat embarrassed, mumbling my apologies. Survivors still live here growing old in this pleasant city on Hiroshima Bay, a place now known for its tasty oysters, its huge Mazda car plant, and its haunting peace dome and museum.

Schoolchildren sing as they place folded paper cranes inside the children's memorial and tourists are unable to fight back their tears. For more than six decades pacifist Hiroshima city has been shouting to a world deaf to the city's experiences. Its museum tells the story of the American atrocity in stark detail. There is no mention of Japan starting the war.

President Harry Truman, 16 hours after the blast, reveals that the bomb is 2000 times greater than the largest ever used. The force from which the sun draws its power has been loosed against those who brought war to the Far East. He warns that the United States is now prepared to 'rapidly obliterate' every Japanese productive enterprise above ground:

> It was to spare the Japanese people from utter destruction that the ultimatum of July 26 was issued at Potsdam. Their leaders promptly rejected that ultimatum. If they do not now accept our terms they may expect a rain of ruin from the air, the like of which has never been seen on this earth.

The Japanese are not yet ready to accept, and on 9 August

another atomic bomb devastates the city of Nagasaki, and some 35,000 are killed and 60,000 injured. On the same day the Soviet Union declares war on Japan.

Admiral Ugaki, formerly Yamamoto's chief of staff, is at the Suginoi hotel on the wooded hillside overlooking beautiful Beppu Bay on Kyushu island on the Inland Sea, 150 kilometres southwest of Hiroshima. 'Now this country is going to fight alone against the whole world,' Ugaki writes in his diary after hearing of the Soviet declaration of war.

Ugaki, who so admired the willingness of the young men heading off to their deaths in midget submarines, is in charge of new secret weapons being mass produced for the final American assault. Now there is no pretence about recovering the crew. The new five-man *Koryu* midget submarine is fitted with a bomb in the nose and is designed for ramming ships. He is also in charge of the greatly accelerated Kamikaze aircraft operations from the southern island of Kyushu, seen as the key to holding back the enemy. Every day, young men and boys are flying away to their deaths against the Americans. Between late 1944 and the end of the Okinawa campaign, 2550 Kamikaze missions are flown, sinking 45 ships, mostly destroyers. No capital ship larger than an escort carrier has been sunk.

Ugaki gets word of the atomic bomb exploding over Hiroshima. 'We must think of some countermeasures against it immediately, and at the same time I wish we could create the same bomb,' he writes.

Navy authorities at Kure rush medical supplies into nearby Hiroshima and assist in rescue operations. Waiting suicide attack boats filled with explosives are moved from the marine training division at Ujina, about four kilometres from centre of the blast, and the base is turned into a hospital. The centre reports to Tokyo that the destructive power of the bomb is enormous, but 'with sufficient preparation and safety measures, it is nothing to be afraid of'.

On 9 August, a student cadet pilot, navy Sub-lieutenant Toshimasa Hayashi, 25, from the faculty of economics at Keio Gijuku

University, rises to a glorious morning with breathtakingly deep blue skies and a sharp touch of autumn. He and his fellow student cadet pilots have been drowning their bitterness in alcohol, 'enraged with indignation' about their situation. They deeply resent the off-hand manner in which they have been treated by the navy's professional officers.

Hayashi writes: 'I will live and die for my fatherland, my comrades of the 13th class, all those senior fighting men who are members of the "students mobilised for war" program, and lastly, for my own pride. I shall do so cursing all the while the Imperial Navy, which to me merely means a certain group of officers who graduated from Etajima...' He takes off in his new Ryusei dive bomber, vowing to slam it into an enemy carrier. It plunges into the sea and Hayashi is dead.

Some of the young men marked for suicide are luckier. Tokuro Takei, of Hamamatsu, in the western Shizuoka prefecture, joined a navy youth pilot training scheme at the tender age of 14. The average age of boy graduates in 1944 was 15. Fortunately for Takei, the surrender came before he could kill himself. It's most unlikely his reflections will ever appear at Etajima:

> We did not want to die – at least not like that. We were not afraid to fight, but we wanted to come home to our families alive after the fighting was over. And nobody except for the admirals and generals believed all that 'die for the emperor' business. We were fighting to protect our homeland and, most of all, our families.

Such is the fanaticism of the Imperial Navy chief, Admiral Toyoda, that even after the atomic bombs on Hiroshima and Nagasaki, he continues to resist surrender. Toyoda argues that the United States can't have more than a limited amount of radioactive material, which could produce only a few bombs. The naval chief believes that world opinion will intervene to stop the US from perpetrating another such 'inhuman atrocity'.

On 11 August, Toyoda sends an order calling for 'positive action against enemy task forces ... while strengthening our attacks on Okinawa at the same time'. But he has no fleet. That day Ugaki's chief intelligence officer, a look of horror on his face, brings the admiral 'the hateful news' in a radio broadcast from San Francisco: Japan has applied for acceptance of the Potsdam proclamation provided the emperor's status is unchanged.

Ugaki rants at 'those selfish weaklings' advocating surrender: 'Even though it becomes impossible for us to continue organised resistance after expending our strength, we must continue guerrilla warfare under the emperor and never give up.'

Next day, Toyoda and the new navy minister, Admiral Mitsumasa Yonai, send an ambiguous message to naval commanders. It says that with the entry of the Soviets against Japan, the crisis of the empire has worsened, so that 'we should fight until the last man'. But the message goes on to say the government has entered peace negotiations with the Allied powers, 'so we are requested to follow national policy in a well organised manner ... ' Yonai favours surrender. Toyoda doesn't. So Toyoda sends his own private and confidential telegram to his commanders calling for 'continuous operations by all means with firm determination'.

Ugaki continues to send boys to their deaths in Kamikaze attacks on the Americans at Okinawa.

On 15 August 1945, for the first time in history, the high-pitched voice of the Japanese emperor is heard on radio. Japanese are stunned. Many listen weeping, other bewildered, barely able to understand Hirohito's formal court language. But the gist becomes clear soon enough. Hirohito is ordering the Japanese people to 'endure the unendurable':

> After pondering deeply the general trends of the world and the actual conditions obtaining to Our Empire today, We have decided to effect a settlement of the present situation by resorting to an extraordinary measure.
>
> We have ordered Our Government to communicate to the

Governments of the United States, Great Britain, China and the Soviet Union that Our Empire accepts the provisions of their Joint Declaration.

To strive for the common prosperity and happiness of all nations as well as the security and well-being of Our Subjects is the solemn obligation which has been handed down by Our Imperial Ancestors, and which We lay close to heart.

Indeed, We declared war on America and Britain out of Our sincere desire to ensure Japan's self-preservation and the stabilization of East Asia, it being far from Our thought either to infringe upon the sovereignty of other nations or to embark upon territorial aggrandizement.

But now the war has lasted for nearly four years ... [it] has developed not necessarily to Japan's advantage, while the general trends of the world have all turned against her interest.

Moreover, the enemy has begun to employ a new and most cruel bomb, the power of which to damage is indeed incalculable, taking the toll of many innocent lives. Should We continue to fight, it would not only result in an ultimate collapse and obliteration of the Japanese nation, but also it would lead to the total extinction of human civilization.

Hirohito does not use the word surrender.

The Grand Naval Command, as it is now absurdly called, through the Kure naval station, orders the suspension of attacks against Okinawa and against the Soviet Union. Ugaki feels ashamed. As he hasn't yet received a formal ceasefire order, he decides to lead his men in ramming enemy vessels at Okinawa: 'I hope ... all the Japanese people will overcome all hardships expected to come in the future, display the traditional spirit of this nation more than ever, do their best to rehabilitate this country, and finally revenge this defeat in the future.'

Ugaki is driven to the nearby Oita airfield. He appears to be in a good mood. He drinks farewell sake with his staff officers and in a perverse act allows them to strip his rank insignia from his uniform. He stands on a folding chair and addresses 21 youthful flyers lined up before him wearing Kamikaze headbands.

'Will you all go with me?' he asks. 'Yes, sir!' they reply, raising their arms into the air. Ugaki, smiling, poses for a photographer before his two-man aircraft and then climbs into the navigator's rear seat.

Five hours after takeoff and now in darkness, Ugaki radios a final message: 'I am going to proceed to Okinawa where our men lost their lives like cherry blossoms, and ram into the arrogant American ships, displaying the real spirit of the Japanese warrior.' He concludes, 'Make our empire last forever... The emperor, Banzai!' and Ugaki and his pilot are never heard from again.

No American ships are hit. There are reports of American fighters shooting down aircraft that night off Okinawa. Ugaki does not return.

True to form, he can't go without one last vicious, blood-thirsty act; taking with him all 21 supportive flyers – those zealous and sad Kamikaze boys – whose lives are wantonly and uselessly wasted, mostly for the sake of one man's 'face' and his wicked pretensions to glory.

It is 15 August 1945, and the 'father of the Kamikazes', Admiral Takijiru Onishi, the spiritualist from the Etajima academy who was ruled as 'ungentlemanly', squats on the floor of the second floor study at his official naval residence at Shibuya, Tokyo. The suicide squads have taken the lives of 6310 Japanese – boys and young men – and killed or badly injured over 15,000 Allied servicemen.

Onishi now has the grand title Vice Chief of the Naval General Staff, but it is a hollow designation as there is no longer an Imperial Navy. He has done everything in his power to prevent surrender, but, undaunted, claims: 'If we are prepared to sacrifice 20 million Japanese lives in a "special attack" effort, victory will be ours!'

Now all is lost, Onishi withdraws a sword from its scabbard, seizes it with both hands, the shining blade facing his abdomen, and drives it home into his body in great spurts of blood. With difficulty, Onishi wrenches the sword sideways, withdraws it, and then stabs himself in the chest and throat.

His friend, Yoshio Kodama, a civilian right-wing extremist who will go on to become one of Japan's richest moguls, finds Onishi covered in blood. The man who has engineered the wasteful deaths of thousands of young patriots has used Kodama's sword to commit ritual suicide *seppuku*. But Kodama's sword is blunt. Onishi talks with Kodama during the 12 hours it takes him to die: 'I have no way of apologising to the people and to the emperor. I feel that just by disembowelling myself, I cannot apologise sufficiently to my men who died on those "special attack" planes and to their bereaved families. But, I have no other way of making atones to them.'

Onishi clasps Kodama with his blood-stained hands and pleads for the youth of Japan to 'bear up against every hardship' which the new age will bring and 'build up with heart and soul the new Japan'.

Despite it being a navy without ships, the Imperial Navy towards the end had more influence over events than did the army. The emperor trusted the navy in the dying days of the war and in particular trusted the admirals Suzuki and Yonai, according to Captain Toshikazu Ohmae. Fluent in English, Ohmae had been in charge of missions and movements of ships within the Naval Affairs Bureau. He also served as a battle-hardened staff officer on several of Japan's important fleets and became chief of the operations section of Naval General Staff.

After the war American interrogators regarded Ohmae highly for his knowledge and intelligence. He also gave an insight into early 1942 thinking when Japan was making plans for the isolation of Australia. Unlike Sadatoshi Tomioka, Ohmae thought the Imperial Navy's plans to invade Australia had little to do with gaining further natural resources:

It was thought that such key areas as Darwin in the north and Townsville, Brisbane and Sydney on the east coast should be occupied. The Navy was responsible for New Guinea, New Britain and the Solomons and Australia figured heavily in its plans ... By invading Australia the supply of war materials, particularly airplanes, gas and oil which had already begun to flow from the United States, would be stopped.

Rear Admiral Baron Sadatoshi Tomioka, as he is now at the age of 45, gazes out from an American destroyer at the massive array of Allied warships at anchor in Tokyo Bay. It is Sunday, 2 September 1945. The sky is dull, heavy with low-hanging cloud. In the distance, Tomioka can see the battleship USS *Missouri*, where Japan's official surrender will take place in an hour or two.

If Ugaki presented the greatest threat to Australia within Combined Fleet, then Baron Tomioka, with his sophisticated manner, educated background and influence, was his counterpart – Australia's greatest enemy within the Naval General Staff in Tokyo.

He has been forced to join the formal Japanese surrender party. 'You lost the war,' navy supremo Admiral Toyoda tells him, 'you go!' Thus the raving fanatic who fought against surrender long enough for scores of thousands more Japanese to be slaughtered avoids his duty, threatening to suicide if he is forced to attend. As the destroyer nears the battleship, Tomioka thinks of honourable death; *hari-kari* might the warrior's answer.

Toyoda will be charged as a war criminal, and tried in October 1948. He is accused of allowing Japanese naval personnel under his command to 'abuse, mistreat, torture, rape, kill, and commit atrocities and offences' against innumerable people, including non-combatants. He pleads not guilty and is the only one of the accused major war criminals found not guilty on all counts. He lives peacefully in Japan until 1957, when he dies of a heart attack aged 72.

Toyoda's opposite number in the army, General Yoshijiro

Umezu, will be found guilty of conspiracy to wage aggressive war against China and the western powers and will be sentenced to life imprisonment. On this terrible day, Umezu has also threatened to kill himself if he is forced to take part in the surrender ceremony, but Emperor Hirohito himself commands him to attend. Cancer kills Umezu in 1949.

Before the surrender ceremony, naval officers who flock to Tokyo, wanting the war to continue, are calmed by Tomioka, the rationalist, who has thought hard enough about the future to know that the coming peace will not be serene: 'With the end of World War II, there is sure to be a confrontation between the democracy and communism, that is between the US and the Soviet Union. In the rift between them, Japan can find a chance to regain its feet.'

Tomioka and eight others now walk across the gangway from the destroyer to board the *Missouri*, led by Foreign Minister Mamoru Shigemitsu. The Japanese are saluted by American officers. Shigemitsu, in topper and tails, limps and leans heavily on his cane, having lost his leg to an assassin's bullet 15 years earlier. He makes a painful progress across the battleship's quarterdeck to a ladder leading up to the deck where the ceremony is about to begin.

Every inch of the *Missouri* is jam-packed with sailors, officers and representatives of the Allied Press. Sailors and photographers hang from the most precarious places, to get a glimpse of the vanquished. The supreme commander General Douglas MacArthur steps to the microphone. He tells the world that this gathering is not taking place in a spirit of distrust, malice or hatred: 'It is my earnest hope and indeed the hope of all mankind that from this solemn occasion a better world shall emerge out of the blood and carnage of the past . . .'

Shigemitsu and Umezu sign the surrender document while Tomioka and the other Japanese stand in three neat rows, waiting, expressionless. Tomioka is awed at the lack of obvious contempt demonstrated by MacArthur and the Americans in general. Yet he is angered by the presence of the Soviet delegation. They are part-

Asian, he feels, but they ignored Japan's desperate plea to act as a peacemaker and then they stabbed Japan in the back by invading Manchuria in the last days of the war.

Among those who sign the historic document of surrender is Australia's commander-in-chief, General Sir Thomas Blamey, who in 1942 thought that Western Australia could easily fall prey to the Japanese.

On 21 August 1945, in 'a personal message of farewell' to the Australian forces, MacArthur recalled the period as the 'lowest ebb' of the Allied cause in the south west Pacific, 'as the enemy hordes plunged forward with almost irresistible force to the threshold of your homeland'. 'There you took your stand and with your Allies turned the enemy advance on the Owen Stanleys and at Milne Bay in the fall of 1942, thus denying him access to Australia and otherwise shifting the tide of battle in our favor.'

Ten days after the surrender ceremony, US military police arrive at a modest house at Setagaya in Tokyo, to arrest the former prime minister, Hideki Tojo. They hear a shot, and when they reach the study they find the former leader with a pistol in hand and blood spreading on his shirt. The pistol clatters to the floor and Tojo slumps into a chair.

A reporter from the *New York Times* has been permitted to witness the arrest. Tojo manages to speak: 'The Greater East Asian War was justified and righteous. I am very sorry for the nation and all the races of the Greater Asiatic powers. I would not like to be judged before a conqueror's court. I wait for the righteous judgement of history.' Rushed by ambulance to hospital, the general is saved to face trial for war crimes.

In the last interview he gives, Tojo insists that Japan had no plans for the physical invasion of Australia or New Zealand: 'We never had enough troops to do so. We had already far out-stretched our lines of communication. We did not have the armed strength or the supply facilities to mount such a terrific extension of our already over-strained and too thinly spread forces. We expected to occupy all New Guinea, to maintain Rabaul as a holding base, and to raid

Northern Australia by air. But actual physical invasion – no, at no time.' Tojo was reported by the Australian newsman, Richard Hughes.

Tojo's memory must have faded. In early 1942, the Japanese prime minister had told Prince Naruhiko Higashikuni: 'I think we will have few problems occupying not only Java and Sumatra but also Australia if things go on like this. We shouldn't think about peace at this time.'

Lord Edward Russell of Liverpool, the soldier, lawyer and historian, described Hideki Tojo as perhaps the most prominent and most blameworthy of all the Japanese major war criminals: 'The barbarous treatment of prisoners and internees was well known to Tojo. He took no adequate steps to punish offenders and to prevent the commission of similar offences in the future.' Tojo is found guilty of war crimes by the International Military Tribunal for the Far East, and executed by hanging in Sugamo prison, Tokyo, on 23 December 1948.

Sadatoshi Tomioka is not charged with war crimes. He cooperates with American intelligence officials wanting to know everything about the Imperial Navy. After the war, he heads a formal Japanese study group charged with reviewing the operation and history of the Imperial Navy. The group analyses mistakes made by the Imperial Navy, including presumably, a few of his own.

Surprisingly, Tomioka even exerts some influence on the future defence direction of Japan's armed forces. His views are much favoured by writers and historians, since he is articulate and readily available to recount his memories. He becomes known as one of the wartime 'moderates' and 'liberals', even though his record shows that he long advocated aggressive war against the United States.

Tomioka helps to edit the official Japanese navy history, *Senshi Sosho*, an immense work of 102 volumes, produced by Japan's National Institute for Defense Studies, the main policy research arm of Japan's Ministry of Defense. As Japan's sole official military history research centre, the institute, and Tomioka's substantial contribution, map the Japanese war history. Tomioka also writes his own books on the progress of the war in the Pacific.

But Tomioka's views, especially on naval history and tradition, penetrate even further. He becomes a member of the Japanese government's 12-man commission for the setting up of a Japanese defence program, which contributes to the establishment of the Japan Self-Defense Forces.

Tomioka dies in 1970, at the age of 73. His ageing son, Sadahiro Tomioka, lives on at Shimoseya, Yokohama, but doesn't like to talk about the baron, noting that he didn't see much of his father when he was associated with the Imperial Navy.

28

NOT THE WAR BUT THE GAME

On Japan's 'one day of the year', the Yasukuni shrine near the Imperial Palace in Tokyo is jam-packed with sombre-faced mourners. Next door, Shinto priests in flowing robes work to control large crowds entering the palatial *yushukan*, or national war museum.

It is 15 August, the anniversary of the Japanese surrender. My Japanese host has suggested that we meet at the shrine on this day of remembrance. 'It will be good for you and good for me,' he says, but at the appointed hour he fails to materialise. I find myself the only European among thousands of Japanese.

Strutting young radicals of the extreme right, clad in black and prominently displaying the Imperial Navy flag on their jumpsuits, demonstrate noisily against the failure of the prime minister to visit the shrine on this day. Loudspeakers blare nationalistic slogans; riot police wait with their water cannon in the side streets.

A few of the young protestors glare at me, but not a soul offers any other discourtesy. Mostly, I do not exist. The only other foreigner that I can detect in the throng, a black American, seeks me out. 'This is really scary,' he says with a nervous smile, for there is more than a hint of fascism at Yasukuni.

1942

It's not all tense symbolism, however. An old man wearing his soldier's uniform plays wartime tunes on an accordion, and a crowd gathers around under the trees to listen quietly. There is no clapping or laughter. Old people are remembering. The younger people must be thinking, 'so this is what it must have been like'.

Japanese mourners, two guards directing them, approach the shrine in waves, dozens at a time, laying flowers, bowing, and saying brief prayers for the war dead; families still grieving for their loved ones. Yasukuni *Jinja* is dedicated to all Japan's war dead, and is the most controversial war shrine in Japan, since it brazenly commemorates major war criminals, including General Tojo, among the war dead.

To the victims of Japanese aggression in World War II, the shrine's rhetoric is inflammatory. Its website has a simple explanation for Japan's War of Greater East Asia: 'To maintain the independence and peace of the nation and for the prosperity of all Asia, Japan was forced into conflict.'

At the vast museum, the crowds, mostly younger people, inch their way past exhibits of Japan's wartime weaponry and military feats from ancient times, leading up to and including the Pacific war. In the entrance hall a steam locomotive, the C56, is displayed: it's the engine used at the opening ceremony of the great feat of the Japanese Thai–Burma railway. There is no mention whatsoever of the estimated 100,000 Asian labourers and the 60,000 Allied POWs who died of disease, injury, brutality or starvation during the railway's construction. The first sin of omission.

In one of the crowded exhibition halls, a little girl, happily playing, runs her hand along the black metal coffin of a *Kaiten* human torpedo; I involuntarily shudder at the awfulness of these death machines. The end result was often death for the sad boy inside, urged on to his sacrifice by his instructors, extremist Imperial Navy officers who made sure that before he set off on his mission, the young man wrote of his willingness to die as an example to others.

Further along the hall, there's an exhibit featuring a map of

Asia and the Pacific under the heading, 'The Campaign Plan, 2nd Phase, Feb–April 1942.' The Japanese story board describes Japan's 'future planning operations': 'When victories in the initial offensives were far more spectacular than anticipated, Japanese strategists altered the original more prudent plans.' A dotted blue line encircles the whole of the top end of Australia, about one quarter of the continent. The Japanese lettering across the top end reads: 'Australia invasion manoeuvres/operations'. The map shows thrusting arrows pointing south from the Moluccas (in the Dutch East Indies) to Darwin and from Port Moresby to far north Queensland. New Caledonia and Fiji are similarly singled out.

Another exhibit is dedicated to the Sydney midget submarine raid; its text revels in the tale of how the Australian naval authorities of 1942 gave four of the dead submariners funerals with full military honours. The exhibition also contains a photograph of the youthful submariner Keiu Matsuo, 'who was killed in action after sinking an enemy warship in the heavily guarded Sydney naval port'. The caption runs on: 'In respect for the gallant soul of a Japanese naval officer, the Australian navy recovered his body and conducted a naval funeral.'

There is another photo, showing Matsuo's mother aboard a boat in Sydney Harbour in 1968, when she was aged 83. She is assisted by two Australian sailors to make a traditional offering to the dead, pouring sake into the harbour. A poem Matsuo's mother wrote to her son after hearing of his death is displayed, along with hundreds of letters and poems from young men killed in action.

This correspondence has been neatly vetted to eliminate those young Japanese who wrote of their fear and hatred at being forced to commit suicide. Every exhibit is calculated not only to honour Japan's war dead, but to instil fervent nationalism. Yet Mrs Matsuo's verse is still as moving as the day she wrote it in deep despair:

The blossom that was raised to fall for His Majesty's cause
Yet how lonely is my garden after the storm.

1942

This war memorial produces mixed emotions.

On the way out, a large story board covering a wall tells us that despite Japan's defeat in the war, the country's actions brought welcomed independence to many countries of Asia that had previously been under the colonial yoke. These 'liberated countries' and their early nationalist leaders are pictured. The crowd takes it all in. Unquestioning Japanese school students make notes as they shuffle along in the queue. But there are no words here about Japan's violent subjugation of Asian countries, or the brutal treatment she inflicted on countless local people and Allied POWs.

The Shinto priests encourage post-war generations to understand why Japan went to war:

> Isn't it a fact that the West with its military power invaded and ruled over much of Asia and Africa and that this was the start of East-West relations?
>
> Japan's dream of building a Great East Asia was necessitated by history and it was sought after by the countries of Asia.

By late 1941 Japan's cause of international peace and justice had been proclaimed by the government, drummed into every citizen and taught by rote to every schoolchild. Voices were becoming shriller by the week. Boys at school drilled daily with toy rifles and were taught the great Japanese military victories of the past. Above all, they worshipped His Imperial Majesty, for whom Japanese would give up their lives, as in the words of the slow, mournful battle dirge, *Umi Yukaba*:

> Across the sea,
> Corpses in the water,
> Across the mountain,
> Corpses heaped upon the field;
> I shall die only for the emperor,
> I shall never look back.

Every schoolboy knew that the objective of Japanese expansion was neither the attainment of capitalist supremacy over other nations nor the accumulation of colonies. What Japan taught was the quest for trade, harmony and peace with the nations of East Asia and to lead those countries into mutual happiness and prosperity. This enforced leadership and prosperity was Japan's right and responsibility. As Japanese foreign spokesmen repeatedly put it, 'Japan is the pioneer of a new age; she is the hope of a new Asia.'

Singapore's founding Prime Minister, Lee Kuan Yew, as a youth witnessed the brutality of the Japanese occupation and almost became a victim of the massacres that claimed many thousands. He has written that successive Japanese governments, their leaders, academics and most of the media have chosen not to talk about evil Japanese war deeds:

> Unlike the Germans they hope that with the passing of the generations these deeds will be forgotten, and the accounts of what they did buried in dusty records. When they refuse to admit them to their neighbours, people cannot but fear that it is possible for them to repeat these horrors.

The Shinto priests and their extremist backers make it clear that they are outraged that some school textbooks are being made to acknowledge the truth that Korean 'comfort women' during the war were forced to become prostitutes for Japanese soldiers. 'The textbooks depict as a historical fact the story of Asian women who were forced into prostitution by the Japanese Army. Imparting this story to students who are still young and immature has become a great problem since last year.'

My companion in this research tour of Japan, the Chinese Singaporean, well remembers the Korean comfort women and their wartime suffering in Singapore. Willie Phua, for years a news cameraman, as a child ran messages for the Japanese. His mother worked as a cook in the officers' brothels in Cairnhill Road.

Finally, the Yasukuni *Jinja* museum has what it calls 'a message for the future' justifying its remembrance of war criminals among the 2,466,000 Japanese war dead honoured as *Kami* (deities):

There were 1,068 'Martyrs of Showa' who were cruelly and unjustly tried as war criminals by a sham-like tribunal of the allied forces ... these martyrs are also the *Kami* of Yasukuni *Jinja*.

A former Japanese prime minister, Junichiro Koizumi, has prayed at Yasukuni shrine, offering his respects to those who died in the war, and insisting that his visits are not an attempt to glorify Japan's past militarism. 'Through its colonial rule and aggression,' he has said, 'Japan caused tremendous damage and suffering to the people of many countries, particularly those of Asian nations.' But the Yasukuni museum has a different message and today's young people read the story boards avidly and move on in the crowd, accepting it all as the truth.

At Etajima, the historic Imperial Navy Academy from 1888 to 1945 is still there, under a new name, in its fabulous setting beneath Mount Furutaka on the Bay of Hiroshima, a short trip from Kure or Iwakuni across the Inland Sea. The former academy now combines Japan's first naval service school and the officer candidate school. As Japanese leaders become more emboldened in remembering the past in a better light, it seems only a matter of time before the Japanese call their 'Maritime Self-Defense Force' a fully-fledged navy.

This is the place that nurtured the Imperial Navy's officers. Etajima not only survives, it unashamedly revels in the past. Today's naval training base boasts that Etajima was, until 1945, recognised as one of the three greatest naval academies in the world. The British connection can be seen readily in the splendid buildings.

NOT THE WAR BUT THE GAME

Etajima's great ceremonial hall is like a cathedral; a grand white granite building of two floors fronted by three massive doors topped by arched windows and surrounded by manicured Japanese pine. Outside, the summer heat is oppressive. Inside, the air is delightfully crisp. Footsteps echo on the white stone floor devoid of seating. You can hear a pin drop. Two flags predominate on what appears to be a stage. One is the national flag of Japan. The other is another symbol that once provoked hatred. The flag of the Imperial Navy is now that of Japan's modern day Maritime Self-Defense Force. Upon this vast altar you imagine the diminutive and much-loved commander-in-chief Admiral Yamamoto, and the imperial princes, speaking quietly about duty and honour to proud graduates who hang on every word and who consider themselves the 'elite'.

When the end came it was ignoble for the Japanese. Australian troops made up the main body of the British Commonwealth Occupation Forces (BCOF) stationed in and around bombed out Kure in the post-war period from February 1946. The Australians headed through the innumerable islands of the Inland Sea, disarming the Japanese and disposing of weapons, bombs and poisonous gas, even setting foot on tiny Hashirajima, whose once great anchorage was now devoid of Japanese ships, apart from the half-sunk hulks nearby. The commander-in-chief, Australian General Sir John Northcott, in 1948 moved his headquarters to Etajima, untouched by bombs, and occupied the very buildings of the former Imperial Navy. The citadel of remembrance of the Imperial Navy's glory – the museum at Etajima – was used as the Australian and British servicemen's club. It contained a bar and their theatre, the 'Roxy'. The classic ceremonial hall became the garrison's Christian church.

The Australian occupiers, with a strict policy of non-fraternisation, were not liked by the Japanese and were known at first for their arrogance. In time, relations improved. Australian soldiers fraternised, despite the rules. Eventually, 650 Australian servicemen in the Kure area married Japanese and, after a long fight with the bureaucracy, gained the right to take their brides home, most to spend their lives together.

The Etajima Educational Museum is an impressive Hellenic-style building with six great columns. The guidebook to the Etajima base says the old Imperial Navy indoctrination of service to the emperor is no longer given to young recuits. They are trained to serve, not the emperor, but concepts such as 'freedom' and 'the people'. I pause for a long time before two framed photographs which induce in me feelings of disbelief. Both are portraits of Vice Admiral Takijiru Onishi, the nasty, big-eared, proud-looking 'father of the Kamikaze', the relentless killer of boys. Some of the youths sent off to crash their planes on to American ships weren't old enough to shave.

Beneath the photographs, today's Japanese naval cadets are able to read this glowing tribute to the man who entered the academy at 17 as a little thug:

> As Commander in Chief, Naval Air Fleet, Admiral Onishi was greatly loved and respected by his men of the Kamikaze special attack corps. He desperately but unsuccessfully put forth his utmost effort in an attempt to turn the tide of the war. When he received the Imperial edict to terminate the war, he left a farewell statement and fulfilled his responsibility to his men by nobly committing *harakiri* (ritual suicide).

During the war, the words of the Kamikaze had a significant propaganda role, often broadcast and included in wartime newspapers, encouraging others to extreme sacrifices. Today, Japanese institutions revere the letters of the departed Kamikaze youth. The pilots were told that their wills and letters would be displayed as writings by 'the heroic souls' or *eirei*, as one pilot who survived, Masamichi Shinta, later wrote:

> I knew the *tokkotai* [Kamikaze] pilots would die like dogs. When I was selected to be one of 36 *tokkotai* out of 200 trained

to be *tokkotai* pilots, I sank into the depths of despair. I was told to write my will so that they can display it at the Exhibition Hall for Education. Of course, we could not say what we really thought and felt. So we had to lie. It was taboo to express our true thoughts.

Etajima's homage to Onishi and the Kamikaze reminds me of the *Kaiten* at Yasukuni. I try to suppress the question because it seems racist, but it gains root and I can't dismiss it – just what sort of a race would sacrifice its young men in such a callous manner and then serve up the story, publicly and unapologetically, as inspired nationalism to be venerated six decades later? Just what sort of a race is it that can concoct such barbaric and assured deaths for young people, knowing too that their latest secret weapon is, at best, a shoddy technological disaster?

Such behaviour seems to exceed desperation. You might revere and mourn the youthful operators, but not those men with so much blood on their hands who so willingly sacrificed their young knowing the boys had no chance of survival whatsoever. The same exasperated anger can be reserved for the Americans who knowingly dropped atomic bombs on cities crowded both with military personnel and large numbers of civilians. Where does the barbarity of nations end?

I look at the green booklet in my hands, and shake my head in wonder at its words: 'Today we regard the old Imperial Japanese Navy with respect and affection as having shown us our national superiority.'

'Our national superiority'! They are the strident nationalistic words of yesteryear. Yet this unapologetic message is not one published in the 1940s, but the guide to Etajima published and distributed by Japan's Maritime Self-Defense Force in 2007.

It's the thoughtless acceptance by many contemporary Japanese of this sort of official rhetoric that grates. A friend showing a Japanese student the scenic sights at Caloundra, on Queensland's Sunshine Coast, points out to the girl a memorial to the hospital ship, the *Centaur*, which was torpedoed by a Japanese submarine in 1943. She reads the inscription and turns away angrily: 'That's a lie!', and quickly leaves the company of her surprised host.

Why are such people, sufficiently clever to help resurrect their nation from utter defeat and transform it into a world leader in technology and manufacture, and to build a better life for future generations, still as unquestioning as their parents and grandparents were in a very different era?

The air commander over Pearl Harbor, Rabaul and Darwin, Mitsuo Fuchida, wrote that, in the final analysis, the root cause of Japan's defeat lay deep in the Japanese national character: 'There is irrationality and impulsiveness about our people which results in actions that are haphazard and often contradictory.'

Japanese naval historian professor Sadao Asada concludes that the failure of naval leadership, including that of General Staff chief Admiral Nagano, to control pressures from unruly subordinates was a significant factor in Japan going to war. Admiral Shigeyoshi Inoue, the aggressive Fourth Fleet commander, after the war said that naval leaders simply did not have the courage and resources to control their radical middle echelon officers from 'whipping up a belligerent spirit'.

There were multiple Japanese threats to Australia. Admiral Inoue had been one of those keen to invade. In early May 1942 he had instructed his carrier striking force in its first attempt to invade Port Moresby, after landing troops and destroying the town, to then cross the Coral Sea, 'and launch air strikes on Allied air bases at Townsville and Cooktown', if the situation allowed. The Battle of the Coral Sea forced Inoue's fleet to turn back to Rabaul and he was unable to unleash his considerable force on Australia. It was a near thing. What might have followed?

David Horner, professor of Australian defence history, has said the events of 1942 presented the Australian government and its military high command with greater challenges than at any time since Federation. For the first and only time since white settlement, Australia faced the prospect of a foreign invasion. The Curtin government, Horner said, had to watch helplessly while the Japanese overran Rabaul, Ambon and Timor and bombed Darwin:

> Australia's political and military leaders were fully justified in believing that the country was under a real threat of invasion. But, unknown to the Australians, Japanese Army and Navy leaders were deep in argument about whether to invade Australia.

Horner was referring to an invasion threat existing between January and March 1942. He believes that by April 1942 intelligence was indicating that Japan was not planning to invade Australia, adding, 'Of course, Japan could have changed its plans if events had turned out differently later in 1942.'

General MacArthur's words that John Curtin 'saved Australia in her hour of need' and that the Diggers 'turned the tide on the enemy advance' on the Kokoda trail and at Milne Bay in 1942, thus 'denying access to Australia', became part of Australia's history and lore.

But were these words mere rhetorical flourish, the type of which MacArthur was supremely capable? It is more recently argued by some that Australian success in the Milne Bay and Kokoda campaigns could not have saved Australia because, by towards late 1942, the Battle of Midway had decimated the Japanese fleet and Japan had not the ships for an invasion force.

In fact, the Japanese fleet was largely intact, with the major exception of the loss of four important carriers, as historian Paul S. Dull points out. Among the Japanese ships surviving at the end of 1942 were five carriers, eight battleships, 14 heavy cruisers and 18 light cruisers. Midway, while a key to the eventual defeat of the Japanese, was but the second of five great battles in the Pacific in which aircraft did all the hitting. After Midway, the Imperial

Navy then was not prepared to say the war was lost, although Yamamoto might have believed so. But he returned to Hashirajima, fleets were rearranged to support ongoing operations, and new planning for the ultimate 'decisive battle' began.

The credible operations planner Captain Toshikazu Ohmae was typical. He told his American interrogators: 'As for myself, after Coral Sea and Midway, I still had hope.' Australia, indeed, was far safer with the loss of Yamamoto's four major carriers. But had the Japanese been adequately supplied and strongly reinforced and been able to advance that little bit further on to Port Moresby over the Kokoda track and also to occupy Milne Bay as an air base in southern Papua around September 1942, would Australia have been ripe for invasion? The logical answer is that Japan by then would not risk its remaining carriers without suitable air cover to invade Australia and army opposition would have been even greater. But this view relies on the expectation of logical thinking within the Imperial Navy. The capture of Port Moresby and/or Milne Bay might have led to further navy 'victory fever', belligerence, audacity and idiocy. Invasion in late 1942 would have been unlikely in these circumstances, yet anything would have been possible.

Did John Curtin bring the troops home to fight in New Guinea and did he overrule Churchill attempting to divert Australian troops to places already doomed? The simple answer is yes, he did.

General Douglas MacArthur's air chief, General George C. Kenney, held a lifelong belief that Japan originally intended to invade Australia:

> How much extra effort expended by the Japanese in the Philippines detracted from carrying out their original plan to seize New Caledonia and Fiji, thus cutting our route to Australia, is difficult to estimate, but certainly if that had happened there

would have been no Battle of the Coral Sea, Port Moresby would probably have fallen, and the Japs would then have been able to carry out the next phase of their plan, which was an invasion of Australia itself.

The weight of evidence is that there were various Japanese plans, mostly – but not all – emanating from the Japanese Imperial Navy, to invade Australia. Yet it is not suggested that a final planning order for an invasion of Australia ever reached the approval stage or that Imperial General Headquarters ever agreed with such an action. The closest was agreement for a future 'temporary invasion of Darwin', subject to strict, if not almost impossible, conditions from the army, put to Emperor Hirohito by the combined chiefs. But the proposal was shelved as the war moved on. However, for several months important and/or influential elements within the Imperial Navy were pressing strongly and repeatedly for invasion and such a possibility of invasion presented a real and imminent danger to an unprepared Australia. An occupation of parts of Australia's remote north, especially Darwin, was for a time in early 1942 very much on the cards, as Japanese sources clearly show.

But did Japan really have the *capacity* to invade a militarily weak Australia in 1942? Dr Steven Bullard, of the Australian War Memorial, thinks not. Overconfidence, he has written, led to the Japanese proposals to continue the advance south to invade all or part of the Australian mainland, but:

We now know that Japan at the time had neither the capacity to seriously threaten Australia's long-term freedom nor the intention to occupy and subjugate the Australian people. Instead, Japanese Imperial Headquarters adopted a policy to consolidate its new territories in anticipation of the expected Allied counter-attacks in the region.

*

1942

The expansive foyer of the international hotel at Shimbashi, Tokyo, is a place of subdued elegance. I am waiting, not knowing quite what to expect. Professor Hiromi Tanaka seeks out the foreigner and, with friendly courtesies, we adjourn to a quiet alcove.

We have met before only by email, but I have read his remarks concerning Australia and the Imperial Navy and I am keen to talk to him further. Once the war began, he has written, the unexpected speed and success of Japan's offensives led to an expansion of the scope of operations to the Lesser Sunda and Solomon Islands. As a result, 'navy planners began to take Australia into serious consideration, seeing it as an imminent threat'.

With a generous head of greying hair, Tanaka looks like the professor of history that he is. He teaches at the National Defense Academy at Yokosuka, at the entrance to Tokyo Bay, and is a recognised expert on Japan's naval history. Yokosuka was one of the main wartime arsenals for the Imperial Navy. Apart from being a naval base, battleships and aircraft carriers and navy planes were built on its shores. Now Yokosuka is also home to the US Seventh Fleet. The academy is one of the places where young men and women train to become officers of Japan's three services of the Self-Defense Force. It trains Japanese officer cadets to develop 'a broad perspective and a scientific and logical way of thinking'. That point soon becomes pertinent.

We settle into soft armchairs in the quiet lounge with its heavy drapes and discreet chat. Waitresses intrude with iced water and cola. Professor Tanaka is keen to talk. Indeed there is an unexpected urgency in his manner. He has brought with him a young assistant who translates, and it's quickly obvious that both these men are passionate about the subject.

We begin by discussing Japanese naval officers including Baron Sadatoshi Tomioka, the charming, sophisticated man who was one of those who wanted to capture Australia. Tanaka knows all about him, including his work after the war as head of an academic think tank set up to study why the Imperial Navy made so many stupid mistakes.

He has no doubts whatsoever that invasion of Australia was a deadly serious option in 1942. 'It is all there,' he tells me, 'in *Senshi Sosho*', the 102-volume official war history series funded by the Japanese government and compiled by the National Institute for Defense Studies. In fact, Tomioka was a major contributor to the series.

'But why invade Australia?' I ask Tanaka, explaining that I cannot see the logic in it. Tomioka had said that Japan's top leaders thought they had a good chance to bring the war to a negotiated peace fairly early 'considering the favourable development of the war in Europe where Germany had become an irresistible force' and possible developments in international politics. Yet, there was no plan, no discussion, no concept of how a favourable, negotiated peace would be reached and conducted after smashing Pearl Harbor and trampling across the nations of Asia and the Pacific. Was the USA expected to submit, to just give up and say, 'OK, we surrender'? It was Mad Hatter stuff, and very hard for a Western researcher to understand.

I sense the professor is restraining himself. I have missed the point. He shakes his head. 'Stop!' he seems to be saying, 'You are looking for logic. You won't find it!'. When he speaks, he says: 'I believe the Japanese Imperial Navy opinion was not very logical or rational. In fact, the navy was very illogical . . .'

According to Tanaka, Imperial Navy officers first began thinking about taking over Australia in a future war as early as 1935: 'There was a time when the navy officers were influenced by the *Mein Kampf* of Hitler and they reflected on what we will do if necessary. It was not a healthy plan and was pretty crazy, I believe. The most scary part of this fascist state approach was that even extraordinary and crazy things can be regarded as healthy and rational and normal.'

Unsatisfied, I probe the reason for the Imperial Navy's interest in Australia. Tanaka patiently explains that at the outbreak of war the planners didn't think a takeover of Australia was possible, but 'because the initial operations went much better than expected, for the first time they began to think realistically about taking over Australia'. After taking over New Guinea, they thought, 'Here's this continent, let's go and get them.' But why, I ask again? Tanaka is becoming frustrated with my obtuseness:

> They didn't really chase after anything! Probably those officers thought they wanted some big place that they could control. I agree that they said they had a purpose, to prevent Australia becoming a big American base, but if they thought about their purpose seriously and carefully, rationally, they wouldn't think about it [taking Australia] seriously.

I'm not convinced, and Tanaka now is quietly imploring me to understand. The reason for his obvious loathing of the Imperial Navy becomes clear. He has spent the last five years studying the plight of the Japanese army in New Guinea. His work includes studying field reports, reminiscences and letters home from stranded Japanese soldiers who would never return, from troops whose supply lines were cut off from Japan, reducing them to hunger and decimation. He feels for these men as though he were there.

Rarely, says Tanaka, would the Imperial Navy lift a finger to help these soldiers. Over the long years of war the Combined Fleet would not even come down to the front line in New Guinea to help the embattled army. And 220,000 Japanese troops were killed in the campaign. It was just as well that the invasion of Australia as demanded by the navy never took place, he says, because the navy would have dropped the troops off and then completely abandoned them, satisfied that they had done their bit.

Tanaka says that apart from everything else, the navy was scared about losing their big ships. I have read that during the war both army and navy men at the front were deeply embittered and derisive about what they called the 'Hashirajima fleet' and the men of those ships who spent most of their war swinging at anchor off Hashirajima island or hunting and fishing and feasting ashore, rather than fighting, or doing much the same while anchored in the Truk lagoon.

Professor Tanaka can barely restrain his derision as he relates how the *Yamato* would cruise backwards and forth from Hashirajima to Truk in the Caroline islands, a great distance north of the front line in New Guinea. 'And what did the *Yamato* and the others do?' Tanaka asks with disdain. 'They cruised up and down, wasting precious oil, and spent months at anchor at Truk and at Hashirajima, never engaging the enemy, perhaps talking about the big decisive battle from which the navy will emerge victorious. And if everything was lost, then so be it. At least they'd be remembered for taking the big decision to fight the Americans.'

The professor's study has left him embittered about the Imperial Navy and this bubbles to the surface when I press him: 'You must understand that the Imperial Japanese Navy was such an irresponsible organisation; they never wanted to take responsibility. Coming to Australia and occupying one small beach was considered a navy responsibility, but after the takeover, they would have withdrawn, and left the rest to the army, saying the rest was an army responsibility.'

When I ask 'but why?' Tanaka's young interpreter almost explodes in the swiftness of his reply. I'm not even sure that he has had time to take in the professor's words. Clearly he knows the professor's thinking. He translates with Tanaka's emotion:

The navy didn't give a shit about those who would take over Australia! Their attitude was, we would land the troops to take part in the invasion of Australia and then they would leave it all to the army to do all the work. The reason they could think about this invasion was that they didn't have to think realistically. The navy would not carry any food, not a single grain of rice for the army . . .

I'm taken aback. I've heard of army–navy antagonism, but in wartime Japan surely this outright loathing wasn't the norm. We discuss some of the chief Imperial Navy proponents for invading Australia.

Tanaka says they were numerous: 'There were so many high ranking officers, including those in the Navy General Staff, who were arguing about attacking Australia. Also in the Combined Fleet. Arguing about attacking and invading Australia. It wasn't just the initiative of junior officers involved in this talk. It was official conversation because the navy officially submitted it to the army. The navy military orders [planning] section officers visited the army strategic section. They were always visiting the army pushing this point of view between February and March 1942 about invading Australia.'

Our conversation goes on for an hour and a half; finally, I close my notebook. But Professor Tanaka hasn't finished. It's a subject dear to his heart. He doesn't say it but those Japanese soldiers left to rot in the jungles of New Guinea by the Imperial Navy cannot be forgotten and the lesson must come out.

What comes through loud and clear is Tanaka's absolute revulsion at those who directed the Imperial Japanese Navy: their so-called honour, their puffed-up gall and their careless inhumanity. I reopen my notebook and he opens his heart: 'You know, some Japanese navy officers thought that letting the Emperor live and survive is the most important thing that needs to be done. They saw their mission as to die beautifully in the battlefield for the emperor. Sometimes I wonder if these Japanese were really determined to win the war or not.'

I look at him quizzically. Surely not? But it is an issue with which he has struggled:

> You see, their view was "I joined this match game and that's good enough. The result is not important." I wonder how many officers were really serious, mentally, about winning the war. No matter how much you try and think about it, I wonder if they really wanted to win the war. That's my personal opinion, really.

This is pretty heavy stuff, I think, coming from a man the Japanese government pays to teach history to aspiring officers of Japan's considerable defence force. Is Tanaka a voice in the wilderness? Or are his views another stream of influential thinking for the younger generation of Japanese?

We wrap it up, and walk across the spacious hotel foyer. I'm saying my thanks when Professor Tanaka stops me. He is standing directly before me, looking me right in the eyes. He is very quiet and very close: 'When you write your book, it must be strong,' he says, and his eager assistant quickly translates. 'Yes, my publisher would want that,' I respond, not quite understanding. The teacher of Japan's modern day warriors is speaking softly, without excitement, but I can see there is turbulence inside.

The history professor bows gently and says goodbye and turns. Then, just before he goes out into the heat of a Tokyo mid-summer evening, he hesitates. There is anxiety written on his face and he wills me to understand:

> No. No. I mean that when you write your book you must make this point about the illogical nature of those men, the Imperial Navy, and make it very strong. Make it so the people will take notice. This is important. Don't hold back. This is the real interest and the truth. That is the way it was.

Epilogue

BOYS, RESTING PEACEFULLY

It's the cold morning of Monday, 1 June 1942. Now, one final time, the young submariners will defy the Australian enemy.

Katsuhisa Ban and Mamoru Ashibe have endured a terrible battle and battering inside Sydney's great harbour. Escaping through Sydney Heads in the early hours of the morning, they turn their unreliable vessel north, past the towering sheer cliffs at the harbour entrance. They have wilfully and knowingly turned in the opposite direction from the only course that offered rescue – the mother subs are waiting at a southerly rendezvous point to retrieve them.

Now the *M-24* has settled on the ocean's bottom about 80 metres down. The horror, panic and excitement of the overnight attack with its gunfire, explosions and flight have faded. After all the mayhem, noise, determination, and raw fear, the special attack mission is about to end as the two young men always knew it would. They will die at sea, sealed in their metal tomb.

The sad, boyish commander, Sub-lieutenant Katsuhisa Ban, 23, probably hands a cup of cold sake to his engineer-navigator, Petty Officer Mamoru Ashibe, 24, and in the confined space, filling his own cup, both of them exhausted, drenched in sweat, and now icy cold, they proudly drink a toast to Emperor Hirohito and the victory they have just achieved. They have done what they intended to do – under fire, against all odds, they have launched their torpedoes at a great enemy ship and seen and felt the explosions follow. They could not have done more.

Now Ban, with resignation, stretches his arm forward towards his comrade and friend and purposely pulls the trigger of his Nambu 14.8 mm pistol, shooting his navigator in the head. The deafening noise reverberates in the restricted space of the control room, and both Ban and the submarine's interior are drenched in blood. Shocked and terrified, Ban quickly puts the pistol to his mouth and pulls the trigger. So there they will rest, far from home, washed by the sea, just another two Japanese boys among many millions going to a glorious death, their submarine disturbed only by the occasional scraping of a fishing net from Australian trawlermen working overhead.

This end of two bright young men by suicide must continue to be speculative, but it is the best educated guess, based on the history of the midget submariners and of those who knew them. That they were encouraged and goaded into such action by their naval elders is clear. One of Japan's old warmongering admirals, Nobumasa Suetsugu, as commander-in-chief of the Combined Fleet in 1933, had ordered research into midget submarine development. Described by British diplomats as 'impetuous and unrestrained', the old admiral told the *Japan Times* in 1942 that only Japanese could undertake such a feat as the Sydney raid because they never expected to return alive:

> They certainly make the Gods weep. 'You cut through my flesh and I will cut through your bone', that is the traditional spirit of the Japanese Army and Navy, and the present great results must have been based on this spirit.

*

1942

On a warm, sunny November day in 2006, a most unlikely bunch of mates are about to solve a great Australian maritime mystery. Calling themselves the 'No Frills Boys', these seven amateur divers, who mostly live along Sydney's northern beaches, have spent their spare time exploring this beautiful stretch of coastline. They enjoy plunging into the local waters looking for objects of interest, such as uncharted wrecks.

Their battered dinghies have seen better days and their underwater detection system in one of the tinnies – their only piece of 'fancy' detection equipment – is a humble fish finder, purchased for $200. But these men are experienced divers. They have developed techniques for diving with a single tank, and can go deeper than most.

Amateur adventurers and explorers in their own right, they are always on the lookout for something different on the sandy ocean floor. They dream of some day finding the much sought after *M-24*, although none of them actually expects to.

In August 2006, when the winter swells were up and they were about five kilometres off Long Reef beach, the little fish finder detected a blip on the ocean floor where, from their knowledge, there really should not have been anything. But because of the rising swell, it was too dangerous then to dive, so the location was marked on a chart and set aside for another day.

Now Alan Simon, a retired company director from Mona Vale, is first in the water, along with Tony Hay, a bus driver. The other five divers follow – retired printer Phil Hendrie, electrician Dave Muir, plumber Dave Arnold, mortgage broker Greg Kerns and builder Paul Baggott.

The men descend 70 metres or more to the sandy floor. Moving along it for several minutes, Alan Simon perceives an object looming in the distance. He thinks he can make out, through shoals of fish, a hull and a conning tower. 'We can kind of talk under water and when I saw the props at the stern, I yelled at Tony, 'Sub, sub, sub!' Simon just knows it is Ban and Ashibe's long-lost *M-24*: 'We knew as soon as we laid eyes on it, we knew the stories behind it, and most divers around here have it in the back of their minds when they are out in the water.'

Tony Hay sees the wreck almost at the same time: 'We saw this long shape with a little lump sticking out of it, and my heart started going and I was thinking, no, it couldn't be!' The other five divers arrive, and the extent of the find begins to dawn on them as they move about gently touching the wreck, examining it thoroughly.

The two boys who trained so earnestly from their base on the Inland Sea of Japan have been found at last. 'It is so peaceful down there, it is just incredible, an amazing site,' Simon says. The submariners will not be disturbed. The divers circle around under lights in the dark, deep water. There is damage that looks like 20-mm machinegun bullet holes on the forward deck of the hull, leading them to think that the *M-24* might have slowly sunk. Other theories quickly emerge, including that the sub crashed into the seabed, which might explain the damage to the vessel's bow.

The No Frills Boys dive on the wreck five or six times in November, carefully measuring and photographing it. They keep their discovery to themselves until they reveal it to the *60 Minutes* television program. A final dive is videotaped and aired on 26 November 2006.

The Australians never lose sight of the importance of the wreck and of the memory of the Japanese boys Ban and Ashibe. They take nothing from the site, treating it as a war grave, as Simon explains: 'Although we felt elated, we felt the site demanded tremendous respect because we believe the two crew are still in there. Although it is unfortunate that what those submariners did cost the lives of 21 sailors, it was an incredibly brave thing to do.'

On television, Australian and Japanese people see the amateurs make their last dive on the *M-24* before strict government regulations come into force prohibiting divers from going anywhere near the wreck. With the camera rolling, Simon casts a wreath into the water with the words: 'On behalf of the No Frills divers and all the divers that found this wreck, we'd like to donate this wreath as a mark of respect for the two Japanese sailors that died on this submarine.'

After the program, questions naturally arise about how the Royal Australian Navy will treat the memory of the two submariners who fired the torpedo that killed 21 mostly Australian naval ratings. Will it mirror the funeral honours bestowed on the midget submariners in 1942? The answer is soon forthcoming in a private, joint ceremony involving modern day chiefs of the Australian and Japanese navies.

In early February 2007, the then chief of staff of the Japanese Maritime Self-Defense Force, Admiral Eiji Yoshikawa, makes a goodwill visit to Australia with his staff, and asks to lay a wreath at Garden Island in memory of the 21 victims of the torpedoing of the *Kuttabul*. Yoshikawa is invited aboard the anti-submarine escort, HMAS *Newcastle*, to visit the site of the wreck. The ship leaves the scene of the tragedy at Garden Island and heads over the waters traversed by Katsuhisa Ban and Mamoru Ashibe. Through Sydney Heads, the warship turns to port, just as Ban and Ashibe did in the early hours of 1 June 1942.

Off the great jutting point called Long Reef, the *Newcastle* cuts her engines and drifts silently in the swell. The chief of the Royal Australian Navy, Vice Admiral Russ Shalders, steps forward before the ship's company and his Japanese visitors, and recites a brief prayer. Then Admiral Yoshikawa steps forward and, together, the chiefs of the navies of Japan and Australia throw a wreath into the waters of the protected zone above the midget sub. Yoshikawa also drops over the side a letter written by Mamoru Ashibe's brother Itsuo, aged 83, of Wakayama city on the Inland Sea, who is visiting Sydney at the time with a Japanese television crew.

The voyage to Long Reef is a purely naval affair. No members of the press have been informed, and the RAN makes a brief statement afterwards saying that the ceremony provided the opportunity to recognise the sacrifice of two brave sailors 'based on an enduring respect between professional sailors and the operational circumstances in which these men died'.

Although he is in Sydney, Mr Ashibe is not present. Instead, the elderly gentleman, clutching a framed photograph of his brother, places flowers at the Garden Island memorial to the victims from the *Kuttabul*, and then takes a boat tour of the various harbour sites pointing out the exploits of the midget submariners.

Itsuo Ashibe has long remembered his brother's liking for sake, and has brought with him a small bottle of the favourite brand Mamoru always enjoyed. Frail Mr Ashibe takes a sip from it himself, then pours the rest of the sake into Sydney Harbour. He smiles, happy that he has made the pilgrimage and has shared a final drink with Mamoru.

Katsuhisa Ban's brother, Kazutomo, 74, a retired doctor from Hekinan, near Nagoya, welcomes the news that the *M-24* has been found, and that the site has been declared protected. He's grateful that the submarine will not be raised: 'I feel relieved that we now know the exact place he died. Now I think we should leave him to rest in peace. What will be found? Probably nothing. It benefits nobody.'

What is not mentioned about the *M-24* lying peacefully on the bottom is the manner in which the two young men died; the probability that Ban and Ashibe died in a double suicide just as they always knew they would. There's good reason for believing this is how they died.

Before they set off for the attack on Sydney, Ban and the other submarine commanders met Admiral Yamamoto. The midget sub commander Teiji Yamaki, who was injured and could not take part in the Sydney raid, was present when Yamamoto insisted that the submariners make every effort to return from their operation. But the young men already knew in their hearts that if they did not defy the commander-in-chief they would put all at risk:

We told him we would do our best to find a way to return after completing our task, but we all knew this was really a remote chance. We believed that to leave the support submarine waiting like a sitting duck for our return would put the lives of 100 crew in danger so we planned to do maximum damage with our torpedoes and the submarine.

Maritime archaeologist Tim Smith from the New South Wales Heritage Department says the *M-24*'s hatch was found locked down and the ladder was in the stowed position; proof that Ban and Ashibe never left the sub. They did not detonate their scuttling charges and, historically, the midget submariners committed suicide by shooting each other.

The American historian Gordon W. Prange encapsulated the greatest unresolved question concerning the submariners from the Japanese midgets: 'The entire mood and atmosphere of the midget submarine operation had been sacrificial from the beginning. While the airmen worked with cool logic and a tough determination to shed buckets of blood for results but not one drop for gestures, there seemed to be an almost ghoulish insistence upon immolating the midget submariners for nothing.'

The clumsy midget submarine raid on Sydney was not a prelude to invasion, nor was the bombing of Darwin and northern Australia. Despite the bravery and fatalism of those boys who came from the alluring beauty of the Seto Inland Sea, the Sydney raid was an unimportant sideshow in comparison with the real and imminent threat of a Japanese invasion of Australia being actively debated in Japan early in that terrible year of 1942.

When they reached Kure, at the end of the war, the occupying forces discovered serried rows of midget submarines in the final stages of manufacture. This is fate. Hundreds of young men marked for assured death are saved by the surrender to resume their place in society.

Ban and Ashibe were but two young men among 2.4 million Japanese war dead. Japan's war cost the lives of 17,501 Australians and millions of others. How many more, though, had the brash captains and the bellicose admirals of the Inland Sea had their irrational way?

Of all the foibles, war is the worst, equalled only by ignorance and disinclination to discover and admit the truth of it.

> *I'm fed up to the ears with old men dreaming up wars for young men to die in.*
> George McGovern

NOTES

Chapter 1

3: **Consequently some historians . . .** Chief among these doubters is Dr Peter Stanley, the former principal historian at the Australian War Memorial in Canberra, who has been outspoken on the subject, and whose words are quoted here. 'Threat made manifest', *Griffith Review*, Spring 2005, p. 15.

5–6: **Description of the** *Nagato*: Agawa, *The Reluctant Admiral*, p. 14. Navy heritage in Churchill, *The Second World War, Volume Three: The Grand Alliance*, pp. 455–56; Kaplan, Philip, *Battleship*, pp. 90, 196.

Chapter 2

9–10: **Background on Kuroshima and AMO Operation.** Prange Papers, Tomioka interviews, including interview August 1947, no. 5; Prange, *At Dawn We Slept*, pp. 98–99; Fuchida and Okumiya, *Midway*, pp. 51–52, 73.

10: **Our Empire, for the purpose of self-defence and self-preservation . . .** Ike (ed./trans.), *Japan's Decision for War*, pp. 135–36.

10: **The armed forces dominated Japanese government . . .** See Togo, *The Cause of Japan*, pp. 115–17.

11: **Etajima and bashings by Japanese naval officers.** Mitsuru, *Requiem for*

1942

Battleship Yamato, pp. 21–22, 40–41; Yutaka Yokota in Cook and Cook, *Japan at War, an oral history*, p. 312; and Rear Admiral Takagi Sokichi in Asada, *From Mahan to Pearl Harbor*, p. 163.

13: **Army and navy ministers also reported directly**... Ienaga, *The Pacific War, 1931–1945*, pp. 34–35, pp. 38–39.

13: **Footsteps echoed in the cavernous entrance**... Navy ministry description in Spurr, *A Glorious Way to Die*, pp. 82–83.

14–17: **Tomioka and Kuroshima debate.** Prange, *At Dawn We Slept*, p. 104; Prange Papers, Tomioka interview, no. 8, 7 August, 1947. Kuroshima after the war said the biggest mistake of his life was that while the Pearl Harbor attack was being planned, he did not prepare for the occupation of Hawaii. Kuroshima interview no. 1 with Gordon W. Prange, 28 November 1964.

14: **He privately had been referring to his guest Kuroshima as 'Yamamoto's foggy staff officer'.** Toland, *The Rising Sun*, p. 159.

16: **Kuroshima argued that the Imperial Navy needed to deliver a crushing blow**... Tomioka and Yoshida, 'Comparison of Japanese and American Naval Strength and Estimate of Future Developments', US Army, *Statements of Japanese Officials on WWII, Vol. 1–2 (1947–1950)*.

16: **Yet even the establishment in Japan was now caught up**... Tsunoda, *Final Confrontation*; selected translations from Morley (ed.) *Taiheiyo Senso e no Michi, Kaisen Gaikoshi*, p. 111.

16: **Now they strongly insisted on war**... Yoshida, *Kaigun Sanbo (A Naval Staff Officer)*, p. 292.

16: **Tomioka feared that once the war in the Pacific started**... Prange Papers, Tomioka interview no. 19, 24 November 1947.

17: **Admiral Yamamoto was a gambler**... Prange Papers, Tomioka interview no. 5.

17: **Tomioka had little time for Admiral Nagano**... Prange Papers, Tomioka interviews nos. 20, 8 December 1947 and 26, 17 February 1948.

18: **Nagano meekly sent word**... Prange Papers, Tomioka interview no. 5. On staff officers' influence, including Tomioka's: Watanabe (ed.), *Who Was Responsible? From Marco Polo Bridge to Pearl Harbor*, p. 110; Asada, *From Mahan to Pearl Harbor*, 177.

19: **He found Australia to be 'virtually naked, militarily'**... Ivan Chapman, *Iven G. Mackay*, p. 234.

20: **I find I am growing old**... Curtin letter to Elsie, 30 September 1941, JCPML 00402/37. Curtin became prime minister on 7 October 1941.

NOTES

21: **Japan is ready and waiting...** Curtin letter to Elsie, 3 March 1941, JCPML 00402:36.

21: **Australia wants peace in the Pacific...** 'Digest of Decisions and Announcements, No. 2', Australian Parliament, 18 October 1941, JCPML00110/7.

21: **Should Britain be defeated...** Lutzow quoted in *Time*, 10 November 1941, and in NAA A981, JAP 185, part 2. Evatt's response is drawn from the same article. Kawai's official title was 'Minister', but in every respect he was Japan's ambassador to Australia.

Chapter 3

23: **Ugaki couldn't hide his pleasure.** The vice admiral wrote in his diary: 'It was a great success that he could have made them agree with us in the arrangements for the AMO Operation. I heard that the commander in chief had already made up his mind to step down if this agreement had not been reached.' 22 October 1941, *Fading Victory*, p. 13.

24: **Ugaki had urged Yamamoto to replace him.** 'He [Admiral Nagumo] is not fully prepared to advance in the face of death and gain results two or three times as great as his cost by jumping into the jaws of death with his men as well as himself.' Ugaki diary, 22 October 1941, *Fading Victory*, p. 13; Dull, *A Battle History of the Imperial Japanese Navy 1941–1945*, p. 10.

24: **He resolved to work for the success of the plan...** 'Once it was definitely decided to attack Pearl Harbor I worked for the success of the plan as did every loyal Japanese naval officer.' Prange Papers, Tomioka interview no. 20, 8 December 1947.

24: **I desire you who are in the active service to prepare wholeheartedly, expecting the worst.** Ugaki diary, *Fading Victory*, p. 16, 29 October 1941, quoting Fukudome.

24: **Who would dare draw back...** Ugaki diary, *Fading Victory*, 29 October 1941, p. 16.

25: **They figured that England might drop out of the war...** Prange Papers, Tomioka interview no. 28, 16 April 1949.

25: **Fukudome was coming around...** Fukudome, US interrogation in Tokyo of 4 May, 1949, p. 6, in Prange Papers.

26: **It is better to strike and be defeated...** Prange Papers, Tomioka interview no. 28.

1942

26: **Ugaki's poem about death.** Ugaki diary, 31 October to 7 November 1941, *Fading Victory*, pp. 17–22; see also editors' note on suicide, p. 43.

28: **The British view of Sugiyama.** The British embassy in Tokyo had seen General Sugiyama as a great friend: 'To Japanese he stands as the embodiment of common sense, wide experience, native ability and successful achievement. To foreigners, especially Englishmen (of whom he is genuinely fond), he possesses a fund of humour and semi-reticence that is decidedly attractive.' Report by British Ambassador Sir Robert Craigie to Halifax, 6 November 1940, The [British] National Archives, FO 371/24744, F5517.

28: **General Sugiyama explained the proposed targets...** Minutes of the Imperial Conference, November 5 1941, in Ike (ed. and trans.), *Japan's Decision for War*, pp. 208–39.

28: **Hirohito's questions re. the war plan.** In Bix, *Hirohito and the Making of Modern Japan*, pp. 422–23.

28: **India and Australia are excluded from this map.** Minutes of the Imperial Conference, 5 November 1941, in Ike (ed. and trans.), *Japan's Decision for War*, pp. 208–39.

28: **Tojo's resolve to go to war.** Minutes of the Imperial Conference, 5 November 1941, in Ike (ed. and trans), *Japan's Decision for War*, pp. 208–39.

29: **Military dominance of government.** Liaison conference description in Togo, Shigenori, *The Cause of Japan*, Simon & Schuster, New York, 1956, pp. 115–117 (published in Japanese as *Jidai no Ichimen* in 1952).

29: **The connection between Australia and India and the British mother country will be broken...** Minutes of the Liaison Conference, 15 November 1941, in Ike (ed. and trans.), *Japan's Decision for War*, p. 248.

30: **Secret Togo intercept.** 19 November 1941, NAA A5954, 558/1.

30: **The Japanese Government has no intention of moving down on Australia by military force...** *Sydney Morning Herald*, 29 April 1941. On the other hand, the Japanese press portrayed Kawai as a correct supporter of Japanese expansion. The *Japan Times* on 6 January 1941 had reported: 'Kawai is a pioneer in the new Asia sphere.'

30: **Kawai, 'man of two faces'.** Interviews with author, October 2002, Masumi Kawai, son, and Toshiro Takeuchi, friend; Wurth, *Saving Australia*, pp. 9, 215.

32: **I do not believe in the inevitability of a conflict in the Pacific...** *Sydney Morning Herald*, 4 March 1941.

NOTES

32: **Curtin appeasement and meetings with Kawai.** Wurth, *Saving Australia*, p. 36, pp. 40–47, pp. 60–72. Curtin family memories of the war and the family relationship with Kawai: Ross, *John Curtin*, 2nd edn, p. 23; recollections of Curtin by Kim Beazley, former leader of the Federal Opposition, to author in Canberra, 10 September 2003.

33: **General Sydney Rowell's letter to his men.** Rowell, *Full Circle*, p. 99.

33: **Kawai meets Curtin, 'Is it to be war?'** Gavin Long diary, AWM 67, 1/3, pp. 26–27.

34: **Kondo background.** Fuller, *Shokan*, p. 264–65; Prange, *At Dawn We Slept*, pp. 283–84, p. 433.

Chapter 4

36: **Wording on monument to midget submariners.** See <http://www.wgordon.web.wesleyan.edu/kamikaze/monuments/specialsub/index>.

37: **Learn the peculiarities of these harbours and commit them to your memory.** Kazuo Sakamaki, translated by Toru Matsumoto, *I Attacked Pearl Harbor*, p. 34. (Spelling for Sydney was Sidney.)

38: **My mother talked a lot . . .** Kazutomo Ban interviewed by Robert Gilhooly in November 2006. Additional Ban background from an essay by a classmate of Ban's, Yutaka Toyoda, in the possession of the wife of Ban's brother Itsuo Ashibe, who died in 2005; additional detail in Lind, *The Midget Submarine Attack on Sydney*, pp. 20–21.

38: **He didn't tell our parents or other brothers . . .** Itsuo Ashibe interviewed by ABC-TV's Tokyo correspondent Shane McLeod, *7.30 Report*, 19 December 2006. Additional background on Ashibe from Lind, *The Midget Submarine Attack on Sydney*, p. 21.

39: **Letters from Mamoru Ashibe to sister Mikiyo and an unnamed recipient.** Early January, 10 January and 24 April 1941, courtesy of Itsuo Ashibe and Shane McLeod, ABC.

40: **Visit to the *Akagi*.** Ugaki diary, 17 November 1941, Matome Ugaki, *Fading Victory*, pp. 24-25.

40: **Description of Matsuo's spying mission.** Thomas Unger, *Honolulu Advertiser*, 7 Dec 2001; Prange, *At Dawn We Slept*, pp. 314–319; Carruthers, *Japanese Submarine Raiders 1942*, p. 45; Burlingame, *Advance Force Pearl Harbor*, pp. 49–52.

41: **Farewell letter from Mamoru Ashibe to his mother.** Written early

December 1941, courtesy of Itsuo Ashibe and Shane McLeod, ABC.
42: **As Japanese of the era would describe it, the young men were like cherry blossoms...** Ohnuki-Tierney, *Kamikaze, Cherry Blossoms and Nationalisms*, pp. 132, 135–36, 164–65.
42: **Gone with the spring...** Poem from the Ugaki diary, 11 May, 1945, *Fading Victory*, p. 610.
42: **None of us was a volunteer.** Sakamaki, *I Attacked Pearl Harbor*, p. 30.
42: **I was unable to look them straight in the face...** Sakamaki, *I Attacked Pearl Harbor*, pp. 34–35.
42: **The effect was like a sudden magic blow.** Sakamaki, *I Attacked Pearl Harbor*, pp. 15–17.
43: **Earlier, Yamamoto, in a discussion with Shimuzu, had expressed concern...** Prange, *At Dawn We Slept*, pp. 340–341; Agawa, *The Reluctant Admiral*, p. 266.
43: **Before departing, the submariners had their pictures taken...** Ugaki diary, 10 December 1941, *Fading Victory*, p. 51; Prange, *At Dawn We Slept*, p. 337.
43: **I, Kazuo Sakamaki, was being buried as of that moment.** Sakamaki, *I Attacked Pearl Harbor*, pp. 15–18.
43: **The surprise attack on X-Day will be an entirely unexpected storm.** Ugaki diary, 19 November 1941, *Fading Victory*, pp. 25–26.
44: **I stood on the deck and watched the coastal hills disappear...** Sakamaki, *I Attacked Pearl Harbor*, pp. 18-19.
44: **British expectations of Japan's immediate intentions.** Diary of Joe Alexander, 1 December 1941, MS2389, NLA and 2 December, 1941.
45: **Japanese newspaper report re Thailand.** *Japan Times*, 2 December 1941.
45: **Japan's assessment of the Allies' response to Japan's attack.** Joint recollections of Hattori, Sugita and Tomioka for US military historical staff in Tokyo, 6 April 1949, US Army, Statements of Japanese officials on World War II, Vol. 1 and 2, 1949–50.

Chapter 5
47: **The emperor told Yamamoto...** Agawa, *The Reluctant Admiral*, p. 246.
47: **Yamamoto's movements.** Agawa, *The Reluctant Admiral*, pp. 242–46. Also see 'Admiral Yamamoto's Sweetheart', *Weekly Asahi*, 18 April, 1954, quoted in Goldstein and Dillon (eds), *The Pearl Harbor Papers*, p. 126.

NOTES

47: **Yamamoto's mistress, Chiyoko Kawai.** *Weekly Asahi*, 18 April 1954 quoted in Golstein and Dillon (eds), *The Pearl Harbor Papers*, Brassey's, Dulles, Virginia, 2000, p. 126 and in Agawa, *The Reluctant Admiral*, pp. 58–65, 69 [Miss Kawai was not related to Tatsuo Kawai.]

48: **Behaviour of staff officers in planning meetings,** Hoyt, *Yamamoto*, p. 145; also numerous references in the Ugaki diary, *Fading Victory*.

48: **One by one I counted them.** Fuchida and Okumiya, *Midway,* pp. 27–28.

49: **The effectiveness of our attack was now certain...** Fuchida Okumiya, *Midway*, p. 28.

49: **Back in the operations room of the *Nagato*, Yamamoto woke from his siesta.** Toland, *Rising Sun*, p. 222.

49: **I torpedoed enemy battleship with great war result...** Ugaki diary, 8 December 1941, *Fading Victory*, pp. 43–45.

49–51: **Account of Sakamaki's disastrous mission.** Craddock, *First Shot*, pp. 79–81; Prange, *At Dawn We Slept*, pp. 493–501.

51: **I wanted to go back, but there was no strength left in me.** Sakamaki, *I Attacked Pearl Harbor*, pp. 44–46.

52: **Emperor Hirohito's Imperial Rescript.** *Japan Times*, 8 December 1941.

52: **Tojo's explanation of the war to the Japanese people.** *Japan Times*, 8 December 1941.

52–53: **Roosevelt's declaration of war.** 8 December 1941, SEN 77A-H1, Records of the United States Senate, Record Group 46, US National Archives.

53: **Men and women of Australia...** Curtin's radio address announcing war with Japan, Curtin broadcast, DDA, no. 10, 8 December 1941, pp. 19–22, JCPML 00110/15.

53: **Description of the *Suikosha* naval club.** *Suikosha* background in History of the Masonic Temple, Tokyo. <http://www.japan-freemasons.org>

54: **Hostility within the Naval General Staff.** Prange Papers, US interrogation of Shigeru Fukudome, 14 December, 1945.

54: **The Japanese naval officers who knew America realised the tremendous power she could eventually generate...** Prange Papers, Tomioka interview no. 19, 24 November 1947.

54: **The officers were wild with joy over the news...** Prange Papers, Fukudome interview no. 6, 19 May 1950.

54: **Nothing could hold back our Imperial Navy...** Diary of Commander Sadamu Sanagi, 8 December 1941, in Prange, *At Dawn We Slept*, p. 540.

55: **Nagano's congratulatory telegram.** Ugaki diary, 8 December 1941, *Fading Victory*, pp. 43–45. Perception of Navy pre-Pearl Harbor: Prange Papers, Tomioka interview no. 21, 15 December 1947, Naval General Staff view of Southern Operation: Prange Papers, Tomioka interview no. 28, 16 April 1949.

55: **We had lost the command of every ocean except the Atlantic.** Churchill, *The Second World War, Volume Three: The Grand Alliance*, p. 483.

56: **When Ugaki learned that none of the ten crewmen had returned...** Ugaki diary, 8–9 December 1941, *Fading Victory*, p. 44, pp. 50–51.

Chapter 6

57: **The loss of relatively antiquated battleships at Pearl Harbor.** United States Strategic Bombing Survey: Summary Report (Pacific War) 1 July 1946. Washington, D.C.: United States Government Printing Office, 1946. <http://www.marshall.csu.edu.au/Marshalls/html/WWII/USSBS_Summary.html>

57: **Mood in Tokyo.** Togo, *The Cause of Japan*, p. 227. Togo's character: Yoshida, *The Yoshida Memoirs*, p. 21.

58: **It can truthfully be said that Australia has weakened her own defences and security for the Empire cause...** C.E. Gauss, US mission report 25, 17 September 1940.

58: **Today the war rages in Australian waters...** Curtin at Royal Automobile Club, Melbourne, luncheon, 11 December 1941, DDA No. 11, 8 December–16 December 1941, JCPML 00110/16.

59: **The most probable form of attack on mainland Australia...** 'Defence of Australia and adjacent areas', presented to war cabinet, 11 December 1941, NAA A5954, 768/13; Advisory war council minutes of 12 December 1941, A5954, 813/1.

59: **On 11 December, Australia's war cabinet announced the immediate call-up of a further 100,000 army personnel.** War cabinet minutes, 12 December 1941, NAA A5954, 807/1.

60: **Curtin's secret press briefings.** See Lloyd and Hall, *Backroom Briefings, John Curtin's War*, pp. 1–9.

61: **God help us and above all God bless Britain.** Alexander diary, 10–11 December 1941, NLA MS2389.

62: **Curtin on Australians' subconscious view about Americans,** *Herald*,

Melbourne, 27 December 1941.

63: **The senior air wing commander of the carrier task force that attacked Pearl Harbor, Captain Mitsuo Fuchida, witnessed the self-importance of the men of Yamamoto and Ugaki's Combined Fleet...** Fuchida and Okumiya, *Midway*, p. 49.

64: **Yamamoto and the eastern operation.** Stephan, *Hawaii Under the Rising Sun*, pp. 1–2.

64: **Australia one of three targets.** Yamamoto's 'Eastern Operation' orders to Ugaki, 9 December 1941, in the Japanese war history series *Senshi Sosho, Daihon'ei Kaigunbu: Daitoa senso kaisen keii*, vol. 2, pp. 242–43, p. 300, p. 318; Stephan, *Hawaii Under the Rising Sun*, pp. 92–95; Ugaki, *Fading Victory*, 9–13 December 1941, pp. 45–54. In some wartime notes, Japanese officers at times appeared to refer to India when they meant British Ceylon (now Sri Lanka).

65: **Tomioka's intentions regarding Rabaul.** Tomioka interview with US Intelligence officers, Tokyo, 10 September 1947, US Army, *Statements of Japanese Officials on WWII*, vols 3 and 4, no. 61232.

66: **The way to operations in the southern areas has been paved opportunely.** Ugaki diary, *Fading Victory*, 14 December 1941, p. 54.

66: **Never shall an enemy set foot upon the soil of this country...** Curtin in Parliament, 16 December 1941, DDA No. 11, 8–16 December 1941.

66: **Evacuation planning.** *Herald*, Melbourne, 17 December 1942.

66–67: **Professor Elkin's assessment of Australian morale.** Letter from Elkin to Curtin, 17 December 1941, NAA A1608, AK29/1/2.

67: **Comments on national mood.** Alexander diary, 28–29 December 1941, NLA MS 2389.

67–68: **Mackay's assessment speaking of Japanese troops on Australian soil.** Mackay to Forde, 17 December 1941, Chapman, *Iven G. Mackay, Citizen and Soldier*, p. 250; David Day, *John Curtin*, p. 436; report of Mackay to Minister for Army, 17 December 1941, Lloyd Ross Papers, NLA MS 3939, Box 31.

Chapter 7

69: **Tomioka's visit to the *Nagato* and discussions with Ugaki.** Ugaki diary, 5 February 1942, *Fading Victory*, p. 85; also 16 December 1941, p. 55.

70: **Tanaka smelt a rat, correctly suspecting that Yamamoto wanted to** capture Hawaii. *'Gyomu Nisshi'*, Tanaka, 12 December 1941 in Boei-cho, *Daihon'ei, Kaigun*, 2:248 and 2:312; also quoted in Stephan, *Hawaii Under the Rising Sun*, pp. 97–99.

70: **What a mean spirit it [the army] has!** Ugaki diary, 16 December 1941, *Fading Victory*, p. 55.

71: **Prince Higashikuni's diary.** Higashikuni, *Ichi-kozoku no Senso Nikki* (War Diary by an Imperial Family Member), p. 106.

72: **On 27 December, Ugaki decided to assume responsibility for all planning of the eastern operation, including Hawaii** ... *Daihon'ei Kaigunbu: daitoa senso kaisen keii*, vol. 2, p. 318.

72: **Until now Yamamoto's Combined Fleet had demonstrated a more radical approach to war operations than the rest of Japan's military leadership.** Stephan, *Hawaii Under the Rising Sun,* pp. 94 and 96.

72: **Crucially, Baron Tomioka had been won over to the Combined Fleet's point of view.** *Senshi Sosho* Boei-cho, *Daihon'ei Kaigunbu: Daitoa senso kaisen keii*, vol. 2, p. 248, pp. 312–314; *Senshi Sosho* Boei-cho, *Chubu Taiheiyo*, 1: 515; Stephan, *Hawaii Under the Rising Sun*, pp. 96–100.

72: **At first he opposed the Hawaii operation as beyond Japan's capacity.** Eastern operation discussions, *Senshi Sosho*, Boei-cho, *Middowei kaisen*, p. 29; *Senshi Soshu* Boei-cho, *Daihon'ei, kaigunbu*, 2:335; Takagi, *Taiheiyo senso to rikukaigun no koso*, p. 54; Tanemura, *Daihon'ei kimitsu nisshi*, p. 117; Stephan, *Hawaii Under the Rising Sun*, pp. 100–101.

73: **Of the major plans under consideration, an attack on Australia was the one most enthusiastically advocated by the operations division of Naval General Staff...** Agawa, *The Reluctant Admiral*, p. 294.

73: **Matsuoka and Oceania.** AAP report in *SMH*, 25 February, 1941.

73: **At the same time, they will endeavour to secure communications with Australia...** Pre-war Japanese Estimate of Allied Strategy, joint interview with Takushiro Hattori, Ichiji Sugita and Sadatoshi Tomioka, 5 April 1949, Prange Papers.

73: **Tomioka told of his own radical answer to counter such action:** Tomioka interview with US Intelligence officers, Tokyo, 10 September 1947, vols 3 and 4, no. 61232.

74: **The idea of simply cutting Australia off had existed from the beginning of the war and in fact Combined Fleet Operations Order No. 1 had alluded to it.** Prange Papers, Kuroshima interview no. 1, 28 November 1964, pp. 3–4.

NOTES

74: **John Curtin's Boxing Day address.** DDA no. 13, 26 December 1941, pp. 7–9 in David Black, *In His Own Words*, pp. 192–93.

75: **But changing the 'lackadaisical Australian mind', as Curtin put it, wasn't easy.** Curtin, *Herald*, Melbourne, 27 December 1941.

75: **He felt even worse, later in a prison camp in the US, when he learned that his midget was touring America on the back of a large truck.** Craddock, *First Shot*, p. 74, pp. 87–88.

75: **US warning about Japan's new midget submarines used at Pearl Harbor.** Cablegram from Australian Legation, Washington, received 17 December 1941, NAA A5954, 531/4.

75: **Yet production of the A-class midget submarines, and experiments with three-man submarines in the Kure area of the Inland Sea, proceeded . . .** Agawa, *The Reluctant Admiral*, p. 266.

76: **Ugaki meets Matsuo and Yamanda.** Ugaki diary, 3 January 1942, *Fading Victory*, p. 67.

76: **Yamanda and Matsuo argued that significant advances had already been made . . .** *Senshi Sosho*, *Sensuikan* (submarine) volume NLA OJ 3393.7207, V98.

76: **As it turned out, Yamamoto was just as blinded by the bravery, passion and effort of the young submariner proponents . . .** Yamamoto to Admiral Sankichi Takahashi, 19 December 1941, Goldstein and Dillon (eds), *The Pearl Harbor Papers*, pp. 120–121.

76: **Susumu Ito.** Interview with author at Iwakuni, 11 August 2007, interpreter Kyal Hill.

77: *I-21* **submarine details.** From Ito, Hackett and Kingsepp, <http://www.combinedfleet.com/sensuikan.htm>

Chapter 8

79: **Official correspondence about Singapore.** Curtin to Churchill, 26 December 1941 in Churchill, *The Second World War, Volume Four: The Hinge of Fate*, p. 21. Bowden in letter to Department of External Affairs, 8 December 1941, Evatt Collection, Flinders University.

80: **Without any inhibition of any kind, I make it quite clear that Australia looks to America . . .** *Herald*, Melbourne, 27 December 1941.

80: **Joe Alexander's response to Curtin's article.** Alexander diary, 28–29 December, 1941, NLA MS 2389.

80: **Churchill was furious**... Churchill to Curtin, 29 December 1941, JCPML 00869.
81: **The British had at first opposed General Sir Thomas Blamey's request to relieve Australian troops at Tobruk.** Odgers, *100 Years of Australians at War*, p. 123.
81: **Former Australian Labor Party leader and prime minister Billy Hughes further antagonised the relationship**... Peter Cochrane, *Australians at War*, p. 135.
82: **Churchill later publicly regretted his 'traces of impatience' with Curtin**... Churchill, *The Second World War, Volume Four: The Hinge of Fate*, pp. 20–21.
82: **We begin the new year with great anxiety for the future of Australia.** Alexander diary, 1 January 1942, NLA MS2389.
82: **On 5 January 1942, Curtin wrote to his wife of his frustrations**... Curtin to Elsie, 5 January 1942, in Ross, *John Curtin*, p. 254.
83: **Churchill correspondence with Curtin from Washington,** 9 January 1942, NAA A5954, 555/4. 'Jumpy' comment: Day, *John Curtin*, p. 442. Details of White House stay: Roy Jenkins, *Churchill*, pp. 673–74.
83: **Pressure on Australia.** Liaison conference 10 January 1942, Hattori, Takushiro, *Dai Toa Senso Zenshi*, (*The Complete History of the Great East Asia War*) p. 99, (US military translation held by the University of Maryland).
84: **At Hashirajima, the aggressive Admiral Ugaki was also experiencing frustration.** He also wrote: 'In any case, we must establish our plan by the end of February. I have decided to have staff officers study it.' Ugaki diary, 29 December 1941 and 1 January 1942, *Fading Victory*, pp. 63–65, p. 68.
85: **Ugaki debated the options in his diary.** Ugaki, *Fading Victory*, 5 January 1942, p. 69.
85: **Captain Yoshitake Miwa had become a Combined Fleet air staff officer**... Miwa had been a junior assistant in the Japanese embassy in Washington while Yamamoto was a naval attaché in the American capital. Seven years before the war, while in London, Yamamoto had written to Miwa: 'I feel keenly that the time has come for this mighty empire rising in the east to devote itself, with all due circumspection, to advancing its own fortunes... I sense the day may not be so distant when we shall have Britain and the United States kowtowing to us.' Yamamoto to Miwa, 10 November 1934, Agawa, *The Reluctant Admiral*, pp. 38–39.

85: **Miwa background and quotes.** *Senshi Sosho,* Boei-cho, Boei Kenshujo (ed), *Nanto homen kaigun sakusen,* vol. 1, p. 354; Agawa, *The Reluctant Admiral,* pp. 37–38 and Prados, *Combined Fleet Decoded,* p. 27.

85: **On 6 January 1942, Miwa advocated a huge expansion of Japanese ambitions...** Ugaki diary, 5 January 1942, *Fading Victory,* pp. 68–69; Frei, *Japan's Southward Advance and Australia,* p. 162. Tomioka background: Agawa, *The Reluctant Admiral,* pp. 294–96. Debate between army and navy: Toland, *The Rising Sun,* pp. 302–304.

85: **Tomioka's men in Naval General Staff were also actively working on their own plan...** Prados, *Combined Fleet Decoded,* p. 279. Also see Frei, *Japan's Southward Advance and Australia,* p. 166.

86: **Having achieved the completion of stage one of the campaign, operations to blockade the United States and Australia...** Records of Shinichi Tanaka quoted in *Senshi Sosho: Minami Taiheiyo Rikugun Sakusen,* (War history series: South Pacific area army operations (1), Port Moresby-Guadalcanal first campaigns), pp. 119–66.

87: **Australia was being taken very seriously...** Hiromi Tanaka, in the *Journal of the Australian War Memorial,* 'The Japanese Navy's operations against Australia in the Second World War', issue 30, April 1997.

87: **Admiral Nobutake Kondo, who led the southern invasion operations, ran into army obstructions during the initial invasion of Malaya.** Kondo, 'Some Opinions Concerning the War', 28 February 1947, in Goldstein and Dillon (eds), *The Pacific War Papers,* p. 310.

88: **The service ministers claimed authority...** Ienaga, *The Pacific War, 1931-1945,* p. 35. Planning structure: Fuchida and Okumiya, *Midway,* p. 49.

88: **An observer in the navy ministry commented...** Chihaya, 'An Intimate Look at the Japanese Navy', in Goldstein and Dillon (eds), *The Pearl Harbor Papers,* p. 326.

88: **Professor Tanaka agrees...** 'In a way that's why Japan couldn't win the war. There was no agreement... what always amazed me was how they could conduct such a big war without having a proper decision-making process. Always the army and the navy were at odds and there was no-one who could bring them together.' Hiromi Tanaka interview with author, 16 August 2007.

88–89: **Hashida's spying mission.** Hashida spying detailed in letter from Walsh, British consul general Batavia, to Australian foreign minister

Stewart, NAA A2880/1, 19 March 1941; undated security report in NAA A8911/1.2, c 1946; Hashida file, NAA A816, 25/301/176.

89: **Naval spy Yanase.** Wurth, *Saving Australia*, p. 76, Japanese residence Craig-y-Mor, p. 75, NAA C443, part 1, J2.

90: **A direct move towards Australia from the Japanese bases grew more probable, Curtin was told.** Defence chiefs' appreciation of invasion of Australia to Curtin, 16 January 1942, NAA A5954, 555/4 and Chiefs of Staff paper 4, 29 January 1942, NAA A2671, 31/1942.

90: **The Americans were also assessing Australia's situation.** Gerow to board of economic warfare, 17 January 1942, RG 165, WPD 4630, National Archives and Record Administration, Washington; Jacobsen, 'US Grand Strategy and the Defence of Australia', in *The Battle of Coral Sea 1942*, conference proceedings, pp. 21–22.

91: **Tojo's speech to the Diet.** *Japan Times*, 21 January 1942.

91: **Mitsuo Fuchida's observations of the Rabaul raid.** Fuchida and Okumiya, *Midway*, p. 37.

92: **Imperial General Headquarters announcement on Rabaul and Kavieng.** *Asashi Shinbun* (newspaper), 25 January 1942, in *Senshi Sosho*, Boei-cho Boei Kenshujo Senshishitsu (ed), *South Pacific army operations*, Vol. 1.

92: **Tomioka on Rabaul.** Statement 10 September 1947, no. 61232, US Army, statements of Japanese officials on World War II, vols. 1 and 2.

92: **On 26 January King instructed the commander-in-chief of the US Pacific Fleet, Admiral Chester W. Nimitz, to detach a cruiser and two destroyers to the ANZAC command...** Lundstrom, *The First South Pacific Campaign*, p. 29.

92: **Curtin on Rabaul.** *Age*, 22 Jan 1942.

Chapter 9

93: **Kondo's movements.** Kondo introduction in Fuchida and Okumiya, *Midway*, p. ix.

94: **He saw Japan as having two planning options: attacks on India or Australia.** Kondo, 'Some Opinions Concerning the War', a study prepared for Gordon W. Prange, 28 February 1947, in Goldstein and Dillon (eds), *The Pacific War Papers*, p. 311.

95: **Marco Polo Bridge incident.** A definitive battle between China's National Revolutionary Army and the Japanese army, outside Beijing.

NOTES

It opened the second phase of the Sino–Japanese War.

95: **Inoue's support for an invasion of Australia.** Lundstrom, *The First South Pacific Campaign*, p. 40. Inoue's character and his aggressiveness in the South Pacific: Frank, *Guadalcanal*, pp. 21–23.

95: **CANBERRA IS INDIGNANT, a headline in the *Nichi Nichi* daily reported** ... *Nichi Nichi*, 27–28 January 1942.

96: **Case of the SS *Holbrook*.** Minutes of the advisory war council 19 January 1942, NAA A5954, 813/2, item 669, p. 418.

96: **With some sort of attack on Darwin appearing imminent** ... Lockwood, Douglas, *Australia's Pearl Harbour*, p. 68.

96: **Mackay's fears about troop numbers.** Chapman, *Iven G. Mackay*, p. 252.

97: **Exchange between Generals Sturdee and Wavell.** War cabinet minutes 29 January 1942, NAA A5954, 807/2.

97: **One, invade Ceylon at the end of May/June** ... *Senshi Sosho Boei-cho Boei Kenshujo, Senshishitsu, Minami Taiheiyo Rikugun sakusen* (War History Series: South Pacific Area Army Operations (1), Port Moresby-Guadalcanal first campaigns), vol. 1, p. 355.

98: **Hirohito's biographer, Herbert P. Bix, described this action as 'the first step of a plan to isolate and ultimately attack Australia'.** Bix cited four separate sources for this claim. Bix, *Hirohito and the Making of Modern Japan*, pp. 445–46.

98: **Churchill to parliament.** 27 January 1942, *Parliamentary Debates*, House of Commons Official Report, National Archives UK.

98–100: **British and American intelligence assessments re an invasion of Darwin.** Intelligence reports, National Archives UK, Cabinet minutes 27 January and 5 February 1942, 'Possible Japanese action against Australia and New Zealand', CAB 79/17/30 and CAB 79/18/7; US version of the same Joint Intelligence Committee in London assessment, CCS 18, 31 January 1942, President's secretary's file, Box 1, US-UK Chiefs of Staff, Combined Staff Planners, 'Possible Action against Australia and New Zealand', CPS 10, 13 February 1942, President's secretary's file, Box 1, US-UK Chiefs of Staff file, FDR Library, Hyde Park, NY.

100: **Even the Germans knew** ... Raeder in Churchill, *The Second World War, Volume 4, The Hinge of Fate*, p. 124.

100: **On this lay-out of Japanese forces it seems very unlikely that an immediate full-scale invasion of Australia could take place.** Prime minister to chiefs of staff committee, 13 March 1942, in Churchill, *The Second World War, Volume Four: The Hinge of Fate*, p. 154.

101: **Ugaki's observations on the midget submarine practice.** Ugaki diary, 31 January 1942, *Fading Victory*, p. 81.

102: **I refrained from giving my decisions, in order to save the face of the staff officers**... Ugaki diary, 29 January 1941 to 3 February 1942, *Fading Victory*, pp. 80–83.

102: **During the 1930s a system**... Dull, *The Imperial Japanese Navy 1941–1945*, p. 5. Tomioka and Ishikawa on 'pressure from below': see Asada, *From Mahan to Pearl Harbor*, pp. 174–77.

103: **Tojo's diminishing enthusiasm for Australian invasion.** Tojo and Hattori in Boei-cho in *Senshi Sosho*: Boei Kenshujo Senshishitsu (ed), *Minami Taiheiyo Rikugun sakusen* (War history series: South Pacific area army operations (1), Port Moresby–Guadalcanal first campaigns), Chapter 3, translated by Dr Steven Bullard.

Chapter 10

104–105: **Rifle shortage.** Curtin to Forde on rifles, 3 Febuary 1942, NAA A367, M1416, 46.

105: **At Victoria Barracks in Sydney, Brigadier Joseph Lee**... Lee letter 3 Feb 1942 AWM collection, RCO2304.

105: **Intelligence warning of Japanese carrier action in Java and the Torres Strait.** Bleakley, Jack, *The Eavesdroppers, the best kept secret of World War 2*, pp. 24–25.

106: **Port Moresby bombing and looting.** Stuart, *Port Moresby, Yesterday and Today*, pp. 134–35.

106–107: **Tol and Waitavalo plantation massacres.** Summary report of Sir William Webb, NAA A1006, H45/580/2/8/1.

107: **He put forward an idea that was to have long-term political ramifications, and shock the Australian population**... Mackay in a document 'Courses open to the enemy' in Chapman, *Iven G. Mackay*, p. 252.

107: **Memo from Mackay to Forde.** Chapman, *Iven G. Mackay*, pp. 253–57.

107: **Mackay's assessment would be the start of acrimonious political debate to be known as 'The Brisbane Line'**... The issue became a major political scandal in Australia in 1943 with the establishment of a royal commission. Mackay later claimed that the term was effectively a 'beat up' by politicians and others. The army was directed not to use the term 'Brisbane Line' and Mackay's ideas did not become official policy. Chapman, *Iven G. Mackay*, p. 264.

108: **The high command in Tokyo is against an invasion of Port Darwin.** Ugaki diary, 5 February 1942, *Fading Victory*, p. 85.

108: **He said that they had no concrete plan about the next operation...** Ugaki diary, 6 February 1942, *Fading Victory*, p. 86.

109: **Ishikawa's proposal to invade Australia.** Frei, *Japan's Southward Advance and Australia*, p. 166. (The Greater East Asia Co prosperity sphere was intended to be a self-sufficient bloc of Asian nations led, if not controlled, by Japan.)

109: **After the war Tanaka would tell US interrogators...** Willoughby (ed.), *Reports of General MacArthur*, Vol. II, Part I, p. 132n.

109: **Yamamoto signal to Nagumo.** Lockwood, *Australia's Pearl Harbor*, pp. 6–7.

110: **Fadden's report on lack of rifles.** Advisory war council minutes, 11 February 1942, NAA A5954, 813/2.

110: **Menzies and Evatt clash.** CPD, Australia, 16 December 1941, pp. 1069–90.

110: **Newspaper reports based on reports from listening posts.** *Japan Times*, 12 and 14 February 1942.

111: **Tomioka's view only token force was needed to take Australia.** In Frei, *Japan's Southward Advance and Australia*, p. 166.

111–112: **Fuchida's explanation of the Darwin strikes.** Fuchida and Okumiya, *Midway*, pp. 38–39.

112: **It was Tomioka who sparked the Australia-first school of strategy.** The strategy was based on fear of an American counteroffensive from Australia, based on air attacks. Fuchida and Okumiya, *Midway*, pp. 54–55.

113: **Evacuation debate, Australian War Cabinet.** War cabinet and advisory war council minutes, 4 February 1942, NAA A5954, 807/2; Evacuation, war cabinet minute no. 1850.

113: **Air raid shelter expenditure.** War cabinet minutes 26 January 1942, NAA A5954, 807/2.

114: **There was fear in Canberra of a Japanese invasion.** Hasluck, *Diplomatic Witness*, p. 44.

114: **Fall of Singapore.** Australians did not learn the terrible details until later; 1789 Australian soldiers were among many thousands of dead. Casualty

1942

figures in Odger, *100 Years of Australians at War*, pp. 135–39. Bowden's execution in Wurth, *Saving Australia*, pp. 175–76.

Chapter 11

116: **Ugaki's war poem.** Ugaki diary, 5 February 1942, *Fading Victory*, p. 86.

117: **Navy food and drink.** Spurr, *A Glorious Way to Die*, p. 79. Conditions elsewhere in Japan: *The United States Strategic Bombing Survey: Summary Report (Pacific War) 1946*, <http://www.anesi.com/ussbs01.htm#thamotjc.>

118: **Onishi visit.** Ugaki, *Fading Victory*, pp. 99–100. Onishi background and cherry blossoms, Ohnuki–Tierney, *Kamikaze, Cherry Blossoms, and Nationalisms*, pp. 163–64. (Onishi is sometimes recorded as 'Ohnishi'.)

120: **Sturdee on bringing the troops home,** his appreciation of 15 February 1942 in Wigmore, *Australia in the War of 1939–1945, Series One, The Japanese Thrust*, appendix 5.

121: **US Army headquarters report that it was evident that Japanese seizure of the entire region could not be long delayed.** Report of Organization and Activities, United States Army Forces in Australia, AG GHQ 314.7, USAFIA and Operation Journal of 19th Bombing Grp., 8 Dec 41–2 Feb 42, G–2 Historical Section, GHQ, FEC.

121: **Roosevelt changes US policy towards defence of Australia.** In Lundstrom, *The First South Pacific Campaign*, pp. 51–52.

122: **The fall of Singapore opens the Battle for Australia.** Curtin statement, DDA, no 19, 16 February 1942; also in the *Times*, London, dateline Melbourne 16 February 1942.

122: **Tojo's speech to the Diet.** *Japan Times*, 16 February 1942.

122: **We naval planners thought exclusively about self-existence and self-defence.** Asada, *From Mahan to Pearl Harbor*, p. 287.

123: **Comments by Kiwao Okumura.** *Japan Times*, 16 February 1942.

123: **The astonishment and confusion of the Australian authorities are beyond imagination.** Board of Information, Ministry of Foreign Affairs, 18 and 23 February 1942, Diplomatic Records Office, Tokyo.

123–125: **Yamashita's invasion planning.** Potter, *A soldier must hang*, pp. 11–14, and Bergamini, *Japan's Imperial Conspiracy*, p. 873.

125: **Hattori's confirmation of Yamashita's support for invasion.** Yamashita and Yamamoto plan listed in Bergamini, *Japan's Imperial Conspiracy*, pp. 898–90, quoting Hattori, *Dai Toa Senso Zenshi* (*The Complete History of the Great East Asia War*), 1:357–58.

126: **Invasion of Australia with five army divisions.** Toland, *The Rising Sun*, pp. 302–303. Toland interviewed both Tomioka and Hattori, among others, for this chapter of his book. Also see Frei, *Japan's Southward Advance and Australia*, pp. 167–169.

127: **Yamamoto's mind passed through this range of options.** *Senshi Sosho: Boei-cho Boei Kenshujo Senshishitsu* (ed), *Minami Taiheiyô Rikugun sakusen*, Chapter 3, Planning and cancellation of the US–Australia blockade, Imperial HQ conception of stage two operation.

127: **Japan's official war history also records that the Army chief General Sugiyama warned his Navy counterpart, Admiral Nagano, to beware that an invasion of Australia could slide out of control . . .** *Senshi Sosho*, Army operations in the South Pacific area: Papua campaigns 1942–1943, (as in previous note), also see Ugaki diary, *Fading Victory*, p. 68; Frei, *Japan's Southward Advance and Australia*, pp. 168–169 and p. 219, Boei-cho, Boei Kenshujo, Senshishita, *Daihon'ei kaigunbu, rengokaitai*, Vol. 2, p. 309, and Boei-cho, Boei Kenshujo, Senshishita, *Nanto homen kaigun sakusen*, Vol. 1, p. 355.

128: **Baron Tomioka repeatedly pushed the navy's invasion plan.** Frei, *Japan's Southward Advance and Australia*, p. 162; Tomioka background also in Agawa, *The Reluctant Admiral*, pp. 294–296; Tomioka and Pearl Harbor in Prange, *At Dawn We Slept*, pp. 104–105, p. 297, p. 437 and Parrish and Marshall, *The Simon and Schuster Encyclopedia of World War II*.

128: **Hattori rejects Tomioka's arguments.** Statement concerning operational perimeter on the Pacific Front by Takushiro Hattori, to the US Historical section, 5 October 1947, annexed paper, 16 August 1949, doc. 55412, Records of US Army, Far East Command, statements of Japanese officials on WW2, vols. 1–4.

128: **Tomioka counters.** Tomioka, *Kaisen to shusen: Hito to kiko to keikaku* (The opening and closing of the war: the people, the mechanism, and the planning), pp. 117–18.

129: **Hattori teacup incident.** Statement concerning operational perimeter on the Pacific Front by Takushiro Hattori, to the US Historical section, 5 October 1947, annexed paper, 16 August 1949, doc. 55412, Records of US Army, Far East Command, statements of Japanese officials on WW2, vols. 1–4.

129: **Australian propaganda. The spearhead of the Japanese hordes reaches south**... AWM ARTV09225; *Sydney Morning Herald* 16 February 1942.

129: **Home Security booklet.** Cochrane, *Australians at War*, p. 137.

130: **Reminiscences of Maroubra resident re military installations there.** Helena Iris (Joy) Wurth, 26 December 2006.

131: **The destination to which they should now proceed is obviously Australia which is in imminent danger of attack which is an essential allied base**... Cable, Curtin to Churchill, 19 February 1942, NAA A816, 52/302/142.

131: **Deliberations of Australian war cabinet and advisory war council.** War cabinet meeting 18 February 1942, item 1897 Defence of Australia, A5954, 807/2; Advisory war council meetings 18–19 Febuary 1942, A5954, 813/2; news of raid to AWC, *Sydney Morning Herald* 20 February 1942; Oral history with Gladys Joyce, 3 July 1997, JCPML 00210.

132: **Shedden comment.** Hasluck, *Diplomatic Witness*, p. 44.

132: **Burying the silver.** Guy Owen-Jones talking about his Uncle Charlie, to the author, Brisbane, 3 July 2008.

Chapter 12

133–134: **Description of Darwin raid and casualties.** Lockwood, *Australia's Pearl Harbour*, pp. 57–59.

134: **Fuchida's comments on Darwin's air defences.** Fuchida and Okumiya, *Midway*, p. 40.

134: **Newspaper reports of the raid.** *Herald*, Melbourne, 19 February 1942; *Sydney Morning Herald*, 20 February 1942.

135: **Signs of panic and looting in Darwin.** Report of Justice Lowe, NAA A431, 1949/687.

135: **We must face with fortitude**... Curtin, DDA, no. 19, 19 February 1942, p. 9 in Black, *In His Own Words*, p. 199.

135: **Advertisements soon appeared in newspapers telling Australians how to behave if they heard air raid sirens wailing.** Bolt (ed.), *Our Home Front*, p. 123.

135–136: **Japanese newspaper reports of the raids.** *Asahi*, 21 February 1942; *Yomiuri*, 21 February 1942; *Chugai Shogyo*, 21 February 1942; *Mikako*, 22 February 1942.

136: **Raid a prelude to invasion of Timor and Java.** Odgers, *100 Years of Australians at War*, p. 141, Fuchida, *Midway*, pp. 39–40.

137: **Yamaguchi plan for invading Australia and elsewhere.** Boei-cho, *Daihon'ei, Kaigunbu*, 2:304-307; Stephan, John S, *Hawaii Under the Rising Sun, Japan's Plans for Conquest After Pearl Harbor*, University of Hawaii Press, Honolulu, 1984, pp. 101–105; Yamaguchi background, Fuchida and Okumiya, *Midway*, p. 93 and Prange, *At Dawn We Slept*, p. 111; table manoeuvres, Ugaki, *Fading Victory*, 20–24 February 1942, pp. 92–94.

137: **While I realise the Japs are moving rapidly...** Roosevelt to Curtin, 20 February 1942, Churchill, *The Second World War, Volume Four: The Hinge of Fate*, pp. 139–140.

137: **Churchill to Curtin re Burma.** 20 February 1942, Churchill, *The Second World War, Volume Four: The Hinge of Fate*, p. 138.

138: **Cablegram from Churchill to Curtin defending Burma transfer.** 22 February 1942, NAA A816, 52/302/142.

138: **Cablegram from Curtin to Churchill.** 23 February 1942, NAA A3196, 1942/11.

138: **Churchill to Governor of Burma.** 25 February 1942, *The Second World War, Volume Four: The Hinge of Fate*, p. 145.

139: **Roosevelt to Churchill with copy of cable to Curtin.** 23 February 1942, Churchill, *The Second World War, Volume Four: The Hinge of Fate*, p. 144.

139: **Eisenhower assessment.** Eisenhower memo to Marshall, 'Strategic conceptions and their applications to Southwest Pacific', 28 February 1942, courtesy research library of the George C. Marshall Foundation, Lexington, Virginia.

140: **We've got to go to Europe and fight.** Eisenhower in Frank, *Guadalcanal*, p. 9; Lundstrom, *First South Pacific Campaign*, pp. 50–51; Morton, *United States Army in World War II, The War in the Pacific, Strategy and Command*, p. 219.

140: **MacMahon Ball commentary.** Greenwood and Harper, *Australia in World Affairs 1956–1960* pp. 243–55, 257–62.

141: **The Lowe report on Darwin.** Report of Justice Lowe, NAA A431, 1949/687 and post–war release of the report, *Herald*, Melbourne, 5 October 1945. This scathing report on Darwin would not be made public until the month after the Japanese surrender in 1945.

141: **Attacks by land-based bombers and fighters.** Shindo, Hiroyuki, *Japanese operations against the Australian mainland in the Second World War:*

A survey of Japanese historical sources, Japan–Australia Research Project, Australian War Memorial.

141: **Darwin raided 64 times.** Darwin raids in Australian War Memorial's website: <http://www.awm.gov.au/encyclopedia/air_raids>; Lockwood, *Australia's Pearl Harbour*, p. 221.

141: **Fate of the HMAS** *Perth*. HMAS *Perth*, Sea Power Centre Australia, Australian HMA ship histories, <http://www.navy.gov.au/spc/history/ships/perth1.html>.

141: **Japanese advances.** Odgers, *100 Years of Australians at War*, p. 143.

141: **That great, vast Indonesian archipelago stretching from west of Malaya down so close to northern Australia…** Among the appalled Australians watching the catastrophe unfold was Sir John Latham, who was ill in Singapore. Latham, on leave as chief justice of the High Court of Australia, had been Australia's envoy in Japan until just before the outbreak of war when he went to Singapore for treatment. He returned to Australia before Singapore fell. As far back as August 1941, Latham had warned the Australian government that Australia faced invasion, as distinct from sporadic raids, if the East Indies islands were occupied: 'In the case of Australia exhaustion of our oil supplies would lead to our defeat by an enemy which controlled the Dutch East Indies and was free to deal with Australia at leisure, which is a case (really the case) which we have to consider.' Latham 'Invasion of Australia' document, 15 August 1941, Latham Papers, NLA MS 1009/65/648–50.

142: **Japanese raids at Broome.** Interview W.F.A. (Gus) Winckel, 'Dimensions in Time', ABC TV, filmmaker David Batty, broadcast 23 April 2002; Winckel in the website of the Netherlands Ex-Servicemen and Women's Association, <http://www.neswa.org.au>.

143: **Impact of WA raids on Curtin.** Curtin 3 March 1942 in DDA no. 20, 21 February to 6 March 1942, JCPML 00110/25.

144: **Admiral King's views on Australia's vulnerability.** King memorandum to Roosevelt, 5 March 1942, PSF, Box 3, King file, Franklin D. Roosevelt Library, Hyde Park, New York; Jacobsen, 'US Grand Strategy and the Defence of Australia', in *The Battle of the Coral Sea 1942*, conference proceedings.

144: **We cannot in honor let Australia and New Zealand down.** Morison quoting King to Roosevelt, *History of the United States Naval Operations, Coral Sea, Midway* etc, Vol. 4, p. 246.

NOTES

145: **Points in the Australia area.** Japanese Basic War Plan, 1941, *Navy Operation Plans and Orders, 1941–1944*, recovered from CA NACHI, ATIS, G-2, GHQ, SWPA, translation no. 39, part VIII, in Willoughby, *Reports of General MacArthur*, Vol. I; Morison, *History United States Naval Operations, Coral Sea* etc, Vol. 4, p. 246–247.

145: **American feature article about Australia.** *Washington Post*, 22 February 1942.

145: **King thought the invasion of Australia had begun.** Clay, *Silent Victory*, pp. 191–92.

Chapter 13

146: **As early as 1936 Curtin had told parliament...** Stargardt, *Australia's Asian Policies*, p. 159.

146: **Curtin's frustration over lack of aircraft.** Lloyd Ross, 'The story of John Curtin', *Sun Herald*, June–August 1958, JCPML 00415.

147: **Curtin's stress levels.** Letter from Curtin to Boote, 25 February 1942, in Black, *Friendship is a Sheltering Tree*, p. 217; Don Rodgers in his papers, NLA MS1536, 1936–1978, box 9.

147: **Curtin's nervous energy.** Don Rodgers in his papers, NLA MS1536, 1936–1978, box 9.

147: **Curtin's loneliness.** Gladys Joyce, oral history, 3 July 1997, JCPML 00210; Lloyd Ross, 'The story of John Curtin', *Sun Herald*, 27 July 1958.

148: **Lord Gowrie on Curtin.** Gowrie letter from Windsor Castle, date unknown, to Lloyd Ross, Ministry of Port War Reconstruction, Sydney, Gowrie Papers, National Library of Australia, MS2852/1/8, 42/50, 5/14 and other references.

149: **War cabinet room details.** Author's visit of 2005; Hannan, *Victoria Barracks Melbourne*. The room was established in September 1939, when Robert Menzies was prime minister.

149: **Defence chiefs' appreciation, 27 February 1942.** Ordered by war cabinet 18 February, NAA A5954/563/1.

150: **Defence of Fremantle.** Appreciation of chiefs of staff, 27 February 1942, NAA A5954, 563/1 and A2671, 96/1942; Horner, *Crisis of Command*, pp. 44–45.

151: **Future policy and strategy for conduct of the war in the Pacific paper.** Minutes of the advisory war council meeting and the war cabinet meeting

1942

28 February 1942, NAA A5954, 813/2 and A5954, 808/1.

151: **Australia's troop strength in early 1942.** Long, *The Six Years War*, p. 182.

151–152: **Sir Guy Royle.** Hadley, Huebert and Crickard, *A Nation's Navy*, p. 329.

153: **Japanese army's assessment.** *Senshi Sosho*, Boei-cho Boei Kenshujo, *Daihon'ei Rikugunbu [3] Showa 17 nen 4 gatsu made* (Imperial Headquarters Army Department, vol. 3, up to April 1942). The meeting of 27 February is discussed on pages 474–475, of volume 35.

154: **Sugiyama's opening comments on Australia.** Sugiyama, Gen, *Sugiyama Memo/Sanbo Honbu hen*, Hara Shobo, 1989, Tokyo, pp. 41–45. (The *Sugiyama Memo* refers to the published war diaries in Japanese of Hajime Sugiyama.)

155: **Admiral Oka's view.** Sugiyama/*Sugiyama Memo*, ibid. Oka background: Toland, *The Rising Sun*, p. 303. Offensive plans in Hattori statement, US Historical section, 5 Oct, 1947, annexed paper, doc. 55412, Records of US Army, Far East Command; Fuller, *Shokan*, p. 278.

156: **Muto's view.** In Sugiyama, *Sugiyama Memo*, pp. 41–45.

156: **Muto's remarks to Togo.** In Togo, *The Cause of Japan*, pp. 228–229. Muto background: Toland, *The Rising Sun*, p. 258. In April 1942 Muto became chief of staff to General Yamashita in the Philippines and went on to northern Sumatra. The troops under his command committed widespread atrocities. After the war Muto was hanged by the Allies. Russell, *The Knights of Bushido*, p. 232.

156: **Tojo's complaint about invasion for natural resources.** Sugiyama, *Sugiyama Memo*, pp. 41–45.

156: **Conference decisions.** ibid.

157: **The liaison conference goes on to discuss Japan's future resource needs.** ibid pp. 41–45; *Senshi Sosho*, Boei-cho Boei Kenshujo, *Daihon'ei Rikugunbu* (Imperial Headquarters Army Department), vol. 3, p. 478.

157: **Shimada's views on Australian resources.** Shimada in *Sugiyama Memo*, pp. 41–45, agenda item 4. Shimada seeing emperor: Kido, *Kido Koichi nikki*, (Kido Koichi Diaries), pp. 927–928.

158: **Kawai on Curtin and Yampi Sound and 'guaranteed Australia's safety'.** Wurth, *Saving Australia*, pp. 36–40, pp. 81–82; Kawai, 'John Curtin: The Politician', written in Japanese for the Japan Australia Society, Tokyo, June 1962. (In the late 1930s, long before coming to Australia, Kawai wrote in his book, 'there are good prospects for sending iron ore from

Western Australia.' Kawai, Tatsuo, *The Goal of Japanese Expansion*, pp. 51–52).

158–159: ***Japan Times* on Australian invasion.** *Japan Times*, 25 February 1942.

Chapter 14

160: **Shortage of shipping.** Ugaki diary, 26–28 February 1942, *Fading Victory*, pp. 95–96.

160: **Loss of midget sub.** Ugaki diary, 1–4 March 1942, *Fading Victory*, pp. 99–101.

161–162: **Tanaka's minutes of 4 March meeting.** Tanaka, diary notes of meeting in *Senshi Sosho, Boei-cho Boei Kenshujo, Daihon'ei Rikugunbu* vol. 3, pp. 512–514; also see Bullard, *Japanese army operations in the South Pacific Area*, pp. 79–80.

162: **Navy and army positions at 4 March conference.** Ibid, Tanaka notes.

163: **Final resolution of 4 March.** Ibid, Tanaka notes.

163–165: **Yamamoto's plan for Midway revealed, and Navy General Staff agreement for it given.** Prange Papers, Kuroshima interview no. 1, 28 November 1964.

165: **7 March conference.** Sugiyama, *Sugiyama Memo*, pp. 48–55. (The Tokyo liaison conference of 7 March 1942 is also cited by Bix in *Hirohito*, p. 446; Toland, *The Rising Sun*, p. 303; Frei, *Japan's Southward Advance and Australia*, p. 171.)

166: **The influential hard-liner...** Admiral Oka in Sugiyama, *Sugiyama Memo*, pp. 48–55.

167: **General Tanabe.** Sugiyama, *Sugiyama Memo*, ibid.

167: **Admiral Oka.** In Sugiyama, *Sugiyama Memo*, ibid.

168: **The 7 March conference finally determined the 'Outline of war guidance suggested for implementation', but its intentions were far from clear.** The first paragraph of the outline stated that 'in order to cause England to surrender and destroy the United States' will to fight, we must continue to expand on the war results already obtained'. However, army participants successfully argued that the following be added: '... while developing the political and war situation into one from which Japan will be unbeatable in the long-term, we shall wait for an opportunity to take proactive measures.'

168: **Sugiyama's analysis of the 7 March conference.** 'Explanation of materials'

1942

in war outline guidance, [summary of debate, especially about Australia], Sugiyama, *Sugiyama Memo*, p. 11. Translated by Kyal Hill, Tokyo.

168: **Japanese invasion of Lae etc.** Odgers, *100 Years of Australians at War*, p. 146.

169: **In relation to Australia and India, the army allowed inclusion in the text of a 'temporary invasion of Darwin' as 'a future option to demonstrate positive warfare.'** *Daihon'ei rikugunbu*, vol.3, pp. 512–22. One military historian, Henry Frei, greatly downplays the value of this reference to the temporary invasion of Darwin, writing that, 'if and when the situation allowed; that is, if [nationalist Chinese leader] Chiang Kai-Shek could be brought down and the Soviet threat diminished. In reality, this meant little more than never.' Frei, *Japan's Southward Advance and Australia*, p. 171.

169: **Defence chiefs to Hirohito.** Hattori, Takushiro, *Dai Toa Senso Zenshi, (The Complete History of the Great East Asia War)*, p. 119 of US military translation, held by the University of Maryland.

169: **The navy knew they had lost ground.** Ibid, Hattori, p. 52.

170: **Ugaki's interpretation of the 14 March liaison conference.** Ugaki in diary entry, 14 March 1942, *Fading Victory*, p. 104.

170: **Ugaki's comments on MacArthur's arrival in Australia.** Hoyt, *The Last Kamikaze*, p. 48.

171: **Briefing by General Gordon Bennett.** Minutes of the war cabinet, Melbourne, 4 March 1942, NAA A5954, 808/1; Bennett, *Why Singapore Fell*, pp. 217–218.

171: **Elkin's advice to PM Curtin.** Elkin to Curtin, 5 March 1942, NAA A1608, AK29/1/2.

172: **US military leadership's view of Australian morale.** Clark to Brett, 15 March 1942, SWPA G2 journals, 98–GHQ–1–32, RG 407, WNRC; James, *The Years of MacArthur, 1941–1945*, vol. 2, p. 114.

172: **US assessment of Australia's vulnerability in early 1942.** Report of Organisation and Activities, US Army Forces in Australia, AG GHQ 314.7, based on 'Appreciation by Australian Chiefs of Staff', 27 February 1942, G3. GHQ, SWPA Journal file prior to 5 April 1942 in Willoughby (ed), *Reports of General MacArthur*, vol. 1, CMH Pub 13.

173: **Curtin's cablegram to Sir Earle Page.** 12 March 1942, NAA A2671, 96/1942. In a post-war review of Australia's plight, conducted by General MacArthur's general staff in Tokyo in 1945, the Americans agreed with the hopelessness of the Australian position in 1942: '... by the middle of March the Japanese were approaching the doorstep of Australia. Darwin ... had already been severely bombed. Townsville had also been subjected to air raids. With each passing day, the Japanese were forging new links in their chain of encirclement and preparing new strikes against Australia and her lifeline to the outside world.' US assessment based on 'Appreciation by Australian Chiefs of Staff', 27 February 1942 and 5 March 1942, G-3, GHQ, SWPA; Journal File prior to 5 April (MS) in Willoughby (ed.), *Reports of General MacArthur*, vol. 1, p. 27.

174: **RAAF at Port Moresby.** RAAF Museum, Point Cook <www.raaf.gov.au/raafmuseum/exhibitions/heritage>
175: **Menzies on Curtin's attitude to the US.** Dickover in memorandum of conversation with Menzies, in report to Washington, 24 March 1942, US Legation mission report from Canberra.

Chapter 15

176: **Defence and security orders and expenditure.** Minutes of the advisory war council, 4 March 1942, NAA A5954, 209/4. War cabinet minutes, NAA A5954, 808/1, 1942, meetings 28 Febuary – 29 July.
177: **Curtin's personal fears.** Daughter Elsie Macleod, oral history interview, 10 May 1994 and 20 February 1995, JCPML 00012.
177: **Presbyterian moderator's letter to Curtin.** Button letter to Curtin and letter to newspapers, 11 March 1942, NAA CRS M1416, 4.
178: **Curtin said an alarming thing today.** Alexander diary, 9 March 1942, NLA MS2389.
178: **Hong Kong atrocities.** Alexander diary, 9 March 1942, NLA MS2389; Lindsay, *The Lasting Honour*, p. 153.
179: **Secret demolition orders.** Demolition orders in NAA BP262/2, 9352, Curtin letter to Queensland Premier, 30 July 1942, and war cabinet NAA A2671, 182/1942.
180: **General Blamey's arrival.** Hetherington, *Blamey*, pp. 134–36.
181: **MacArthur's views of Australia's defences.** MacArthur, *Reminiscences*, pp. 161–63.
181: **Curtin broadcast to US.** *Sydney Morning Herald*, 16 March 1942.
182: **Curtin's account of MacArthur's view that invasion unlikely.** Minutes of the advisory war council, 26 March 1942, NAA A5954, 3/5. MacArthur

also quoted in advisory war council minute 869, Canberra, 26 March 1942, NAA A5954, 563/1.
182: **Churchill's qualified promise of help.** Cablegrams Churchill to Curtin 30 March and 1 April 1942 in advisory war council minutes, NAA A5954, 814/1.
183: **While the chiefs of Britain's three armed services tended to agree with their prime minister, they were much more circumspect than Churchill...** The British chiefs were the First Sea Lord, Sir Dudley Pound, Air Chief Marshal, Charles Portal, and chief of the General Staff, General Sir Alan Brooke.
183: **British defence chiefs' assessment.** Appreciation by chiefs, High Commissioner London to Curtin, 3 April 1942, War Cabinet agendum no 96/1942, NAA 2671, 96/1942.
184: **This report was part of Curtin's Easter reading.** Sent on Good Friday and read by Curtin the following day, on 4 April.
184: **Blamey on Western Australia.** Blamey remarks to Curtin in Alexander diary, 27 March 1942, NLA MS2389; Hetherington, *Blamey*, pp. 134–136.
185: **General Brett and 'Probable immediate Japanese moves in the Proposed New Anzac Area'.** Defence appreciation of 5 March 1942, NAA A5954, 563/1.
186: **The Australian Chiefs of Staff would be virtually compelled to yield the northern part of the continent to the Japanese should they attempt an invasion.** Assessment based on US signals in April 1942, G–3 GHQ, SWPA Journal and AHQ Opn Instr No 50, 9 April 42, G–3, SWPA Admin 370 (S) in Willoughby (ed.), *Reports of General MacArthur*, Vol. I, p. 34.
186: **Blamey remarks to Curtin.** Curtin secret briefing with press, Alexander diary, 27 March 1942, NLA MS2389.
187: **Curtin tells war council that MacArthur agrees with US–Australian assessment.** Advisory war council minute 893, Defence of Australia: Appreciation for Dr Evatt, 8 April, 1942, NAA A5954, 563/1.
187: **Curtin's briefing to Gavin Long.** Diary of Gavin Long dated 2 October 1943, referring to his notes of April 1942, AWM67, 1/3. (The emphasis was Curtin's.) On India, Churchill, *The Hinge of Fate*, p. 91.

Chapter 16

188: **Gowrie to George VI.** 14 April 1942, Gowrie papers, NLA MS2852/5/14.

189: **Lost production through strikes.** Alexander diary, 15 April 1942, NLA MS2389.

189: **Strike at Lithgow small arms factory.** Alexander diary entry, 13 April 1942, NLA MS2389.

189: **Civilian morale committee report to Curtin.** 4 April 1942, NAA A1608, AK 29/1/2.

189: **Loss of the HMAS** *Vampire.* Alexander diary, 16 April 1942, NLA MS2389.

190: **Curtin exchange with Churchill over troop reinforcements.** Curtin to Churchill, 14 April 1942, NAA A5954, 563/1. Rounding the Cape: especially see NAA A5954, 563/1, Churchill to Curtin, 30 March and 1 April, 1942.

191: **Ugaki on farewell to midget submariners.** Ugaki diary, 16 April 1942, *Fading Victory*, p. 111.

191: **Matsuo family farewell.** Jenkins, *Battle Surface!*, pp. 154–156.

192: **Ban's reaction to missing selection.** Stephen Lunn and Jonathon King, *Weekend Australian*, 'War on Our Doorstep', 25–26 May 2002.

192: **In time, he will be forced to accept that the proposal might well have been foolhardy.** Tomioka, *Kaisen to Shusen*, pp. 116–18.

192: **Kuroshima and Tomioka agree that Midway can be supported, if the Aleutians are included.** Prange Papers, Kuroshima interview no. 1.

194: **Yamamoto's Port Moresby priorities.** Frei, 'Japan's southward advance and Australia in the final stage', p. 6.

194: **Port Moresby was the key.** Morison, *History of the United States Naval Operations*, vol. 4, 'Coral Sea' etc, p. 10.

195: **Atrocities on New Britain.** Alexander diary, 17 April 1942, NLA MS2389; Webb report summary into atrocities, NAA A1006, H45/580/2/8/1.

195: **India suggested as target.** 'Magic' diplomatic summary SRS 575, 18 April 1942, War Department, Office of Assistant Chief of Staff, Record Group 457: Records of the National Security Agency/Central Security Service, US National Archives and Records Administration, Maryland.

196: **He had received the news through highly secret Magic radio intercepts of the Japanese Navy.** The British and Australians called these the Ultra intercepts. See Bleakley, *The Eavesdroppers*, p. XV.

1942

196: **Japanese military build-up near New Guinea.** Alexander diary, 28 and 29 April 1942, NLA MS2389; Curtin in the *Times*, London, datelined Canberra, 29 April 1942.

197: **Curtin gave review of war in which he said the Government regarded an outright Japanese attack on Australia as a constant and undiminished.** Alexander diary, 28 and 29 April 1942, NLA MS2389.

197: **Ugaki is brimming with confidence.** Ugaki diary, *Fading Victory*, 1–3 May 1942, pp. 118–121.

197: **Nagumo's carrier force will launch air strikes against Sydney.** Prange, Goldstein and Dillon, *Miracle at Midway*, McGraw-Hill, New York, 1982, pp. 30–31.

197: **Yamamoto on offensive and war games on *Yamato*.** Fuchida and Okumiya, *Midway*, pp. 95–99.

198: **Great things are in train.** Lloyd Ross writing in the *Sun Herald*, 27 July 1958.

198: **Curtin's speech about announcing the Battle of the Coral Sea.** Curtin speech 2 May 1942, JCPML00652/1/10.

199: **Curtin broadcast after Battle of the Coral Sea.** *Sydney Morning Herald*, 9 May 1942.

199–200: **The Battle of the Coral Sea.** See Dull, *The Imperial Japanese Navy*, pp. 115–129, Toland, *The Rising Sun*, pp. 322–25, 337.

200: **Ugaki disgusted by failure to take Moresby.** Ugaki, *Fading Victory*, 7 May 1942, p. 124.

201: **Roosevelt seeks MacArthur's advice.** 6 May 1942, R–6-4, B.15:F3 'WD 4 April to 8 June 1942', MacArthur Memorial & Historical Center, Norfolk, Virginia.

201: **MacArthur on Japanese plans.** 11 May 1942, NAA A5954, 3/5.

201: **MacArthur's request for aircraft carriers for Australia.** Radio message to Roosevelt, 8 May 1942, in Willoughby (ed.), *Reports of General MacArthur*, Vol. I, pp. 38–39.

201: **Request for carriers declined.** Lundstrom, John B., *The First South Pacific Campaign*, pp. 134–135.

201–202: **Governor-General Mike Jeffery.** Speaking at a service to commemorate the Battle of the Coral Sea, Australian–American Memorial, Canberra, 3 May, 2007.

Chapter 17

203: **This is the first of at least three reconnaissance flights the Japanese make over Sydney before launching their midget submarine raid.** Report of an unnamed participant officer in the operation quoted in *Senshi Sosho, Sensuikan shi*, (Submarine operations),Vol. 98, pp. 160–161; Also documents relating to 'Midget submarines, Japan Naval operations', typed Japanese translation into English, quoting p. 339, NLA MS3108, prepared by Japan's Defense Training Institute.

204: **Industrial disputes continue in coal industry.** Alexander diary, 14 May 1942, NLA MS2389.

204: **Curtin, frustrated, pleads to Parliament...** Commonwealth Parliamentary Debates, vol. 170, 13 May 1942, pp. 1140–1141; Black, *In His Own Words*, pp. 205–6.

204: **New liquor hours.** *Sydney Morning Herald*, 9 April 1942.

204: **Rush on clothing.** *Herald*, Melbourne, 9 May 1942; *Sun News Pictorial*, 9 and 14 May 1942.

204: **Joe Alexander on clothing rush.** Alexander diary, 13 May 1942, NLA MS2389.

205: **Attack on the *Wellen*.** Sinkings, AWM 54, 622/5/9 Japanese campaign against Australian coastal shipping; Navy Board report on Sydney attack, 1 August 1942; Gill, *Royal Australian Navy 1942–1945*, pp. 61–64.

205: ***I-28* sinking.** Carruthers, *Japanese Submarine Raiders 1942* p. 85.

205: **Ashibe to Mikiyo.** Letter, 18 May 1942, courtesy of brother Itsuo Ashibe, translated by Kyal Hill, Tokyo.

207: **Katsuhisa Ban to one of his brothers.** Undated letter of April 1942 from the collection of brother Itsuo Ban, translated by Rob Gilhooly, Tokyo.

207: **Final dinner with Ban.** Teiji Yamaki interviewed by Stephen Lunn, *Weekend Australian*, 25–26 May 2002.

208: **Ban's final letter.** Teiji Yamaki and Iwao Ban interview, Stephen Lunn, *Weekend Australian*, 25–26 May 2002.

208: **Description of Chuman, leader of the midget submarine fleet.** Friends of Chuman quoted in *Japan Times*, October 1943. (Note: In some documents and publications, Chuman's name is given as 'Chuma'.)

209: **Ugaki mulls over Coral Sea Battle.** Ugaki diary, 25 May 1942, p. 129.

209: **Hirohito's and Tojo's speeches.** *Japan Times*, 28 May 1942.

210: **Yamamoto letter to Chiyoko Kawai.** 27 May 1942 in Agawa, *The Reluctant Admiral*, p. 310.

211: **Details of vessels sent to the Midway and Aleutian islands invasions.** Ugaki diary, 25 and 28 May 1942, *Fading Victory*, pp. 128–130; Toland, *The Rising Sun*, p. 326.

Chapter 18

213: **Evatt cable to Curtin.** 28 May 1942, NAA A4764,1. Curtin cable to Evatt on invasion: 13 May 1942, DAFP, Vol. 5, 487.

213: **Psychological warfare.** *Senshi Sosho, Boe-icho, Papua campaigns: Port Moresby-Guadalcanal first campaigns*, Chapter 3, Planning and cancellation of the US–Australian blockade, 'various issues concerning the operation'.

214: **Boy who saw the Japanese.** Ian Spring, of Chiswick, New South Wales, to the author, 14 December 2006.

215: **Brownout policy.** Minutes of the war cabinet, 24 and 25 January 1942, NAA A5954, 807/2.

215: **Evening reconnaissance flight and attack order.** In translation of *Senshi Sosho, Boe-icho*, 'Midget submarines, Japan-Naval operations, Submarines New South Wales – Sydney Naval operations' in 'Documents relating to the Rabaul & Kavieng operations and the attack on Sydney Harbour by the Japanese submarines', NLA MS3108, pp. 339–342.

216: **Ito's memories of his flight.** Ito writing in a veterans' journal in Japan in 1988, as reported by Stephen Lunn and Jonathon King, 'War on our Doorstep', *Weekend Australian*, 25–26 May 2002; Ito interview with Peter George, *Rewind*, ABC-TV, 10 October 2004 and with the author in Iwakuni, 11 August 2007.

216: **Dulhunty sighting of Ito's flight.** Phil Dulhunty, *Rewind*, 10 October 2004.

217: **Susumu Ito's interview with author.** 11 August 2007.

217: **Wilson reports plane.** Lt Cdr P.F. Wilson in Gill, *Royal Australian Navy, 1942–45*, pp. 72–73.

218: **Navy Office summary report on midget attack.** Dated 1 August 1942, AWM 124, 4/474.

218: **Diego Suarez midget sub attack.** O'Neill, *Suicide Squads*, pp. 47–48; Craddock, *First Shot*, pp. 110–12, p. 192; Carruthers, *Japanese Submarine Raiders 1942*, pp. 90–94; Burlingame, *Advance Force Pearl Harbor*, pp. 388–93.

220: **Ugaki on the way to Midway.** Ugaki diary, 29–31 May 1942, *Fading Victory*, p. 131.

Chapter 19

221: **End of May approaches.** Alexander diary, 31 May 1942, NLA MS2389.

222: **Katsuhisa Ban and Masao Tsuzuku letters.** Quoted in Lind, *The Midget Submarine Attack on Sydney*, p. 21; preparations in *Senshi Sosho, Boei-cho*, Vol. 98, *History of Submarines (Sensuiken shi)*, pp. 160–161.

222: **Physical description of entry to midget sub.** In report to the Navy Office, NAA B6121/3,162K; also *Senshi Sosho* (as above).

224: **His thoughts are interrupted by the sudden splashing of oars.** Horace Doyle reminiscences, AWM PRO3229.

224: **Loop station failures.** Navy Office summary, Japanese Midget Submarines Attack on Sydney Harbour, 1 August 1942, AWM 124, 4/474, p. 4-5.

225: **James Cargill's account of finding sub.** In letter to Rear Admiral Muirhead-Gould of 3 June 1942, archives, Maritime Services Board of NSW, Sydney.

226: **The *Yarroma* returns.** The chart indicates there is only 10 feet of water – too shallow for depth charges. (10 feet = 3.04 metres.)

226–227: **Muirhead-Gould's report of the attack.** Official report of Rear-Admiral in Charge of Sydney Harbour Defences, B.S. 1749/201/37, 16 July 1942, AWM54, MP2026/21/22. Also see Carruthers, *Japanese Submarine Raiders 1942*, pp. 233–45. Background on Muirhead-Gould: NAA A6769, MUIRHEAD-GOULD GC.

227: **He turns the gun on himself and presses the trigger again, simultaneously exploding the sub's demolition charges.** The Japanese war history compiled by wartime submariner officers simply records that the *M-27* had become entangled in the net and lost all mobility, 'so its crew committed suicide'.

227: **The bodies of Chuman and Omori were later recovered in the wreckage of the *M-27*...** Mervin Lynam typescript AWM MS1257; Part of Navy Office summary, 'Japanese Midget Submarines Attack on Sydney Harbour', 1 August 1942, AWM 124, 4/474.

228: **Gowrie's account of the deaths onboard the *M-27*:** Gowrie to George VI, 9 June 1942, and attached draft of same letter, NLA MS 2852/5/14.

228: ***Lolita* showered with hot debris.** Horace Doyle reminiscences, AWM PRO3229.

228: **Recollections of James Nelson.** Carruthers, *Japanese Submarine Raiders 1942*, p. 136.

1942

229: **Anderson's riposte to Muirhead-Gould.** Carruthers, *Japanese Submarine Raiders 1942*, p. 136.

229: **Encounter with ammo-laden freighter.** Horace Doyle reminiscences, AWM PRO3229.

229: **Navy workboat almost hit by fire from the USS *Chicago*.** Earnest Jamieson recollection in AWM PRO3013.

230: **Gregory's account from the *Canberra*.** Mackenzie Gregory interview in Australians at War Film Archive no. 0071, Department of Veterans' Affairs, Canberra, Mullion Creek Productions; Navy News, Dept of Defence, 1 October 2001; Archive, Gregory biography, Naval Historical Society of Aust. Inc., Victorian Chapter.

230: **On shore, anti-aircraft gunner Phil Dulhunty witnessed Sydney under attack...** Dulhunty interview, *Rewind,* ABC-TV, 10 October 2004.

231: **The *Kuttabul* is hit.** Earnest Jamieson recollection in AWM PRO3013.

231: **Ban's sub escapes.** Navy Office summary report on midget attack, dated 1 August 1942. AWM 124, 4/474.

232: **Aboard the *Kuttabul*.** Neil Roberts' statement, AWM PO2534.001. Colin Whitfield's statement, *Navy News*, 24 June 2002; *Sydney Morning Herald* 2 June 1942.

232: **Unnamed seaman's account.** *Sydney Morning Herald*, 2 June 1942.

233: **Percy Wilson puts the Garden Island lights out.** Gill, *Royal Australian Navy 1942–45*, p. 73.

233: **Navy informs RAAF about mother sub off Cronulla.** Sub signals 1 June 1942, NAA B6121/3, 162K.

234: **Jim Mair recollections to the author.** 14 November 2007. Mair now resides at Caloundra, Queensland.

235: **Other civilian recollections.** The late Patricia Black: details from her son, Professor Alan Rix, the University of Queensland, 30 January 2007. Helen Ekin, of Cootamundra: interview with the author, 31 January 2007.

235: **Gregory's view of Sydney's defence.** Mackenzie Gregory interview in Australians at War Film Archive no. 0071, Department of Veterans' Affairs, Canberra, Mullion Creek Productions; Navy News, Dept of Defence, 1 October 2001; Archive, Gregory biography, Naval Historical Society of Aust. Inc., Victorian Chapter. Gregory retired from the RAN in 1954 with the rank of Lieutenant Commander.

NOTES

Chapter 20

237: **Ferries keep operating.** Muirhead-Gould in appendix B preliminary report, 22 June 1942, BS 1518/201/37.

238: **Gowrie describes attack to George VI.** Gowrie to George VI, 9 June 1942 and attached draft of same letter, NLA MS 2852/5/14. (Naval authorities had mistakenly told Gowrie that four submarines, instead of three, had attacked Sydney.)

238–239: *Sea Mist* **action.** In Navy Office summary report, 1 August 1942, AWM 124, 4/474.

239: *Yarroma* **damaged in action.** Carruthers, *Japanese Submarine Raiders 1942*, pp. 159–61.

239: **Matsuo's letter to parents.** Letter Keiu Matsuo dated 15 April 1942, from display at Educational Museum, Etajima academy.

240: **Conditions on the wreck of the** *Kuttabul*. Bullard statement in AWM 419/014/020, PR 86/241.

240: **Bullard's discovery of the** *M-22*. Ibid, Bullard statement.

241: **Circumstances of Matsuo and Tsuzuku's deaths.** Navy Office summary report, 1 August 1942, AWM 124, 4/474, p. 8.

241: **Position of submariners' bodies.** In Lind, *The Midget Submarine Attack on Sydney*, p. 49.

242: **Navy signals re subs.** Submarine signals 31 May/1 June 1942, NAA B6121/3, 162K.

242: **1941 warning about midget subs.** Cable from director military operations and intelligence to all commands, 4 May 1941, AWM 505/4/9.

244: **MacArthur on Curtin.** MacArthur, *Reminiscences*, p. 161.

245: **Curtin's recall of MacArthur's comments.** Discussions with the Commander-in-Chief in which Curtin quotes MacArthur, NAA A5954, 3/5, 1 June 1942.

246: **In view of the strategical importance of Australia . . .** NAA A5954, 3/5; Wurth, *Saving Australia*, p. 163; *Herald*, Melbourne, 27 December 1941.

247: **Code-breaking.** Smith, *The Emperor's Codes*, pp. 168–180; Bleakley, *The Eavesdroppers*, pp. 4–6.

247–248: **MacArthur reveals news that Battle of Midway is about to occur.** Discussions with the Commander-in-Chief in which Curtin quotes MacArthur, NAA A5954, 3/5, 1 June, 1942.

248: **Telegram to Ugaki re midget subs.** Gwyer and Butler, *Grand Strategy*, Volume 3, pp. 494–497.

248: **Newspaper reports of Sydney raids 2 June.** *Sydney Morning Herald*, 2 June 1942. *Age*, 2 and 3 June 1942.

250: **Curtin at Melbourne Town Hall.** DDA no. 31, 2–5 Jun 1942, JCPML 00110/36; *Age*, 3 June 1942 including Corser and Makin comments.

Chapter 21

251: **Ugaki learns of midget subs' failure.** Ugaki diary, *Fading Victory*, 2 and 3 June 1942, pp. 135–136.

252: **Makin's statement to parliament.** *Sydney Morning Herlad*, 4 June 1942.

252: **Curtin hints of new naval engagement.** Alexander diary, 3 June 1942, NLA MS2389.

252: **Revelation of the intercepted signal.** Alexander diary, 8 June, 1942, NLA MS2389. (The emphasis in the quote is the author's.)

252: **Curtin thought now was time for offensive.** Alexander diary, 8 June 1942, NLA MS2389.

253: **Ugaki's diary reflections on midget subs' fate.** Ugaki diary, original translation for 5 June 1942 held at the Archives of Industrial Society, University of Pittsburgh. (Note: This portion of Ugaki's diary does not appear in *Fading Victory*.)

254: **Rescue of *Iron Chieftain* crewman.** Papers of Ernest Jamieson, AWM PRO3013.

254: **Signal re sub sighting Vaucluse Bay.** Sub signals, 3 and 4 June 1942, NAA AB6121/3, 162K.

254–255: **Attacks on shipping.** NAA A9519, 2 (Attacks – Naval – Submarines), Gill, *Royal Australian Navy 1942–1945*, pp. 74–76.

255: **Midway naval code intercepts.** Dull, *The Imperial Japanese Navy*, pp. 116–117.

255: **Admiral Chuichi Nagumo, aboard the carrier *Akagi*, launched his planes against Midway.** Ugaki diary *Fading Victory*, Friday 5 June 1942, p. 149.

256: **Yamamoto's response to the losses.** Agawa, *The Reluctant Admiral*, pp. 316–20.

256: **Japanese airmen's criticism of the Hashirajima fleet.** Fleet comment in Fuchida and Okumiya, *Midway*, pp. 240–41.

256: **Damage to the *Hiryu*.** Agawa, *The Reluctant Admiral*, p. 317.

256: **Yamaguchi's response.** Fuchida and Okumiya, *Midway*, pp. 197–98; Toland, *The Rising Sun*, p. 340.

NOTES

257: **Ugaki's reflections on the failure at Midway.** Ugaki diary *Fading Victory*, Friday 5 June 1942, p. 152.

257: **Japan's false claims re the Sydney raid.** Hiraide broadcast of 5 June, transcript in the *Japan Times*, 6 June 1942.

258: **Japanese newspaper accounts of Madagascar and Sydney raids.** *Japan Times*, morning edition, 6 June 1942. *Japan Times*, evening edition, 6 June 1942. *Nichi Nichi*, 6 June 1942.

259: **Emperor Hirohito's reaction to Midway.** Kido, *The Diary of Marquis Kido*, entry of 8 June 1945.

259: ***Wilcannia* depth charges a sub.** *Sydney Morning Herald*, 6 June 1942.

259: **Frank Forde broadcast.** 6 June 1942, ABC.

259: **Miners' strikes.** *Sydney Morning Herald*, 9 June 1942.

260: **Gowrie to George VI.** 9 June 1942, Gowrie papers, NLA 2852/5/14, p. 3.

Chapter 22

261: **Submarine shelling of Sydney and Newcastle.** The order to shell Sydney and Newcastle was given by the commander of the Eastern Advanced Attachment, Captain Hanky Sasaki, during the submarine campaign against shipping off the east coast. *Senshi Sosho, Boei-cho, Sensuikan Shi* (Submarines) vol. 98, p. 160.

261: **Jim Mair recollections.** 14 November 2007. (He might have been hearing shells being fired from coastal batteries.)

262: **Attack on the Hirschs' flat.** *Sydney Morning Herald*, 8 June 1942.

262: **Response in the streets.** *Sydney Morning Herald*, 8 and 9 June 1942.

263: **Joan Hamilton's experiences.** Walter Hamilton, son, interview with author, 18 January 2007.

264: **Ito and Newcastle shelling.** Susumu Ito interview with author, 11 August 2007; shelling background from Gill, *Royal Australian Navy 1942–45*, pp. 77–78, *Newcastle Morning Herald* and *Sydney Morning Herald*, 8 and 9 June, 1945.

264: **Hitchcock family reminiscence.** John Hitchcock, of Wahroonga, Sydney, interview with author, 5 February 2007.

264: **Warning about children's sensitivity.** Home Security pamphlet in 'Personal Papers of PM Curtin', NAA M1415, 162, p. 73.

265: **Gowrie correspondence.** Gowrie to George VI, 9 June 1942, and attached draft of same letter, MS 2852/5/14.

1942

265: **Six-month anniversary of the war in the Pacific.** *Japan Times*, 8 June 1942.

266: **Curtin on Midway.** Alexander diary, 8 June 1942, NLA MS2389.

266: **Curtin on liberty loan,** statement 11 June 1942, in DDA, no. 37, 5 to 24 June 1942, JCPML00110/37.

266: **Japan lies about Midway.** Toland, *The Rising Sun*, pp. 329–42; Agawa, *The Reluctant Admiral*, pp. 321–22.

267: **Tomioka's attitude before and after Midway.** Tomioka and atmosphere at Naval General Staff in Fuchida and Okumiya, *Midway*, p. 215, also p. 443 of the 1992 new edition; Tomioka, *Kaisen to Shusen*, p. 118.

267: **Aircraft losses.** Fuchida and Okumiya, *Midway*, p. 250. Fukudome's assessment in Yoshida, *Kaigun Sanbo*, p. 294.

267–268: **MacArthur's assessment of Australia's position.** MacArthur at the advisory war council meeting, 17 June 1942, NAA A5954, 814/1. On invasion possibilities: Galloway, *The Odd Couple*, p. 101.

268: **Curtin continues to fear invasion.** Curtin briefing, 1 July 1942, in Lloyd and Hall, *Backroom Briefings*, pp. 50–51.

268: **MacArthur briefing to Canberra journalists.** 17 July 1942, in Lloyd and Hall, *Backroom Briefings*, pp. 64–66.

269: **Curtin national broadcast.** 17 June 1942, JCPML 00652/2/9.

270: **Port Moresby, prelude to occupation of northern Australia.** Dull, *The Imperial Japanese Navy 1941–1945*, p. 133, quoting *Boei-cho Boei Kenshujo Senshishitsu*, vol. 34, pp. 22–23.

271: **Japan ... has made a landing in Papua which threatens our important advanced base at Port Moresby ...** Curtin to Churchill, 30 July 1942, NAA A4763.

271: **Renewed shipping losses by submarine.** Attacks – Naval – Submarines, NAA A9519, 2.

Chapter 23

273: **Newspaper article re dead submariners.** *Age*, 2 June 1942.

273: **Raising of the *M-27*.** Sub signals, 5 June 1942, NAA B6121/3, 162K.

274: **Objections to the submariners' military funeral.** *Sydney Morning Herald*, 9 June 1942.

274: **Muirhead-Gould's response to objections.** *Sydney Morning Herald*, 22 June 1942.

NOTES

274: **Account of funeral.** Major G.B. Walker to Muirhead-Gould, 8 June 1942, Hedinger to Kawai, c. 15 June 1942, NAA 3741/5, V/11189.

274: *Nippon Times*' **account of Kawai's response to the deaths.** 29 March 1943. (*Nippon Times*, formerly *Japan Times*.)

275: **Kawai's poem.** Kawai family remembrance book, *Manazuru*, Tokyo, 1968, courtesy Masumi Kawai, Tokyo.

276: **He had put his staff to work gathering intelligence of military value, as his friend and commercial secretary at the time, Taijiro Ichikawa, later confirmed.** Ichikawa interview with the author at Tsujido, Japan, 25 October 2002.

276: **Background on Kawai, and Evatt's correspondence with him.** Evatt letter to Kawai, 4 March 1942, NAA A981/4, Cons 12, part 2. Evatt in Parliament on Kawai, CPD, vol. 169, Evatt ministerial statement, 26-27 November 1941, pp. 972-78; Evatt's sympathy for Japan in Wurth, *Saving Australia*, pp. 96–97, p. 108, p. 120, pp. 155–56, p. 169, p. 212.

276: **I gazed every morning and night at the coffers...** *Nippon Times*, 29 March 1943.

276: **Kawai poem,** in the Kawai family remembrance book, *Manazuru*, edited by Taro Kawai, after Kawai's death in 1966.

276: **Thank-you letter.** Kawai to Swiss consul Hans Hedinger for onpassing, dated 13 August 1942 and Hedinger to Hodgson 20 August 1942, NAA MP1185/8, 1877/13/320.

277: **Kawai's interview in the** *Times***.** 1 September 1942.

278: **Kawai leaves without farewelling Curtin.** Paper entitled 'John Curtin, the politician' written in Japanese in June 1962, for the Japan Australia Society in Tokyo by Tatsuo Kawai, the society's president.

278: *Asahi* **report.** In the *Asahi* and the *Japan Times*, 16 September 1942.

279: **Kokoda campaign.** Ryan (ed.), *Encyclopaedia of Papua and New Guinea*, vol. 2., pp. 1216–18, Odgers, *100 Years of Australians at War*, pp. 155–57. Author's reporting from the Kokoda Trail for *Sydney Morning Herald* and ABC Radio, May–June 1977.

281: **Australian youths fighting at Kokoda.** Minutes of the advisory war council, 19 May 1942, NAA A5954, 814/1.

282: **Forde anecdote.** Horner, 'Remembering 1942: High Command and the Kokoda Campaign', conference, Australian War Memorial, 2002.

282: **Japanese officer's diary.** Copy of translated diary, ATIS translation No 2, 11 November 1942, p. 23, in *Reports of General MacArthur, Japanese Operations*

1942

   in the Southwest Pacific Area, Vol. II, Part 1, 1950, compiled from Japanese demobilization bureaux records, Library of Congress card no. 66–60007.
282: **Blamey sacking Rowell.** Horner, *Crisis of Command*, pp. 183–87; Day, *John Curtin*, p. 486.
283: **Curtin asks Roosevelt to review 'beat Hitler first' policy.** Curtin to Dixon (for Roosevelt), 11 September 1942, Department of Foreign Affairs and Trade, Defence: Special collection II, bundle 5, Strategical policy – SWPA, file no. 3, 48/1942.
283: **Roosevelt's response.** Roosevelt to Curtin, 16 September, NAA A981, WAR 33, Attachment C.
284: **Troop numbers.** Bruce to Curtin 18 September 1942, DFAT, Defence: Special collection II, bundle 5, Strategical Policy – SWPA, file no. 3, 48/1942. (Curtin's troop figures are at August–September 1942.)
284: **Churchill unrelenting.** Note by Bruce of conversation with Churchill, London, 21 September 1942, NAA, M100, SEPTEMBER 1942.
284: **Tojo boasts of occupying Perth.** *Sydney Morning Herald*, 24 September 1942.

Chapter 24
285: **Author interview with Eric Damai at Gona.** *Sydney Morning Herald*, June 3 1977.
286: **Tojo's attitude to Japanese wartime atrocities.** Berlin broadcast of Tojo's remarks, 27 July 1942, monitored in New York: *Sydney Morning Herald*, 29 July 1942. Tojo and crimes against prisoners: Russell, *The Knights of Bushido*, p. 237.
287: **Casualties in New Guinea.** Odgers, *100 Years of Australians at War*, pp. 156–57.
287–288: **MacArthur recalls Kokoda's significance.** MacArthur, *Reminiscences*, pp. 161–63. MacArthur unequivocally pressed the issue in a communiqué on 2 July 1945 when speaking in praise of the 7th Division which had made a third major landing in Borneo. He said: 'It is fitting that the Australian 7th Division which in July three years ago met and later turned back the tide of invasion of Australia on the historical Kokoda Trail ... should this month secure ... the most lucrative target in our East Indies sector ...' MacArthur communiqué 1182 in Willoughby, *Reports of General MacArthur*, Vol. 1, p. 380.

288: **Possible advance to Australia.** From a paper by Professor Hiromi Tanaka to a symposium held at the Australian National University 19–21 October 2000, translated by Steven Bullard and Akemi Inoue, Australia–Japan Research Project, Australian War Memorial.

288: **We are not defending New Guinea of course, we are defending Australia.** Curtin quoted at press briefing in diary of Fred Smith, in Lloyd and Hall, *Backroom Briefings*, pp. 88–92.

288: **Curtin still worried about a Japanese offensive, but doubted their supply lines.** Curtin quoted at press briefing in diary of Fred Smith, in Lloyd and Hall, *Backroom Briefings*, pp. 88–92.

289: **Memorialisation of the Sydney raiders.** Domei's Toshio Ando in the *Japan Times*, 7 October 1942. Report of Curtin broadcast: *Japan Times*, 7 October 1942; *Chugai Shogyo*, 7 October 1942.

289: ***Kamakura Maru* arrival details.** *Japan Times*, 10 October 1942 and *Nippon Times*, 29 March 1943; Wurth, *Saving Australia*, pp. 215–20.

291: **... I feel that you can be reassured as to the adequacy of troops available ...** Roosevelt to Curtin, 2 December 1942, Papers of Lloyd Ross NLA MS3939/11/37.

291: **The two together may soon place us in what may be a very precarious position.** Curtin to Roosevelt, 8 December 1942, Papers of Lloyd Ross NLA MS3939/11/37.

291: **Ito's flight over Sydney and later reminiscences.** Interview with author, 11 August 2007.

292: **We leapt up and fled as fast as our legs would carry us.** Jim Mair, recollections to author, 14 November 2007.

293: **Kawai realises he has to go.** Kawai in *Sydney Morning Herald*, 23 February 1959, and in family remembrance book, *Manazuru*.

293: **Citation for dead submariners.** Domei news report on Yamamoto and Navy Ministry statements picked up from Batavia, 27 March 1943, AWM54, 622/5/6.

294: **Kawai interview.** Kawai in *Yomiuri* newspaper, reprinted in *Nippon Times*, 29 March 1943.

294–296: **The ashes propaganda.** NAA A3269, T42, 'Propaganda, Ashes of Enemy Dead'. This scheme had remained secret for decades until the author discovered it, revealed in a closed and confidential security file at the National Archives of Australia in Canberra. All the material quoted is from this file, unless cited separately below.

1942

297: **Dubinsky's report of search for plane.** 18 September 1943 in Keogh casualty file, NAA A705, 166/22/111.

297: **Chaplain's letter to widow.** Shea's American report of 22 September 1943, in Keogh's casualty file, NAA A705, 166/22/111.

297: **Wreck still visible.** Report from Justin Taylan, 2003.<http://www.pacificwrecks.com/aircraft/b-24/42-40984.html>

Chapter 25

299: *Yamato and Musashi* **at Truk.** Yoshimura, *Battleship Musashi*, pp. 134–37.

300: **German observation of Japanese at Truk.** US Strategic Bombing Survey (Pacific), Interrogation of Japanese Officials, OPNAV-P-03-100, Interrogation NAV no. 70 USSBS NO. 359, 11 November 1945.

300: **Japanese request for battleships.** Peattie, *Nan'yo*, pp. 261–62.

300: **Protracted campaign at Gona–Buna.** Curtin quoted at press briefing 8 December 1942, in diary of Fred Smith in Lloyd and Hall, *Backroom Briefings*, p. 110.

301: **New Guinea casualties.** Dull, *A Battle History of the Imperial Japanese Navy*, p. 180.

301: **Curtin's address to parliament.** Curtin in parliament on 10 December 1942, JCPML00110/52.

302: **Curtin's Christmas greeting to Menzies.** 24 December 1942, in NLA MS4936/1, folder 16.

302: **Return of the 9th Division.** Curtin quoted at press briefing 15 January 1943, in diary of Fred Smith in Lloyd and Hall, *Backroom Briefings*, p. 125.

303: **Build-up near Torres Strait.** Notes of advice from MacArthur to Curtin in NAA A5954, 524/6, 16 March 1943.

303: **MacArthur abandoned the Brisbane Line.** MacArthur HQ briefing in McCarthy, *South-West Pacific Area – First Year, Kokoda to Wau*, p. 112, notes.

304: **Yamamoto leaves Truk and IJN decline,** Yoshimura, *Battleship Musashi*, p. 136–37; Imperial Navy strength details, Summary Report, Pacific war, Marshalls, United States Strategic Bombing Survey, 1 July 1946.

305–306: **Ugaki's account of fatal attack and his own survival.** Ugaki, 'special entry', 18 April 1944, *Fading Victory*, pp. 352–54; Agawa, *The Reluctant Admiral*, pp. 350–60.

NOTES

307: **Rabaul bunker and devastation today.** Author's visit to Rabaul in 1999 to witness the volcanic damage, chiefly caused by Mt Tavurvur in 1994.

308: *Mutsu* **explosion.** IJN *Mutsu*, Tabular record of movement, <www.combinedfleet.com/Mutsu.html>

310: **Morale declines at Rabaul.** Okumiya and Horikoshi, *Zero!*, pp. 222–23. Description of Rabaul: Sakaida, *The Siege of Rabaul*, pp. 8 and 23.

310: **General Curtis Le May.** Wainstock, *The Decision to Drop the Atomic Bomb*, p. 2.

310: **Ugaki on gloomy future of the IJN.** Ugaki diary, *Fading Victory*, 21 June 1944, p. 415.

311: **Hirohito's warning on Saipan.** *Senshi Sosho: Daihon'ei kaigunbu, rengo kantai (6): dai sandankai sakusen koki*, p. 21.

311: **Baron Tomioka knew the significance of the fall of Saipan.** Prados, *Combined Fleet Decoded*, p. 583.

312: **Tomioka on Onishi.** Prange Papers, Tomioka interview No. 26. Onishi background: Fuller, *Shokan Hirohito's Samurai*, pp. 280 and 281; Fuchida and Okumiya, *Midway*, p. 21.

312–313: **Onishi's Kamikaze pilot scheme.** Toland, *The Rising Sun*, p. 568; Ohnuku–Tierney, *Kamikaze*, pp. 159–160.

314: **Curtin and HMAS** *Australia***.** Day, *John Curtin*, p. 554; transcript of interview with Robert Hartley, p. 19, Battye Library, Perth.

Chapter 26

315–316: *Kaiten* **pilot Naoji Kozu.** In Cook and Cook, *Japan at War, an oral history*, pp. 312–319.

316: **Hashimoto recalls** *Kaiten***s.** Thomas and Morgan-Witts, *Ruin from the Air*, p. 118.

316: **Japanese remnant naval strength.** Frank, *Downfall*, p. 206.

316–317: **Iwojima battle.** Toland, *The Rising Sun*, pp. 638–69, Bix, *Hirohito*, pp. 483–84.

320: **Toyoda order.** Toland, *The Rising Sun*, p. 690.

321: **Memories of Admiral Ito.** Prange Papers, Tomioka interview No. 26.

322: **I must state in all honesty that I have doubts about this plan.** Ito, quoted in Spurr, *A Glorious Way to Die*, p. 49.

322: **Ensign Yoshida's memories of the** *Yamato* **send-off.** Yoshida, *Requiem for Battleship* Yamato, p. 23.

415

323: **Ito chooses to die.** Spurr, *A Glorious Way to Die*, p. 289.

323: **Yoshida's memoir of the *Yamato*'s sinking.** Yoshida, *Requiem for Battleship* Yamato, pp. 116–17.

324: **Ugaki's mocking of new cabinet.** Ugaki, *Fading Victory*, 8 April 1945, pp. 577.

324–325: **Curtin, speech for third victory loan.** 12 March 1945, JCPML 00652/1/18.

325: **Curtin's death.** Elsie Curtin writing in *Woman*, 9 April 1951, JCPML 00577/5.

326: **He was one of the greatest wartime statesmen . . .** MacArthur, *Reminiscences*, p. 298.

326: **MacArthur photo.** Signal Corps, US Army, Curtin Family Collection, JCPML00376/124.

326: **You have given me a deep well of content and met the urges of my nature completely.** Letter from John Curtin to Elsie Curtin, 30 September 1941, JCPML 00402/37.

326: **I do not care who knows it . . .** Fadden, *They called me Artie*, pp. 80–81.

326: **Of John Curtin, I can say, as I believe we all can say . . .** Menzies, quoted in A.W. Martin, *Robert Menzies* vol. 2, p. 30.

327: **The palace burns.** Toland, *The Rising Sun*, pp. 744–45.

Chapter 27

328: **The high command's theory was that the nearer the battlefields to Japan . . .** Togo, *The Cause of Japan*, pp. 291–92.

329: **The first 500-pound bomb crashes into the bridge of the battleship, smashing the pilot house.** Account of the bombing of the *Nagato* on 15 July 1945. IJN *Nagato*, Tabular record of movement, Hackett, Kingsepp and Ahlberg, 18 July 1945, <www.combinedfleet.com/nagatrom.htm>

330: **I hope that I too will never forget about my mother's tender love . . .** Inoue in Yamanouchi and Quinn (eds/trans) *Listen to the Voices from the Sea*, p. 264.

330: **Potsdam Proclamation.** Hasegowa, *Racing the Enemy*, Stalin, Truman and the surrender of Japan, pp. 155–60.

331: **Army and navy leak official discussions of Japan's position.** Togo, *The Cause of Japan*, pp. 312–13.

NOTES

332: **Atomic explosion description by US airman Bob Caron** in *Enola Gay*. Thomas and Morgan-Witts, *Ruin from the Air*, pp. 427–31.

332: **I glanced at my watch.** Ogura, *Letters from the End of the World*, p. 17.

333: **If they do not now accept our terms, they may expect a rain of ruin from the air...** Truman, 6 August 1945, US State Department publication no. 2707, The International Control of Atomic Energy, pp. 95–97 and Papers of Eben A. Ayers, Harry S. Truman Library, Independence, Missouri.

334: **Now this country is going to fight alone against the whole world.** Ugaki diary, 6 August 1945, *Fading Victory*, p. 654.

334: **Kamikaze raids and US shipping.** US Strategic Bombing Survey, summary report (Pacific War), 'Conversion of Japanese air forces to Kamikaze forces'.

334: **We must think of some countermeasures against it immediately...** Ugaki diary, 7 August 1945, *Fading Victory*, p. 655.

335: **I will live and die for my fatherland...** Hayashi in Yamanouchi and Quinn (eds/trans) *Listen to the Voices from the Sea*, pp. 247–50.

335: **We did not want to die – at least not like that.** Takei in Sheftall, *Blossoms in the Wind*, p. 119.

335: **Toyoda continues resisting surrender.** Frank, *Downfall*, p. 270.

336: **Ugaki rants at those advocating surrender.** Ugaki diary, *Fading Victory*, 11 August 1945, pp. 658–59.

336: **Toyoda sends his own orders.** Ugaki diary, *Fading Victory*, 12 August 1945, p. 660.

336–337: **Hirohito radio address.** Imperial Rescript, 14 August 1945, Diplomatic Records Office, Tokyo; *Nippon Times*, 16 August 1945.

337: **Ugaki decides to lead his men in one last mission.** Ugaki diary, *Fading Victory*, 15 August, 1945, pp. 663–64.

338: **I am going to proceed to Okinawa where our men lost their lives like cherry blossoms.** Ugaki diary, *Fading Victory,* Epilogue by editors Goldstein and Dillon, pp. 665–66.

338: **If we are prepared to sacrifice 20 million Japanese lives in a 'special attack' effort, victory will be ours!** Onishi in Toland, *The Rising Sun*, p. 828.

338–339: **Onishi's suicide.** Kodama, *I Was Defeated*, pp. 172–73; Lamont-Brown, *Kamikaze*, p. 171; Toland, *The Rising Sun*, p. 855.

339: **The emperor trusted the navy.** Ohmae quoted on Australia in US

1942

Interrogation Files, G-2, Historical Section, GHQ, Far East Command in Willoughby, (ed.), *Reports of General MacArthur, The Campaigns of MacArthur in the Pacific*, Vol. I, *Decision to Take the Offensive*, p. 38 n and, on navy influence, in United States Strategic Bombing Survey, Interrogation of Japanese Officials, Nav no. 43, USSBS no. 192, 30 October, 1945.

341: **Surrender.** Harries, *Sheathing the Sword*, p. 189; Toland, *The Rising Sun*, pp. 866–67.

341: **MacArthur's speech.** MacArthur, *Reminiscences*, p. 315.

341: **Soviet Union presence.** MacArthur, *Reminiscences*, pp. 311–317; Toland, *The Rising Sun*, pp. 867–69.

342: **MacArthur's farewell as Supreme Commander of the Allied Forces in the South West Pacific.** MacArthur in CINCAFPAC Radio no. 210555 to PM Chifley of Australia with enclosure, 'Personal Message of Farewell to Australian Forces, 21 August 1945, C/S GHQ S, Aust 952 in Willoughby (ed.), *Reports of General MacArthur*, Volume I, p. 392.

342–343: **Tojo's last interview.** Richard Hughes of the Sydney *Daily Telegraph*, 10 May 1950, in Gill, *Royal Australian Navy 1939–1943*, p. 643. Hughes had written glowingly of Japanese progress during a visit to Japan just before the war in 1941 and was praised for his reporting by Japanese officials in Australia. After the war Hughes in Tokyo associated with, praised and worked with a former Japanese officer, ex-colonel Masanobi Tsuji, who ordered the killing of scores of thousands of civilians and prisoners in Singapore and Manila. Hughes even assisted Tsuji with some of his literary efforts and praised him as a brave and patriotic Japanese. Wurth, *Saving Australia*, pp. 62–63, 246; Hughes, *Foreign Devil: Thirty Years of Reporting From the Far East*, pp. 220–22.

343: **Tojo contemplated invasion of Australia.** Higashikuni, *Ichi-kozoku no Senso Nikki*, p. 106.

343: **Official view of Tojo's culpability.** Russell, *The Knights of Bushido*, p. 237.

344: **Tomioka's son.** Author's brief telephone conversation with Sadahiro Tomioka, via translator, August 2007.

Chapter 28

346: **To maintain the independence and peace of the nation.** Author visit to museum, 15 August 2007, Yasukuni shrine website, Q & A. <http://www.yasukuni.or.jp/english/>

NOTES

347: **Yasukuni Museum,** map showing Australia invasion, text translated by Robert Gilhooly, Tokyo.

348: **Isn't it a fact that the West ...** Yasukuni message, <http: www.yasukuni.or.jp/english/>

348: ***Umi Yukaba*** **translation.** Willoughby (ed.), *Reports of General MacArthur, The Campaigns of MacArthur in the Pacific*, Vol. II, part I, p. 43.

349: **Japan is the pioneer of a new age; she is the hope of a new Asia.** Kawai, *The Goal of Japanese Expansion*, p. 114.

349: **Lee Kuan Yew on Japanese war deeds.** In his memoir, *The Singapore Story*, p. 83.

349: **Comfort women.** Yasukuni commentary, <http://www.yasukuni.or.jp/english/qanda>

352: **I knew the *tokkotai* [Kamikaze] pilots would die like dogs.** Matsui, *Gakuto Shutsujin Goju-nen*, pp. 117–18; Ohnuki-Tierney, *Kamikaze, Cherry Blossoms and Nationalism*, p. 190.

353: **Our national superiority.** Guide booklet, undated, 'Welcome to Etajima!' of the JMSDF First Service School, Etajima.

354: **There is irrationality ...** Fuchida and Okumiya, *Midway*, p. 247.

354: **Failure of naval leadership.** Asada, *From Mahan to Pearl Harbor*, pp. 295–96.

354: **... navy planners began to take Australia into serious consideration, seeing it as an imminent threat.** Hiromi Tanaka in the *Journal of the Australian War Memorial*, issue 30, April 1997.

354: **Inoue and proposed carrier strikes on Townsville and Cooktown.** Lundstrom, *The first Pacific campaign*, p. 68.

355: **Prospects of Japanese invasion.** Paper, *High command and the Kokoda campaign*, Professor David Horner, 31 May 2002, History Conference, Remembering 1942, presented by the Australian War Memorial. Professor Horner is an official war historian. Kenney, *The MacArthur I Know*, pp. 193–4.

355: **Did Curtin and the Diggers save Australia?** On the mind and strength of the Imperial Navy after Midway, see Dull, *A Battle History of the Imperial Japanese Navy*, pp. 168, 175, 343–44; Ohmae's view of fighting capacity, US Strategic Bombing Survey, Interrogation of Japanese Officials, No. 30, No. 192, 30 October 1945.

357: **Did Japan have the capacity to invade Australia?** Dr Steven Bullard, senior historian, Australian War Memorial, in his introduction to *Japanese*

Army Operations in the South Pacific Region, in which he has translated extracts of *Senshi Sosho, Minami Taiheiyo Rikugun sakusen*, vols. 1 and 2, (Guadalcanal, Buna campaigns.).

358–363: **Tanaka interview with the author.** 16 August 2007, Tokyo.

Epilogue

365: ***Japan Times*, 6 June 1942, and Suetsugu background.** The National Archives, London, FO 371/24744, F5517, list of biographies, Craigie to Halifax, 13 December 1940.

366–367: **Discovery of the *M-24*.** Diver interviews from Channel 9, *60 Minutes*, 26 November 2006, reporter Liam Bartlett, producers Stephen Taylor and Julia Timms; *The Bulletin* magazine, 'Tomb of the Lost Raiders' by Stephen Taylor, 5 December 2006; *Manly Daily*, 28 November 2006 and 6 December 2006. (After engaging a celebrity agent, the amateur divers could not be interviewed by the author.)

368–369: **Joint private RAN–Japanese ceremony off Long Reef.** Author's account in feature, 'Sake and a salute to submariners', *Sydney Morning Herald*, 19 February 2007, including statement issued to author by the RAN in response to questions, 15 February 2007, attributed to 'a Defence spokesperson'. Ashibe brother visit to Sydney Harbour, courtesy NHK Television, Sydney office.

369: **Kazutomo Ban comments.** 'Insight' section, 'Small submarine, big questions', *Sydney Morning Herald*, 13 December 2006, Bob Wurth and Rob Gilhooly.

369: **Yamaki interview.** *Weekend Australian*, 'The Longest Night', Stephen Lunn (Tokyo) and Jonathon King (Sydney), 25–26 May 2002.

370: **Evidence submariners 'stayed with their vessel'.** Maritime archaeologist Tim Smith with the New South Wales Heritage Department interviewed by the author, 26 December 2006. On midget sub wreck, minister Shinichi Hosono, Embassy of Japan, Canberra.

370: **The entire mood and atmosphere of the midget submarine operation had been sacrificial from the beginning.** Prange, *At Dawn We Slept*, p. 349.

370: **Wartime death toll.** Tanaka, Hiromi, *The Japanese Navy's operations against Australia in the Second World War*, Journal of the Australian War Memorial, issue 30, April 1997.

SELECT BIBLIOGRAPHY

Books and articles

Agawa, Hiroyuki, *The Reluctant Admiral, Yamamoto and the Imperial Navy*, Kodansha International, Tokyo, 1982.

Asada, Sadao, *From Mahan to Pearl Harbor, The Imperial Japanese Navy and the United States*, Naval Institute Press, Annapolis, 2006.

Bennett, H. Gordon, *Why Singapore Fell,* Angus and Robertson, Sydney, 1944.

Bergamini, David, *Japan's Imperial Conspiracy*, Heinemann, London, 1971.

Bix, Herbert P., *Hirohito and the Making of Modern Japan*, HarperCollins, New York, 2000.

Black, David, *Friendship is a Sheltering Tree, John Curtin's Letters 1907 to 1945*, John Curtin Prime Ministerial Library, Perth, 2001.

_____, *In His Own Words, John Curtin's Speeches and Writings*, Paradigm Books, Curtin University, Perth, 1995.

Bleakley, Jack, *The Eavesdroppers, The Best Kept Secret of World War 2*, Kana, Melbourne, 1992.

Boei-cho Boei Kenshujo Senshishitsu (ed.), *Senshi Sosho* (Japanese War History Series, part of 102 volumes), Military History department of Asagumo Shinbunsha (National Institute for Defense Studies), Tokyo, 1968. In Japanese.

_____, *Senshi Sosho, Sensuikan* (Submarine) volume, *Asakumo Shinbun Sha*, Tokyo, 1979, NLA OJ 3393.7207, V98 and other references. In Japanese.

Bolt, Andrew (ed.), *Our Home Front 1939-1945*, Wilkinson Books, Melbourne, 1995.

Bullard, Steven, *Japanese Army Operations in the South Pacific Area: New Britain and Papua Campaigns, 1942-43*, Australian War Memorial, Canberra, 2007.

Burlingame, Burl, *Advance Force Pearl Harbor*, Naval Institute Press, Annapolis, 2002.

Carruthers, Steven L., *Japanese Submarine Raiders 1942*, Casper Publications, Sydney, 2006. (Previously titled *Australia Under Siege*, Solus Books, Sydney, 1982.)

Chapman, Ivan, *Iven G. Mackay, Citizen and Soldier*, Melway, Melbourne, 1975.

Chida, Takeshi (ed.), *History of Kure 2, Kure as seen by BCOF*, Kure City Historical section, Kure, 2006.

Churchill, Winston, *The Second World War*, Cassell, London, 1948-1954. (Reprint Society editions consulted.)

Clay, Blair, *Silent Victory, the U.S. Submarine War against Japan*, Lippincott, Philadelphia, 1975.

Cochrane, Peter, *Australians at War*, ABC Books, Sydney, 2001.

Cook, Haruko Taya and Cook, Theodore F., *Japan at War, An Oral History*, New Press, New York, 1992.

Craddock, John, *First Shot, The Untold Story of the Japanese Minisubs That Attacked Pearl Harbor*, McGraw-Hill, New York, 2006.

Daihon'ei, *Communiques issued by the Imperial General Headquarters: from December 8, 1941 to June 30, 1943*, Mainichi, Tokyo, 1943.

Day, David, *John Curtin: A Life*, HarperCollins, Sydney, 2000.

_____, *The Great Betrayal: Britain, Australia and the Onset of the Pacific War, 1939–1942*, Oxford University Press, Melbourne, 1992.

_____, *Reluctant Nation, Australia and the Allied Defeat of Japan 1942–1945*, Oxford University Press, Melbourne, 1992.

Dower, John W., *Embracing Defeat, Japan in the Wake of World War II*, Norton/New Press, New York, 1999.

_____, *War Without Mercy: race and power in the Pacific war*, Pantheon Books, New York, 1986.

SELECT BIBLIOGRAPHY

Dull, Paul S., *A Battle History of the Imperial Japanese Navy 1941–1945,* Naval Institute Press, Annapolis, 1978.

——————, *Guadalcanal, The Definitive Account of the Landmark Battle*, Penguin, New York, 1992.

Frank, Richard B., *Downfall, The End of the Imperial Japanese Empire*, Penguin, New York, 2001.

Frei, Henry P., *Japan's Southward Advance and Australia*, University of Hawaii Press, Honolulu, 1991.

Fry, Gavin, *et al* (eds), 'The Battle of Coral Sea 1942, Conference Proceedings, 7–10 May 1992', Australian National Maritime Museum, Sydney, 1993.

Fuchida, Mitsuo and Okumiya, Masatake, *Midway, the Battle that Doomed Japan: The Japanese Navy's Story*, US Naval Institute, Annapolis, Maryland, 1955.

Fuller, Richard, *Shokan, Hirohito's Samurai, Leaders of the Japanese Armed Forces, 1926–1945*, Arms and Armour Press, Cassell Imprint, London, 1992.

Galloway, Jack, *The Odd Couple: Blamey and MacArthur at War*, University of Queensland Press, St Lucia, 2000.

Gill, G. Hermon, *Royal Australian Navy 1942–1945*, Collins, Sydney, in association with the Australian War Memorial, Canberra, 1985.

——————, *Royal Australian Navy 1939–1942*, Australian War Memorial, Canberra, 1968.

Goldstein, Donald M. and Dillon, Katherine V. (eds), *The Pearl Harbor Papers: Inside the Japanese Plans,* Brassey's, Dulles, Virginia, 2000.

——————, *The Pacific War Papers: Japanese Documents of World War II*, Potomac, Washington, 2004. (Also see Ugaki, Matome)

Greenwood, G. and Harper, N.D. (eds), *Australia in World Affairs 1956–1960*, Cheshire for the Australian Institute of International Affairs, Melbourne, 1963.

Grose, Peter, *A Very Rude Awakening,* Allen & Unwin, Sydney, 2007.

Hadley, Michael L., Huebert, R.N. & Crickard, F.W., *A Nation's Navy: In Quest of Canadian Naval Identity*, McGill-Queen's Press, Montreal, 1996.

Ham, Paul, *Kokoda*, HarperCollins, Sydney, 2004.

Hannan, Agnes, *Victoria Barracks Melbourne, A Social History*, Australian Defence Force Journal Production, Canberra, 1995.

Harries, Meirion and Susie, *Sheathing the Sword: The Demilitarisation of Japan*, Maćmillan, New York, 1989.

Hasegawa, Tsuyoshi, *Racing the Enemy, Stalin, Truman and the Surrender of Japan*, Belknap Press, Cambridge, 2005.
Hasluck, Paul, *Diplomatic Witness: Australia's Foreign Affairs, 1941–1947*, Melbourne University Press, 1980.
——————, *Australia in the War of 1939–1945, The Government and the People*, Australian War Memorial, Canberra, 1952.
——————, *The Government and the People, 1942–1945*, Australian War Memorial, Canberra, 1970.
Hattori, Takushiro, *Dai Toa Senso Zenshi*, (*The Complete History of the Great East Asia War*), Hara Shobo, Tokyo, 1965. In Japanese. (US military translation in English held by University of Maryland.)
Hetherington, John, *Blamey: The Biography of Field-Marshal Thomas Blamey*, F.W. Cheshire, Melbourne, 1954.
Higashikuni, Naruhiko, *Ichi-kozoku no Senso Nikki*, (*War Diary of an Imperial Family Member*) Nihoa Shuhosha, Tokyo, 1957. In Japanese.
Horner, David, *Crisis of Command: Australian Generalship and the Japanese Threat 1941–1943*, Australian National University Press, Canberra, 1978.
——————, *Blamey: The Commander-in-Chief*, Allen & Unwin, Sydney, 1998.
——————, *Defence Supremo: Sir Frederick Shedden and the Making of Australian Defence Policy*, Allen & Unwin, Sydney, 2000.
——————, *High Command, Australia and Allied Strategy, 1939–1945*, George Allen & Unwin, Sydney, in association with the Australian War Memorial, Canberra, 1982.
——————, *Inside the War Cabinet: Directing Australia's War Effort, 1939–45*, Allen & Unwin, Sydney, 1996.
Hoyt, Edwin P., *The Last Kamikaze, the Story of Admiral Matome Ugaki*, Praeger, Westport, 1993.
——————, *Yamamoto, the Man who Planned the Attack on Pearl Harbor*, The Lyons Press, Guilford, Connecticut, 1990.
Hughes, Richard, *Foreign Devil: Thirty Years of Reporting from the Far East*, Andre Deutsch, London, 1972.
Ienaga, Saburo, *The Pacific War, 1931–1945*, Pantheon Books, New York, 1978.
Ike, Nobutake (ed./trans), *Japan's Decision for War: Records of the 1941 Policy Conferences*, Stanford University Press, 1967.
Jacobsen, Marc, *The Battle of the Coral Sea 1942: Conference Proceedings*,

SELECT BIBLIOGRAPHY

7-10 May 1992, US Grand Strategy and Australia, Australian National Maritime Museum, Sydney, 1992.

James, Dorris Clayton, *The Years of MacArthur, 1941-1945* (vol. 2), Houghton Mifflin, Boston, 1975.

Jenkins, David, *Battle Surface! Japan's Submarine War Against Australia 1942-44*, Random House, Sydney, 1992.

Kaplan, Philip, *Battleship*, Aurum Press, London, 2004.

Kawai, Tatsuo, *The Goal of Japanese Expansion*, Hokuseido Press, Tokyo, 1938.

Kennedy, Paul M., *Strategy and Diplomacy 1870–1945* (eight studies), Allen & Unwin, London, 1945.

Kenney, George C., *The MacArthur I Know*, Duell, Sloan and Pearce, New York, 1951.

Kido, Koichi, *The Diary of Marquis Kido, 1931–45: Selected Translations into English,* University Publications of America, Maryland, 1984.

Kodama, Yoshio, *I Was Defeated*, Asian Publication, Tokyo, 1951.

Krug, Hans-Joachim; Hirama, Yoichi; Sander-Nagashima, Berthold. J., Niestle, Axel, *Reluctant Allies, German–Japanese Naval Relations in World War II,* Naval Institute Press, Annapolis, 2001.

Lamont-Brown, Raymond, *Kamikaze: Japan's Suicide Samurai*, Cassell, London, 1997.

Lee Kuan Yew, *The Singapore Story*, Marshall Cavendish and The Straits Times Press, Singapore, 1998.

Lind, Lew, *The Midget Submarine Attack on Sydney*, Bellrope Press, Sydney, 1990.

Lindsay, Oliver, *The Lasting Honour, the Fall of Hong Kong 1941*, Sphere Books, London, 1978.

Lloyd, Clem and Hall, Richard, *Backroom Briefings: John Curtin's War*, National Library of Australia, Canberra, 1997.

Lockwood, Douglas, *Australia's Pearl Harbour, Darwin 1942*, Cassell Australia, Melbourne, 1966.

Long, Gavin, *The Six Years War, Australia in the 1935–45 War*, The Australian War Memorial and the Australian Government Publishing Service, Canberra, 1973.

Lundstrom, John B., *The First South Pacific Campaign: Pacific Fleet Strategy, December 1941–June 1942*, Naval Institute Press, Annapolis, 1976.

Lunn, Stephen and King, Jonathan, 'War on Our Doorstep, The Longest Night', 60th anniversary feature in the 'Weekend Inquirer', *Weekend*

1942

Australian, 25–26 May 2002.

MacArthur, Douglas, *Reminiscences*, Crest Books, New York, 1965, McGraw-Hill, 1964.

Manchester, William, *American Caesar: Douglas MacArthur 1880-1964*, Hutchinson Australia, Melbourne, 1978.

Martin, A.W., *Robert Menzies, Volume 2, 1944–1978: a life*, Melbourne University Press, 1999.

Matsui, Kakushin, *Gakuto Shutsujin Goju-nen*, Asahi Sonorama, Tokyo, 1994.

McCarthy, Dudley, *South-West Pacific Area: First Year, Kokoda to Wau*, Australian War Memorial, Canberra, 1959.

Morison, Samuel E., *The Two Ocean War, A Short History of the US Navy in the Second World War*, Little, Brown and Co., Boston, 1963.

_____, *History of the United States Naval Operations in World War Two*, Little, Brown & Co, Boston, 1947–1952 (15 volumes).

Morley, James William (ed.), *The Fateful Choice: Japan's Advance into South East Asia, 1939–1941*, Columbia University Press, New York, 1989.

_____, *The Final Confrontation: Japan's Negotiations with the United States, 1941*, Columbia University Press, New York, 1994.

Nagata, Yuriko and Nagatomo, Jun, *Japanese Queenslanders: a History*, Bookpal, South Brisbane, 2007.

Odgers, George, *100 Years of Australians at War*, New Holland, Sydney, 1994.

Ogura, Toyofumi, *Letters from the End of the World, A Firsthand Account of the Bombing of Hiroshima*, Kodansha International, Tokyo, 1997.

Ohnuki-Tierney, Emiko, *Kamikaze, Cherry Blossoms and Nationalisms*, the University of Chicago Free Press, 2002.

O'Neill, Richard, *Suicide Squads*, Salamander, London, 1981.

Parrish, Thomas and Marshall, S.L.A., *The Simon and Schuster Encyclopedia of World War II*, Simon & Schuster, New York, 1978.

Peattie, Mark R., *Nan'yo, The Rise and Fall of the Japanese in Micronesia, 1885–1945*, University of Hawaii Press, Honolulu, 1992.

Potter, John Deane, *A Soldier Must Hang: The Biography of an Oriental General*, Four Square, London, 1963.

Prados, John, *Combined Fleet Decoded, The Secret History of American Intelligence and the Japanese Navy in World War II*, Naval Institute Press, Annapolis, 1995.

Prange, Gordon W., *At Dawn We Slept*, Penguin, New York, 1991.

_____, (with Goldstein, Donald W., and Dillon, Katherine V.)

Miracle at Midway, McGraw-Hill, New York, 1982.
Richie, Donald, *The Inland Sea*, Stone Bridge Press, Berkeley, 2002.
Ross, Lloyd, *John Curtin, a biography*, Melbourne University Press, 1996.
Rowell, S.F., *Full Circle*, Melbourne University Press, 1974.
Ryan, Peter (ed), *Encyclopaedia of Papua and New Guinea*, Melbourne University Press and University of Papua and New Guinea, 1972.
Sakaida, Henry, *The Siege of Rabaul*, Phalanx, St Paul, 1996.
Sakamaki, Kazuo, *I Attacked Pearl Harbor*, translated by Toru Matsumoto, Associated Press, New York, 1949.
Sheftall, M.G., *Blossoms in the Wind: Human Legacies of the Kamikaze*, New American Library, New York, 2005.
Skulski, Janusz, *The Battleship Yamato*, Naval Institute Press, Annapolis, 1988.
Spurr, Russell, *A Glorious Way to Die: The Kamikaze Mission of the Battleship Yamato, April 1945*, Sidgwick and Jackson, London, 1981.
Stanley, Peter 'Threat made manifest', *Griffith Review*, Griffith University, Brisbane, Spring 2005.
Stargardt, A.W., *Australia's Asian Policies: The History of a Debate 1839–1972*, Institute of Asian Affairs, Otto Harrassowitz, Hamburg, Wiesbaden, 1977.
Stephan, John J., *Hawaii Under the Rising Sun: Japan's Plans for Conquest After Pearl Harbor*, University of Hawaii Press, Honolulu, 1984.
Stuart, Ian, *Port Moresby, Yesterday and Today*, Pacific, Sydney, 1970.
Sugiyama, Hajime, *Sugiyama Memo/Sanbo Honbu hen*, Hara Shobo, Tokyo, 1989.
Takeyama, Michio, *The Scars of War: Tokyo during World War II*, Rowman & Littlefield, Lanham, 2007.
Tanaka, Hiromi, *The Japanese Navy's Operations Against Australia in the Second World War*, Journal of the Australian War Memorial, issue 30, April 1997.
Thomas, Gordon and Morgan-Witts, Max, *Ruin from the Air: The Atomic Mission to Hiroshima*, Sphere, London, 1978.
Togo, Shigenori, *The Cause of Japan*, Simon & Schuster, New York, 1956.
Toland, John, *The Rising Sun: The Decline and Fall of the Japanese Empire 1936–1945*, Penguin, London, 2001.
_____, *But Not in Shame*, Random House, New York, 1961.
_____, *Infamy, Pearl Harbor and its Aftermath*, Berkley Books, New York, 1983.
Tomioka, Sadatoshi, *Kaisen to Shusen: Hito to kokio to keikaku* (The opening

and closing of the Pacific war: The people, the mechanisms, and the planning), Mainichi Shinbunsha, Tokyo, 1968. In Japanese.

Ugaki, Matome, *Fading Victory: the Diary of Admiral Matome Ugaki, 1941–45,* translated by Masataka Chihaya, with Donald M. Goldstein and Katherine V. Dillon, University of Pittsburgh Press, Pittsburgh, 1991.

US War Department, *The World at War, 1939–1944*, War Dept. publication, Washington, 1945.

Waley, Paul, *Tokyo Now and Then, an Explorer's Guide*, Weatherhill, New York, 1984.

Warner, Peggy, and Sadao, Seno, *The Coffin Boats: Japanese Midget Submarine Operations in the Second World War*, Cooper, Secker & Warburg, London, 1986.

Watanabe, Tsuneo, (ed.), *From Marco Polo Bridge to Pearl Harbor: Who was Responsible?,* Yomiuri Shimbun, Tokyo, 2006.

Werner, Herman O., and Langdon, Robert M. (eds), *The Japanese Navy in World War II*, US Naval Institute, Annapolis, 1969.

Wigmore, Lionel, *The Japanese Thrust*, Australian War Memorial, Canberra, 1957.

Willoughby, Charles A. (ed.), *Reports of General MacArthur: The Campaigns of MacArthur in the Pacific*, (two volumes) US Department of the Army, US Government Printing Office, Washington, 1966.

Wurth, Bob, *Saving Australia: Curtin's Secret Peace with Japan*, Lothian (Hachette Livre), South Melbourne, 2006.

———, 'Small submarine, big questions', Insight feature, with Rob Gilhooly, *Sydney Morning Herald*, 13 December 2006.

Yamanouchi, Midori and Quinn, Joseph L., (trans), *Listen to the Voices from the Sea, (Kike Wadatsumi no Koe),* The University of Scranton Press, 2000.

Yoshida, Mitsuru, *Requiem for Battleship* Yamato, Naval Institute Press, Annapolis, 1985.

Yoshida, Shigeru, *The Yoshida Memoirs*, Houghton Mifflin, Boston, 1962.

Yoshimura, Akira, *Battleship* Musashi*, The Making and Sinking of the World's Biggest Battleship*, Kodansha International, Tokyo, 1991.

National Archives of Australia, Canberra

A367, Security investigations

A431, Darwin and the Northern Territory

A461, Prime Minister's Department, correspondence files

SELECT BIBLIOGRAPHY

A705, Air correspondence files
A816, Department of Defence
A981, War records
A1006, including report of Sir William Webb
A1608, Prime Minister's Dept (war)
A2670, War Cabinet Agendum
A2671, War Cabinet Agendum, including copies of cables
A2682, Advisory War Council minutes
A2684, Japanese midget submarines
A2703, Cabinet minutes
A3196, Outward cable copies
A3269, Propaganda, Ashes of Enemy Dead
A4763, Ninth Division, AIF
A5954, The Shedden collection
A6121, Navy historical files
A6769, Navy officers' files
A8911, Intelligence
A9519, Attacks, Naval, Submarines
M100, Papers of Stanley Melbourne Bruce
M1415, Personal papers of Prime Minister Curtin

National Library of Australia
Joseph Alexander, diary, MS2389
Documents relating to the attack on Sydney Harbour, MS3108
Lord Gowrie, papers, MS2852
Sir John Latham, papers, MS1009
Don Rodgers, papers, MS1536
Lloyd Ross, papers, MS 3939

Australian War Memorial
Bill Bullard, statement AWM 419/014/020, PR 86/241
Director Military Operations cable, AWM 505/4/9
Horace Doyle, reminiscences, AWM PRO3229
Earnest Jamieson, reminiscences, AWM PRO3013
Japanese attacks on Australian shipping AWM 54, 622/5/9
Brig. Joseph Lee, AWM RC 02304
Gavin Long, diary, AWM 67, 1/3

Midget Submarine Attack on Sydney Harbour, AWM MP1587/1, Signals B6121/3
Mervin Lynam, typescript, AWM MS 1253
Muirhead-Gould, Report from Rear-Admiral-in-Charge, AWM52, MP2026/21/22
Navy Office summary report on midget attack, AWM 124, 4/474
Newspaper advertisements (propaganda), AWM ARTV09225
Neil Roberts, statement, AWM PO2534.001

John Curtin Prime Ministerial Library
Elsie Curtin, wife of John, writing in *Woman*, JCPML 00577/5
John Curtin, 'Digest of Decisions and Announcements and Important Speeches by the Prime Minister, 21 February to 3 March, 1942'. DDA, JCPML 00110/25
Herbert Evatt, as above
John Curtin, DDA 2–5 June 1942, JCPML 00110/36 and 5–24 June 1942, JCPML 00100/37
_____, broadcast, 17 June 1942, JCPML 00652/2/9
_____, loan speech, 12 March 1942, JCPML 00652/1/18
_____, letter to wife Elsie, 30 September 1941, JCPML 00402/37
Gladys Joyce, oral history, JCPML 00210
Frederick McLaughlin to Hector Harrison, on Curtin, JCPML 00472/4
Elsie Macleod, daughter of John and Elsie Curtin, oral history, JCPML 00012
Don Rodgers, personal papers, JCPML 00463/1
Lloyd Ross, on Curtin, JCPML 00415

University of Maryland Libraries
Gordon W. Prange Papers, Special Collections, University of Maryland Libraries
Prange interviews: Admiral Sadatoshi Tomioka, Admiral Shigeru Fukudome, Admiral Kameto Kuroshima
US Interrogation: Admiral Shigeru Fukudome

University of Pittsburgh
Prange Collection, including original Ugaki translations and photographs from *Fading Victory*, Goldstein and Dillon. (This is a separate archive resource to the University of Maryland.)

Other archival sources

Eisenhower memo to Marshall, research library of the George C. Marshall Foundation, Lexington, Virginia.

Franklin D. Roosevelt Library, US-UK Chiefs of Staff file, Hyde Park, New York. Files on President Roosevelt and Admiral Ernest J. King.

Nakahara, Yoshimasa (Captain) diary, *Nisshi kaiso*, Library, Institute of Defense Studies, Japanese Defense Agency, Tokyo.

National Archives and Records Administration, Maryland, 'Magic' diplomatic summary SRS 575, 18 April 1942, War Department, Office of Assistant Chief of Staff, Record Group 457: Records of the National Security Agency/Central Security Service.

Operation Journal of 19th Bombing Grp., 8 Dec 41–2 Feb 42, G–2 Historical Section, GHQ, FEC.

Rikugunsho Dainikki, (Document Files of the Military of the Army, 1868 to 1942), National Institute for Defense Studies, Tokyo.

'Report of Organization and Activities', United States Army Forces in Australia, AG GHQ 314.7, USAFIA.

Senji Nisshi and *Sento Shoho* (action reports produced by Imperial Naval units during the Sino-Japanese War, the Russo-Japanese War, World War I and the Greater East Asian War), National Institute for Defense Studies, Tokyo. In Japanese.

US Strategic Bombing Survey (Pacific), Interrogation of Japanese Officials, Tokyo, November, 1945.

Author interviews in Japan

Professor Takeshi Chida, chief editor, Kure City Historical Section, Kure

Taijiro Ichikawa, friend of Tatsuo Kawai

Susumu Ito, wartime pilot

Tadashi Kanai, Japan–Australia Society, Tokyo

Masumi Kawai, son of Tatsuo Kawai

Toshiro Takeuchi, friend of Tatsuo Kawai

Akihiko Tanaka, Diplomatic Record Office, Ministry of Foreign Affairs, Tokyo

Professor Hiromi Tanaka, Japan Self-Defense Force

Kazuhiro Tomizuka, Diplomatic Record Office, Ministry of Foreign Affairs, Tokyo

Kazushige Todaka, director, Kure Maritime Museum

Author interviews in Australia
Helen Ekin
Walter Hamilton
Tim Harlock
John Hitchcock
Shinichi Hosono
Jim Mair
Guy Owen-Jones
Professor Alan Rix
Tim Smith
Ian Spring

Other interviews
Itsuo Ashibe, interview with Shane McLeod, *The 7.30 Report*, ABC-TV, 19 December 2006
Kazutomo Ban, interviewed by Robert Gilhooly
Ashibe, Mamoru, letters courtesy of his brother Itsuo Ashibe of Wakayama
W.F.A. 'Gus' Winckel, interview with David Batty, *Dimensions in Time*, ABC-TV, 23 April, 2002

Newspapers
Asahi
The Age
Argus
The Australian
Chuga
Daily Telegraph
Herald
Honolulu Advertiser
Japan Times
Kokumin
Mikako,
Newcastle Morning Herald
Nichi Nichi
Shogyo
Sun Herald
Sydney Morning Herald

SELECT BIBLIOGRAPHY

The Times
Washington Post
Weekend Australian
West Australian
Yomiuri

Websites

Australia Japan Research Project, Australian War Memorial, including part translations by Dr Steven Bullard of *Senshi Sosho*, the Japanese war history series, as relating to Australia, <http://ajrp.awm.gov.au/ajrp/ajrp2.nsf/>

Australian Dictionary of Biography, Online edition, <http://www.adb.online.anu.edu.au>

Churchill, Winston, debate in House of Commons, 27 January, 1942, <http://www.ibiblio.org/pha/policy/1942/420127a>

Combined Fleet background site: <http://www.combinedfleet.com/kaigun.htm>

Combined Fleet operations order 1, 5 November 1941 mentioning Australia, US Army in World War II, Strategy and Command, The First Two Years. <http://www.ibiblio.org.com/hyperwar>

Darwin raids in Australian War Memorial's website: <http://www.awm.gov.au/encyclopedia/air_raids>

Hackett, Bob and Kingsepp, Sander, information on Japanese warships <http://www.combinedfleet.com>

HMAS *Perth*, Sea Power Centre Australia, Australian HMA ship histories, <http://www.navy.gov.au/spc/history/ships/perth1.html>

Interview with Gus Winckel. Netherlands Ex-Servicemen and Women's Association, <http://www.neswa.org.au>

Ourasaki monument, <http://wgordon.web.wesleyan.edu/kamikaze/monuments/ourasaki/index.htm>

Summary Report, Pacific war, Marshalls, United States Strategic Bombing Survey: Summary Report (Pacific War) 1 July 1946. Washington, D.C.: United States Government Printing Office, 1946. <http://marshall.csu.edu.au/Marshalls/html/WWII/USSBS_Summary.html>

Suikosha naval officers' club, background in History of the Masonic Temple, Tokyo, <http://www.japan-freemasons.org>

Wartime conditions in Japan: The United States Strategic Bombing Survey: Summary Report (Pacific War) 1946, <http://www.anesi.com/ussbs01.htm#thamotjc>

ACKNOWLEDGMENTS

Legends and myths inevitably surround stories of nations at war. This book is based on research of facts and accounts of politics and war and has had no interest in myth and legend.

Deep inside the National Library of Australia on Lake Burley Griffin in Canberra, just beyond the Asia collection reading room, there is a usually darkened hall of reference books, among which can be found 102 weighty volumes of the war history series of *Senshi Sosho* in Japanese; a veritable sleeping treasure.

Professor John J. Stephan, of Honolulu, advised that when seeking evidence of Japan's wartime intentions, *Senshi Sosho* was always a good starting point. He should know. John Stephan is the author of *Hawaii Under the Rising Sun* and he documented Japanese plans to invade Hawaii after the Pearl Harbor attack. Like the Japanese plans to invade Australia, the course of the war would intervene. I am appreciative of Professor Stephan's assistance during my research.

Senshi Sosho was compiled by the Military History Department of the National Institute for Defense Studies in Tokyo, which is the main policy arm of Japan's Ministry of Defense. I am grateful for being able to include these references and to the officers of the National Library's Asia collection, especially Mayumi Shinozaki, Chikako Murata and Yumiko Clifton. The *Senshi Sosho* volumes were compiled between 1966 and 1980. One of *Senshi Sosho's* senior editors and contributors was Sadatoshi Tomioka, the former captain and later rear admiral who, as a war planner in the Imperial Navy's General Staff, was one of the leading advocates of an invasion of Australia in 1942.

Tomioka is prominent in this narrative and I also draw briefly from his own work, *Kaisen to shusen: Hito to kiko to keikaku (The opening and closing of the Pacific war: the people, the mechanisms and the planning)* for which I am grateful.

Valuable documents of great assistance were the Papers of Gordon W. Prange at the University of Maryland Libraries. Prange was chief of General Douglas MacArthur's large historical staff section in Tokyo between 1946 and 1951. Professor Prange, as he was later, became known for his major books on the Pacific war. He died in 1980, but his papers left a treasure trove of material, including interviews and copies of US interrogations with almost all of the surviving Japanese generals and admirals of note in the war. Prange told Tomioka in a letter on 28 May 1955: 'I consider you the ultimate authority on all questions affecting the Operations Section of the Naval General Staff...' Prange left the transcripts of at least 28 separate interviews with Tomioka together with statements by the war planner on many issues, including his proposal that Japan should invade Australia.

Donald M. Goldstein, or 'Goldie' as he has become known, and Katherine V. Dillon co-authored with Prange the famous landmark book on Pearl Harbor, *At Dawn We Slept*. Goldstein was a close associate of Prange. Goldstein served for 22 years as a US Air Force officer. He wrote many of his own acclaimed war histories and at time of writing was a Professor of Public and International Affairs at the Graduate School of Public and International Affairs at the University of Pittsburgh. I am indebted to Professor Goldstein for his friendly assistance and access to his archives, including historic photographs, in the Prange Collection at the University of Pittsburgh.

Professor Goldstein, along with Katherine Dillon, edited the remarkable record *Fading Victory, The Diaries of Admiral Matome Ugaki, 1941–1945*, and I am grateful to Professor Goldstein and the book's publisher, the University of Pittsburgh Press, for permission to quote extensively from this valuable historical record of the Imperial Navy at war. Among other things, the diaries of Ugaki – Admiral Yamamoto's chief of staff – provided an insight into Combined Fleet and Naval General Staff thinking about the possibility of invading Australia, Hawaii and other places in the so-called 'second stage' operations. The diaries also expose details of Ugaki's fascination with, if not hero worship of, the young men pressed in to duty on midget submarines, including those boys who perished at Sydney.

A particular thrill for one who gets joy from musty archives was the discovery of additional pages of Admiral Ugaki's diary commentary on the midget submariners who died in the attack on Sydney, which had not been published in *Fading Victory* or elsewhere before this. ('Although they claimed that our attack was unsuccessful ... their souls could rest free from anxiety for having done so.') Marianne Kasica, Archives of Industrial Society, the University of Pittsburgh, is to be thanked for her willing assistance. Thanks also must go to Jennie A. Levine who, as the then curator of Historical Manuscripts at the C. Hornbake Library, at the University of Maryland Libraries, similarly was extremely helpful, as was the curator of the Prange Collection, Eiko Sakaguchi.

Baron Tomioka's nemesis who opposed an invasion of Australia, Colonel Takushiro Hattori, head of the Operations section of Army General Staff and one-time private secretary to Prime Minister Tojo, like Tomioka, took to writing war history after Japan's conflict. His great tome originally published in 1953, *Dai Toa Senso Zenshi (The Complete History of the Great East Asia War)* was translated by the US military in Tokyo and was provided to me by the University of Maryland Libraries.

Other sources of great interest on the subject of the invasion threat to Australia included the work of the wartime conference minute-taker General Hajime Sugiyama in his *Sugiyama Memo*, and the *Reports of General MacArthur*, compiled by General Charles Willoughby in two volumes published by the US Department of the Army in four large books in 1950. My regards to James W. Zobel of the MacArthur Memorial for his assistance in obtaining extract pages and charts from Willoughby's *Reports*. Thanks also to the Harry S. Truman Library, Independence, Missouri, the National Archives and Record Administration and the Franklin D. Roosevelt Library, Hyde Park, New York, for the provision of wartime archives.

American author of *Hirohito and the Making of Modern Japan*, Professor Herbert P. Bix, readily allowed me to quote from his Pulitzer Prize winning work and also volunteered his agreement about the crucial behaviour of radical 'middle echelon' naval officers who so pressured their superiors, a role seemingly far above their station. Bix was cautious on the general subject, venturing to me: 'Although a ground invasion [of Australia] was not in the short-term offing, middle echelon officers probably "contemplated" landings if the grand plan had unfolded smoothly'. Bix credits John J. Stephan with being the first to unearth the significance of the behaviour of these middle-echelon officers in the Imperial Navy.

The Swiss scholar on Japan's wartime history, the late Henry P. Frei, wrote a fine academic work, *Japan's Southward Advance and Australia* (University of Hawaii Press) in 1991. As part of a history ranging from the sixteenth century to World War II, the book tells the story of short-lived Imperial Navy proposals for invading Australia and the army's implacable opposition. This is a significant work from which I quote briefly, yet, in the margins, I do question a few of Frei's observations, including commentary on Admiral Yamamoto opposing invasion of Australia. This opposition indeed might have come later, when the commander-in-chief turned his attention elsewhere, but there is some indication of his early support for the proposition. Frei says 'middle-echelonists' within Combined Fleet submitted a plan at the end of January 1942 to Naval General Staff which insisted, among other things, that 'Port Darwin must be taken.'

Frei notes that Combined Fleet staff planners and Yamamoto did not always see 'eye to eye'. However, other commentators, me included, find difficulty in reaching Frei's conclusion that Yamamoto was solidly against invasion of Australia and that his juniors went to General Staff with a plan – behind Yamamoto's back, virtually – involving the capture of Darwin. Moreover, as Frei says, Combined Fleet and General Staff got together on 24 February 1942 and strongly pressed for an invasion of Australia. Would they do this behind Yamamoto's back? It is doubtful. This was not their *modus operandi*. Remember, these people lived and worked on the same flagship, which for the most part was not overly pressed with combat duties. The technique of the hot-blooded staff officers was to exert considerable influence and pressure for their radical plans, not to outwit their much-loved commander-in-chief. Certainly Yamamoto had other priorities as time went on and he turned his attention towards Midway and the much sought-after 'definitive battle' with the US Pacific fleet. But even at that stage in early May 1942, Admiral Ugaki aboard the *Yamato* and his planners were openly debating offensives beyond Midway and Hawaii, even the carrier bombing of Sydney. Yamamoto was aboard the *Yamato* at that time and there is no record of him interfering in this debate or opposing it.

Frei's contention that Combined Fleet did not 'look south' is also at odds with the remarks of people such as Captain Mitsuo Fuchida, Yamamoto's wing commander over Pearl Harbor, who wrote: 'The Hashirajima headquarters continued to focus its attention exclusively on the southern area.' As Fuchida said, 'Combined Fleet, rather than the Naval General Staff, often played the dominant role in shaping fleet strategy.'

On the issue of timing and how it affects perceptions, Frei's correct reporting of General Tojo's opposition to an invasion of

Australia, which is clearly recorded at liaison conferences, should also be read in conjunction with Tojo's earlier quoted remarks to Hirohito's uncle, Field Marshal Prince Naruhiko Higashikuni, recorded in Higashikuni's *Ichi-kozoku no Senso Nikki, (War Diary by an Imperial Family Member)*: 'I think we will have few problems occupying not only Java and Sumatra but also Australia if things go on like this.'

Further, I am not sure if Frei appreciated the full extent of influence and power the middle echelon officers exerted in thrusting Japan southward, as emphasised by many expert naval historians. Frei's accurate observations about their involvement in proposals to invade Australia nevertheless regrettably have allowed a few Australian historians and history lecturers blithely to dismiss Japanese invasion proposals for Australia as nothing more than the petty work of 'a few middle echelon officers', which considerably misunderstands and underrates their role and the case. I also question Frei's contention that there was no intention of a 'resources grab' in plans to invade Australia when Tomioka, in particular, says it was part of the strategic mix.

In this research project I came to learn that you must expect the unexpected and the unimagined. Professor Hiromi Tanaka, who teaches tomorrow's Japanese officers at the National Defense Academy at Yokosuka overlooking Tokyo Bay, in answers of some passion, provided me with a strong insight into the Imperial Japanese Navy and its shortcomings. He was unequivocal about the intentions of Japanese naval officers to invade Australia and set their motives, or lack of them, in unambiguous language, helping me to understand the illogicality and irrationality of the Imperial Navy. The ideals of Japan's future navy and its grasp on security blended with human values are in good hands if it adheres to the advice of Hiromi Tanaka.

Thanks also to Bill Gordon, of Cromwell, Connecticut, for assistance with information on the midget submarine base near Kure, and Tony Tully of the excellent combinedfleet.com site for valuable information on the Imperial Navy.

ACKNOWLEDGMENTS

In four research visits to Japan since 2002 I have had the pleasure of visiting an old friend, Toshiro Takeuchi, owner of the Hotel Ichibo-kaku perched on the hill overlooking the bay of Sagami and the Izu peninsula at beautiful Manazuru. He was both friend and neighbour to the first Japanese ambassador to Australia, Tatsuo Kawai, until Kawai's death in 1966. Tak-san, a humble foot soldier who served in Manchuria and later became world president of the YMCA, brings to life the character of Kawai, the diplomat's love of Australia and John Curtin and events in wartime Japan. He still grieves for his many young classmates killed in the war. I will never forget sitting with Tak over sake at our first meeting in 2002 and asking, ever hopefully: 'You can't remember whether he spoke about Prime Minister John Curtin?' And Tak replied, setting me back: 'He mentioned that. As he was a personal friend, above the official line . . .' and then a host of stories of Curtin and Kawai tumbled out. Neither will I forget my first visit during a storm to Kawai's exquisite little Japanese villa house perched on a hilltop, behind Tak's inn. Toshiro Takeuchi is generous not only with his time and hospitality, but also his precious memories.

Masumi Kawai has generously provided me with the same kind hospitality, but also the valuable writings, documents and photographs of his father, Tatsuo, copies of which are now in a collection at the John Curtin Prime Ministerial Library at Curtin University, Perth. Masumi Kawai knows Australia well; having formerly been Mitsui Australia's mining chief and a regular visitor to the Curtin family house at Cottesloe, Perth, when John Curtin's widow, Elsie was still alive, a woman he remembers with great affection.

On my last visit to Japan I was in good company with friend Phua Tin Tua (Willie) and professional translator and friend Kyal Hill, both of whom made travel through the bay of Hiroshima on the Inland Sea, even in summer heatwave conditions, pleasant and informative. Professor Takeshi Chida, chief editor of the Kure City historical section, was a big-hearted host and guide with a great knowledge of the region and of Australia's occupation there after the war. He introduced me to Kazushige Todaka, director of the Kure Maritime Museum, also an expert on Japan's naval history, especially the super battleship *Yamato*. Meeting a very active Susumu Ito, the pilot who flew over wartime Sydney Harbour and who stood on the deck of a submarine while it shelled Newcastle, was a very special occasion. It was enlightening to see Ito's confident, forthright character of old emerge as he spoke of his past.

Photojournalist Rob Gilhooly of Tokyo was of great assistance in the production of this book with interviews conducted in Japanese, information, translations and photographs, both contemporary and archival.

In Australia, my thanks go especially to Professor Alan Rix, of the University of Queensland, who, with his extensive knowledge of Japan, has long been a sounding board and a source of worthy advice. The director of the Historical Publications and Information section of the Department of Foreign Affairs and Trade in Canberra, Dr David Lee, too has always been available with support and encouragement.

I have deep gratitude to the John Curtin Prime Ministerial Library at Curtin University in Perth, especially director Imogen Garner, manager Lesley Wallace and David Wylie, who have been supportive over the research life of two books with their ongoing assistance in all matters pertaining to John Curtin. The library's extensive electronic research archive has been a boon for those researching the former prime minister and the era.

I am also appreciative of the Australian War Memorial in Canberra and its officers, whose considerable archives include a wealth of highly valuable material on Australia's wartime history. In particular, the AWM was able to supply the detailed eyewitness accounts of those involved in the midget submarine attacks on Sydney Harbour which began on the night of 31 May 1942. The AWM is also a valuable source of excellent photographs. Special thanks to senior historian Dr Steven Bullard.

No book on Australia's history can be written without access to the archival riches in the National Archives of Australia, with its head office and main reading room in Canberra, and offices in all Australian capitals. Over some six years, I have visited these reading rooms and accessed countless files and corresponded with the NAA with mostly agreeable results.

The former Consul-General of Japan in Brisbane, Hajime Nishiyama, has been most supportive of my research and I have welcomed my discussions and time with him.

My appreciation also to noted historians Professor David Day and Professor David Horner for their insights and for permission to quote from their works.

Memories of families in wartime in Australia, supplementing recorded oral histories, were given freely, including those from Helen Ekin, Walter Hamilton, Tim Harlock, John Hitchcock, Jim Mair, Ian Spring, Joy Wurth and Alan Rix.

I thank my friend Norm McCormick, who has an insightful view of World War II, Bob Duncan for his interest and encouragement, Vince Madden for his friendship and in joining me on our visit to the ruins of Rabaul, and the members of the H&HTP historical society who have suffered my work for so long.

My agent, Trish Lake at Freshwater Pictures, remains forever supportive. At Pan Macmillan, thanks to Tom Gilliatt, Sarina Rowell and Mary Verney. Editor Sybil Nolan had a sometimes testy author with whom to work but she improved the end product with considerable professionalism.

To my good wife, Jenny; what can I say, but hearty and respectful thanks for suffering the writer – the loneliest profession in the world, at least until the study door opens.

And, finally, there was the naval lieutenant who guided us around the Etajima base in the summer of 2007. On showing us a midget ramming submarine with a bomb in the nose, he smiled and commented, 'Hundreds of these were built near the end of the war', adding compassionately, 'fortunately, none of them were used.'

INDEX

ABDA command 97, 121,
Abukuma 111,
Adelaide 125,
Agawa, Hiroyuki 73,
Age 253,
Akagi 40, 44, 49, 52, 91, 111, 211, 255–256,
Albany 184, 186,
Aleutians 165, 192, 196, 210–211,
Alexander, Joseph 44, 61, 67, 80, 82, 177–178, 189–190, 195, 196, 204, 221, 252, 266,
Allara 271,
Anami, Korechika 331,
Ambon 173, 355,
Anderson, Herbert 228–229,
Andrew, Reg 238–239,
Ariga, Kosaku 323,
Arizona 52,
Arnold, Dave 366,
Asada, Sadao 354,
Ashibe, Itsuo 38, 368–369,
Ashibe, Mamoru 38–39, 41, 192, 205, 208, 224, 229–233, 236, 237–238, 252, 259, 364–370,
Ashibe, Mikiyo 38–39, 205–206,
Atago 34, 93, 94, 247,
Auchinleck, Claude 81,
Auckland 212,
Australia 200, 313–314,
Australia
    no invasion protagonists 3, 287, 373n,
    Japanese invasion discussion/ planning 5, 64–65, 69–70, 71, 72–74, 84–86, 87, 88, 94–95, 97, 103, 108–109, 111, 112, 123–129, 137, 149, 152–159, 161–170, 192, 193, 194, 270, 340, 347, 355, 359–363, 398n,
    occupation in Kure area 7, 8, 350–352,
    cuts to trade with Japan 10,
    Australian Imperial Force (AIF) 17, 19, 57–58, 79–82, 96, 130, 131, 137–138, 139–140, 147, 152, 171,

1942

180–181, 187, 234, 245, 250, 278, 283, 291, 302,
defence assessments of Japanese danger 19, 22, 33, 58–59, 67–68, 74, 79–80, 82, 90, 105, 107, 113, 121, 146–147, 148–152, 171, 172, 173–175,183, 184, 185–186, 187, 189, 270, 283, 303,
Australian Labor Party (ALP) 19, 20, 32, 81, 302,
preoccupied with war elsewhere 19, 22, 57–58, 80, 82, 144, 145, 147,
public threats from Japan to Australia 19, 91, 92, 94, 122, 123, 135–136, 158–159, 209–210, 257–258,
Australian concern about Japanese invasion 19, 21, 22, 33, 58, 66, 67–68, 74, 79–80, 90–92, 96, 105,107, 113–114, 129, 132, 134, 140, 141, 142, 146–147, 148–152, 154, 171–173, 183–184, 185–186, 196, 212, 249
defence forces' unpreparedness 22, 33,57–58, 82, 96, 97, 104–105, 106, 110, 120, 130, 133, 143, 146, 149–150, 154, 172, 173–175, 179, 181, 185–186, 187, 202, 203, 217, 225,250, 270, 271, 283, 289, 303,
Royal Australian Navy 28, 104, 105, 141, 151, 179, 181, 200, 217, 218, 223–246, 254, 267, 270, 272, 274, 289–290, 292, 294, 295, 313–314, 347, 368–369,
intelligence and propaganda 30, 105, 129, 140, 195–196, 292–295, 243, 294–297, 354–355,
relations with Britain 31, 32, 66, 79–83, 110, 130, 137–138, 187, 189–190, 212–213, 245–246, 268, 270–271,
Thailand invasion accusations 45,

War Cabinet 53, 59, 96, 113, 130, 146, 149, 176, 179, 281,
lax public attitude despite Japan's threat 61–62, 74–75, 177, 188, 264,
blackouts/brownouts 62, 135, 215, 216,
US reinforcements 62, 83, 95, 121, 143, 146, 152, 176, 201,
evacuations of civilians and industry 62, 66, 113, 132,
Australian Parliament 66, 110, 196–197, 198, 204, 252, 324, 326,
industrial disputes and lost production 66, 96, 176–177, 189, 204, 259–260,
morale 66–68, 171–172, 177, 178, 181, 188–189, 259, 264,
censorship 67, 234, 243–245,
Churchill's dismissal of invasion in force 79–83,
Japanese intelligence 89, 274, 276–277, 278,
Royal Australian Air Force 90–91, 105–106, 131, 141, 142, 174–175, 181, 185–186, 254, 255, 267, 279, 296–297,
Advisory War Council 96, 110, 113, 131, 149, 187, 267–268, 281,
British concern about Japanese invasion of Australia (or part) 98–99, 148, 183–184,
US concern about Japanese invasion of Australia 100, 121, 143–144, 172–173, 185–186, 201, 285–286, 301, 325–326, 352–353, 354, 387–388,
Citizen Military Forces (CMF- Australia's militia) 106, 154, 250, 270, 281–283, 286,
Japanese atrocities on Australians 106–107, 115, 125, 178, 178, 194–195, 286,

446

INDEX

Australian cities prepare for war 113–114,
war fears in Canberra 114, 177,
Australians captured in Singapore 115, 195,
Australian War Memorial, Canberra 120, 297, 357,
Battle for Australia 122,
Yamashita's invasion plan 123–125,
return of servicemen from overseas 130, 131, 137–138, 140, 147, 148, 245, 291, 302,
defence low on US priority list 140,
base for counteroffensive 151, 245–246,
Hirohito postpones invasion proposal 169,
defeatism and 'make peace' movement 171, 172, 177–178, 265,
government war spending 176,
white Australia policy 176, 178,
scorched earth policy 179–180, 181–182,
Blamey on W.A. invasion 183–184, 186,
northern Australia to 'yield to Japanese' 186,
rationing, panic shopping 204,
Japanese attacks on Australian shipping 205, 218, 253–255, 259, 267, 269–272,
censorship 241–242,
prime minister's war conference 244,
funeral service for Japanese 252, 274, 290, 293, 294, 347,
conscripts sent overseas 299–300,
discovery of midget M-24 off Sydney 366–370,
war dead 370–371,
Ayatozan Maru 285,
Azuma 12,

Baggott, Paul 366,
Bali 149,
Balmoral, Sydney 235,
Ban, Iwao 208,
Ban, Katsuhisa 37–38, 41, 192, 205–208, 222, 226, 229–233, 236, 237–238, 242, 259, 259, 364, 367–370,
Ban, Kazutomo 37–38, 369,
Bangkok 45,
Barwon 254,
Batavia 89,
Bateman's Bay 272,
Beasley, Jack 176, 178,
Bellevue Hill, Sydney 262, 264,
Bennett, Gordon 171,
Bergamini, David 125,
Bingera 229–231, 254,
Bismarck archipelago 95, 109, 112, 196,
Bix, Herbert P. 98,
Black, Patricia 235,
Blamey, Thomas 81, 180, 184–185, 186, 282–283, 298, 304, 342,
Bode, H.D., 227,
Bondi, Sydney 62, 234, 261–262, 292, 290,
Bora Bora 144,
Borneo 44, 57, 83, 90, 122, 173,
Boote, Henry 147,
Bougainville 291, 304–306, 307, 309, 310,
Bowden, Vivian 80, 115.
Brain, Lester 142–143,
Brett, George H. 172, 185–186, 187, 221,
Brisbane 99, 107, 124, 127, 173, 174, 186, 255, 294, 325, 340,
Brisbane Line controversy 107–108, 303–304, 388–389n,
Britain
    trains Japanese navy 6, 62,
    Royal Navy 6, 11, 55, 98, 121,122, 151–152, 189, 193, 210, 219, 227, 242, 243, 326,
    War with Japan 16, 22, 29, 31, 32, 45, 52, 58, 60, 73, 79, 80–82, 87, 96,

110–111, 113, 120, 122, 131, 138,
144, 154, 157, 163, 167, 175, 208,
210, 285, 337, 351,
  British Army 19, 97, 102, 121, 178,
  182, 190,
    Relations with Australia 21, 31,
    32, 66, 79–82, 137–138, 189–190,
    212–213, 245–246, 270–271,
  British Empire 58, 85, 94, 154,
  158–159, 175, 246,
  British defence assessment of
  Australia 98–99, 183–184, 270–271,
  rules out Japanese invasion of
  Australia 213,
Broome, 142–143, 173,
Bruce, Stanley 284,
Bullard, Bill 240–241,
Bullard, Steven 357,
Buna 279, 286–287, 300–301,
Burma 5, 34, 103, 121, 123, 124, 126, 131,
136–139, 140, 145, 150, 169, 173, 183,
302, 317,
Burnett, Charles 60, 149,
Button, C.N. 177,

California 52,
Canada 105, 179,
Canberra 230, 235, 255, 299,
Canberra 58, 66, 96, 114, 135, 177, 181,
188, 189, 204, 212, 221, 244, 266, 325,
Cape Moreton 255,
Cape of Good Hope 182, 190,
Cape York Peninsula 59, 100, 270,
Cargill, James 225–226,
Caroline islands 84, 268,
Carruthers, Steven 238,
Celebes 83, 90, 122, 145, 173,
Centaur 354,
Ceylon 5, 64, 89, 97, 136, 137, 138, 157,
158, 167, 196, 201,
Chiang Kai-shek 71,
Chicago 200, 217–218, 227, 229–231,

233–236, 242, 299,
Chihaya, Masataka 88,
Chikuma 111,
China 10, 28, 30, 31, 34, 38, 52, 57, 63, 95,
103, 126, 139, 153, 157, 169, 183, 194,
330, 336, 340, 241,
Chiyoda 42, 101, 192, 206,
Chuman, Kenshi 208, 223–225–228, 273,
Churchill, Winston
  Japanese army/navy heritage 6,
  Britain to 'let Thailand rip' 44.
  situation 'not hopeless' 55.
  Australians ill advised and panicky
  60,
  plans limited defence of Singapore
  79,
  Australians not felt 'weight of war',
  80–81,
  Australia lacking proportion 82,
  Australians 'jumpy' about invasion
  83,
  Roosevelt's visitor 83,
  US troops for Australia 83,
  doubts mass invasion of Australia 98,
  silence on Darwin invasion forecast
  100,
  Curtin demands troops home 130,
  131, 137–138,
  diverts Australians to Burma
  137–139,
  qualified support if Australia invaded
  182,
  opposes Australian offensive proposal
  187,
  delays in suggested reinforcements
  190,
  Magic intercepts on India invasion
  195,
  disagreements with Curtin 79–81,
  137–138, 146–147, 268, 271, 278,
  focus on beating Germany 212–213,
  282,

INDEX

no immediate danger 284,
City of Canterbury 277–278,
Clark, F. S. 172,
Coast Farmer 270,
Colvin, Ragner 60,
Combined Fleet (see Imperial Navy),
Cooktown 354,
Coolana 271,
Coote, Ray 240–241,
Coral Sea 144, 194, 196, 200, 216, 354,
Coral Sea battle 199–202, 209–210, 221, 227, 250, 256, 258, 267–268, 269, 301, 356, 357,
Corser, Bernard 249,
Cottesloe 20, 31, 32, 104, 147,
Cox, William 296–297,
Craig-y-Mor 89,
Crace, John 200,
Cremorne, Sydney 230,
Crete 19, 79,
Cronulla, Sydney 233,
Curtin, Elsie (wife) 20, 147, 302, 326,
Curtin, Elsie (daughter) 31–32, 147, 177, 302, 325,
Curtin, John Francis (son) 20, 302, 325,
Curtin, John
    background, becomes prime minister 20, 21, 60,
    on British/US priorities 21,
    mood swings 21, 147,
    health 20–21, 147, 302, 314, 325,
    early concerns about invasion 21, 32, 146, 312,
    Kawai secret meetings 31, 33,
    home at Cottesloe 31, 32, 104,
    appeasement 32,
    Kawai visits Cottesloe home 32,
    Kawai warns of war 33,
    Thailand attack expected 44,
    seeks peace talks with Japan to continue 44,
    Japan at war, 'our darkest hour' 53,
    wartime Japanese invasion concerns 58, 66, 74–75, 128, 146–147, 283,
    secret press briefings 60–61,
    warning to Japan 66,
    on industrial problems 66,
    on Singapore 79,
    'inexcusable betrayal' 79–80,
    'looks to America' 80–81, 246,
    9th Division return debate 81, 130, 137–138, 140, 148, 245, 291, 302,
    fall of Rabaul 92,
    troops drilling with broomsticks 104,
    Battle for Australia statement 121–122,
    diversion of troops to Australia 130, 131, 137–138, 245, 291, 302,
    announces first Darwin attack 135,
    refuses troops for Burma 137–138,
    enemy comes ever nearer 143,
    anger at Allies' treatment of Australia 79–80, 146–147, 187, 268, 271, 283,
    Gowrie's friendship 147–148,
    vividly imagines Japanese takeover 177, 178, 179,
    scorched earth policy 178–180,
    Australia 'last bastion' 181,
    bitter, seeks major offensive 187,
    announces Coral Sea battle 198,
    invasion menace capable hourly 199,
    on strikers 204,
    hears of US-Britain's 'beat Hitler first' 212–213, 283,
    rebuked by MacArthur on relationship 244–246,
    hears of Midway battle 247–248,
    defies enemy to land large force 250,
    tells press about secret intercepts 252,
    praised by Lord Gowrie to King 265,
    Midway removes some danger 266,
    Japanese shelling 'childish' 266,
    criticises Churchill and Roosevelt 268,

Australia could still be lost 269,
critical of British in Pacific 271,
Kawai wishes Curtin a brave fight 278,
tells Roosevelt of Japanese invasion threat 283,
Moresby secure 288,
deep gratitude and thanksgiving 301,
conscripts overseas 301–302,
Kamikaze attack 313–314,
heart attack 314,
grim days of 1942 reversed 324,
dies 325,
love of Elsie 326,

Damai, Eric 285–286,
Darwin 58, 59, 69, 88, 89, 90, 96, 97, 98, 100–101, 105, 108, 110, 112, 125, 130, 131, 150–151, 154, 173, 180, 182, 183, 186, 289, 355,
Darwin, air raids 98, 99, 109, 111, 131–136, 140–141, 256, 302, 355, 370,
Darwin, invasion scenarios 69, 97–100,108–109, 125, 126,169, 173, 185, 304, 340, 347, 357,
Davao 93,
Dechaineaux, E.F. 313,
Dickover, Earle R. 175,
Diego Suarez 218–219, 293,
Dili 108, 136,
diplomacy, East Indies 10, 28, 32, 34, 53, 59, 64.
diplomacy, Japan-US pre-war 10, 17, 27, 29, 45.
Doyle, Horrie 223–226, 228, 229, 239,
Drakeford, Arthur 281,
Dubinsky, Stephen 296–297,
Dulhunty, Phil 216–217,
Dull, Paul S. 102–103, 355,
Durnford, John 60,
Durreenbee 271–272,

East Indies (Dutch, now Indonesia) 10, 28, 32, 34, 53, 59, 64, 80, 90, 91, 98, 100, 112, 122, 123, 131, 138, 141, 142, 149, 150, 153,174, 347,
Echunga 255,
Eden 271,
Eisenhower, Dwight D., 139–140,
Elizabeth Bay, Sydney 226,
Elkin, A.P. 66–67, 171–172,
Ellice islands 144,
Enola Gay 332,
Enterprise 77,
Etajima naval academy 2, 11, 23, 56, 311, 335, 338, 350–353,
Evatt, Herbert 21, 79, 80, 110, 148, 178, 181, 212–213, 274, 276,
Eyers, Harry 225–227,

Fadden, Arthur 110, 326,
FELO intelligence group 294–297,
Fiji 70, 85, 92, 97, 99, 100, 103, 108, 127, 137, 143, 151, 157, 158, 164, 171, 173, 184, 192, 194, 197, 214, 347, 356,
Finschhafen 168,
Forde, Frank 67, 96, 104–105, 107, 110, 130, 131, 259, 281,
Formosa (Taiwan) 312, 321,
Fort Dennison, Sydney 230,
Fort Scratchley, Newcastle 263–264,
Frei, Henry 126, 398n
Fremantle 145, 150, 174, 180, 183, 184, 186, 205,
Fuchida, Mitsuo 48–49, 63, 91, 111–113, 134, 351, 354,
Fujii, Shigeru 170,
Fujita, Nobuo 130,
Fukudome, Shigeru 17, 24, 25, 54, 70, 137, 152, 161, 267,

Gabo island 254,
Guadalcanal 296–297, 298,
Gauss, Clarence E. 58,

Germany 6, 18, 19, 21, 25, 29, 45, 81, 84, 89, 94, 95, 97, 100, 139, 162, 196, 201, 212, 262, 284, 317, 359,
George S. Livanos 269–270,
George VI 188–189, 228, 238, 260, 264–265,
Gerow, Leonard T. 90–91,
Gona 279, 285–286, 301,
Gowrie, Alexander 147–148, 188, 228, 238, 260, 264–265,
Gowrie, Zara 238, 264,
Greater East Asia Co-prosperity Sphere 109, 122, 123, 136, 157, 162, 183, 265–266, 342, 348, 349, 350,
Greece 19, 79,
Gregory, Mackenzie 230, 235–236, 406n,
Grew, Joseph C. 29,
Guadalcanal 193, 298–299, 300, 310,
Guam 52, 95, 316,
Guatemala 267,

Haddelsey, L 254,
Haguro 326,
Hainan 34, 157,
Hamilton, Joan and family 263,
Hara, Yoshimichi 28,
Haruna 34, 93, 299, 329, 330,
Hashimoto, Mochitsura 316,
Hashirajima, island and anchorage 1–8, 9, 14, 23, 26, 33, 34, 40, 52, 55, 63, 69, 74, 76, 84, 111, 116, 136,160, 163, 190, 209, 211, 220, 256, 267, 299, 306, 308, 330, 332, 351, 356, 360,
Hashida, Sei 88–89,
Hasluck, Paul 114, 132,
Hattori, Takushiro 45, 103,125, 126, 128–129, 169–170,
Hattori, Tsuneo 31,
Hawaii 39, 44, 49–51, 56, 71, 101, 144, 155, 247, 248, 303,
Hawaii (invasion scenario) 64–65, 69–70, 84, 86, 97, 102, 110, 127, 137, 153, 162, 167, 197, 198, 254,

Hay, Tony 366, 367,
Hayashi, Toshimasa 332–333,
Hedinger, Hans 272, 274,
Hendrie, Phil 363,
Hermes 189,
Hiei 111,
Higashikuni, Naruhiko 71, 343,
Hiraide, Hideo 257–358,
Hiroshima bay and city, 2, 6–9, 11, 69, 116, 306, 329, 334, 335, 350,
Hirohito 13, 24, 27–29, 45, 47, 52, 86, 87, 98, 168–169, 209, 239, 258–259, 265, 293, 311, 317, 323, 327, 336–337, 341, 348, 357, 362,
Hiryu 44, 111, 136, 211, 255–257,
Hisamatsu, Daimyo 53.
Hitchcock, Catherine and family 264,
Hitler, Adolf 100, 124, 128, 283, 324, 359,
Hobart 200,
Holbrook 96,
Home Security Dept. 129,
Hong Kong 15, 52, 74, 90, 122, 178,
Hopkins, Harry 121,
Hori, Tomokazu 123,
Horii, Tomitaro 281,
Horner, David 354,
Hosho 247,
Houston 142,
Hughes, Richard 71–72, 343, 418n,
Hughes, William 81,
Hyuga 330,

Imperial General Headquarters 87, 91–92, 97, 128, 168, 200, 266, 282, 357,
Imperial Army
    trained by Germany 6,
    originally less moderate and cautious than Navy 6,
    Australia, early consideration 28, 29, 45, 359,
    army-navy disagreements 70–71, 87–88, 89, 90, 103, 108–109, 111–112, 127, 128–129, 152–159,

161–170, 192–194, 299–300, 307, 328, 361–362,
General Staff opposes Hawaii invasion 70–71, 86,
seeks unassailable position 86,
opposes invasion of Australia 88, 108–109, 112, 126, 127, 128–129, 153–157, 161–170, 192,
Army ministry 88,
General Staff opposes capture of Darwin 108,
Yamashita's Australia invasion plan 123–126,
opposes Midway plan 193–194,
psychological warfare against Australia 213–214,
favours Port Moresby invasion 214, 270,
defeat in Kokoda campaign 287, 300–302,
against surrender 331,
Imperial Navy
Combined Fleet 4, 10, 12–18, 23, 24–26, 33–34, 35–40, 41–44, 47–52, 55, 62–65, 69–70, 72, 74, 75, 84, 93–95, 97, 98, 101, 102–103, 108–109, 111–113, 117, 126–127, 128–129, 136, 153, 163–171, 190–191, 192–194, 198–200, 208–210, 219–220, 246–247, 249–258, 266–267, 278, 290–291, 298, 300, 302–306, 308–311, 315–324, 328–329, 339, 354, 355–363,
Navy strength at start of war 5,
Navy life 5, 6, 26, 34, 117, 209, 299–300, 322, 335,
Australia invasion, discussion/planning 5, 64–65, 69–70, 72–74, 84–86, 87, 88, 95, 97, 103, 108–109, 125–129, 136, 149, 152–158, 161–170, 193, 256, 347, 359,
brutality towards subordinates 11,

Naval General Staff 12, 14, 16, 18, 24, 25, 53–55, 63, 65, 70, 72, 84, 85–86, 93, 97, 103, 108–109, 112, 119, 126, 149, 153, 157, 161–170, 192, 193, 194, 209, 258–259, 308, 309, 315–324, 330, 335, 338, 339, 340, 354, 358–363,
Naval Ministry 13, 26, 54, 88, 108, 111, 157, 161, 317, 319,
'decisive battle' at sea 15, 25, 64–65, 72, 102, 193, 300, 358,
middle echelon officers' freedom and power/*gekokujo* 16, 48, 63, 86, 102–103, 126, 354,
Midget submarines 35–39, 42–44, 49–51, 56, 75, 101, 160–161, 190–192, 201, 203–207, 214, 216–217, 219–243, 246–247, 249–251, 255–257, 271–277, 287–289, 290–292, 293, 316, 345, 361
midget submarine defects 50, 101, 160–161, 228,
Midway attack, first, 52.
Navy officers club, *Suikosha*, Tokyo 53, 110, 152,
battleships obsolete 117–118,
Onishi and Kamikaze 'special attack' forces 118,
Asia's liberation not an issue 122,
attacks on Australian shipping 205, 218, 253–255, 259, 267, 269–272,
fleet as at April 1945 317,
Toyoda and 'fight to glorious death' 320,
Yamato death toll 323,
Grand Naval Command 337,
end-of-war influence 339,
fleet strength after Midway 355,
I class large submarines:
I-10 219,
I-16 75,
I-21 77, 90, 214, 216, 222, 253, 261–264, 272,

INDEX

I-22 41, 43, 206, 222, 231, 232, 240, 251,
I-24 43, 49, 90, 206, 222, 235, 253, 259, 261–263, 272,
I-25 130,
I-27 206, 222, 253, 254, 272,
I-28 205, 206,
I-29 203, 205, 214, 220, 253, 255,
I-58 316,
I-121, 90,
I-123, 90,
Imperial Palace 27, 29, 86, 87, 169, 293, 317, 327, 346,
Inagaki, Kiyoshi 50–51, 56, 242,
India 5, 28, 45, 64–65, 73, 82, 83, 84, 89, 94, 123, 124, 128, 139, 145, 150, 154, 156,157, 167–168, 169, 183, 187, 195, 196, 201,
Indochina 10, 45, 93, 158,
Inoue, Hisashi 330,
Inoue, Shigeyoshi 16, 95, 354,
Iron Chieftain 254,
Iron Crown 255,
Ise 330,
Ishikawa, Shingo 16, 103, 109,
Ishino, Jikyo 192,
Italy 45, 95,
Ito, Seiichi 17, 54, 112, 165–166, 321–323,
Ito, Susumu 76–78, 216–217, 263–264, 291,
Iwakuni 2, 48, 76, 293, 332, 350,
Iwojima 316–317,

Jamieson, Ernie 229–231, 254,
Japan
    oil shortage 3, 16, 32, 304, 328,
    Japanese discussion or planning on attacks and invading Australia 5, 28, 64–65, 69–70, 71, 72–74, 84–86, 87, 88, 91–92, 94–95, 97, 103, 108–109, 111, 112, 123–126, 127–129, 137,152–157, 161–170, 192–194, 197–198, 254, 270, 339, 341–343, 349, 359–363,
    economic sanctions by West 10, 37,
    encirclement by West 19, 21,
    warns Australia 19, 91, 92, 122, 123, 135–136, 158–159, 208, 255–256, 258,
    peace 'conversations' with US 24,
    Imperial conferences (emperor, government, army, navy) 27, 86–88, 169,
    Government crippled by armed forces 29,
    liaison and communications conferences (government, army, navy) 10–11, 29, 83, 86–88, 152–158, 161–168,
    declares war 52,
    buoyant public morale 57,
    neutrality pact with Russia 71,
    National Diet (parliament) 69, 73, 75, 91, 122, 209, 213,
    intelligence efforts against Australia 31, 88–89, 276–278,
    exploits Australia-Britain relationship 31, 32, 95–96, 110–111, 154, 278,
    atrocities by armed forces 106, 107, 115, 125, 178, 194–195, 286, 340, 343, 349,
    cherry blossom symbols of youthful sacrifice 118,
    threats and propaganda against Australia 91, 94, 122, 123, 135–136, 158–159, 209–210, 257–258, 278, 289,
    continuous raids on Darwin 135–140,
    coal production 156,
    iron ore mining/steel production 157–158,
    shipping shortages 170,
    claims great victory in Coral Sea 199,
    attacks on Australian shipping 205, 218, 253–255, 259, 267, 269–272,

mid-1942 empire and losses 265–266,
celebrates first six months of war 266,
starvation in Kokoda campaign 282,
praise for RAN over submariners 289–290, 293, 294,
food shortages, mass bombings 316–319, 324, 327,
Supreme Council for the Direction of War 328, 330,
armed forces demand fight to death 331,
atomic bombs on Hiroshima and Nagasaki 331–334,
Hirohito's surrender broadcast 336–337,
Self-Defense force 343–344, 350–352, 353, 357, 368,
war dead 350, 370,
Java 71, 93, 97, 99, 105, 109, 120, 121, 136, 141–142, 145, 149, 173, 177, 185, 188, 288, 343,
Jeffery, Mike 201–202,
Jervis Bay 267, 269, 270,
Johore Bahru 101–102,
Joyce, Gladys 131, 147,

Kaiten human torpedo 37, 119, 120, 315–316, 346, 353,
Kaga 44, 91, 111, 211, 255,
Kaku, Tomeo 257,
Kamakura Maru 278, 290–291,
Kamikaze 2, 118, 312–314, 317, 321, 322, 324, 334–335, 336, 337–338, 352–353,
Kanji, Matsumura 264,
Kashima 95,
Kavieng 92, 95, 310,
Kawai, Chiyoko 47, 210,
Kawai, Tatsuo 22, 30–31, 33, 89, 115, 157–158, 273–278, 289–291, 293–294, 349, 375n, 396n,
Kawai, Tatsuo, Melbourne residence *Carn Brea* 30–31, 273, 275–376,

Kaya, Okinobu 155, 167,
Kenney, George C. 356,
Keogh, Gerard 296–297,
Kerns, Greg 366,
Kido, Koichi 27, 258–259,
King, Earnest J. 92, 143–145, 201,
Kings Cross, Sydney 262,
Kinoshita, Toshiko 191,
Kirishima 111,
Kirribilli, Sydney 238, 264,
Kodama, Yoshio 339,
Koepang 97, 108, 136, 141,
Koiso, Kuniaki 324,
Koizumi, Junichiro 350,
Kokoda campaign 140, 200, 270, 279–284, 285–288, 300, 301, 302, 342, 355, 412n,
Komatsu, Teruhisa 190,
Kondo, Nobutake 34, 87–88, 93–95, 246–247,
Kongo 34, 93, 299,
Korean 'comfort women' 349,
Kormoran 104.
Koryu (submarines) 334,
Kota Bharu 48,
Kotani, Etsuo 111,
Kozu, Naoji 315–316,
Kuantan 55,
Kurahashijima 35,
Kuroshima, Kameto 9, 11–18, 23–24, 70, 102, 164, 192–193, 374n,
Kurozumi, Seishi 278,
Kure, Australian occupation 6, 7, 8, 351–352,
Kure, port, arsenal, industrial centre 2, 8, 9, 34–37, 40–42, 75, 116, 118–120, 207, 210, 239, 308, 315, 317–318, 321, 332, 334, 337, 350, 351, 370,
Kure City Naval History and Science Museum (Yamato museum) 119–120,
Kusaka, Jinichi 307,
Kuttabul 231–233, 240–242, 252, 365, 368, 369,

INDEX

Lae 97, 168, 296, 298, 308,
Lamon Bay 93,
Latham, John 394n
Lauriana 233,
Lazzarini, H.P. 264,
Lee, Joseph 105,
Lee Kuan Yew 349,
LeMay, Curtis 310,
Lexington 200,
Leyte 312, 313, 317,
Libya 19, 145,
Lingayen Gulf 93,
Lithgow 58, 60, 189,
Lloyd, C.E.M. 282,
Lolita 226, 228,
London 81, 181, 183, 212, 270, 284,
Long, Gavin 187,
Long Reef, Sydney 366, 368,
Lourenco Marques 277–278, 289,
Lowe, Charles 134, 140–141,
Lundstrom, John B. 95, 121,
Lutzow, Friedrich 21,
Luzon 48, 93,

(Midget submarines.)
M-13 160–161,
M-22 222, 233–234, 239, 240–242,
M-24 206, 222, 226, 229, 252, 364–370,
M-27 223, 226–229, 230, 273,
MacArthur, Douglas
    arrival in Australia 140, 170, 180,
    'I shall return' 180,
    defence of Australia key problem 181,
    doubts 'full-scale', but not 'piecemeal', invasion 182,
    hopelessness of Australia 186, 398n,
    officers yield part of Australia 186,
    seeks US ships and planes 187,
    warns Roosevelt of Australian disaster 201,
    rebukes Curtin about US-Australia relationship 244–246,
    critical of Britain's effort for Australia 245,
    tells Curtin about Midway plan 247–248,
    Australia's defence assured 267, 268,
    offensives begin 269, 298,
    worried about Port Moresby 282,
    saving Australia from invasion 287–288,
    northern Australia menaced 303,
    defends Australia in New Guinea 304,
    lands at Leyte 312,
    Curtin preserved Australia from invasion 325–326, 355,
    at Japan's surrender 341,
    on Japan's intentions towards Australia 342,
Mackay 179,
Mackay, Iven 19–20, 67–68, 96–97, 107, 388–389n,
MacMahon Ball, W., 140,
Madagascar 36, 190, 218–219, 257–258, 286,
Maejima, Toshihade 39–40.
Magic/Ultra intelligence intercepts of Japanese traffic 46, 105, 145, 195–196, 247, 252, 255, 305,
Mair, Jim and family 234–235, 261, 292,
Makin, Norman 249, 252,
Malaya 15, 28, 34, 45, 52, 55–57, 67, 74, 79–80, 88, 90, 93, 96, 98, 99, 101, 121, 122, 124, 138, 141, 153, 171, 173, 195, 246, 327,
Malay barrier 59, 90, 100, 149,
Manazuru 293,
Manchuria 10, 109, 126, 157, 342,
Manila 44, 48, 62, 82, 93, 122, 123, 125, 156, 174, 180, 312,
Manly, Sydney 214–215, 238.
Manunda 134,
Marianas 310, 311,

455

Maroubra, Sydney, 130,
Marshall islands 329,
Marshall, George C. 187,
Maryland 52.
Masumoto, Shizuka 206,
Matsuo, Keiu 39–41, 75–76, 191, 222, 234, 239–242, 273, 347,
Matsuoka, Yosuke 73,
Maya 34,
McCarthy, Dudley 304,
Melbourne 30, 33, 58, 67, 75, 88, 89, 90, 96, 107, 105, 121, 125, 149, 173, 174, 177, 201, 204, 224, 243, 244, 250, 253, 267, 273, 276, 277, 314,
Menzies, Robert 19, 20, 31, 32, 60, 110, 151, 175, 302, 326,
Merimbula 271,
Middle East 19, 58, 80, 96, 130, 137, 139, 140, 145, 147, 149, 180, 181, 183, 245, 302,
Midget submarines (see Imperial Navy),
Midway preparation and battle, 52, 64, 85, 86, 126–127, 136, 137, 163–165, 171, 192–193, 197, 198, 210–211, 212, 220, 246–247, 249, 251–252, 255–257, 260, 266, 267, 268, 269, 301, 302, 355–356,
Millar, Malcolm 142–143,
Milne Bay 279, 283, 287, 342, 355,
Miners' Federation 259–260,
Missouri (surrender ceremony) 340–342,
Miwa, Yoshitake 85, 384n,
Morison, Samuel Eliot 144, 194,
Moruya 272,
Mosman, Sydney 230, 235, 238,
Muir, Dave 366,
Muirhead-Gould, Gerard 205, 226–229, 230, 232, 233, 235, 237, 242, 243, 249, 254, 273–274, 276, 289,
Musashi 299, 304, 308,
Muto, Akira 123, 152–156, 161, 396n,
Mutsu 247, 308–309,

Nagako (empress) 71,
Nagano, Osami 13, 17–18, 54–55, 112, 127, 168, 258–259, 311, 354,
Nagara 256,
Nagasaki 334, 335,
Nagato 1, 5, 6, 9, 12, 23–24, 34, 40, 41, 43, 47–49, 52, 54, 55, 69–70, 75–76, 84, 85, 101, 116, 117, 247, 308, 328–330,
Nagumo, Chuichi 24, 40, 48, 91, 109, 197, 211, 255, 375n,
Naruto 247,
National Defense Academy 87, 358,
National Institute for Defense Studies 359,
Nauru 176, 277,
Nelson, James 228,
Neptuna 134,
Nevada 52.
New Caledonia 59, 90, 91, 99, 100, 103, 108, 127, 137, 144, 150, 151, 157, 158, 173, 174, 184, 185, 194, 197, 214, 347, 356,
Newcastle 368,
Newcastle 59, 60, 107, 131, 150, 205, 218, 242, 271,
Newcastle shelling from Japanese submarine 261, 263–264, 266,
New Guinea 59, 84, 90, 91, 95, 99, 103, 126, 147, 150, 152, 168, 171, 194, 196, 197, 205, 214, 279–283, 287, 288, 294, 304, 307, 309, 310, 339, 340, 342, 359, 361, 362,
New Hebrides 90, 144, 194,
New Zealand 28, 53, 55, 64, 82, 85, 98, 100, 121, 122, 137, 144, 149, 150, 151, 171, 173, 201, 202, 218, 253, 279, 283,
Nimitz, Chester W. 92, 200,
North Africa 19, 96,
Noumea 214, 255,
Nowra 270,

Oahu 40, 50, 49, 56, 75, 77,
Obon season 2–3,

Ogura, Toyofumi 332,
Ohmae, Toshikazu 339, 356,
Oka, Takasumi 152, 155, 161, 166,
Okinawa 118, 316, 317, 321, 322, 324, 332, 334, 336–338,
Oklahoma 52.
Okumiya, Masatake 309–310,
Okumura, Kiwao 123,
Omori, Takeshi 208, 223, 225–228, 273,
Onishi, Takijiro 118, 311–313, 338–339, 353,
Orestes 267,
Ott, Eugen 196,
Oulanhan, Richard 145,
Ourasaki Beach 36, 39, 206, 227,
Owen-Jones, Charles 132,
Owen Stanley Range 270, 280, 296–297, 301, 342,
Oyoda 306, 330,

Page, Earle 173,
Palau 105, 111, 316,
Palmyra 70, 137,
Papua 59, 98, 194, 200, 214, 270–271, 287, 300, 301, 356,
Pearl Harbor, planning carrier strike force raid 9–18, 22, 23–27, 39–40, 47.
Pearl Harbor, planning midget submarine raid 9, 36.
Pearl Harbor carrier force attack 33–34, 48–49, 50–55, 256,
Pearl Harbor midget submarine participation 41–44, 49–51, 56, 76–78, 101, 251,
Pearl Harbor victory, effect on Navy 62–63,
Penang 191, 327,
Penguin, 235,
Pennsylvania 52,
Perkins 227,
Perth 141,
Perth 67, 96, 201, 284, 314,

Philippines 15, 28, 34, 45, 52, 57, 80, 90, 93, 98, 99, 105, 153, 246, 311, 325, 356,
Phua, Willie 349,
Port Hacking 222, 233,
Port Kembla 59, 60, 84, 107, 150,
Port Moresby 59, 84, 88, 95, 97, 106, 109, 131, 150, 151, 169, 173, 174, 183, 185, 193–194, 196, 198, 199–200, 209, 214, 250, 270–271, 279–284, 286–288, 293, 297, 324, 347, 354,
Potter, John Deane 123,
Potsdam Proclamation 330, 331, 335, 336,
Prange, Gordon W. 197, 370,
Prince of Wales 55,
Proud, John 294–297,

Queen Mary 180, 235,

Rabaul 59, 65, 84, 91–92, 95, 106, 121, 128, 194, 195, 200, 252, 280, 281, 285, 300, 301, 304–310, 342, 354, 355,
Raeder, Erich 100.
Ramillies 219,
Rangoon 100, 136–138,
Redding, H.R. 274,
Repulse 55,
Roberts, Neil 231,
Rockhampton, Qld 107, 110,
Rodgers, Don 131, 147,
Roosevelt, Franklin D.
    Curtin pleas for ongoing talks 44,
    personal message to Hirohito 46,
    on Pearl Harbor attack 52–53,
    Curtin's time of great crisis 79,
    Churchill at White House 83,
    grave concern for Australia 121, 143,
    US reinforcements for Australia 121,
    wants Australians in Burma 137–138,
    against return of Australian troops 139,
    warned by King about Australia 144,
    orders MacArthur to escape 180,

warned by Brett and Australian defence chiefs 185–187,
seeks advice on Australia 201,
criticised by Curtin 268,
thinks Australia will survive 283–284, 291,
dies 324,
Rose Bay, Sydney 229, 262, 263, 292,
Ross, Lloyd 147,
Rowell, Sydney 33, 282–283,
Royal Australian Air Force (see Australia.)
Royal Australian Navy (see Australia.)
Royle, Guy 149, 151–152, 187,
Russia and Soviet Union 45, 70, 71, 84, 86, 99, 103, 109, 139, 169, 170, 183, 184, 331–330, 333, 336, 341,
Russell, Edward 343,

Saipan 211, 311,
Sakamaki, Kazuo 42–44, 49–51, 56, 75, 242,
Salamaua 97, 168, 298,
Samoa 70, 85, 97, 99, 100, 103, 108, 127, 137, 143, 157, 158, 164, 171, 184, 192, 194, 214,
Sanagi, Kowashi 152,
San Michele 233,
Saratoga 190,
Sasaki, Akira 48.
Sea Mist 238, 239,
Senshi Sosho (Japan's war history series) 64, 86, 119, 127, 270, 272, 343, 359,
Shalders, Russ 368,
Shea, Thomas F. 297,
Shedden, Frederick 132, 148, 244,
Shigemitsu, Mamoru 341,
Shimada, Shigetaro 13, 69, 157, 161, 311, 317,
Shimizu, Mitsumi 42–43,
Shinta, Masamichi 352–353,
Shoho 200,

Shokaku 44, 91, 200,
Simon, Alan 366–368,
Singapore 4, 32–33, 45, 52, 55, 58, 59, 67, 71, 74, 79–82, 93, 97, 99, 100, 102, 108, 110, 111, 124, 349,
Singapore battle and capture 114–115, 120, 121–123, 130, 133, 137, 149, 171, 173, 177, 187, 188, 195, 269,
Smith, Fred 300–301,
Smith, Tim 270,
Solomons 84, 95, 103, 199, 283, 289, 291, 298–299, 300, 301, 308, 340, 358,
Soryu 44, 111, 136, 211, 255, 256,
Spender, Percy 113,
Spring, Ian 214–215,
Stalin, Josef 103,
Steady Hour 238,
Sturdee, Vernon 60, 96–97, 120, 130, 149, 281,
Suetsuga, Nobumasa 365,
Suikosha, naval officers club 53–54,
Sugita, Ichiji 45.
Sugiyama, Hajime 27–28, 86, 127, 154, 156–158, 168–169, 376n,
Sumatra 71, 93, 99, 121, 149, 173, 343,
Sutherland, R.K. 244,
Suva 144,
Suzuki, Kantaro 321, 328, 337,
Suzuki, Suguru 39.
Sydney 104.
Sydney 37, 58, 59, 60, 61–62, 66–67, 75, 76, 88, 89, 99, 107, 113–114, 124, 125, 126, 127, 130, 131, 176, 178, 196, 205, 259, 272, 286,
Sydney Harbour reconnaissance and midget raid 36, 38, 41, 76–78, 88, 130, 190, 192, 203, 205–209, 214–218, 220–245, 248–249, 251–253, 257–259, 273–276, 289–291, 293–295, 347, 364–370,
Sydney shelling, 261–263, 266,
Syria 19,

Taiyo Maru 39–40,
Takada, Toshitane 16,
Takamatsu, Nobuhito 117,
Takao 34,
Takei, Tokuro 335,
Tanabe, Moritabe 166–167,
Tanaka, Hiromi 87, 88, 288, 358–363, 385n,
Tanaka, Shinichi 70, 109, 152, 161, 163, 214,
Tasmania 173,
Tathra 271,
Tautog 205,
Tennessee 52.
Timor 34, 59, 64, 97, 98, 99, 108, 135, 136, 141, 145, 149, 173, 288, 355,
Thai-Burma railway 195, 346,
Thailand 10, 27, 34, 44, 45, 52, 57,
The Lodge, Canberra 147,
Thursday island 173,
Tjilatjap 141,
Tobruk 19, 81,
Todaka, Kazushige 119–120,
Togo, Heihachiro 11,
Togo, Shigenori 29, 30, 57, 155–156, 165, 196, 328, 331,
Tojo, Hideki
    forms extremist cabinet10,
    opinion on Pearl awaited 24,
    urges war with US 27,
    resolves early December attack 28–29,
    war declaration explained, 52,
    occupying not only Java 'but Sumatra and Australia' 71–72,
    no mercy in crushing Australia 91,
    no consensus on Australia invasion 103, 126,
    urges Australia to avoid 'useless war' 122,
    opposes invasion of Australia 124, 127, 167, 342,
    Australia debate, too many invasions 155–156, 165,
    Australia orphan of Pacific 209–210,
    Japanese troops will take Perth 284,
    Asians 'welcome Japan' 287,
    forced to resign 317,
    last interview, mentions Australia, 342–343,
    shoots himself 342–343,
    hanged for war crimes 343, 346,
Tokyo, 9, 11, 13, 18, 26, 29, 30, 45, 53, 57, 59, 63, 65, 72, 74, 83,86, 91, 102, 103, 108, 110, 111, 128, 135, 136, 152, 160, 161, 186, 199, 257, 266, 284,293, 308, 311, 318–320, 324, 336, 340–349, 357, 363,
Tol and Waitavalo atrocities 106, 195,
Toland, John 126,
Tomioka, Sadahiro 119, 344,
Tomioka, Sadatoshi
    background 14–16,
    Pearl Harbor plan opposed14–18,
    favours war with US 16,
    sees no way to defeat US 16,
    hawk hardliner 16,
    superiors criticised 17,
    Pearl Harbor plan supported 24–26,
    Army meetings 45,
    on eve of Pearl Harbor 54,
    can't defeat US 54,
    meets Ugaki re second stage of war 69,
    proposes invasion of Australia 72–74, 95,
    Rabaul as airbase for Australia 65, 92,
    misunderstands Hawaii operation 69–70,
    steps to Australian mainland 95,
    token force can take Australia 111,
    'Australia-first' strategy 112,
    liberation of Asia not an issue 122,
    use Kwantung Army in Australia 126,

459

1942

worried most about Australia 128–129,
Australia invasion shelved 169,
logic in Army's invasion doubts 192,
'we can take Australia' 193,
Midway's shattering defeat 267,
embattled Rabaul chief 306–309,
importance of Saipan 311,
disagrees with Onishi 312,
on irrational behaviour 320–321,
at Japan's surrender 340–342,
becomes war historian 119, 343,
helps set up new navy, dies 344,

Tone 111,
Tonga 144,
Torres Strait 100, 105, 303,
Townsville 131, 150–151, 173, 186, 194, 340, 354,
Toyoda, Soemu 310, 319–321, 323, 331, 335, 336, 340,
Tripartite Pact 25, 95,
Truk 65, 84, 95, 105, 191, 192, 197, 205–208, 252, 299, 306, 310, 361,
Truman, Harry S. 324, 330, 333,
Tsutsumida, Tamaye 275, 293,
Tsuzuku, Masao 222, 234, 239–242, 273, 290,
Tulagi 95, 199, 298,

Ugaki, Matome
    background 12, 23,
    Washington Treaty 12,
    pleasure at Kuroshima's mission 23,
    anger at Pearl Harbor opponents 24,
    happiness at Pearl Harbor planning 26, 41,
    boys like cherry blossoms 42,
    admiration for midget submariners 43–44, 101,
    vacates room for subordinates 48,
    listens to Pearl Harbor attack 49,
    Pearl Harbor result 'trivial' 55.
    British sinkings, 'no greater victory' 55.
    worries about midget submariners 56, 220,
    studies Hawaii, Australia and India invasion 64, 69–70, 84–85,
    favours southern operations 65–66,
    army's 'mean spirit' 70,
    impressed with new midget subs 101,
    Tokyo's indecision on second phase 102,
    defers to subordinate officers 102–3,
    plan to capture Darwin, army opposition 108,
    demands offensive action 108, 160,
    confident army will join navy in offensives 170,
    tries to fathom MacArthur 170,
    submariners' 'determination to die' 191,
    war games and carrier attacks on Sydney 197,
    sarcasm over Coral Sea victory 200,
    celebrates second stage operations 209,
    hears no survivors from Sydney raid 251–253,
    on Midway disaster 255–257,
    with Yamamoto on fateful flight 304–306,
    dream of victory ends 310–311,
    navy forms cabinet 322,
    as Kamikaze chief 334,
    wishes for atom bomb 334,
    raves against surrender talk 336,
    takes Kamikaze pilots to death 337–338,
Umezu, Yoshijiro 331, 340–341,
United States
    United States Navy 6, 10, 15–16, 51–52, 57, 64, 90, 92, 121, 122, 126, 127, 143, 144, 164, 174, 197,

199–201, 210, 217–218, 229–231,
233–236, 255–257, 266, 285,
298–300, 304–305, 310, 311, 313,
316–317, 322, 328–329,
trade embargo with Japan 10,
Washington Treaty 12,
war with Japan, 15–16, 22–25, 27, 28,
41, 45, 50, 51, 52–53, 57, 58, 64, 79,
80, 83, 86, 87, 94, 117, 129, 157, 162,
163, 164, 167, 210, 212, 257, 283,
317, 330, 331–333, 336, 339,
talks with Japan in Washington 25,
reinforcements for Australia 62, 83,
95, 121, 143, 146, 152, 174, 201,
245–246,
United States Army 62, 72, 91, 121,
122, 139–140, 143, 152, 172, 181,
187, 255,
mainland US attacked by Japan 77,
US defence assessments of Australia
91, 99–100, 121, 143–144, 172–173,
185–186, 201, 245–246, 268,
285–286, 301, 354,
United States Air Force 141, 174,
221, 296–297, 311, 317–319, 322,
325–327, 328–329,

Vampire 189–190,
Vaucluse, Sydney 254,
Victoria Barracks, Melbourne 30, 33, 67,
75, 120, 148–149, 171, 177, 244,

Wake 52, 95,
Wamberal 267,
War loans 131,
Ward 50.
Ward, Eddie 204,
Washington 25, 64, 75, 83, 85, 91, 99, 121,
144, 172, 181, 183, 186, 201, 212, 270,
298, 331,
Watanabe, Yasuji 49.
Watson's Bay, Sydney 223,

Wavell, Archibald 81, 97,
Webb, William 106–107,
Wellen 205, 218,
Weneker, Paul 300,
West Virginia 52,
Western Australia 104, 142, 145, 150, 158,
173, 184–185, 186, 316, 342,
Wewak 307,
White Australia policy 176, 178,
Whitfield, Colin 231–232,
Whittle, George 240–241,
William Dawes 271,
Whyalla 230,
Whyalla 254,
Wilcannia 259,
Wilson, Percy 217–218, 232–233,
Wilson, Peter 263,
Winckel, Gus 142,
Wollongong 255,
Woollahra, Sydney 262,
World War 1 20, 31, 84, 105, 212,
Wyndham 143,

Yahagi 318, 322, 323,
Yamaguchi, Tamon 136–137, 256–257,
Yamaki, Teiji 206, 207–208, 369–370,
Yamamoto, Isoroku
 on board *Nagato* 6,
 Pearl Harbor 10–12, 24, 47–49,
 background 12,
 threatens resignation over Pearl
  Harbor 17,
 midget submariners meeting 40,
 midget submariners must be
  recovered 43, 76,
 visits wife and mistress prior to war
  47,
 'climb Mt. Niitaka' 47,
 hears reports of Pearl attack 49.
 Americans not to be underestimated
  41,
 looks to invasion of Hawaii 64, 69–70,

1942

attitude fleet commanders' plans 94,
inspects midgets with Ugaki 101,
orders raid on Darwin 109,
transfers flag from *Nagato* to *Yamato* 117,
reportedly opposed to Australian invasion 126,
pleas to submariners to attempt return 190–191,
maintains offensive 197,
learns of Midway defeat 255–256,
declares submariners 'hero gods' 293–294,
life on flagship at Truk 299–300,
killed on Bougainville flight 304–306, 308,
defied by midget submariners 369–370,
Yamamoto, Yuji 25, 110,
Yamanda, Kaoru 75–76,
Yamashita, Tomoyuki 74, 120, 123–126, 127, 128,
Yamato 1, 6, 116, 117, 120, 136, 137, 160, 164, 190, 191, 192, 197, 209–211, 219–220, 246–247, 252, 255, 256, 299, 312, 361,
Yamato museum 119,
Yamato sinking 118, 136, 299, 310, 317–323,
Yampi Sound 158,
Yanase, Mitsumi 89, 275–278,
Yandra 233,
Yano, Shikazo 95,
Yarroma 223, 226–229, 237, 239,
Yasukuni shrine and museum 345–350, 353,
Yokosuka 358,
Yonai, Mitsumasa 336, 339,
Yoshida, Mitsuru 322–323,
Yoshikawa, Eiji 368,
Yorktown 197, 255,

Zealandia 133,
Zuiho 211,
Zuikaku 44, 91, 200, 313,

Bob Wurth is a Queensland writer on the Asia-Pacific region. He is a former foreign correspondent for the Australian Broadcasting Corporation and ABC manager for Asia, and later, Queensland.

His previous books are *Justice in the Philippines, Father Brian Gore, the Church, the State and the Military*, ABC Books, Sydney, 1985 and *Saving Australia, Curtin's secret peace with Japan*, Lothian Books, South Melbourne, 2006.

The principal translator of Japanese documents for this book was Kyal Hill, of Tokyo, who also acted as interpreter for some interviews. Other translations were by Robert Gilhooly, Tokyo, and Dr Steven Bullard, Canberra.

Bob Wurth can be contacted via www.1942.com.au